LONG TERM

LONG ♡ TERM

SCOTT HERRING &
LEE WALLACE, EDITORS

With a foreword by
E. PATRICK JOHNSON

ESSAYS ON QUEER COMMITMENT

Duke University Press *Durham and London* 2021

Designed by Courtney Leigh Baker
Typeset in Minion Pro, Trade Gothic, and Besom by
Westchester Publishing Services

Library of Congress Cataloging-in-Publication Data
Names: Herring, Scott, [date] editor. | Wallace, Lee, [date] editor.
Title: Long term : essays on queer commitment / Scott Herring and
    Lee Wallace, editors.
Description: Durham : Duke University Press, 2021. |
    Includes bibliographical references and index.
Identifiers: LCCN 2020046536 (print) | LCCN 2020046537 (ebook)
ISBN 9781478013327 (hardcover)
ISBN 9781478014232 (paperback)
ISBN 9781478021544 (ebook)
Subjects: LCSH: Commitment (Psychology) | Interpersonal
    relations. | Relationship quality. | Time perception—Social
    aspects. | Same-sex marriage. | Queer theory.
Classification: LCC BF619 .L66 2021 (print) | LCC BF619 (ebook) |
    DDC 158—dc23
LC record available at https://lccn.loc.gov/2020046536
LC ebook record available at https://lccn.loc.gov/2020046537

Cover art: Graffiti on restroom wall, Oscar Wilde Memorial
Bookshop. 1969. Photo by Diana Davies, Manuscripts and Archives
Division, The New York Public Library.

Duke University Press gratefully acknowledges the Office of the
Vice Provost for Research and the Department of English at
Indiana University, which provided funds toward the publication
of this book.

CONTENTS

Wouldn't Take Nothing for My Journey

Nothing awakens the senses like death. Although we don't know (unless we are psychics, oracles, or other intermediaries) if we continue to sense after death, those of us left in the wake of death know all too well the plethora of emotions that rain down upon us after the loss of a loved one. Nonetheless, death is the one event that we are compelled to commit to—in the long and short term—because we can't predict, at least with any precise certainty, its arrival, only its inevitability. We do have some agency, I suppose, around when death might happen if we choose suicide, but even in that instance death may choose not to take the bait. It might, for instance, decide that we have much more living to do, despite our feelings of despondency, depression, or desire to exist in another realm. It is in this way that death is a queer phenomenon: a thing to which one must commit because it has committed itself to us but also something that remains elusive, even in its seeming finality. The interstitial space that precedes death—the anticipation and uncertainty of its arrival—and that which follows—the unknowingness of the afterlife—link it to queer affects/effects with long-term implications. Death, then, becomes an apropos allegory for long-term queer commitments.

To wit, many of the essays in this volume index death as the ghost of queer affiliations: the waiting with and on loved ones who are ill, managing a life-threatening disease, the impending death of a relationship or pet, the purgatory of incarceration, the death wish for gay marriage alongside a valuing of its "afterlife," and so on. These authors' engagement with death, I believe, is coincidental, as opposed to an ideological alignment with queer theorists who focus on antisociality and the death drive. They also do not easily align with the counterideology of queer utopia; rather, these authors sidestep those polemics in pursuit of something more nuanced about how long-term commitment affectively registers and effectively responds to queer attachments. As the editors of this volume suggest, these authors "stay around long enough to consider the ramifications of indentured commitments—familial, financial, institutional—that might wax and wane across time." The concern, then, is not death in and of itself, but death as a temporal and spatial metaphor for how queers commit to commitment in ways that supersede the obvious tautology of such a construction and in ways that are not in bed with heteronormativity. These authors' promiscuity acutely disavows normativity that flows in either direction—hetero or homo—in an attempt to cheat death at its own game.

Thus, these essays ironically account for how we as queers commit to life and living despite a contemporaneous world in which we are constantly under siege. If we think about how queer existence has been sustained by queer *persistence*, we quickly come to understand the relationship between commitment and the long term. There is a gospel song titled "I Believe I'll Run On," the recurring line of which says, "I believe I'll run on, see what the end's goin' be" (Oprah Winfrey used it as the theme song for her talk show one season!). Although the song is about having faith that things will get better at the end, it's also about endurance and commitment to the journey. Indeed, the song encapsulates the ambiguity of the "end" because it is an unspecified designation (the finish line? Death? Heaven?). Nonetheless, the speaker is going to run, not walk, toward whatever the unspecified state/place because they are committed to the *process* of the journey. Queers, then, have a unique relationship to commitment because we are in a constant process of becoming and unbecoming, and sometimes in ways—like running—that are exhausting. But there is also joy and pleasure in the pursuit of that place that dare not speak its name: unknown, unnamed, unmoored, undone. What we, as queers, have reaped from our undying cathexis to commitment is both the solemnity that follows each and every reminder that white-supremacist heteropatriarchy reigns supreme and the jubilance that stems from our radical resistance to the same. But for our long-term commitment to care for one another, we would have never survived the hold of the slave ship, the concentration camp, McCarthyism, HIV/AIDS, Don't Ask, Don't Tell, DOMA, and dare I say, Trumpism, although that remains to be seen.

The essays collected here wade into troubled waters but find a life buoy by way of rhetorical flourishes that convincingly argue for the focus on commitment to postmarriage equality. Collectively, they shore up the notion that long-term commitment is not anathema to the radicality, nonnormativity, and transgressive politics that have come to be associated with queer culture. However, they also note that even the more conservative formations of long-term commitment (e.g., gay marriage) have radical material implications that are often overlooked or ignored. Some might construe my suggestion here as equating commitment with a progress narrative of queer equality toward a path of hetero or homonormativity. Yes and no. Yes, in the sense that queer fortitude has afforded many of us (despite the fact that race and class status still make progress elusive to some) access to certain rights. No, in the sense that the goal or even the by-product of commitment is not necessarily "progress" or access to rights or commodities. Sometimes, the commitment is for commitment's sake, for the experience to live inside the liminal space of queerness, unencumbered. For example, when someone "gets their life" on the dance floor—that liminal space where the body is committed to the exhilarating exhaustion of moving to the pulse of the music. Or that liminal space where the body is committed to the touch, the taste, the sound, the sight, the smell of passionate sex. Or that liminal space where the body is committed to marching, chanting, rallying, laying prostrate in the street, for the right to love and fuck as many or as few or whomever it desires. Or that liminal space where the body is committed to the care of a lover, spouse, parent, pet, plant, or other sentient being because to commit to the care of and for an "other" is to assure our redemption in the long term. For in the long term there will be a reckoning. And in the long term, those who come after will look afresh on how we did and did not commit—not to the end, but to the journey.

E. PATRICK JOHNSON

INTRODUCTION

A Theory of the Long Term

SCOTT HERRING AND LEE WALLACE

In the back-end world of computer programming there is a protocol called a "pre-commit" that checks code for errors before intended changes are made permanent. In this cryptographic schema, the opposite of commitment is "rollback," the protocol by which tentative tweakings of code are discarded along with all data saved since work began. The error-proofing protocols put in place around relational database management systems have no equivalent in the front-end world of interpersonal relationships, where the codes of commitment are all the richer for not deleting but keeping the many flaws, mistakes, and gestures of reparation that make up a committed life. The essays in this collection address durational commitments of the kind that might be thought at odds with the instantaneous likability metrics built into contemporary social media, which buoy up our sense that the world runs on good feelings alone, just as they resist the idea that the social, sexual, and emotional dimensions of relationships can be compressed into text-friendly initialisms such as LTR (long-term relationship), STR (short-term relationship), or LDR (long-distance relationship).

As coeditors committed to the slow task of rewriting each other's sentences to the point where they blended into a uniquely standardized voice, one of the few things we struggled with was the grammar of this collection's title. When referencing the "long term," did we mean a noun—as in "serving a long term"—or an adjective—as in "long-term prognosis"? Or was it something else we were trying to capture, say the point at which the compound adjective starts to register as a phenomenon in its own right, hardening off as something called the "longterm"—a consolidation of effects brought about by engaging the idea of the long term? Long-term commitments, long-term relationships, long-term sentences, long-term ambitions, long-term writing projects, long-term institutionalization, long-term climate change—all of these seem to point to a shift in our affective apprehension of how duration might be weathered, to use a phrase that turned up in the environmental humanities to catch at the changes attendant on materially living through time: "weathered bodies, weathered houses, weathered cars, weathered clothes, weathered relationships, weathered dreams."[1] Certainly, our contributors had no problem understanding what we meant when we first raised the idea of this collection with them. As soon as we prompted them with our title— sometimes hyphenated, sometimes not, depending on which one of us was at the keyboard—they anticipated our thinking and engaged us on themes the two of us had already been scoping out in the long, informal conversations that have marked our getting to know each other across the last several years: mortality, change, viability, dependence, and care.

This casual responsiveness confirmed our initial hunch that the long term has emerged as a structure of feeling while many of us have been resisting it, particularly in the context of gay marriage debates and the queer critique of homonormativity. As Raymond Williams famously pointed out, changes in our shared apprehensions of the world—whether intuitive or critical—do not happen overnight, nor is overnight the time frame we invoke here. It has been two decades, for instance, since Lauren Berlant edited "Intimacy," the award-winning special issue of *Critical Inquiry.* Subsequently expanded into a volume that appeared two years later, "Intimacy" helped to recast the personal field of love and sex across transnational domains of citizenship, capitalism, race, and ethnicity.[2] In so doing, "Intimacy" laid the groundwork for future affective and political coordinates of queer studies as decisively as Eve Kosofsky Sedgwick's *Epistemology of the Closet* had facilitated its fin-de-siècle concerns ten years earlier. Many of the tightly argued ideas put forward by Berlant and her contributors about intimate publics and the role that mediated sentiments play in civil belonging remain critically influential, just as the collection's outlier formal contributions—such as Sedgwick's account of her post-chemo psychotherapy, one of several pieces relying on autobiographical experimentation to break the usual code of academic impersonality—reimagined theory from the ground up and enabled new iterations of personal writing to flourish within the field.[3]

Looking back at that landmark millennial volume, however, it is also obvious that in the twenty years since then the social infrastructure that determines what counts as private and what counts as public around intimacy and queerness has been transformed in many ways, not all of them predictable. The world of 2000, for instance, is still the world of Bill Clinton and Monica Lewinsky, a place where—for all the mediated interpenetration of public and private interests represented in that peculiarly American sex scandal—sexuality and virtuality have yet to mutually implant in ways that are taken for granted in a smartphone-enabled world. Although the ideas in Berlant and Michael Warner's coauthored contribution, "Sex in Public," stay as current as the day they were minted, the everyday context that the essay points to has evolved. Written at a moment when Google was still being conceived by some Stanford doctoral punks, the form of the internet undergirding "Sex in Public" is not the ubiquitous filter for everything that it has become. Thus, when Berlant and Warner refer to the various tacit and explicit sexual publics that swell in the interstices of American national culture, they could not have anticipated the public-private affordances of geosocial networking applications such as Grindr.[4] Rereading their turn-of-the-century essay from the vantage point of now also reveals that, back then, the cause of gay marriage was not yet a highly mobile global juggernaut but could be neatly represented by a handful of conservative stooges within the gay movement—Andrew Sullivan, William N. Eskridge Jr.—and thus presents something of an easy target for what will toughen into the antinormative impetus that subtends Queer Theory, Mark II.[5]

Rather than emphasize innovation around sex and the technological extension of nonproximate queer communities, the essays gathered here proceed from the assumption that the time is right for further rethinking of intimacies postmarriage equality, a social phenomenon that has arrived in many jurisdictions as a customary practice well ahead of its legal implementation. Not everyone, of course, is enamored of this social acceptance, nor do they consider it a legal advance, including many of this volume's contributors. One confirms "the twin homonationalist forces of marriage and militarization"; one considers "the lies and false promises of gay marriage discourse"; one of us elaborates on an "apolitical queer habitus" that manifests in fiction but is not limited to that context. In dialogue with other essays that approach marriage equality and the social legitimation that underscores it more obliquely, these writings contribute to what Warner refers to as "the history of principled critique of marriage in queer politics."[6] That unfinished project remains a long-term enterprise to which we remain wired.

When we rehearse these challenges to normative iterations of marriage equality, we lock arms with forceful critiques originating within queer-of-color theory. A decade after "Intimacy," José Esteban Muñoz would decry "today's hamstrung pragmatic gay agenda" and its devaluation of queer lifeways less indexed to presentist aspiration.[7] Others such as Juana María Rodríguez cite "a reappropriation of family values discourse and political platforms focused on same-sex marriage and homonormative formulations of family life" that exclude "those who are poor, institutionalized, gender-nonconforming, disabled, in alternative domestic relationships, or marginalized by their race or immigration status."[8] Still others, such as Chandan Reddy, have linked the success of rights-based marriage-equality claims to the rise of a racially liberal state that first appeared in the context of the rescinding of twentieth-century prohibitions on miscegenation, a progressive legal advance that strives "to obscure and displace from political legitimacy" a "variety of autonomous black social struggles."[9]

We heed Reddy when we also remind ourselves that long-term commitments can and have operated as technologies of racial normativity and hegemonic whiteness, whether or not they formalized themselves into marital bonds. Perhaps the best example of this technology on the American scene remains Daniel Patrick Moynihan's "The Negro Family: The Case for National Action" (1965), the so-called "Moynihan Report." Part of Lyndon B. Johnson's War on Poverty, the statistically driven sociology animating the report officialized stale tropes of Black dysfunction that acquired a newly intimate profile, such as "family disorganization" and "disintegration of the Negro family structure" that erroneously contribute to a "family pathology" characterized by "divorce, separation, and desertion, female family head, children in broken homes, and illegitimacy," or what might be called diseases of the long term.[10] Queer and antiracist critiques of the liberal ahistoricism driving the Moynihan Report, such as those launched by Hortense Spillers and Roderick Ferguson, continue to stand as necessary correctives that strive to secure breathing room for multiple axes of antinormativity, including those that fail—or are cast outside of—the state's propulsion toward norms of relational durability.[11] Laboring to dislodge totalizing notions of normative white commitment, our contributors are also in agreement with Sara Ahmed's observation that "it is not up to bodies of color to do the work of antiracism" either personally or on an institutional scale.[12]

As they set about diversifying the landscape of the long term, particularly as it intersects with the drive to marriage equality, some of our essayists find themselves in step with Kendall Thomas's valorization of the attempt "to create aesthetic and imaginal space that positions black lives in marital narratives with unexpected and even 'queer' effects." Looking at recent Black cinema, specifically the unlikely double feature made by *Moonlight* (2016) and *Black Panther* (2018), Thomas considers how Black directors have creatively modified a normative script by providing stories of "African American erotic and intimate life *beyond* the binary boundaries of normative whiteness and nonnormative blackness." Filled with wonder by these films and the post-*Obergefell* times of their making, Thomas is moved to ask "Is black marriage queer?" Responsive to the racial violences of the populist era, but not limited to them, these films give Thomas cause to embrace the adaptability of the marriage plot as a narrative means of capturing "whether, why, and how bisexual, heterosexual, gay, and lesbian black people around the world experiment with conjugality by crafting spaces *within* marriage that engage and include intimate relational possibilities *outside* it."[13]

Thomas's interest in queer-of-color marital imaginaries recalls sociologist Mignon R. Moore's thesis that "'normalization' can in itself be radical, depending again on the context."[14] The context for Moore's claim is her experience as "an active participant in the marriage equality movement" and a critic of "marriage equality as a platform for LGBTQ social justice" to the exclusion of "everything else"—a profile we suspect she shares with many of our readers—but also her life experience as a wife, a mother of two, and a not-infrequent churchgoer. Like E. Patrick Johnson's foreword to this volume, Moore invites us to think about the particularities of LGBTQ lives and the multiple ways that people negotiate racial and sexual normativities that may paradoxically result in "radical, even revolutionary behaviour" beyond the usual ken of queerness.[15]

In line with these queer-of-color critiques of the popular embrace of same-sex marriage that ask us to crack open this historically conservative institutional form, our contributors likewise find the present moment to be a vertiginous time of constraint, contradiction, and potential. To move along the critical conversations delineated above, we have collectively flagged a dimension of queer life generally unremarked upon or neglected outside conjugal paradigms either pro or con or somewhere in between. The original essays that make up this volume address queer theoretical ambivalence around commitment by reflecting on long-term queer achievements in all their idiosyncrasy and contextually driven nuance. They consider what queers have committed to—politically, erotically, domestically, psychically—and how these commitments appear now that the legal advent of same-sex marriage has broadly transformed the idea of what some LGBTQ persons want or, in terms of legal and medical benefits, need. Given a wide brief, our authors take prevalent conceptions of what currently counts as queer—the nonidentitarian, the performative, the ephemeral—and expand them to include commitments that overlap with normative impetus toward the long term. Without stepping away from the queer critique of longevity and the normativity embedded in reproductive futurity, they nonetheless stay around long enough to consider the ramifications of indentured commitments—familial, financial, institutional—that might wax and wane across time.[16] Considering topics ranging from the long-term care of household pets to the durational cruelties of incarceration and the queer family as a scene of racialized commitment, they trace the costs and consolations of normativity in queer commitments that last the distance, as well as those that don't.

Building on prior critiques and queerings of long-term marital intimacies, we continue to ask what queer commitment involves, in either its universalizing or minoritizing idioms.[17] In this we follow Ahmed, who in her 2006 book-length thought experiment on the notion of queer phenomenology puts forward the negative proposition that "rather than being a commitment to a line of deviation," a queer commitment "would be a commitment not to presume that lives have to follow certain lines in order to count as lives."[18] Although the word *commitment* carries less psychoanalytic baggage than the more theoretically invested *attachment*, it is not without its philological complications, which suggests to us that commitment has always been defined by its capacity to deviate from itself. The *Oxford English Dictionary* tracks the now pervasive meaning of the word to as recent a date as 1962: "the state or condition of being committed to a partner in a long-term romantic relationship; the action or an act of committing to such a relationship."[19] Intimately tied to the verb *commit*—appearing as late as 1987 as "to resolve to remain in a long-term (monogamous) relationship with another person"—commitment has both a fairly recent and a historically dense definitional life.[20] Although it carries forward earlier usages such as the late sixteenth-century phrasing "to commit marriage," the term's normative associations date largely to the late twentieth century, the period in which the institution of marriage has come under legal pressure to include same-sex couples.[21]

Other usages hint at similarly crossed wires between normative and antinormative messaging. Even the phrase *commitment ceremony*—now understood as a socially performative event "at which a couple in a romantic relationship declare their long-term commitment to one another without becoming legally married"—in the early twentieth-century United States referred to the burial of a corpse, an end-of-life ritual in which the singular materiality of a body is ultimately acknowledged.[22] Although the "usual sense" of commitment remains shackled to legalized marriage, other, less conventional instances of its usage also populate the OED, which notes that commitment can refer to psychiatric institutionalization ("commitment order"), jailing, and increased militarization, all instances that ramp up the normative and antinormative tendencies of the term and parlay them across a highly complex social field that engages notions of sanity, punishment, security, and delinquency.[23]

Our contributors collectively grasp the real-time stakes of these historical vocabularies. Their essays understand the overlaps and discordances between these interrelated usages and point to the myriad modes of commitment that transect the social and how often it is that commitments, voluntary or involuntary, manifest in durational terms, whether in the binding vow or psychiatric sectioning that tithes body and soul to an institution or the recognition— whether slow or instant—that a forward-tending promise has been dishonored or reneged upon. As the somewhat muddy distinction between a commitment and a committal registers, some commitments lay more claim to us than others. Our emotional, spiritual, and fiscal commitments may coincide or run counter to one another. In intimate and professional spheres we can be overcommitted or undercommitted, or both at the same time. Consider, too, how the therapeutic discourse that has developed around intimate obligation catches up even those who avoid commitment as "commitment-phobes," a highly stigmatizing term in the psy-friendly sphere of listicle culture and a phenomenon that one of our pieces considers at length.[24]

We validate the aversion to commitment even as we focus on what one contributor refers to as "the long run" or the span across which the long lasting and the fleeting compete for ongoing outlay. Within the trip-wired world of commitment, where the appropriate level of investment, risk, or restraint is hard enough to call, let alone sustain, the psychoanalyst Adam Phillips sees advantages to "being uncommitted," which he likens to Freud's "notion of free-floating attention." In his counterintuitive and aphoristic style, Phillips entertains the idea that "to be committed to something—a person, an ideology, a vocabulary, a way of going about things—one has first to be committed, perhaps unconsciously, to commitment itself."[25] Unsurprisingly, Phillips has found Herman Melville's Bartleby—whose catchphrase "I would prefer not to" went into extraliterary circulation during Occupy Wall Street as a slogan for passive resistance or noncommital to capitalism—a good figure to think this conundrum through, specifically in relation to the refusal of things that are said to be good for us, such as food or nurture.[26]

In their individual and collective noncompliance, Bartleby and his activist heirs undermine the organizational commitment that industrial psychology deems crucial to prosperous workplace dynamics.[27] Although anyone who works in a world of 24/7 email appreciates Bartleby's wish, Phillips understands that a clear-cut binary between commitment and noncommitment cannot always be assumed, for most commitments come trailing countercommitments or "side-bets," as they are known in the psychology domain.[28] Contra commitment altogether, Phillips advocates flirtation as a reminder of the open-ended fickleness of desire: "If our descriptions of our sexuality are tyrannized by various stories of committed purpose—sex as reproduction, sex as heterosexual romance, sex as intimacy—flirtation puts in disarray our sense of an ending."[29] Like Ahmed, Phillips distrusts commitment to the degree that it promotes not just closure but the idea that some commitments are better than others emotionally, socially, or sexually.

Rather than calibrating commitments against each other in these terms—thruples considered more socially experimental than couples, flings assumed to be less emotionally complicated than LTRs, LDRs thought to deliver the best of both worlds, casual encounters presumed to have fewer strings attached—others have likewise questioned the utility of commitments at all. For instance, Leo Bersani insists that in psychoanalytic terms commitments—particularly the commitment to monogamy—are "inconceivable except as something that blocks circuits of desire": in the Freudian schema the "incestuous monogamous passion" of the infant for one particular person is ultimately renounced in favor of a nonexclusive desire that can fasten on any person. Bersani's insistence that the renunciation of exclusivity provides the "passage from the family to the social" suggests that the high value placed on monogamy in general is done at the cost of the social rather than in its defense.[30] This counterintuitive proposition leads us to ask what is it that commitments are thought to secure when they no longer assume monogamy or longevity as their measure or rationale.

Like Thomas, who is interested in the ways in which queer modes of relationality have been brought into long-term bonds, we do not presuppose that all intimate commitments play to the hard-core rules of loyalty, duty, and constancy. Commitments can be loose or hesitant as easily as harsh or demanding, sometimes driven and other times less compelling. Or they may slip the framework of commitment in favor of something more enigmatic, such as acknowledgment, or at least that is what Berlant proposes in her recent two-hander with Lee Edelman around sex and the unbearable necessity of intimate relationality itself: "Acknowledgment, what we do in the sustained presence of an object, . . . performs our obligation to it by way of a looseness that, from the perspective of drama, can constitute a formally comic scene." Whereas her work on melodrama tends to emphasize the cruel optimism of attachment, particularly maternal attachment, Berlant derives this perspective on comic performance and its capacity to "make routes within the impossible" from two scholars: Sedgwick and Stanley Cavell, whose name is less frequently bandied about in queer circles.[31] Indeed, much of Berlant's work on "the attachment to attachment" has its origins in her attachment to Cavell's work on marriage—specifically American marriage as mediated by popular Hollywood cinema—as a form of public-private intimacy.[32] In *Cruel Optimism*, for instance, she acknowledges her indebtedness to his writing on the uncanniness of the ordinary as "an interesting space . . . for inventing new rhythms for living, rhythms that could, at any time, congeal into norms, forms, and institutions."[33] Earlier, in *The Female Complaint*, she notes that her idea of "whatever optimism," which explicitly connects her work with that of Giorgio Agamben, "is also cognate, I think, with Stanley Cavell's argument in *Contesting Tears*, that love ideally involves a commitment to a mutual continuity without guarantees."[34] More recently, she has acknowledged her interest in Cavell's thinking on the Hollywood comedy of remarriage, a genre that at first glance (and even a second look) seems an unlikely match to queer theoretical interests.[35] In her contribution to a *Critical Inquiry* special issue on comedy, Berlant references Cavell as an outlier among comedy theorists—most of whom insist that humorlessness is key to comedy—in his promotion of remarriage comedy as "a test of the conditions of freedom in relation."[36] Like Berlant, we also think that Cavell is a go-to theorist for anyone wanting to put the comedy back in what might otherwise be read as the cruel optimism of queer commitment.

For those unfamiliar with his idea that the real mark of marriage is re-marriage, Cavell has written, not one, but two books about the same Hollywood movies, as if he understood the need for—or should that be "a commitment to"—getting things wrong before you have a shot at getting them right, a premise that underwrites the seven films he is obsessed by, all of which involve a married couple getting back together after the error of their estrangement.[37] Whereas one of us has elsewhere argued for the critical utility of the notion of remarriage in the context of gay marriage, and does so again in one of the two couple contributions included in this book, for present purposes we follow Cavell in suggesting that perhaps what we want, when we don't want commitment, is enchantment.[38] Understood as a benign process of perpetual reattachment that thrives on change, enchantment delivers us the best version of ourselves in the object to which we continuously yet spontaneously attach. Whether that object be a person, a project, a scene, or an abstraction (like God or America, for enchantments are both specific and generic), and no matter how misconceived that commitment looks to someone outside it (or even on the receiving end of it), enchantment secures attachment, even attachments such as marriages, which some like to think are built on more solid institutional ground. Drawing a long historical and complacently Eurocentric bow, Cavell argues that since the time of Luther and Henry VIII, "it has been a more or less open secret in our world that we do not know what legitimizes either divorce or marriage." Within this context of secular uncertainty, and coincident with the American middle-class acceptance of divorce, a Hollywood comedy genre arises that

> emphasizes the mystery of marriage by finding that neither law nor sexuality (nor, by implication, progeny) is sufficient to ensure true marriage and suggesting that what provides legitimacy is the mutual willingness for remarriage, for a sort of continuous reaffirmation, and one in which the couple's isolation from the rest of the world is generally marked; they form as it were a world elsewhere. The spirit of comedy in these films depends on our willingness to entertain the possibility of such a world, one in which good dreams come true.[39]

This dream world is the world of marriage equality. Although Cavell makes the connection between his interest in the generic reinvestment in marriage represented by the Hollywood comedies of remarriage and the worldly expansion of the institution to include same-sex marriage, he immediately slides out from under the obligation to think of the two forms of marriage together: "While same-sex marriages, or unions, have become common enough to force a consciousness, and elaboration, of the economic and legal consequences for partners and for children reared in such marriages, it is too early yet to know (or I am too isolated in my experience to tell) what new shapes such marriages will discover for their investments in imaginativeness, exclusiveness, and equality."[40] Drawing on their own experience inside or outside marriage-like unions, many of our contributors investigate precisely these contours of commitment, from the creative blockages of palliative caregiving to the inequalities at the core of prison volunteerism, to the changed understanding of what it takes to build enduring queer families now that there is a transnational reproductive market that brokers interracial gamete donation and surrogacy.

Whether they consider films or novels, add to the growing genre of queer life writing, or touch on issues of fiscal or institutional policy, the essays in this collection engage with queer commitments as they are extended and retracted in the bedroom, the classroom, the doctor's office, in multispecies households, state penitentiaries, on the dance floor, and via the virtual byways of contemporary hookup culture. As this summary suggests, the genres of long-term commitment never stand still but, like all genres, bend to accommodate novelty and change, as each of our contributors well understands. Together, these essays orient us to the psychic and affective polyculture that queer commitments can induce. As always, however, our thinking in this area is often outrun by the popular genres themselves. In this introduction's remainder we turn to two subgenres that combine photography and autoethnography in order to capture the intricacies of commitment premarriage and postmarriage equality, a moment in which the distinction between normative and antinormative is often hard to define.[41] Like the theorists of commitment we have drawn on, the popular genres we point to invoke multiple ways of being with someone or something for the duration, however short, long, or indeterminate that time span may be.[42]

Our first example is East Coast–based photographer Sage Sohier's *At Home with Themselves: Same-Sex Couples in 1980s America*, a glossy photobook published in 2014 that documents queer racialized commitments against the backdrop of late twentieth-century norms of the long term. Featuring black-and-white photographs of LGBTQ couples and their families, children, and pets, *At Home with Themselves* is itself a long-term project. Featuring Mexican American, Anglo American, African American, and Filipino subjects, the photographs were taken across a near twenty-year span, from 1986 to 2002, with many couples being photographed twice at least a decade apart. The book is formally divided into two parts: a portfolio of staged portraits followed by transcripts of personal interviews with the subjects from the moment the photographs were taken. Where photograph titles are uniformly minimalist—*Lloyd & Joel, San Francisco, 1987; Lloyd & Joel, Stockbridge, MA, 2002*—the interviews are briefly prefaced with notes about relationship duration, occupation, and general well-being. The sixty or so full-page couple portraits in the book range across gender, race, ethnicity, age, class, and geography, with a concentration of subjects hailing from the demographically queer epicenters of New Orleans, San Francisco, and Boston. Collectively, these photographs testify to "the prevalence, variety, and longevity of gay and lesbian relationships" within the wider context of American urbanity and its domestic life-stylings.[43]

Some of the photographic updates reveal the deaths from AIDS-related causes of previously photographed subjects, but the emotional tone in which this information is delivered shares none of the outrage and militancy historically associated with public activism around the HIV/AIDS crisis. Throughout the book the framing of LGBTQ social trauma—and LGBTQ social justice—remains intimate, as does the visual prominence of the "long-time companion," a relational mode and caretaking identity central to the lives and deaths of many LGBTQ persons in the 1980s and 1990s that went into mainstream circulation via the obituary pages of the *New York Times* and Norman René's 1989 film of the same title. The photographs and verbatim transcripts reflect the long-term relational achievements and challenges of being LGBTQ in the United States from the Reagan years to the time when George W. Bush reprised his father's role in the White House, a period in which the idea of same-sex couples gaining popular support for the right to marry remained a political pipe dream.

Although Sohier's intent is to capture "private love" in the usual routines of domesticity, where couples cook breakfast, get dressed, or share a bathtub together, the book sometimes records a more collective desire for literal marriage or an equivalently public display of intimate commitment (7).[44] Whereas some of the same-sex couples express ambivalence about long-term intimacies, others claim marriage as a jointly held aspiration. *Cindy & Barb's Wedding, Boston, 1986* shows two besuited white women in a crowded kitchen, surrounded by well-wishers, slicing into a pseudo–wedding cake seven years before the Supreme Court of Hawai'i ruled bans on same-sex marriage unconstitutional, thereby super-boosting the US marriage-equality movement (see figure I.1).

Other couples are captured in equally iconic forms of commitment. David and Eric have been *"on and off, for 10 years,"* although the intravenous

FIGURE I.1. *Cindy & Barb's Wedding, Boston, 1986*. Photograph by Sage Sohier. Reproduced with permission.

cannula on Eric's chest and his holding hands with David on an unmade bed conveys the steadfast nature of their relationship to a camera that neither he nor his boyfriend looks at directly (82). In the corner of their bedroom, alongside a chrome IV stand, there is an equivalently tall armless boy mannequin, smooth groin and hips girded in stretch underpants, who stares with them along the same oblique sight line (see figure I.2). Constructing clear, clean frontal frames around LGBTQ couples with nothing to hide, *At Home with Themselves* elsewhere quietly teases away at what counts as longevity. "*Together 45 years; have lived together 36 years*," Lloyd and Joel have also been "*in a threesome with John (not shown) for 23 years*" (91). The couple seen in *Jean & Elaine, Santa Fe, 1988* have been together for less than half a year, whereas George and Tom, two well-preserved Florida retirees in their mid-sixties, talk about Tom's suicide attempt and speak of aging as if it were a liability rather than the jackpot of life.

As these examples make clear, *At Home with Themselves* surveys different understandings and experiences of long-term intimacies. Combining visual documentation with self-reflection, the book is rife with negotiations of change and care as commitments splinter and foster new allegiances in their wake, a dynamic that several of our contributors also detail at length. *Shadow, San Francisco, 2002*, for instance, captures a bearded man seated in

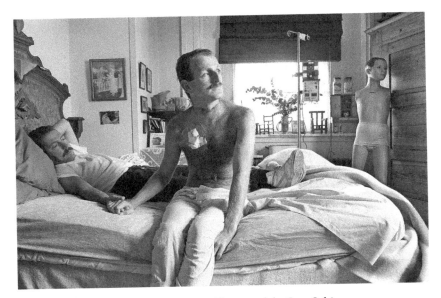

FIGURE I.2. *David & Eric, Boston, 1986.* Photograph by Sage Sohier.
Reproduced with permission.

FIGURE I.3. *Shadow, San
Francisco, 2002.* Photograph
by Sage Sohier. Reproduced
with permission.

a plastic chair, hands clasped, looking directly at the camera. The only solo portrait in the book, the photograph is linked to an earlier couple photograph, *Shadow & Sky, San Francisco, 1987*, and two interview transcriptions, also from 1987 and 2002 (see figure I.3). In the second transcript, Shadow, now aged forty-one, speaks about a decade of transitioning and the intimacies, counterpublics, and family relationships that have sustained him across that time. "I identify as a gay man," he matter-of-factly states. "[I] haven't had a long-term relationship since Sky and I broke up. . . . I've had on-and-off relationships, but they're not like partner relationships" (96).

Although she stays out of sight, Sohier is also implicated in the forms of lesbian, trans, gay, and queer-of-color longevity that she documents. As she acknowledges in the prologue, the origins of the book are in her "lifelong curiosity about my father," who shared apartments with various men for decades, although his relationship with them was never broached conversationally (5). Sohier's photographs of LGBTQ couples are dedicated to her father and his male partner of forty years, an aesthetic surrogate for the domestic life they never openly shared with her or her sister. With regard to its reparative effect, as well as its content, Sohier's book is precisely what we have in mind when we think about what queered commitment entails at this particular moment.

Our second example of the expanding genres of commitment is the Museum of Broken Relationships, founded as a pop-up in Zagreb, Croatia, in 2010, with a landed offshoot opening in Los Angeles in 2016 and shuttering the following year. The antithesis of lover's padlocks attached to wire fences in Cinque Terre or steel trees in Moscow, the museum's globally dispersed sites offer curatorial space for the remnants of failed or finished relationships, whether a former high school crush or a thirty-five-year marriage that ended in divorce. They exhibit "objects donated anonymously by members of the public from all over the world," including, to date, Brazil, China, Qatar, South Korea, Spain, Switzerland, Mexico, Belgium, the United States, the Netherlands, and Ireland. Along with the objects, donors also give accounts of their provenance in broken relationships that the museum terms "brokenships," a tongue-in-cheek neologism that fast becomes sincere.[45]

In its LA instantiation the museum presented as a minimalist white box amid all the tat and trash where Hollywood Boulevard intersects Highland Avenue. When visited in spring 2017, not long before its closing, the immaculate vitrines held running medals, a cheerleader outfit, a piñata, pubic hair, belly-button lint, a used set of silicone breast implants, handwritten notes, and an empty bottle of rum. These queered objects were paired with wall texts prefaced by curatorial notes that specify the time span and the place across which the now broken relationship endured. The rest of the wall text was given over to first-person accounts of marriages that had reached breaking point, soured friendships, abandoned ideals ("this is my breakup with hope"), lost youth, and everyday lives altered by unexpected disability.[46] Yet the more that the visitor wandered and read—or scrolled, if you happen to be in the museum's virtual exhibition—this initial impression of erotic idiosyncrasy gave way to banal uniformity, as if all brokenships were ultimately the same, at least to the degree that they insist on personal uniqueness.

As this sampling of first-person accounts suggests, the Museum of Broken Relationships often archives something other than failed long-term romance even as it exhibits a ton of failed long-term romance. "The museum's concept," the print catalog informs us, "was born when the founders—Olinka Vištica and Dražin Grubišić—wondered what people did with objects that had been meaningful in their relationships."[47] Although it had its origins in the founding couple's broken romance, the museum's brief has subsequently expanded to include broken commitments of any kind as well as those that refuse to break whatever the circumstance. For instance, the Los Angeles museum exhibited a pair of well-worn denim jeans that connects to a heterosexual marriage based in the small town of Hailey, Idaho. The collection label dated this relationship from 1983 to 2009 and informed visitors in the ubiquitous first person that the wearer of the jeans, "my husband, the father of our children, was hit by an elk on his motorcycle one summer evening." The text ran on to say that "he is able to talk, although his reality is very different. He time travels to different decades of his life, locations, and people. He is still there, but I have had to learn how to live with a broken relationship, a one-sided relationship."[48] With one partner cognitively and affectively elsewhere, this relationship is simultaneously over and ongoing. Sitting uncomfortably across genres of disability, trauma, and everyday life, this testimony to a spoiled yet enduring commitment alters how we calibrate attachment and loss, a theme that is also taken up by several of our contributors, who anchor their observations in disability and debility studies, as well as the companion field of mad studies, in order to engage what disability justice activist Leah Lakshmi Piepzna-Samarasinha has called "long-term survivorhood."[49]

Although it is not a nominally LGBTQ archive, the Museum of Broken Relationships has an inclusive approach to documenting attachment and detachment in all its diversity.[50] As a blended museum with virtual and actual displays, the exhibits curated by the Museum of Broken Relationships speak to any number of breached dependencies, many of which have come up in our own thinking in this area. But whether they deal with compulsions to lovers, friends, objects, or substances, the consistent element connecting all these exhibits is narration itself and the need to position oneself, however provisionally, in relation to a no-longer-shared past. Most of these narratives register as both highly personal and strangely impersonal—even the obsessional or violent details register predictably, like the melted cell phone retrieved from an oven. Many of the exhibits also revealed the projects of collation that are part and parcel of falling in love: the kept 3M love notes, the serial regiftings or found items repurposed as tokens, and the claiming of representational ciphers for a shared attachment to the world, such as the assembly of tins, boxes, and books emblazoned with a "mutually loved font."[51] Many of the anonymous donors expressed relief or just a sense of rightness at being able to hand over to the impersonal collecting drive of a museum the custodianship of some personal object they wanted to be without but could not discard. The gift shop accommodated this ambivalence in other ways, peddling an array of T-shirts, coffee cups, books, and other commodities that spoke to the productive alienation of emotion on a broader scale. In this sense the museum's rightful home is Hollywood and the Boulevard of Broken Dreams, the place where the attachment to the fantasy of attachment is played out on an industrial scale, although now the narrational output is meme-like rather than feature-length and commonly accessed in print-to-order publications available online.

When taken together, *At Home with Themselves* and the Museum of Broken Relationships invoke and at times reinforce normative genres of the long term, but they also suggest their compatibility with nonnormative content. This lived tension is explored in this volume as our contributors broach diverse forms of commitment to other people, to animals, to the couple form, to caretaking, to genres, to race, to class, to careers, to prisoners, to therapy, to saving, to practice, to theory. For all the inclusiveness of this list, we are still troubled by what else might have been included and the gaps left by those who reluctantly withdrew from this project because of overcommitment.

Rather than presenting as the last word on commitment and the long term, the original essays that follow open onto a set of theoretical inquiries that invite ongoing attention as a form of what Elizabeth Freeman might call chronic thinking, or observations produced in and of a situation that is persistent rather than resolvable.[52] Featuring case studies drawn from sites such as contemporary Asian American literary fiction, sentimental literature, endurance performance art, HIV/AIDS and personal illness narratives, trans-of-color documentary film, and a threnody of mourning, these essays engage the implications of the long term as their authors have come to know it. Although the collection was never designed with any consensus in mind, as the essays arrived in our inboxes we nonetheless began to sense a shared aesthetic and theoretical adherence to the "experimental critical writing" that Sedgwick reserves for prose and poetry that dilutes the boundaries "between genres, between 'critical' and 'creative' writing, between private and public address, between argumentation and performance"—and between the personal and the impersonal. Sedgwick reminds us that these committed writing styles have been around much longer than any of us and were historically jump-started by "liberatory theoretical movements around race, colonialism, and sexuality."[53] As Johnson's foreword also reminds us, these stylistics have historically functioned as instruction manuals for "how we as queers commit to life and living despite a contemporaneous world in which we are constantly under siege."

We are happy to report that this tradition of committed life writing is alive and kicking within LGBTQ studies, as evidenced in queer feminist autotheory; in trans memoir; in the antiracist ethnography Johnson models in his writing with Black queer Southern women; and in those chapters ahead that eschew the impersonal academic voice in favor of something more queerly indentured.[54] Even as they deal in theoretically rigorous ways with interracial dynamics, coupling and uncoupling, interspecies animacy and technologically driven sound, generational divides and overlaps, cognitive and physical disabilities, incapacity, licit and illicit drug use, kinship, care and stranger intimacy, we also noted how many were unsolicited refreshings of the queer life writing tradition. We hope that readers will take up—and take issue with—all that is laid out in these pages in a way that keeps knowledge production in this area engaged and attentive to its conditions of possibility. In the network-provider speak that perpetually pimps the world while disclaiming it, we invite you to browse further but make no commitment on your behalf.

NOTES

1 Astrida Neimanis and Jennifer Hamilton, "The Weather Is Now Political," *Conversation*, May 22, 2017, https://theconversation.com/the-weather-is-now-political -77791. For a lengthier discussion of weathering, see Neimanis and Walker, "*Weathering*."

2 See Berlant, *Intimacy*.

3 For a reengagement of the personal and impersonal impulses undergirding the theoretical enterprise, see Jagose and Wallace, "Dicktation."

4 For more on twenty-first-century digital innovations of sexual cultures, see Kipnis, *Unwanted Advances*, and Dean, "Introduction: Pornography, Technology, Archive."

5 Berlant and Warner, "Sex in Public," 326.

6 Warner, *The Trouble with Normal*, 98. For further historical and theoretical elaborations of queer marriage, see Franke, *Wedlocked*; Cleves, "'What, Another Female Husband?'"; Chauncey, *Why Marriage?*; Freeman, *The Wedding Complex*; Chenier, "Love-Politics"; and Shelden, *Unmaking Love*.

7 Muñoz, *Cruising Utopia*, 10.

8 Rodríguez, *Sexual Futures*, 35, 36.

9 Reddy, "Race and the Critique of Marriage," 430. See also Reddy, "Time for Rights?"

10 Moynihan, "The Negro Family," 12, 14, 19.

11 See Spillers, "Mama's Baby, Papa's Maybe," and Ferguson, *Aberrations in Black*, 119–23.

12 Ahmed, *Queer Phenomenology*, 177. See also Ahmed, *On Being Included*.

13 Thomas, "Is Black Marriage Queer?," 208, 211.

14 Moore, "Reflections on Marriage Equality," 78. See also Moore, "Marriage Equality."

15 Moore, "Reflections on Marriage Equality," 73, 75, 77.

16 Although these ideas now circulate under the umbrella term the *antisocial thesis*, they are more compellingly encountered in the particularity of their source documents: Caserio et al., "The Antisocial Thesis in Queer Theory"; Halberstam, *The Queer Art of Failure*; and Edelman, *No Future*. For longevity critiques, see Halberstam, *In a Queer Time and Place*; Puar, "Prognosis Time"; and Berlant, "Do You Intend to Die?"

17 See Lowe, *The Intimacies of Four Continents*; Shah, *Stranger Intimacy*; Dean, *Unlimited Intimacy*; Bersani and Phillips, *Intimacies*; and Kunzel, *Criminal Intimacy*.

18 Ahmed, *Queer Phenomenology*, 178.

19 *Oxford English Dictionary*, "commitment," www.oed.com.

20 *OED*, "commit."

21 *OED*.

22 *OED*, "commitment ceremony."

23 *OED*, "commit"; *OED*, "commitment order."

24 A quick (unhyphenated) search on one of our browsers immediately returns the following click-bait headers: "42 Signs You're in Love with a Commitment-Phobe"; "Commitment-Phobe: 7 Signs He's Terrified of Being in a Relationship"; "12 Women Reveal What It Takes to Nudge a Commitment Phobic Man into a Relationship"; "7 Types of Commitment Phobe"; "10 Signs that Your Lover Is Commitment Phobic"; and "10 Things Commitment Phobic Men Need to Know."

25 Phillips, *On Flirtation*, xi, xviii.

26 For his discussion of Bartleby and the lessons his patients with anorexia nervosa have taught him, see Phillips, "On Eating, and Preferring Not To." For a wider discussion of what is at stake in Bartleby's second life on Wall Street, see Castronovo, "Occupy Bartleby."

27 For relevant literatures on organizational commitment, see Mercurio, "Affective Commitment as a Core Essence of Organizational Commitment."

28 For a classic account of the human tendency to hedge one commitment with another one, see Becker, "Note on the Concept of Commitment."

29 Phillips, *On Flirtation*, xviii–xix. See also Kipnis, *Against Love*, 201, where, using Phillips, she "flirts with paradox" in her thoughts on marriage and adultery.

30 Bersani, "Against Monogamy," 11, 6.

31 Berlant and Edelman, *Sex, or the Unbearable*, 89–90, 90. For more of Berlant's thinking around comedy, see Berlant and Ngai, "Comedy Has Issues."

32 Berlant and Edelman, *Sex, or the Unbearable*, 90.

33 Berlant, *Cruel Optimism*, 9.

34 Berlant, *The Female Complaint*, 310.

35 The connection between Berlant and Cavell is pursued further in Wallace, *Reattachment Theory*.

36 Berlant, "Humorlessness," 313.

37 The seven films that obsess Cavell are, in the order in which he discusses them, *The Lady Eve* (Preston Sturges, 1941), *It Happened One Night* (Frank Capra, 1934), *Bringing Up Baby* (Howard Hawks, 1938), *The Philadelphia Story* (George Cukor, 1940), *His Girl Friday* (Howard Hawks, 1940), *Adam's Rib* (George Cukor, 1949), and *The Awful Truth* (Leo McCarey, 1937). Initially discussed in *Pursuits of Happiness*, these same seven films are revisited in *Cities of Words*.

38 See Wallace, *Reattachment Theory*.

39 Cavell, *Pursuits of Happiness*, 142.

40 Cavell, *Cities of Words*, 16.

41 For more on such blurring, see Wiegman and Wilson, "Introduction: Antinormativity's Queer Conventions."

42 For more about the queer dimensionalities of temporality, duration, and repetition, see Freeman, *Time Binds*.

43 Sohier, *At Home with Themselves*, 6. Page references to Sohier will hereafter be given parenthetically in the text.

44 For discussion of the racialized contours of queer domesticity as they emerge in US public health discourse, see Shah, *Contagious Divides*, 77–104. For an equally historical account of the role of domestic food preparation and consumption in the emergence of American gay male identity, see Vider, "'Oh Hell, May, Why Don't You People Have a Cookbook?'"

45 "About Us," Museum of Broken Relationships, Los Angeles, 2016, http://brokenships.la/about.

46 "Betty Boop Doll: 2013 to Present: Los Angeles, California," *Museum of Broken Relationships*.

47 *Museum of Broken Relationships*.

48 "Blue Jeans: 1985 to 2009: Hailey, Idaho," *Museum of Broken Relationships*.

49 Piepzna-Samarasinha, *Care Work*, 237. Piepzna-Samarasinha is responding to Eli Clare's call that we "embrace our brokenness." See Clare, *Brilliant Imperfection*, 160. Further iterations of queer disability studies and queer debility studies can be found in Puar, *The Right to Maim*; Kafer, *Feminist, Queer, Crip*; Chen, *Animacies*; and McRuer, *Crip Times*.

50 The museum's popular transnational spread might therefore be considered alongside recent work on queer archiving such as Richardson, *The Queer Limit of Black Memory*, and Cvetkovich, *An Archive of Feelings*.

51 "Mutually Loved Davida Font: October 2008 to December 2012: Los Angeles, California," *Museum of Broken Relationships.*

52 Freeman, "Hopeless Cases."

53 Sedgwick, "Teaching 'Experimental Critical Writing,'" 104. We have in mind Jean-Paul Sartre's account of committed writing as it appears in *What Is Literature?* See Goldthorpe, *Sartre,* and Berman, *Modernist Commitments,* for more recent accounts of how philosophical ideas around commitment have overlap with experimental writing across the twentieth century.

54 See Johnson, *Black. Queer. Southern. Women.,* 280–322; and Johnson, *Honeypot.*

BIBLIOGRAPHY

Ahmed, Sara. *On Being Included: Racism and Diversity in Institutional Life.* Durham, NC: Duke University Press, 2012.

Ahmed, Sara. *Queer Phenomenology: Orientations, Objects, Others.* Durham, NC: Duke University Press, 2006.

Becker, Howard S. "Note on the Concept of Commitment." *American Journal of Sociology* 66, no. 1 (1960): 32–40.

Berlant, Lauren. *Cruel Optimism.* Durham, NC: Duke University Press, 2011.

Berlant, Lauren. "Do You Intend to Die? Lauren Berlant on Intimacy after Suicide." *King's Review,* March 4, 2015. www.kingsreview.co.uk/laurenberlantonintimacy.

Berlant, Lauren. *The Female Complaint: The Unfinished Business of Sentimentality in American Culture.* Durham, NC: Duke University Press, 2008.

Berlant, Lauren. "Humorlessness (Three Monologues and a Hairpiece)." *Critical Inquiry* 43, no. 2 (2017): 305–40.

Berlant, Lauren, ed. *Intimacy.* Chicago: University of Chicago Press, 2000.

Berlant, Lauren, and Lee Edelman. *Sex, or the Unbearable.* Durham, NC: Duke University Press, 2014.

Berlant, Lauren, and Sianne Ngai. "Comedy Has Issues: An Introduction." *Critical Inquiry* 43, no. 2 (2017): 233–49.

Berlant, Lauren, and Michael Warner. "Sex in Public." In Berlant, *Intimacy,* 311–30.

Berman, Jessica. *Modernist Commitments: Ethics, Politics, and Transnational Modernism.* New York: Columbia University Press, 2011.

Bersani, Leo. "Against Monogamy." *Oxford Literary Review* 20, nos. 1/2 (1998): 3–21.

Bersani, Leo, and Adam Phillips. *Intimacies.* Chicago: University of Chicago Press, 2008.

Caserio, Robert L., Lee Edelman, Jack [Judith] Halberstam, José Esteban Muñoz, and Tim Dean. "The Antisocial Thesis in Queer Theory." *PMLA* 121, no. 3 (2006): 819–28.

Castronovo, Russ. "Occupy Bartleby." *J19* 2, no. 2 (2014): 253–72.

Cavell, Stanley. *Cities of Words: Pedagogical Letters on a Register of the Moral Life.* Cambridge, MA: Harvard University Press, 2004.

Cavell, Stanley. *Pursuits of Happiness: The Hollywood Comedy of Remarriage.* Cambridge, MA: Harvard University Press, 1981.

Chauncey, George. *Why Marriage? The History Shaping Today's Debate over Gay Equality.* New York: Basic Books, 2005.

Chen, Mel Y. *Animacies: Biopolitics, Racial Mattering, and Queer Affect*. Durham, NC: Duke University Press, 2012.

Chenier, Elise. "Love-Politics: Lesbian Wedding Practices in Canada and the United States from the 1920s to the 1970s." *Journal of the History of Sexuality* 27, no. 2 (2018): 294–321.

Clare, Eli. *Brilliant Imperfection: Grappling with Cure*. Durham, NC: Duke University Press, 2017.

Cleves, Rachel Hope. "'What, Another Female Husband?': The Prehistory of Same-Sex Marriage in America." *Journal of American History* 101, no. 4 (2015): 1055–81.

Cvetkovich, Ann. *An Archive of Feelings: Trauma, Sexuality, and Lesbian Public Cultures*. Durham, NC: Duke University Press, 2003.

Dean, Tim. "Introduction: Pornography, Technology, Archive." In *Porn Archives*, edited by Tim Dean, Steven Ruszczycky, and David Squires, 1–26. Durham, NC: Duke University Press, 2014.

Dean, Tim. *Unlimited Intimacy: Reflections on the Subculture of Barebacking*. Chicago: University of Chicago Press, 2009.

Edelman, Lee. *No Future: Queer Theory and the Death Drive*. Durham, NC: Duke University Press, 2004.

Ferguson, Roderick A. *Aberrations in Black: Toward a Queer of Color Critique*. Minneapolis: University of Minnesota Press, 2004.

Franke, Katherine. *Wedlocked: The Perils of Marriage Equality*. New York: New York University Press, 2015.

Freeman, Elizabeth. "Hopeless Cases: Queer Chronicities and Gertrude Stein's 'Melanctha.'" *Journal of Homosexuality* 63, no. 3 (2016): 329–48.

Freeman, Elizabeth. *Time Binds: Queer Temporalities, Queer Histories*. Durham, NC: Duke University Press, 2010.

Freeman, Elizabeth. *The Wedding Complex: Forms of Belonging in Modern American Culture*. Durham, NC: Duke University Press, 2002.

Goldthorpe, Rhiannon. *Sartre: Literature and Theory*. Cambridge: Cambridge University Press, 1984.

Halberstam, Jack [Judith]. *In a Queer Time and Place: Transgender Bodies, Subcultural Lives*. New York: New York University Press, 2005.

Halberstam, Jack [Judith]. *The Queer Art of Failure*. Durham, NC: Duke University Press, 2011.

Jagose, Annamarie, and Lee Wallace. "Dicktation: Autotheory in the Coupled Voice." In "Autotheory Theory," edited by Robyn Wiegman, special issue, *Arizona Quarterly* 76, no. 1 (2020): 109–39.

Johnson, E. Patrick. *Black. Queer. Southern. Women.: An Oral History*. Chapel Hill: University of North Carolina Press, 2018.

Johnson, E. Patrick. *Honeypot: Black Southern Women Who Love Women*. Durham, NC: Duke University Press, 2019.

Kafer, Alison. *Feminist, Queer, Crip*. Bloomington: Indiana University Press, 2013.

Kipnis, Laura. *Against Love: A Polemic*. New York: Pantheon, 2003.

Kipnis, Laura. *Unwanted Advances: Sexual Paranoia Comes to Campus*. New York: Harper, 2017.

Kunzel, Regina. *Criminal Intimacy: Prison and the Uneven History of Modern American Sexuality*. Chicago: University of Chicago Press, 2008.

Lowe, Lisa. *The Intimacies of Four Continents*. Durham, NC: Duke University Press, 2015.

McRuer, Robert. *Crip Times: Disability, Globalization, and Resistance*. New York: New York University Press, 2018.

Mercurio, Zachary A. "Affective Commitment as a Core Essence of Organizational Commitment: An Integrative Literature Review." *Human Resource Development Review* 14, no. 4 (2015): 389–414.

Moore, Mignon R. "Marriage Equality and the African American Case: Intersections of Race and LGBT Sexuality." *differences* 29, no. 2 (2018): 196–203.

Moore, Mignon. "Reflections on Marriage Equality as a Vehicle for LGBTQ Political Transformation." In *Queer Families and Relationships after Marriage Equality*, edited by Michael W. Yarbrough, Angela Jones, and Joseph Nicholas DeFilippis, 73–79. New York: Routledge, 2019.

Moynihan, Daniel Patrick. "The Negro Family: The Case for National Action." Washington, DC: Office of Policy Planning and Research, U.S. Department of Labor, 1965.

Muñoz, José Esteban. *Cruising Utopia: The Then and There of Queer Futurity*. New York: New York University Press, 2009.

Museum of Broken Relationships. Los Angeles: Museum of Broken Relationships, 2016.

Neimanis, Astrida, and Rachel Loewen Walker. "*Weathering*: Climate Change and the 'Thick Time' of Transcorporeality." *Hypatia* 29, no. 3 (2014): 558–75.

Phillips, Adam. "On Eating, and Preferring Not To." In Phillips, *Promises, Promises: Essays on Psychoanalysis and Literature*, 282–95. London: Faber, 2000.

Phillips, Adam. *On Flirtation*. Cambridge, MA: Harvard University Press, 1994.

Piepzna-Samarasinha, Leah Lakshmi. *Care Work: Dreaming Disability Justice*. Vancouver: Arsenal Pulp, 2018.

Puar, Jasbir K. "Prognosis Time: Towards a Geopolitics of Affect, Debility and Capacity." *Women & Performance* 19, no. 2 (2009): 161–72.

Puar, Jasbir K. *The Right to Maim: Debility, Capacity, Disability*. Durham, NC: Duke University Press, 2017.

Reddy, Chandan. "Race and the Critique of Marriage." *South Atlantic Quarterly* 115, no. 2 (2016): 424–32.

Reddy, Chandan. "Time for Rights? *Loving*, Gay Marriage, and the Limits of Comparative Legal Justice." In *Strange Affinities: The Gender and Sexual Politics of Comparative Racialization*, edited by Grace Kyungwon Hong and Roderick A. Ferguson, 148–74. Durham, NC: Duke University Press, 2011.

Richardson, Matt. *The Queer Limit of Black Memory: Black Lesbian Literature and Irresolution*. Columbus: Ohio State University Press, 2013.

Rodríguez, Juana María. *Sexual Futures, Queer Gestures, and Other Latina Longings*. New York: New York University Press, 2014.

Sartre, Jean-Paul. *What Is Literature?* Translated by Bernard Frechtman. London: Methuen, 1950.

Sedgwick, Eve Kosofsky. "Teaching 'Experimental Critical Writing.'" In *The Ends of Performance*, edited by Peggy Phalen and Jill Lane, 104–15. New York: New York University Press, 1998.

Shah, Nayan. *Contagious Divides: Epidemics and Race in San Francisco's Chinatown.* Berkeley: University of California Press, 2001.

Shah, Nayan. *Stranger Intimacy: Contesting Race, Sexuality, and the Law in the North American West.* Berkeley: University of California Press, 2011.

Shelden, Ashley T. *Unmaking Love: The Contemporary Novel and the Impossibility of Union.* New York: Columbia University Press, 2017.

Sohier, Sage. *At Home with Themselves: Same-Sex Couples in 1980s America.* Boston: Spotted Books, 2014.

Spillers, Hortense J. "Mama's Baby, Papa's Maybe: An American Grammar Book." *Diacritics* 17, no. 2 (1987): 64–81.

Thomas, Kendall. "Is Black Marriage Queer?" *differences* 29, no. 2 (2018): 204–12.

Vider, Stephen. "'Oh Hell, May, Why Don't You People Have a Cookbook?': Camp Humor and Gay Domesticity." *American Quarterly* 65, no. 4 (2013): 877–904.

Wallace, Lee. *Reattachment Theory: Queer Cinema of Remarriage.* Durham, NC: Duke University Press, 2020.

Warner, Michael. *The Trouble with Normal: Sex, Politics, and the Ethics of Queer Life.* Cambridge, MA: Harvard University Press, 2000.

Wiegman, Robyn, and Elizabeth A. Wilson. "Introduction: Antinormativity's Queer Conventions." *differences* 26, no. 1 (2015): 1–25.

No one came to see us. No one, except for the UPS man when Jules sent me books from the office, and manuscripts too, so I wouldn't lose my editing touch. I stacked them in the corner of my bedroom, and continued with *Anna Karenina,* even though I knew very well how it ended. I felt as though I had an obligation to go on until the train thundered out of the station.
—ANNA QUINDLEN, *One True Thing* (1994)

1

COMMITTED TO THE END

On Caretaking, Rereading, and Queer Theory

ELIZABETH FREEMAN

From mid-August 2009 to early January 2011, I was committed to care work: by committed, I mean both that I was highly invested in and dedicated to it, and that I was handed the job as if it were a sentence. A decade ago, my mother, Caroline Freeman, was diagnosed with adult myelogenous leukemia, and as the female of her two children and the one with the more flexible schedule, I took on the project of caring for her, initially from three thousand miles away. This meant taking a quarter-long leave from work, getting on a plane every other week, and going from San Francisco to Boston to be with her for seven days running at a time, while she did three months of inpatient chemotherapy. During these weeks in Boston, I left our three-year-old daughter behind with her other mother, who is herself chronically ill, and then picked up the full-time parenting during the alternating weeks that I was home so my partner could recover. After the unsuccessful chemotherapy ended and my mother was pronounced terminal, I moved her out to San Francisco into a nearby apartment and saw her daily while she did "salvage" chemo, intended to extend her life by as many months as possible. And of course I went back to full-time work. Finally, when Caroline decided after nine months that the salvage chemo was doing her more harm than good, I moved her into a hospice that I also visited every day for three months until her death on the night of January 4, 2011, just before my daughter turned five.

During the time I was taking care of my mother while also raising a small child and compensating when necessary for my partner's disability, I could not read anything new. I could only reread: only one book, and not a work of great literature at that. Christina Lupton has described eighteenth-century readers who reread books and sections of books for the purposes of marking the progression of greater and greater critical powers that added up to a life, but I took up this book repeatedly with no greater insight than I started with.[1] The book I read and reread, and not always from start to finish, was Anna Quindlen's *One True Thing*, a 1994 *New York Times* best seller, a book-club selection, a middlebrow work of contemporary American domestic sentimental fiction.[2]

The genre I chose to accompany my complete immersion in familial care-taking for three people was not incidental. American sentimental literature has portrayed care work as the paradigm for familial intimacy: like "family," care work in the United States ideally takes place in the private dwelling, is performed by unpaid consanguineous or affinal female relatives, and is begotten from and an expression of intense love—all of which characterized my own labors, and if I say I was committed to care work the way one is consigned to prison, that is an expression of how grueling it is to do this work in the late-capitalist United States and not of my love for my mother.[3] In any case, the plot of *One True Thing* also exemplifies these ideals, although it initially foregrounds care as coercion rather than as the spontaneous expression of love. The novel's protagonist, Ellen Gulden, is a twentysomething career builder in the cutthroat world of New York publishing, summoned home by her father, George, to take care of her mother, Kate, who has been diagnosed with terminal cancer. Ellen is a daddy's girl who resents the summons but accepts it because she wants to prove to herself that she has a heart and prove to her father that she can fulfill his rather sudden vision of her as a properly domestic woman, even if up to this point he has raised her to compete in a man's world (24). Ellen has grown up feeling "something even more dismissive than contempt" (64) for Kate, whose homemaking projects she has disparaged as confining and old-fashioned because they do not cumulate into lasting interventions in the world like the work of her English professor father supposedly does.

One True Thing follows the pattern of nineteenth-century domestic sentimentalism, in which white female, especially maternal, values triumph over those of capitalism and the world of labor outside the home. Over the course of the novel, Ellen watches the father whom she once admired fail, over and over again, to rise to the occasion of his wife's illness. While George buries himself in pointless research projects and has sex with younger colleagues in his office, Ellen learns the offices of care, and through them she experiences Kate's greater integrity and strength, coming to love and admire her mother. After Kate dies and the coroner orders—implausibly, it must be noted—an autopsy, the novel blends its sentimentalism with the genre of legal fiction. Ellen, having won a high school prize with an essay on euthanasia, goes before a grand jury, which must decide if it will charge her with having hastened her mother's death by administering an overdose of morphine. She goes through her hearing stoically, knowing she is innocent but assuming that George has killed Kate and let her take the fall for it. Only at the very end, long after the jury declines to charge Ellen on the grounds that she took Kate's life out of mercy, do we learn that George too is innocent and had genuinely believed that Ellen committed the murder, however altruistically. After seeing her father for the first time in eight years, Ellen realizes that Kate had hoarded her morphine pills and then committed suicide, proving herself to be stronger than both of them and intending to spare her loved ones the burden of doing away with her. Kate, or perhaps the love and respect she finally engenders in her husband and daughter, or perhaps domestic womanhood itself, is the novel's "one true thing."

Given the specificities of my own family, it is not surprising that this is the novel I read and reread as my mother lay dying. On the one hand, it was an absurd reading choice: my mother was a very butch straight woman with none of the warm, cozy qualities of Kate Gulden. Whereas Kate and Ellen start a mother-daughter book club in which they reread that urtext of ironized domestic fiction, *Pride and Prejudice,* along with the archetypal family drama *Anna Karenina,* my information-technology-specialist mother and I pored over spreadsheets of her finances and passwords to her various electronic devices. On the other hand, *One True Thing*'s descriptions of a fundamentally selfish English professor, a daughter who had to bend to the discipline of her gender just like I did, and a mother who was worth more than the two of them put together just like mine was clearly spoke to my situation. Moreover, I'm a cisgender femme lesbian and thus, I like to say, female-gendered in triplicate, and my reading choice may reflect the fact that many women turn not only to popular fiction for solace but to domestic fiction and romance in particular—indeed, Kate Gulden herself reads pot-boiler Gothic romances as the cancer ravages her body.[4] Finally, and most importantly for my purposes here, I read and reread *One True Thing* because domestic sentimental fiction traffics in spatiotemporalities that resonated with my experiences in my mother's home, the hospital, her waiting-to-die apartment, and the hospice—and with caretaking in general. What was less obvious to me at the time, but what I would like to work out in the space of this essay, is the way that the spatiotemporalities of domestic fiction, of the act of rereading, and of caretaking intersect with one another: this is clear from the cover of *One True Thing,* which shows a bed—possibly a sickbed, possibly the bed of a caretaker—on which lies an abandoned book, open to a particular page. And I'd like to work out how that intersection might be productive for queer theory, particularly for queer theories of relationality and commitment.

Spatially, both caretaking and sentimental literature involve compression. With caretaking, this shrinkage of space is literal. The fictional caretaker Ellen gives up her job, her New York apartment, and her boyfriend to enter Kate's increasingly restricted world of small-town ladies' lunches, Christmas deco-rations, a wheelchair, and eventually an in-home hospital bed; similarly, as caretaker to my mother I had to unbuild both her rich adult world and a large part of mine. Caroline and I began by stripping down her home and removing her identification, clothing, toiletries, and legal papers in prepa-ration for her hospital stay, for we both knew she might never return. And gradually, over the course of her illness, I dismantled her "before" life, helping her distribute her possessions to others, canceling subscriptions and deliver-ies, calling friends and telling them the news, mailing her final "good-bye" Christmas cards. Eventually, after the inpatient chemotherapy failed, I boxed up a small number of her belongings and mailed them to San Francisco, where she started over in a furnished apartment. Just as Ellen moves Kate's life into the living room where the hospital bed fits, I rebuilt my mother's world, fitting it into the parameters of that little apartment as best I could: I organized her kitchen, bought replacements for what we could not bring out to San Francisco, maintained her appointments, rotated food in and out. And finally, I moved Caroline and one small suitcase into a single room at the Zen Hospice Project, where she got out of bed and into a chair every day until three days before her death, when she finally climbed into bed for the last time. Over the course of the sixteen months all this took, my own world telescoped into the home I shared with my partner and child, my car as I commuted to and from work, my office and classrooms, my mother's various locales, and Facebook: I saw almost nobody socially. In short, in fiction and in reality caretaking work presses inward toward the center that is the ill person: just as Ellen moves from New York City to small-town New England to her mother's house to a bedside, so did my mother's surroundings shrink from the whole city of Boston to an apartment in San Francisco to a hospice room to, finally, a single bed, and I cut off work and friends and, to a certain extent, my spouse and child.

Like caretaking, sentimental literature as a genre condenses setting down to the space of the home and even the suffering body. Lydia Sigourney's classically sentimental poem of 1856, "The Sick Child," for example, plunges the reader into a scene of suffocating physical proximity.[5] The speaker is a mother who has given up the fashionable world of dances and now finds herself tending her sick son in the waning light of the "pale nurse-lamp." Her predominant sensation is that of her child's "fevered arms around me." She goes on to stave off her fears of the child dying by entreating him to "Cling closer, round my bosom / Thy feeble arms entwine / And while the life-throb stirs thy heart, / Be as a part of mine." This poem offers a vision of the caretaker and the taken-care-of as so close that they share not only a room and a bed but also a single body, for which the "life-throb" and heart are synecdochal. The deathbed scene in *One True Thing* resonates rather startlingly with this: Ellen sits with her bedridden mother and describes how

> I began to breathe in tandem with her, and when I inhaled it felt as if whole minutes went by as I waited for her to let the air out again and let me do the same. In. Out. In. Out. Perhaps it was because the breaths were so far apart, perhaps I was faint, but after a long while I began to feel as though I was watching the two of us from some corner of the ceiling, looking down on this evaporated woman with her red hair thin and dull now . . . and her daughter next to her. . . . (184)

Here, synchronized breathing joins Ellen and her mother to the extent that they become a unit that Ellen can see apart from herself. In these two examples separated by a century and a half, sentimental literature reduces plot to setting, and setting to the minutiae of the suffering body, in figures of merger between a familial caretaker and her charge that duplicate the

merger of reader and sufferer. Indeed, these mergers are typical of sentimental literature, which is what Linda Williams calls a "body genre," insofar as
it both focuses on the sensations of its characters' bodies and aims to elicit a
bodily response—here, tears—from its readers, thereby lessening the space
between reader and text.[6]

If the space of sentimental literature and caretaking is characterized by
compression, their temporality is characterized by diffusion: suspensions,
elongations, and dilations that belie the figure of a time line or the fiction
of progress.[7] Accordingly, *One True Thing* lingers on the mundane details
of Ellen's days with Katherine, making it feel slow to many readers (if Ama-
zon.com reviews are admissible evidence for reader responses). And Kate's
deathbed scene, in which Ellen seems to watch herself and Kate breathe in
tandem, slows time to nearly a standstill:

> In. Out. In. Out. They breathed in unison, and as I watched them I
> wondered which would stop first. And then one did, the mother, and
> the sound brought me back to myself, out of the daze into which the
> slow repetitive sound had allowed me to fall. There was a sound like
> that a car makes when it won't start on a cold morning, an *eh eh eh*
> deep in my mother's throat. . . . A shudder shook her body, and then
> the sound once more: *eh eh eh,* and one last long inhalation of breath.
>
> I waited for her to exhale, waited for so long, holding her fingers,
> feeling them small under my own. I laid my head down near the foot
> of the bed but I did not let go until I could tell by a faint shift of the
> black outside that it was almost morning. (185)

My mother's death was much the same: I remember counting her last breaths,
her left hand in mine, her right hand in my brother's, as we lay on either side
of her hospital bed like we had lain in her single-mom double bed as small
children for story time. After she was gone, my brother went to a different
room to sleep, but I stayed with her body and got up every half hour or so to
slide my hand under the back of her neck, where she was still warm, until I
fell into an exhausted sleep for a couple of hours very early in the morning,
and then woke up and slid my hand under her one more time, and she was
cold, and I knew she was gone.

As the figures of the "life-throb" that binds Sigourney's mother and child
and the breathing that binds Ellen and her mother suggest, in sentimental
literature the clock and calendar recede, earthly time stands still, and the
temporalities of the body expand. Relying on the body as a chronometer,
Sigourney's mother measures time by the "half-broken sob of thine / Which

tells that sleep is near" and staves off memories of her baby's past in her arms and possible future in a coffin by attending to the "heavy knell" of his breathing. In nineteenth-century sentimental literature, this body-time allows access to the sacred, as the speaker prays that God will give her the strength to surrender "not [to] my will, but thine," altogether relinquishing forward agency. The poem, then, hints at sentimental literature's intervention into linear-progressive time—generally, the time of agency, nation, and capitalist accumulation—for which sentimental literature substitutes a static, unmoving sacred time, sometimes in an overtly religious idiom, and sometimes in related idioms such as mourning, suffering, tending the hearth, and family feeling.[8] In "The Sick Child" we see little of what this sacred time displaces, as it has expanded to quite literally fill the nursery; the poem's only nods to other temporalities are a reference to a past "summer's eve" of dancing and to the "midnight hour" during which the mother breast-fed her newborn. All that is missing from *One True Thing* is the religiosity.

In sum, the space-time of caretaking and of the sentimental consists of compressed, almost eliminated space and expanded, undifferentiated, yet highly saturated time. And the spatiotemporalities of caretaking and of the sentimental overlap to such an extent that doing the former feels like living inside of the latter, and reading the latter can be—at least was, for me—a way of surviving the former. But if a literary genre and a life genre, as it were, could be almost coextensive, what I could not figure out for years was why, during this time of living inside a literary genre, I did not simply read the way I had done for so much of my adult life, using the stretched-out hours and long waits that are inherent to caretaking to read *more* books, *more* works of domestic sentimental fiction. Indeed, I could probably have read the complete run of *Godey's Lady's Book* or every Oprah's Book Club selection during the sixteen months I took care of my mother. But instead I read and reread the same book. *One True Thing* even captures this aspect of my obsession with it: upon hearing about Ellen and Kate's mother-daughter book club, George remarks that Ellen has read *Pride and Prejudice* "a hundred times" (49). So Ellen, too, embarks on a project of rereading domestic fiction, though a distinctly satirical version of it that matches her own skeptical wit, just as she becomes a caretaker. And she finishes, on the night of her mother's death, by "reading the same page of *Anna Karenina* over and over again, the one in which Anna rides on horseback in a black habit, her hair in curls" (183). This shift from reading entire works multiple times to a kind of stuttering rereading of a single passage is closer to what I did while I was taking care of Caroline. Why did Ellen reread, and why did I reread, not just the same novel but the same page over and over and over again? What do rereading and caretaking have to do with each other? And, more to the point of this volume, what are the stakes of figuring out this strange dual commitment for queer theory?

On Rereading

One way to think about rereading is that it is a process of turning time into space, and thereby of transcending time, quite on a par with sentimental literature's reduction of plot to setting and to the body itself. When, every day, I opened *One True Thing* to a random page and began reading, and Ellen reads "*Anna Karenina*, even though I knew very well how it ended" (159) and then gets stuck on the same page, we read with a knowledge of the whole structure of the novel, the way that one can apprehend a short poem's parts almost simultaneously. In fact, the act of rereading a novel brings the centripetal force of the novel's entire structure to bear on a particular passage, pulling the outside in, as it were. This spatialization of the text, in turn, mitigates against the forward movement of plot. One rarely, if ever, immediately rereads a book just for plot. Instead, we reread for the whole. When we reread, that is, formerly diachronous events assume a synchronicity, taking place simultaneously in our mind.[9] In the process of rereading, the progressive-linear time of any novel tilts into monumental, eternal, or sacred time—again, the time of sentimentality. This version of sacred time may be all that nonreligious people like me have with which to think and experience something like the afterlife, a temporality in which the dead person is somehow still present. Perhaps rereading was, for me at least, a rehearsal of the idea that after my mother's death, I could turn back to her, bring the parts of her life that were strung out across a historical time line together into an essence that would still, somehow, coincide with my own present tense, that would accord with Lupton's idea that rereading a work several times over a lifetime and finding different things in it can grant continuity to one's own life almost as an obituary does—but applied to another person. Perhaps Ellen's rereading of the same page of *Anna Karenina* is similar, for she sees the page "as though it's yet another picture on our piano: the horse, the habit, the dark curls" (183), the description merging with the family photos that depict lives across time to create a still life, to cease time's forward movement.

At the same time, rereading the same passage involves not only forestalling the ending but proleptically arriving at it. For I also think I was committed to rereading during my mother's terminal illness precisely for the same reason that Ellen feels "an obligation to go on until the train thunder[s] out of the station" (159): because I knew the ending of Caroline's story. When you know the ending, you are no longer in a rush to get there—you are, in a sense, so committed to the ending that you both read to fend off the inevitable and read everything with the ending in mind. You can linger forever in the middle. In fact, when I do reread like this, I often focus on a single paragraph just as Ellen does with the scene of Anna on horseback, returning to its beginning and reading it several times so that I can experience the ending of the paragraph over and over again, and so that I can read that paragraph as if the ending were already in it. The only other novel I have read this way in adulthood, I should admit, is *Lolita* (1955), which has several paragraphs detailing Humbert's first physical connections with Lolita that align ideally with the act of self-pleasuring and so must be paced accordingly or read and reread in rapid succession—a confession I'm only willing to make because it supports my understanding that body genres often reduce the action of the story to the vagaries of the bodies inside the stories in an attempt to take hold of the readerly bodies they address and instigate bodily mimicry. What may distinguish some body genres—pornography, sentimentality, and perhaps suspense and melodrama—from others, such as horror (which relies on surprise), is the question of timing, the question of when the readerly body is prepared for and can bearably experience the ending it has committed to. If rereading *Lolita* has duplicated for me, on the level of the paragraph, the process of arousal and orgasm, rereading *One True Thing* duplicated for me on the level of the entire novel the process of taking care of my mother, in which I often focused on the most trivial of details, lingering on them, perseverating about them, marking each one as perhaps the last time I would do whatever it was I was doing and so doing it with the end in mind, even as doing it seemed to somehow delay the ending.

It's in the overlap between my rereadings of *Lolita* and my rereadings of *One True Thing* that I might be able to stake a claim for rereading and caretaking as feminine acts, perhaps even queer acts in a feminine key—that is, femme acts. Rereading, like caretaking, is an act of repetition. In deconstruction and the queer theory that has emerged from it, repetition is generally understood to be imperfect and its imperfections productive of new and liberating possibilities for meaning.[10] Matei Calinescu's detailed study of rereading follows this way of thinking, arguing along the same lines as Lupton that through rereading "one becomes aware of the openness of the text, of its degree of indeterminacy, of its irreducible plurality and of one's own crucially important role in shaping and articulating its meanings."[11] And Juliana Spahr connects this deconstructive aspect of rereading with feminine domestic labor. In an article on Gertrude Stein as the writerly paradigm of productive repetition, Spahr cites Gertrude Stein's remark in *The Autobiography of Alice B. Toklas* that "correcting proofs is, as I said before, like dusting, you learn the values of the thing as no reading suffices to teach it to you."[12] Stein's equation of rereading and dusting, Spahr argues, revalues the feminine, articulating "domestic space and the repetitive task" as sites where women in particular can become "shifters of thought patterns."[13] In other words, in Spahr's analysis the feminine, like queer theory's queer, becomes the space of rupture and reorientation.

But Stein's analogy, in which rereading means "learning the values of the thing," or unlocking its hermeneutic potential, does not describe the kind of rereading I did while taking care of my mother. This kind of rereading toward an intensification of meaning is what Victor Nell calls "rereading to heighten consciousness," the kind we want our students to do when they go back over a passage of prose or a poem, seeing what they did not see the first time around.[14] My kind was Nell's "reading to dull consciousness," the kind that either simply induces a trancelike state mitigating against thought or that Karen Odden equates with childlike fantasies that block new possibilities: "*I am all-knowing and can avoid the negative effects of trauma by anticipating frightening events perfectly, every time.*"[15] This latter kind of rereading reduces all meaning to one, the ending, and so does not innovate on meaning: it is, in this way, nonhermeneutic. And in fact, Stein's analogy is strange. Correcting proofs is perhaps the dreariest kind of rereading, and one of the mandates a proofreader has is to introduce *no* substantive changes. The same is true of dusting, which is certainly not supposed to change the dusted object and which may leave something clean momentarily but will be undone relatively swiftly, as if nobody has dusted in the first place. Correcting proofs and dusting are "disappearing" forms of labor, acts of conservation rather than transformation, often relegated to unpaid or low-paid women (Alice B. Toklas for Stein, publishing staff and paid help or ourselves, for most of us). If thought of in terms of proofing and dusting, rereading introduces the possibility of feminine repetition without much difference at all, or with differences that do not accumulate into any kind of breakthrough in agency or understanding: seemingly the antithesis of queer, as indeed I have elsewhere argued that Stein's early writing does in correlating repetition with the chronic.[16] And yet.

In a brilliant book on the temporalities of caretaking, *Enduring Time*, Lisa Baraitser describes just this form of repetition as "repetition without development." She focuses on the forms of stopped or suspended time that emerge in relation to foreclosed futures: deferred endings that do not, even should they come about, promise change. She links these forms of temporality, which include "waiting, staying, delaying, enduring, persisting, maintaining, preserving, and remaining," to the act of caretaking itself. In her view, care work is not respite for or restoration of the productive body, not the renewal of that body in service of capitalism and thus not, precisely, social reproduction or the ongoing reproduction of structures of inequality. Turning the lens from the cared-for body presumed to be on its way to wellness to acts of caretaking that may never end, she sees the latter as a form of work *on* the social itself, a project in which we transcend "the immanence of our own historical moment in precisely the places that it looks simply impossible to happen." In other words, care work changes what looks like historical inevitability, but through acts that do not look in any way historical, event-like, ruptural, or even temporal at all. Baraitser's aim is to think about "social change as occurring in or through a form of chronic time," the time not of illness or pathology but of caring labor.[17]

As someone who has raised a child for thirteen years and counting, who took care of her mother for sixteen months, who was with a chronically ill partner for eleven years, and who saw that partner through kidney failure for eight months while our divorce was pending, I am drawn to this formulation, which allows me to think of that part of my life as something other than my having fallen entirely out of history, my own and the larger political one to which I had thought myself committed. Baraitser is interested in what sustains us, and she and I agree that the act of self-sustenance is not just the dreary reproduction of self-same-ness, but a difficult and delicate accomplishment in an era bent on the destruction of the bodies and souls of all but a small percentage of the population.[18] Nor is the project of sustaining others, so often relegated to white women, people of color, queers of all races, and the poor of all races, historically negligible right now. Moreover, as a literary critic, I am also drawn to the way that Baraitser's formulation may help us break through the hermeneutic model of literary inquiry, where any practice of reading that does not yield new insights is de facto useless: Baraitser allows me to understand how what Michael Warner calls "uncritical reading" intersects with femininity and feminization.[19] If rereading sustained me, sustained my ability to sustain my mother during a time when having a new idea seemed entirely beside the point, was it really just waste or escapism? If caretaking refuses to be a transformative event and the kind of rereading I am describing here refuses to be a hermeneutic one, this does not mean that nothing happens in either transaction. In their introduction to the idea of "surface reading," for example, Stephen Best and Sharon Marcus ask of reading what might well be asked of caretaking: What does it mean to hew closely to an object that does not promise or provide the figure for liberation? What kind of commitment, other than false consciousness, is this?[20] I would add: What does it mean that people of color, straight white women, and white queers have often been figured as liberated by and through reading, even as our reading practices have been curtailed by the obligation to care for others in seriously interruptive environments that do not allow us to read deeply or critically? Is "surface reading" actually the way people with less privilege, in various ways, are forced to read?

These questions seem especially important for a queer theory that has questioned the hegemony of developmental-futural thinking yet in that questioning may have abandoned the necessity of care and the feminized, racialized, class-inflected kinds of seemingly meaningless labor that constitute it. Indeed, Baraitser offers a compelling intervention into queer theory, in particular into the antisocial thesis of Lee Edelman, by way of a revised model of maternal time.[21] Although for Julia Kristeva and others who follow her, including Dana Luciano, maternal time is effectively sentimental-religious time, where forward progression yields to the full presence and simultaneity of eternal and monumental time, Baraitser reimagines maternal time as the time through which attachment between bodies and subjects materializes.[22] It is the "repetitive, obdurate, mundane practices of maternal care," she argues, that make repetition literally "matter" as a bond between the mother and the child.[23] In other words, simple biological reproduction is not the same as mothering; we might even say that mere reproduction cannot, *pace* Edelman, create the future Edelman attributes to it, insofar as a child born but not maintained is swiftly a dead child. Instead, mothering and an attachment to futurity of some sort consist in the acts that extend the mother's body toward the child and create the child's body in response to the mother on a daily basis. Baraitser asks, pointedly, "Can we use maternal time, deliberately embraced as repetitive time, as a way to rethink queer and the time of the death drive?" She does this by rethinking the time of the death drive as "the suspended time of allowing one life to unfurl in relation to another." In other words, both Edelmanian queer theory and theories of the maternal, Baraitser argues, share a "dynamic chronicity, alive to the potentials of not moving on."[24] But the maternal admits the possibility of interdependence and of matter as something built, created, sustained into the future by *practice* rather than just as something emerging intact into and symbolizing a future. Here, staying close to an object that does not contain the potential to liberate us (or itself) is precisely what creates and recreates the social. And this may be what the nonhermeneutic forms of reading I am trying to describe do for the populations who take care of other people: they create a social fabric that is not the same as a critical horizon.

This unfurling of lives in interrelation, we might also say, is a matter of time leaning toward, or tilting into, space and spatialization. Repetition here is not so much incremental extension forward in time, toward the new, as it is dilation outward, overlapping and in coextension with other bodies and their timings. The sentimental "life-throb" that links Sigourney's narrator and her child, the breathing that linked Ellen and Kate and myself and Caroline, may be dehistoricized, but they are modalities of mutual timing in which bodies sync up and intermingle into new entities that one might call care-taking assemblages, if one includes in their contemporary instantiations the professional workers who interface with (or are) modern caregivers; the institutions of medicine, family law, social services, and so on; and the nonhuman substances introduced into the bodies of people who are infirm.

But despite my enormous respect for Baraitser's project, the queer in me also wants to ask this: Why privilege maternity as the paradigm for a care-taking committed to an alternate futurity, when elder care, care of life partners, care of friends, intergenerational eroticism, and teaching and mentoring have been so central to queer life? The answer may lie in how difficult it is to conceptualize any kind of futurity at all without the presence of an in-tergenerational relationship in which the carer is female or feminized, and the recipient of care, or even the reproduced body, is younger and destined to survive rather than to die. I can transport Baraitser's model into male parenting, same-sex intergenerational eroticism, and teaching/mentoring between any and all genders, each of which acts may involve the repetition of perhaps mundane tasks that foment attachments and "matter" bodies and subjects into the future. I have a harder time transporting the model into lateral relationships or into intergenerational ones in which the recipient of care is older and, in fact, has no future but only a finite number of days or weeks whose quality matters much more than their teleology.

Still, Baraitser's sense that the time of repetition creates attachment and hence a thicker social tapestry is, I think, key for getting queer theory out from under fantasies of transgression and newness and out from under the antisocial thesis, and this doubles back toward my sense that a commitment to caretaking and a commitment to rereading might have something to do with one another. If repetition is a fantasy of resistance to or negation of time, it is only this in relation to future-oriented time. It is not a fantasy of resistance to the dilation of time outward, to its stretching backward or doubling on itself, to the texturing or textualizing of time. For example, Patricia Meyer Spacks reminds us that the rereader "can allow herself a state of suspended attention comparable to Keats's 'negative capability,' a condition of receptivity devoid, as the poet says, of irritable reaching after fact and reason—of irritable reaching after anything at all."[25] This lack of reaching echoes Marcus and Best's contention that "attentiveness to the artwork is itself a kind of freedom," even if it does not constitute or produce liberation.[26] Rereading and caretaking are antiteleological, but the space of receptivity opened up by them is not, for all that, antisocial: the form of sociality itself may not be linear at all, but bulbous, distended, and even enlooped. For within the act of repetition, at least as it has been described by theorists of rereading, the past and the present can touch. For example, Spacks describes rereading similarly to Lupton, as an encounter with a past self newly understood in light of subsequent events. Calinescu, another theorist of rereading, reminds us that it can produce the phenomenon of "reverse influence," whereby a later author such as Proust can shed light on, and thus seem to have influenced, an earlier writer like Flaubert.[27] These are all ways of weaving the social fabric more densely, more tightly, more elaborately, across time as well as space. How does care work do the same, considering that at first glance it isolates those doing it and those receiving it, often into dyads that feel rather dysfunctional (as the literature and filmography of caretaking, including *One True Thing*, make abundantly clear)?[28]

The Way We Read Now

In order to answer the question of how caretaking elaborates the social, it seems necessary to turn away from the domestic sentimental genre and toward other kinds of fiction. Susan Sontag's short story "The Way We Live Now" (1986) is an exemplary narrative of caretaking that refuses both the dyadic mother-child paradigm and the child-as-futurity, without reducing to queer antisociality. The story consists of dialogues, or linked monologues, among a set of friends who are visiting, taking care of, and gossiping about an unnamed person with HIV-related symptoms in the mid-1980s. It has in common with sentimental literature a dilation of time into space and a certain plotlessness, but it altogether refuses sentimentality's focused setting, detailed attention to bodies, and direct solicitation of its reader's visceral response. Instead, Sontag's story consists of a linked series of somewhat deadpan declarations without quotation marks, the lack of which makes the attribution of each declaration ambiguous, as the opening sentence illustrates:

> At first he was just losing weight, he felt only a little ill, Max said to Ellen, and he didn't call for an appointment with his doctor, according to Greg, because he was managing to keep on working at more or less the same rhythm, but he did stop smoking, Tanya pointed out, which suggests he was frightened, but also that he wanted, even more than he knew, to be healthy, or healthier, or maybe just to gain back a few pounds, said Orson, for he told her, Tanya went on, that he expected to be climbing the walls (isn't that what people say?) and found, to his surprise, that he didn't miss cigarettes at all and revelled in the sensation of his lungs' being ache-free for the first time in years.[29]

The statement "At first he was just losing weight, he felt only a little ill" seems to come from Max, along with "and he didn't call for an appointment with his doctor." But the latter statement is then attributed to Greg, such that there is an overlap between the voices of Max and Greg. Greg's statement may pick up where Max left off, beginning with "and he didn't call for an appointment with his doctor," progressing to "because he was managing to keep on working at more or less the same rhythm," and finishing with "but he did stop smoking," but again, the last phrase is also attributed to Tanya, who may be pointing this out and then carrying on with "which suggests he was frightened [etc.]." Orson's statement may then pick up where Tanya leaves off, or it may be embedded in Tanya's observations—it is impossible to tell. All told, the structure of Sontag's story is like an elaborate game of telephone, in which in addition to repeating what is heard, each interlocutor adds something to it before passing the whole on to a recipient.

This short story, which might best be characterized as experimental narrative, has become a classic in the literature of AIDS because its structure so perfectly allegorizes its content: during the early years, gossip was how news about HIV and people's seropositivity traveled, in the absence of mainstream media's attention to the virus. Furthermore, the fact that we never learn either the ill person's name or the name of the virus that engenders his symptoms possibly reflects the Centers for Disease Control and Prevention's 1984 study on the "origin" of AIDS in the United States in "Patient Zero" and definitely reflects the refusal of the Reagan administration to mention AIDS.[30] Finally, the story's sequence of gossipy declarations links speakers to one another across time and space just as the HIV virus links people who may never have met one another but share an infected partner. As the story itself says in a moment of meta-commentary, "My gynecologist says that everyone is at risk, everyone who has a sexual life, because sexuality is a chain that links each of us to many others, unknown others, and now the great chain of being has become a chain of death as well" (TWWLN). The story might well be read, though, as a meditation on how this chain of death can be remade into a chain of social "being." For it also allegorizes something that is less immediately tied to the historical moment of its writing and that if anything is even more true than it was in 1986, now that increasing numbers of people are denied access to health care: the way that caretaking is not only temporally but socially centrifugal, and the role of reading and rereading in this movement outward from a center, from the isolated ill person to the social fabric made possible by his attachments and by others' attachments to him becoming manifest as attachments to one another.

First and most obviously, the chain of gossip and reportage in the story distends the circle of visitors, interlocutors, and friends: "It seemed that everyone was in touch with everyone else several times a week, checking in, I've never spent so many hours at a time on the phone, Stephen said to Kate, and when I'm exhausted after the two or three calls made to me, giving me the latest, instead of switching off the phone to give myself a respite I tap out the number of another friend or acquaintance, to pass on the news . . ." (TWWLN). This phone tree, in short, is arboreal, and it has the effect of amalgamating heretofore disconnected strangers into a social field: "Well, everybody is worried about everybody now, said Betsy, that seems to be the way we live, the way we live now" (TWWLN). This reference to the story's title suggests that the way we live "now" (in the mid-1980s, in the 2020s) is in interconnection. It is, precisely, *viral*, in advance of the use of that word to denote the rapid circulation of images and information via the internet. Certainly the repetitions, the readings and rereadings that make something viral on the internet, may indeed produce something new, the way that a virus mutates; an example of this would be the way that memes proliferate more memes. But this is not the story's point. Instead, "The Way We Live Now" allows us to see that what viral phenomena do, more than generate newness, is inaugurate and/or solidify a social field. This emergence of the social *is* the plot of "The Way We Live Now," as the reader gradually comes to understand that each of the names of the twenty-six relatively undifferentiated characters who talk about the unnamed person with AIDS begins with a different letter, and so mean something as a whole rather than as a number of individuals: they constitute less a group of characters than an alphabet, something defined as a set. As one character puts it, "His illness sticks us all in the same glue" (TWWLN). In short, the suspended time and repetitive actions that constitute caretaking make the social matter, materialize the social as a field thick with moving parts that cannot be extracted from it as discrete individuals, although within it individuals can combine and recombine, like letters of the alphabet or like DNA molecules.

Second, "The Way We Live Now" demands, as part of how we apprehend its structure, a rereading of each of its clauses, again linking rereading and caretaking. Take the first part of the opening sentence one more time: "At first he was just losing weight, he felt only a little ill, Max said to Ellen, and he didn't call for an appointment with his doctor, according to Greg." If Max is the speaker of "and he didn't call for an appointment with his doctor," there is no need to reread that clause. But at the point that we realize that that statement is now being attributed to Greg, we have to restart the sentence at "and," carrying through to "but he did stop smoking," after which again we could stop if Greg were the only speaker of that clause. However, "but he did stop smoking" begins Tanya's set of statements, so we are forced to start over with it. These statements that compel the reader to move backward and reread are, as in Baraitser's model of caretaking, the material that binds Max not only to his immediate interlocutor, Ellen, but also to Greg (to whom Max does not actually seem to speak, or perhaps Greg's speech is embedded in Max's). And not only do they describe information gleaned by caretakers, visitors, and those with whom the patient is in communication; they are also an *enactment* of caretaking, insofar as caretakers must constantly manage and pass on information about the recipients of their care to others who cannot be there (a simple way of putting this: caretakers must take care not only of their immediate charges but also of those who want information about the latter). Here, the social binding, the thickening of the social field that I have described, is fostered and enacted precisely by rereading and repetition.

Finally, "The Way We Live Now" links rereading and caretaking to a form of futurity that is not predicated on an ending, although it may be committed to the possibility of one. One character points out that "they'd begun talking about him in a retrospective mode, summing up what he was like, what made them fond of him, as if he were finished, completed, already a part of the past" (TWWLN). But the story rejects this form of tidy closure.

Instead, its last few sentences focus on the potential of narrative itself to suspend time, to create what Gertrude Stein called a "continuous present"[31]: "I was thinking, Ursula said to Quentin, that the difference between a story and a painting or photograph is that in a story you can write, He's still alive. But in a painting or a photo you can't show 'still.' You can just show him being alive. He's still alive, Stephen said" (TWWLN). *Still* is an adverb, but as an adverb of time it has a kind of tense to it, one that connects to the processes of both rereading and caretaking: the tense of being in a present that includes everything leading up to it (and perhaps even what follows it, insofar as rereading and caretaking, as I have described them, take place with some foreknowledge of an ending that may not redeem or transform the present). This is not sentimental literature's "still"-ness of time and place, in which the sacred redeems earthly suffering. But it is a dilation of sorts, in which what takes place in the moment may not be significantly different than what has just taken place: may in fact not simply repeat it but be an extension of it, a thickening of it that conjoins the people in it more than reimagining the horizon toward which they tend or the context in which they do their work. That is not nothing.

"The Way We Live Now" has its own moment of reflection on rereading. The friends of the seropositive man who is the absent center of the story report that he keeps a diary. Quentin suggests to Kate that "the point was that by the very keeping of the diary he was accumulating something to re-read one day, slyly staking out his claim to a future time, in which the diary would be an object, a relic, in which he might not actually reread it, because he would want to have put this ordeal behind him" (TWWLN). Here, to stake a claim to rereading is also to stake a claim on a future in which rereading is not necessary because an ordeal is complete, bounded, discrete. Yet in (re)reading the story from the vantage point of more than thirty years later, we know that even if the unnamed character lives long enough to benefit from the medications that lifted the death sentence from those with HIV, the virus will never be "behind him." He will be in a new kind of time, a queerly chronic time in which, if he is lucky, his attachments will be thicker than ever. If the unnamed character is lucky the way that I have been lucky during and after the periods in which I took care of my daughter, my mother, and my now ex-partner, this character and his former and future caretakers and those to whom he commits his own caretaking work will be not the means for him to live but the ends of living itself. This use of repetition, of time, of acts of sustenance and maintenance, to solidify and extend attachments exemplifies queer commitment.

This essay is for my mother, Caroline Smith Freeman (1939–2011), and for my brother Roger, with whom I was, for this one time, on the same team, Team Mom. I miss them both.

Thanks to Mary Grover for lending her UC Berkeley book-borrowing privileges. Thanks also to UC Davis for the assistance of a Small Grant in Aid of Research.

1 See Lupton, *Reading and the Making of Time in the Eighteenth Century*.

2 Quindlen, *One True Thing*. Page references to this novel will be given parenthetically in the text.

3 On care as the kind of commitment that implies a sentence, see Glenn, *Forced to Care*. Works that explore the economic coercion and exploitation of racialized as well as feminized (though not always female) caretakers include Ehrenreich and Hochschild, *Global Woman*, and Manalansan, "Queer Intersections." The paradigm of disability justice in which caretaking comes from *within* an organized disability community is beautifully examined in Piepzna-Samarasinha, *Care Work*.

4 On women's attachment to domestic fiction and romance, see Radway, *Reading the Romance*, and Odden, "Retrieving Childhood Fantasies."

5 Full text available online at the American Verse Project, University of Michigan Humanities Text Initiative.

6 Williams, "Film Bodies," 3.

7 This dilation and suspension of time is also, of course, characteristic of disability and illness, especially chronic illness. See my "Hopeless Cases," and Samuels, "Six Ways of Looking at Crip Time." On disability and queer/feminist temporality more generally, see McRuer, *Crip Times*, and Kafer, *Feminist, Queer, Crip*.

8 See Luciano, *Arranging Grief*.

9 Galef, "Observations on Rereading," 19–20.

10 See, for example, Butler, *Gender Trouble*.

11 Calinescu, *Rereading*, 113.

12 Stein, *The Autobiography of Alice B. Toklas*, cited in Spahr, "Gertrude Stein and Disjunctive (Re)reading."

13 Spahr, "Gertrude Stein and Disjunctive (Re)reading," 272, 268.

14 Nell, *Lost in a Book*, 229.

15 Nell, *Lost in a Book*, 228, and Odden, "Retrieving Childhood Fantasies," 146.

16 See Freeman, "Hopeless Cases."

17 Baraitser, *Enduring Time*, 56, 13, 17.

18 See Freeman, "Hopeless Cases."

19 See Warner, "Uncritical Reading."

20 Best and Marcus, "Surface Reading," 15.

21 See Edelman, *No Future*.

22 See Kristeva, "Women's Time."

23 Baraitser, *Enduring Time*, 76.

24 Baraitser, *Enduring Time*, 78, 79.

25 Spacks, *On Rereading*, 70.

26 Best and Marcus, "Surface Reading," 16.

27 Calinescu, *Rereading*, 54.

28 A preliminary, very partial bibliography of fiction in which caretaking is portrayed as murderously dyadic would have to include sections of Harriet Jacobs, *Incidents in the Life of a Slave Girl* (1861); Edith Wharton, *Ethan Frome* (1911); Stephen King, *Misery* (1987); Jane Hawking, *Traveling to Infinity* (2007); and Emma Donoghue, *Room* (2010). I'm still taking your suggestions for this bibliography.

29 Sontag, "The Way We Live Now." Further references to this story will be given parenthetically in the text with the abbreviation TWWLN.

30 The relevant study is Auerbach et al., "Cluster of Cases." Importantly, this study focuses on Patient O (as in the letter O), later misconstrued as a zero. At the time of this writing I am unable to ascertain whether or not Sontag read the study, but each of her twenty-six characters has a name beginning with a different letter of the alphabet, which could reflect either the alphabetic aspects of AIDS (formerly GRID, attributed to HIV), the patient at the center of this study, or both.

31 Stein, "Composition as Explanation."

BIBLIOGRAPHY

Auerbach, David M., William W. Darrow, Harold W. Jaffe, and James W. Curran. "Cluster of Cases of the Acquired Immunodeficiency Syndrome." *American Journal of Medicine* 76, no. 3 (1984): 487–92.

Baraitser, Lisa. *Enduring Time*. New York: Bloomsbury Academic, 2017.

Best, Stephen, and Sharon Marcus. "Surface Reading: An Introduction." *Representations* 108, no. 1 (2009): 1–21.

Butler, Judith. *Gender Trouble: Feminism and the Subversion of Identity*. New York: Routledge, 1990.

Calinescu, Matei. *Rereading*. New Haven, CT: Yale University Press, 1993.

Edelman, Lee. *No Future: Queer Theory and the Death Drive*. Durham, NC: Duke University Press, 2004.

Ehrenreich, Barbara, and Arlie Russell Hochschild, eds. *Global Woman: Nannies, Maids, and Sex Workers in the New Economy*. New York: Henry Holt, 2004.

Freeman, Elizabeth. "Hopeless Cases: Queer Chronicity and Gertrude Stein's 'Melanctha.'" *Journal of Homosexuality* 63, no. 3 (2016): 329–48.

Galef, David. "Observations on Rereading." In Galef, *Second Thoughts*, 17–33.

Galef, David, ed. *Second Thoughts: A Focus on Rereading*. Detroit: Wayne State University Press, 1998.

Glenn, Evelyn Nakano. *Forced to Care: Coercion and Care in America*. Cambridge, MA: Harvard University Press, 2012.

Kafer, Alison. *Feminist, Queer, Crip*. Bloomington: Indiana University Press, 2013.

Kristeva, Julia. "Women's Time." Translated by Alice Jardine and Harry Blake. *Signs* 7, no. 1 (1981): 13–35.

Luciano, Dana. *Arranging Grief: Sacred Time and the Body in Nineteenth-Century America*. New York: New York University Press, 2007.

Lupton, Christina. *Reading and the Making of Time in the Eighteenth Century*. Baltimore: Johns Hopkins University Press, 2018.

Manalansan IV, Martin. "Queer Intersections: Sexuality and Gender in Migration Studies." *International Migration Review* 40, no. 1 (2006): 224–49.

McRuer, Rob. *Crip Times: Disability, Globalization, and Resistance*. New York: New York University Press, 2018.

Nabokov, Vladimir. *Lolita*. New York: Penguin, 1987. First published 1955 by Olympia Press.

Nell, Victor. *Lost in a Book: The Psychology of Reading for Pleasure*. New Haven, CT: Yale University Press, 1988.

Odden, Karen. "Retrieving Childhood Fantasies: A Psychoanalytic Look at Why We (Re)read Popular Literature." In Galef, *Second Thoughts*, 126–51.

Piepzna-Samarasinha, Leah Lakshmi. *Care Work: Dreaming Disability Justice*. Vancouver: Arsenal Pulp, 2018.

Quindlen, Anna. *One True Thing*. 1994; repr., New York: Random House, 2006. Page references are to the 2006 edition.

Radway, Janice. *Reading the Romance: Women, Patriarchy, and Popular Literature*. Chapel Hill: University of North Carolina Press, 1984.

Samuels, Ellen. "Six Ways of Looking at Crip Time." *Disability Studies* 37 (2017). http://dx.doi.org/10.18061/dsq.v37i3.

Sigourney, Lydia. "The Sick Child." In *Select Poems*, 91–93. Philadelphia: Parry & McMillan, 1856.

Sontag, Susan. "The Way We Live Now." *New Yorker*, November 24, 1986. www.newyorker.com/magazine/1986/11/24/the-way-we-live-now.

Spacks, Patricia Meyer. *On Rereading*. Cambridge, MA: Belknap Press of Harvard University Press, 2013.

Spahr, Juliana. "Gertrude Stein and Disjunctive (Re)reading." In Galef, *Second Thoughts*, 266–93.

Stein, Gertrude. *The Autobiography of Alice B. Toklas*. First published 1933 by Harcourt, Brace. Available online at http://gutenberg.net.au/ebooks06/0608711.txt.

Stein, Gertrude. "Composition as Explanation." First published 1926 by the Hogarth Press. Available online at www.writing.upenn.edu/library/Stein_Composition-as-Explanation.html.

Warner, Michael. "Uncritical Reading." In *Polemic: Critical or Uncritical*, edited by Jane Gallop, 13–38. New York: Routledge, 2004.

Williams, Linda. "Film Bodies: Gender, Genre, and Excess." *Film Quarterly* 44, no. 4 (1991): 2–13.

2

LOSS AND THE LONG TERM

AMY VILLAREJO

This essay intersperses an account of loss in a long-term queer relationship with three scenes of viewing media. I am interested in how relationality is formally built into different sorts of media texts through three different devices: shot/reverse shot (in the case of television dramedy), seriality (in the case of a web series), and an establishing shot (in the case of a documentary film). Although the examples arrive at different times on different platforms, they share a focus on young queers of color, some of whom are threatened and imperiled and some thriving and joyous. Although it is a marvel to me, a queer child of the broadcast TV of the 1960s, that these images now arrive on my multiple sleek screens, my interest here lies less in the specific affects they compel or incite and more in the very conditions of possibility that endow viewers with a relationship to them—that is to say, those formal mechanisms upon which media rely in order to create relays (of affect, of identification, of relationality, of really anything at all). I find myself—for reasons that I hope become clear in the narrative account—at once at a loss for response and responsive to the loss they record.

Quiet Attachment

Deep in the night, the blades of the ceiling fan slice the air overhead and set my bedroom vibrating on a low hum. Before sunrise, at our little regional airport a few miles away from our house, three airplanes start their engines, two small jets bound for Detroit and Philadelphia and an old prop plane, thankfully retired since I started writing this, heading for Newark. This air network, like media, is an infrastructure of relationality: these planes connect us to our larger worlds. As far away as they seem, I'm surprised that I can hear them clearly every morning; they synchronize with the ceiling fan as a background whir, intensifying as they take off and fly almost directly over our house. As the morning traffic on the street outside gets heavier, the cats and I hear cars and occasionally a truck or school bus rumble by the window. When the sounds are loud enough, they (the cats) turn their ears in bored acknowledgment of the world outside; otherwise, it remains as a receding reality, there for context and contrast.

The humanist cultural geographer Yi-Fu Tuan seeks some account of this sense of ongoing attachment, which he charmingly, even quaintly, describes as "quiet": "Attachment of a deep though subconscious sort may come simply with familiarity and with ease, with the assurance of nurture and security, with the memory of sounds and smells, of communal activities and homely pleasures accumulated over time. It is difficult to articulate quiet attachments of this type."[1] Contrary to Tuan's modest confession of difficulty, this background world is not, actually, all that hard to describe. Accounts of something like quiet attachment have become integral to the strain of theoretical and critical writing that goes under the banner of "political emotions," including Kathleen Stewart's ethnographies, Lauren Berlant's accounts of the everyday, and Ann Cvetkovich's reports from the field(s)—I'm thinking of her writing both on the Michigan Womyn's Music Festival and on depression.[2]

This web of quiet attachment may occupy only a small corner in the current scene of theory and political philosophy, but it has a robust history.

It is what, for example, the philosopher Hannah Arendt called the "human artifice," a stable and durable lifeworld of our making that precedes and outlasts us. It has what she describes as an "enduring permanence."[3] Without it, there is no history. Against the human artifice emerges what she calls, enigmatically and interestingly, the "space of appearance," the realm for human action and speech:

> The space of appearance comes into being wherever men are together in the manner of speech and action, and therefore predates and precedes all formal constitution of the public realm and the various forms of government, that is, the various forms in which the public realm can be organized. Its peculiarity is that, unlike the spaces which are the work of our hands, it does not survive the actuality of the movement which brought it into being, but disappears not only with the dispersal of men—as in the case of great catastrophes when the body politic of a people is destroyed—but with the disappearance or arrest of the activities themselves. Wherever people gather together, it is potentially there, but only potentially, not necessarily and not forever.[4]

The space of appearance is, we might say, virtual: present as potential in the context of the—not absolutely but reliably—solid human artifice and a plurality of humans. It is not simply the web of human relationships, which is also part of our reality, part of that which is between us, because the space of appearance is defined by those specific activities that constitute it: action and speech. Arendt thickens our sense of the lifeworld as now constituted by layered virtualities: the human artifice is that which brings into salience and actuality the space of appearance, which is in turn the precondition for the formal organization of publicness (or "the public realm").[5] For Arendt, without *some* understanding of ongoingness, a feel for the long term, we remain impoverished in our sense of what it means to speak, to act, and to constitute ourselves.

I think that it is something like this thick sense of virtual interrelation *in potentia* that Kath Weston wanted to capture through the anthropological category of kinship in her study, *Families We Choose: Lesbians, Gays, Kinship*, a book published in 1991 (which seems a long time ago) that had enormously important consequences for thinking, particularly about queerness and attachment. Let's zoom in closer toward that nexus. As readers undoubtedly know, Weston's interviews and fieldwork, conducted in the mid-1980s in the San Francisco Bay Area, revealed to her a set of questions about gay families (variously made of lovers, ex-lovers, coparents, sperm donors, biological children, adopted children, extended kinfolk, neighbors, friends, and so on), particularly within the context of a larger condition of the politicization of kinship and the circulation of symbols of kinship (family, love, romance, marriage, etc.) within that field. Her study investigates the ways in which the idea and the ideology of family grant legitimacy to gay and lesbian relationships, but the book neither idealizes nor nostalgically embraces such legitimation; instead, Weston is interested in how private, intimate domains (quiet attachment, the human artifice) become symbolized and freighted as questions of public and political life. The task, then, is less to study normative families (i.e., the nuclear family) and their variations than it is to subject kinship, ideology, and social relations to a historical critique. What I like, still, enduringly, about Weston's book is its appreciation of how different forms of attachment function among a genuinely and deliberately diverse sample, understanding how those folks she studies shuttle between different familial and social compositions all the time, from their families of origin (what many in her study call "straight family") to their families of choice.

What her study focuses on is that process of *making* family: her emphasis is on families we choose, not families we lose. Because her sample skews young, and because her interest is largely in the early years in which adults tend to forge families or consider having children (in whatever configurations), Weston understands attachment largely in terms of bonds chosen and wrought rather than frayed or shattered. Weston is candid about the age of her sample, insofar as it reflected her own situation and experience as a young, queer researcher in the Bay Area in the 1980s.[6] And although *Families We Choose* is peppered with experiences *and* myths of loss—suicide, AIDS/HIV, the symbolic death of parental rejection, and so on—the book nonetheless emphasizes the ways in which queers forge webs of quiet attachment as kin. As will become clear in what follows, my angle on loss has to do less with the anthropology of kinship than with disability, and this essay seeks to weave disability and media together to urge reflection on the order of potentiality that is quiet attachment.

First Channel

Look for a moment at my first example of what queer attachment enables in the realm of multiplatform television. It's a powerful thing: to see narratives that would have been impossible to develop and articulate twenty years ago, especially revolving around young-ish queers of color. *Master of None* (2015–), a series created and attached to the comedian Aziz Ansari, introduces us to

Denise (Lena Waithe), a BFF to Ansari's character, Dev Shah, and a Black lesbian whose coming out features in the season two episode, "Thanksgiving" (air date May 12, 2017). The episode was cowritten by Ansari and Waithe and draws on Waithe's own experiences coming out to her mother—for which she received a 2017 Emmy award, becoming the first Black woman to win for writing on a comedy series. In an unsurprising connection, in her moving Emmy acceptance speech, Waithe thanked her queer chosen family.

As much a stand-alone episode about Denise's family as the episode is a way of writing a history of queer identity, "Thanksgiving" presents six slices of Dev and Denise's Thanksgiving celebrations from their childhood in 1995 through the "present" in 2017. The third generation of a matriarchal family, Denise hosts Dev at the annual dinner, as the Indian American is here a cultural outcast in the normative calculus of American holiday celebrations. On Thanksgiving in 1995, as a young adolescent, Denise struggles to articulate her attraction to other girls; in 1999, Denise comes out to Dev; in 2006, Denise comes out to her mother, Catherine (Angela Bassett); in 2015, Denise invites her girlfriend, Michelle, to dinner; in 2016, she invites a less sympathetic girlfriend, Nikki, to join the family; and in 2017, Michelle rejoins the family dinner and is embraced by Denise, Dev, Denise's mother, Catherine, her aunt Joyce, and her grandmother Ernestine.

All this in a terse thirty-four minutes, where what is at stake is delineating Denise's queerness visually (especially through her butch costuming) and then charting how this queerness, visually guaranteed, comes to be factored into the familial and friendly attachments that form Denise's life-world. Rather than exploring her character's interiority and desire, in other words, the work of this episode is on the shot/reverse shot: on Denise's sense of herself and how that queerness reverberates with others. In the opening teaser, an aerial shot of the Thanksgiving table with young Dev and Denise in 1995 gives us this program's image of familial connection, which is mirrored in the final aerial of Thanksgiving in 2017. In between, however, the visual grammar relentlessly relies on the shot/reverse shot and two-shot pattern, nowhere as powerfully as in the crucial exchange in which Denise comes out to her mother at a diner. As Denise struggles to utter the words "I'm gay" to her mom, the editing almost mimics Denise's discomfort in securing this attachment by juxtaposing a succession of two shots with two entirely different shot/reverse shot framings, ultimately coming to rest on a reverse of Angela Bassett's teary face for the affective punch. Later, in the episode's most touching scene in the Thanksgiving kitchen of 2017, Catherine reaches behind her to grab Denise's hand and to give her approval to Denise's girlfriend, Michelle (Ebony Obsidian), as though pulling Denise into a two shot they both can inhabit happily. Even the dialogue patterns common to sitcoms rely on a verbal kind of "reverse shot" for comic relief, with both Aunt Joyce (Kym Whitley) and Dev alternating as comic counterparts to the mother-daughter heaviness. For all of the episode's innovation in content, then, it still obeys the fundamental laws of televisual attachment through the visual grammar of the reverse shot. I wonder, though, about what happens when there is no reverse shot possible, when we've lost or are in the process of losing again and again the second term of relation.

Andrea's Stroke

Loss is a freighted word, and so let me say what I have lived as loss before I turn to two more media examples refracted by it. My experience of loss is tied to May 8, 2011, when in bed in the midmorning, my partner Andrea surfed the internet on her MacBook and suffered a catastrophic ischemic stroke. That means that a blood clot, the result we later learned of atrial fibrillation (which is a heart murmur, where the heart pauses after beating long enough to generate a pool of blood that can clot before traveling to the brain), lodged itself on the left side of her brain and blocked the delivery of oxygen. What this looked like was that Andrea was slumped on the bed over her computer, drooling on the Chez Piggy T-shirt I had gotten her while sailing in Ontario, unable to speak or move.

We live in a small town, so the ambulance and fire truck both arrived extremely quickly at our house, and on this sunny May morning the guys ran up the stairs and had her on a gurney loaded into the back of the ambulance within a few minutes. In a twist of fate, our best friend, Alison, was driving down our street when the sirens screeched their arrival; her husband had died (not horribly or prematurely, but still) the previous weekend, and she was taking her son Jason to the bus stop for his return to New York after Bill's funeral. So Alison squeezed my hand, and off I drove to the hospital, trailing the ambulance.

I'll leave out the part about how Andrea had suffered what was diagnosed as an "optical migraine" a couple of days earlier, an event that probably, in retrospect, signaled the impending stroke. We'll never know. But the stroke itself caused the emergency room (ER) staff at our regional hospital to call a code blue (emergency lingo for a stroke or heart attack), and because we had managed to get Andrea into the ER shortly after the event, the doctors administered something called tissue plasminogen activator (TPA), an intravenous drug that sometimes helps to dissolve the clot and stimulate blood flow to the affected area of the brain.

It didn't and did "work." In stopping what might have been a fatal ischemic stroke, it in fact caused a secondary event, a kind of reverse effect: Andrea had a hemorrhage in her frontal lobe from the TPA, which caused a new brain injury resulting in a kind of dopey and smiley affect that was completely at odds with what she was actually experiencing. All this was in the first hours in the ER, where I was trying to learn the acronyms of drugs and to keep holding Andrea's cold, still hands while everyone was brisk and efficient and intent and hurrying around in trauma—code blue—mode. After conceding that the TPA did whatever its magic might have been, they sent Andrea into the intensive care unit (ICU), with the hopes that the brain swelling would begin to diminish, and we would thereafter discover who remained, who emerged, from May 8. Maybe I should say as a teeny footnote that on this first day I yanked my right foot in a weird way, perhaps rushing to my car to follow the ambulance, and I consequently had some painful injury to the tendons on the top of my arch for the next two months, causing me to limp pitifully around the hospital. Maybe I should also say that Andrea was sixty-four years old to my forty-seven on that day and described as an "elderly woman" (really?) by the attending neurologist in his report. He kept her in the ICU for a few nights before releasing her to the telemetry floor. This means that her cardiac function was measured 24/7 through body sensors that transmit data to a central nurses' station on the floor. After a few days, the nurses told me that every time I walked (hobbled) into Andrea's room, they could watch her heart beat faster.

Initially, Andrea lost her ability to speak (this is called aphasia). Entirely. She could only really say no (but she could curse like a sailor—that part of speech actually lives in a different part of our brains), and she couldn't tell nurses what hurt or what scared her or what she needed. She was incontinent. She lost movement on the right side of her body, including her entire right arm and her right leg. She lost the ability to tell right from left, and she lost the capacity to understand or execute sequences of any sort (this is called apraxia). Even with her left hand, she couldn't get the spoon to the Jello and the Jello to her mouth without step-by-step instructions. Not that she likes Jello, but she also couldn't come up with any words to tell the food service orderly what she wanted to eat, and not that she could eat just anything, for the right side of her gastrointestinal tract was paralyzed.

Coping with, accommodating to, this situation of the unlivable body is called "rehab."

While Andrea was in the hospital for those long four months, I watched TV or something like it on my mobile devices when I came home each day, trying to shed the stress as I padded around our empty house (which was soon filled with builders adapting our house and bathroom to accommodate a wheelchair). Queer web series were beginning to experiment with new formats: Ingrid Jungermann and Desiree Akhavan premiered *The Slope* that summer of 2011, a multiseason web comedy about a lesbian couple in Park Slope, Brooklyn. Jungermann's *F to 7th* follow-up series from 2013, a similarly deadpan study of Brooklyn queers, succeeded in balancing the work of series regulars (including Jungermann most prominently) with big-name guest stars such as Amy Sedaris, Olympia Dukakis, Janeane Garafolo, and Gaby Hoffmann; that series is now in development at Showtime.

These series that initially present themselves as edgy portraits of marginalized queer communities nonetheless make some money and end up seeming to be profitable *enough* for the world of cable and new-media narrowcasting. Such is the case with *Dyke Central*, a multiepisode "comedic drama centered on masculine-of-center Oakland roommates Alex and Jin," according to the press release. Directed by Florencia Manovil, the series has, of this writing, migrated to the Amazon platform after several years circulating both online and in film festivals, and it is therefore bound to attract greater numbers of viewers and heightened attention.

An ensemble study of queer gender, *Dyke Central* interests itself primarily in the dynamics of a group of California thirtysomething friends whose lives revolve around the Oakland apartment, "dyke central," of the two roommates. A deliberately diverse cast and delightful range of female masculinity, including the fabulous drag king and trans actor Tom Paul, anchor this dramedy, the heart of which is devoted to hanging out, smoking pot, and building complicated love triangles and other shapes. It is structured, in other words, to extend itself through seriality: through the promise of repetition and familiarity across its ten episodes.

The soothing seriality of *Dyke Central*, like that of *F to 7th*, is itself a mode of quiet attachment, one that valorizes minor dramas and everyday encounters, largely in the domestic or public spheres of Oakland queer culture. By presenting characters with almost no attachments to families of origin or complicated work situations (with the exception of Paul's Zack, a therapist), *Dyke Central* records a swirling orbit of pleasant relationality and lovely bodies, free of serious friction or want. Like *Friends* or *Thirtysomething*, it's a world into which one can settle over a number of episodes without fear. For someone living in a world of fear, it's pabulum of the best sort, but it also raises the question of the kind of world building that our queer media might be doing in order to reflect and mediate textures of loss.

Recovery

After several weeks on the telemetry floor, as Andrea essentially learned how to be in the hospital with these constraints, she was transferred to rehab proper, the Physical Medical Rehabilitation Unit (PMRU) at the same hospital, where she spent the period of time that medical insurance will pay for "acute" rehab. (Because no one in a hospital will tell you, ever, what the duration will be of any treatment or stay or procedure or event, I learned the phrase "period of time," which describes all time as though it is horizonless and unsegmented.) In her case that was six weeks. During acute rehab, she had physical, speech, occupational, and recreational therapies, sometimes all four on the same day, during which she regained some language, learned to walk with assistance, learned to use a wheelchair, did some work on her weak arm, and began to assimilate what had happened. That reflection made her both extremely depressed and anxious, but the medications for both interacted poorly with the millions of other medications she was on for spasticity, pain, blood pressure, and atrial fibrillation. So she was just kind of doped up and sad most of the time, trying to rally herself for the many friends who visited regularly and trying to maintain some energy for the daily hard work of therapy.

We seized upon a moment from this interval that we retell often, providing as it does some relief from the overwhelming horror. Her therapists were in the business of constantly trying to assess Andrea's capacities, trying to measure what she knew and could know, what she thought and could think. It wasn't immediately clear, for example, that she could read, for she was unable to speak, but in these early days it was slowly emerging that she had retained much if not almost all of what is called "executive function" (working memory, mental flexibility, and self-control) as well as skills of higher reasoning and reading/writing. Thank the fucking lord. And so one day her speech therapist, Phyllis, asked Andrea how many cats we have, the "correct" answer being I suppose one, which is how many cats we currently had living in our house (Slash the Maine Coon was thriving in the absence of his "brother" Taagie, who had died earlier that spring, hit by a car on our busy street). But Andrea said "two," and Phyllis later came to ask me whether that was right, with I again suppose the theory that Andrea didn't know how to count, which was indeed possible. I suggested that Phyllis ask Andrea herself to clarify her answer, which she did by saying that we had two cats, but one of them was dead.

So much for being able to access humor through aphasia: what made Andrea herself, her personality, her guffaw, her acuity, was lost to these well-meaning skilled therapists, new armies of whom seemed to spring from the hospital halls each shift. As Andrea settled into the routines of rehab, I tried to figure out the consequences of what Marge the nice lesbian social worker kept calling a "catastrophic" brain injury. Was this going to get better? Did any of the "therapy goals" mean anything? Would Andrea be able to come home, ever?

Third Channel

The final example is a fragment of footage of Latina trans activist Sylvia Rivera, which is now accessible on various video-streaming platforms thanks to the uploading efforts of the LoveTapesCollective, an organization loosely associated with the collectively run Lesbian Herstory Archives, which holds the archive of L.O.V.E. (Lesbians Organized for Video Experience), yet another collective, which used half-inch reel-to-reel video portapaks to record lesbian feminist activities from 1972 to 1977. I first saw the footage of Rivera not in the community-based context suggested by this digital trace but embedded in *The Death and Life of Marsha P. Johnson*, a documentary film directed by David France, released in October 2017 on Netflix. France, you will remember, is the director of *How to Survive a Plague*, from 2012, an Oscar-nominated film that he subsequently adapted into a nonfiction history of AIDS activism under the same name. Both of his films rely to a striking degree on archival footage, and the Marsha P. Johnson film, incidentally, has come under scrutiny for its eclipsing of the efforts of another filmmaker, a Black queer/trans woman named Tourmaline (fka Reina Gossett), who had been researching and amassing historical footage for her own documentary about Marsha. (Tourmaline instead made a short film, *Happy Birthday, Marsha!*, that premiered in March of 2018.) The unhappy consequence is that David France—a white, cisgender guy—made a film that ends up on a pay-for-access platform (which is to say, out of reach for many of the folks this film is about), while Tourmaline—a queer/trans artist and filmmaker of color—struggled to find resources for her project.

Marsha P. (the "P" stands for "Pay It No Mind") Johnson was a Black trans woman who lived in New York City, one of those on the front line with the police the night of the Stonewall Riots in 1969. With Sylvia Rivera, the other subject of the film, Johnson founded Street Transvestite Action Revolutionaries (STAR), an organization that provided support and housing for mostly poor trans and queer people in the 1970s. With Rivera, Johnson worked on behalf of incarcerated, homeless, and abused queers, many of them trans women of color like themselves, and they fought tirelessly against the mainstreaming of white, middle-class gay and lesbian respectability. Johnson died in 1992 (a year after Weston's book was published) at the age of forty-seven under mysterious circumstances: her body was found in the Hudson River. Rivera died at age fifty in 2002 of liver disease. Watching *The Death and Life of Marsha P. Johnson*, one cannot help but to be drawn to these incandescent figures, resplendent queens both, whose work continues to inspire young activists (who, like the young queens whom they helped and protected, see them emphatically in kinship terms as the mothers of drag-queen and transvestite New York).

Before I describe the fragment of footage, a word about naming. Sylvia Rivera described herself as a drag queen and disliked the term *transgender*. Seeing a notice about a meeting of the Gay Activists Alliance, she reports that she phoned the listed telephone number and asked, "Do you take drag queens?" In the context of the last years of her life, when she had become partners with a woman, she rejected those who subsequently wanted to call her a lesbian: "I'm tired of being labeled. I don't even like the label *transgender*. I'm tired of living with labels. I just want to be who I am. I am Sylvia Rivera. Ray Rivera left home at the age of 10 to become Sylvia. And that's who I am."[7] If there was any label she embraced unambiguously, it was calling all the young people she helped and loved her children: "I call everybody including yous in this room, you are all my children."[8] It was her way of putting stakes on the future of an inclusive and just community.

Tourmaline is one such young person whose connection to Marsha and Sylvia has guided her art making. Writing in *Teen Vogue* about France's film, she highlights the very piece of archival footage upon which I'll concentrate this reading:

> One of the most profound moments I had was finding the footage of Sylvia Rivera's famous "y'all better quiet down" speech. Watching it, I started to cry feeling how alive these legacies were. It was then that I dreamt of making a film about Sylvia and Marsha's life, to uplift and share their incredible work. I dreamt of a day that black trans women and the people who love us would come away from watching my film

feeling more connected to ourselves and our sense of power and joy and feel more free in the face of struggle.[9]

Sylvia Rivera's "y'all better quiet down" speech took place at the Christopher Street Gay Liberation pride rally in 1973. Like Tourmaline, I find it an incredibly moving piece of footage, miraculously captured and archived (and I don't know by whom—it's uncredited everywhere I've seen it). Tourmaline's art and activism alert her to "how alive" Rivera's legacy is, connecting her struggles to those in the past. Watching it over and over, I'm also awed by how overcoded this four-minute piece of film is by waves of loss. With power, joy, connection, and freedom come impotence, melancholy, severing, and constraint.

How many waves of loss are there in these few minutes of footage? Let's start with the image itself. Speaking as we were of families, it's a piece of footage that documentary scholars and archivists call (in its broadest sense) an "orphan," a piece of film that has been abandoned or neglected. Its provenance remains unknown: although it is archived online, its original source, its maker, is out of frame, beyond our grasp. As the camera initially pans toward Rivera's appearance onstage, we glimpse faces and bodies in the crowd, but they, too, are indistinct and fleeting in an establishing shot. About twenty seconds in, as the crowd boos Rivera before she begins her speech, the frame dissolves into the distortion, lines, and glitches typical of analog videotape. We can see some history in this artifact, then, insofar as this electronic distortion is part of its materiality, part of its inscription: at some point, maybe sometime in the 1980s, the footage was transferred from the medium in which it was born to tape that was then digitized and uploaded as an orphan.

So we have an orphan film about an orphan. Sylvia Rivera was abandoned by her birth father and orphaned at the age of three when her mother committed suicide. At the age of ten, she began living on the streets and working as a prostitute; she was born as "Sylvia" when she was taken in by a community—a chosen family—of drag queens, who baptized her with her new name. Throughout her life, she battled addiction and alcoholism, and she spent parts of her life in New York homeless, living in the gay community on the Christopher Street piers (the Marsha Johnson film has some footage of her giving an interview to Randy Wicker that includes a tour of her room at the encampment). Her experiences on the street attuned her to the marginalization of some queers, not just by the "pigs" and straight men who routinely raped and beat them, but by largely white middle-class gays and lesbians who were advocating for gay liberation.

Not all of these pieces of Sylvia Rivera's life are visible on her body, but the boos that greet her appearance onstage signal something of the rejection and hostility that white affluent members of the community direct toward marginalized queers that was as real in 1973 as it is today. It's in the hair, the jumpsuit, the accent. It was her bitter experience appearing in public at this rally, in fact, that led Sylvia Rivera actually to withdraw from gay liberation for the next twenty-odd years, a political loss that seems absolutely essential to acknowledge and mourn. The Gay Activists Alliance's decision to drop trans issues from a multi-issue platform came at precisely the same moment as this rally, essentially pushing activists like Rivera toward despair. Although she disappeared from activist circles, she nevertheless tended those street children—trans hustlers and poor kids of color—who were then, two decades later, to become the faces of HIV/AIDS as it ravaged New York. Nothing much changed for "street transvestites" and the revolution as a result. Gay power, maybe—revolution, no. Sylvia Rivera recounts this history for us, over and over, and somehow we haven't *registered* the loss as our own.

And so here let me make a broader methodological argument. Any contemporary discourse on queer loss finds itself indebted to Heather Love, whose book *Feeling Backward* affirms a fundamental ambivalence inherent in our relationship to the past: "We are not sure if we should explore the link between homosexuality and loss, or set about proving that it does not exist."[10] In her turn to those texts that speak to the darker side of queer experience, she mines the twentieth-century literary "archive of feeling" (Cvetkovich's helpful phrase) that registers queer pain, depression, regret, violence, damage, despair, shame, and other physical and psychic costs of homophobia. Working against a kind of critical blindness toward modernism's bleakness, Love foregrounds a "backward" canon that might help us linger with the complexity of the past and with the negativity that attaches to the most marginal among us.

I want to take Love's provocation further and argue that this four-minute fragment of film is as capable as a modernist novel of harboring this temporal ambivalence and, further, that our engagement with it *as multiply damaged* is crucial to our critical practice. Let me be clear: I don't mean that Sylvia Rivera the historical person was a cipher for damage; I mean the *image* that circulates, this fragment of film with its patchy resolution, risks becoming detached from its historical web and celebrated. I want it to *indict*. I am not, in other words, making a case that we can choose to read Sylvia Rivera's image and appearance as affirming, joyful, and free instead of reading it as negative, disruptive, and psychically devastating. It's rather that reading it *only* as the former remains blind to history's lessons regarding our own movement's transphobia and misogyny and our own image archive's impoverishment with regard to contradictory structures of feeling. Reading Sylvia as triumph, we lose the despair she felt walking onstage to loud attempts to shame her as she was trying to forge a language of trans affiliation in the face of a white middle-class disdain for those lives, including her own, most precious to her.

What Sylvia actually says during her speech carries with it the force of her sense of marginalization. I want to draw attention to a triangulation she formulates in describing the letters STAR (again, Street Transvestite Action Revolutionaries) received from incarcerated trans people:

> Have you ever been beaten up and raped and jailed? Now think about it. They've been beaten up and raped after they've had to spend much of their money in jail to get their [inaudible], and try to get their sex changes. The women have tried to fight for their sex changes or to become women. On the women's liberation and they write "STAR," not to the women's groups, they do not write women, they do not write men, they write "STAR" because we're trying to do something for them.

I'm drawn to incipient trans theory, staring us in the face: "They do not write women, they do not write men, they write 'STAR.'" "Women" and "men," terms hurled from Sylvia's mouth with astonishing venom: these are synonyms for "you people," "you all" who cannot see the violence and loss she has suffered *on their behalf*. STAR represents something altogether different from these "women" and "men," something to which people who suffer loss can attach: "I have been beaten. I have had my nose broken. I have been thrown in jail. I have lost my job. I have lost my apartment for gay liberation and you all treat me this way? What the fuck's wrong with you all? Think about that!"

Think about that indeed. As Riki Wilchins, founder of the group Transsexual Menace, and others who memorialized Sylvia Rivera upon her death have bleakly observed, 1973 is repeating itself, over and over again: "The earlier expulsion of transvestites by GAA [Gay Activists Alliance] was a harbinger of things to come. In 2002 [much less 2021], butches, queens, fairies, high femmes, drag people, tomboys, and sissies have all but vanished from official gay discourse. They are rarely mentioned in the public pronouncements of major gay organizations." Wilchins is prescient in additionally noting the political unevenness of the category of "gender identity," which has been crucial to the mission statements of queer organizations in the early twenty-first century but is used primarily as a means of addressing the rights and practices of trans people. In fact, Wilchins's organization GenderPAC (Gender Public Advocacy Coalition) found that about a third of gays, lesbians, and bisexuals who experienced workplace discrimination attributed it to the perception that they transgressed gender norms: all who don't fit the ideal of "real" men and women are subject to violence, shaming, harassment, and abuse. Policing the lines between genderqueer, gender nonconforming, trans, LGB, and other identities is as perilous today as it was thirty-five years ago. When Love's book was published, I thought to myself that it had gone far in countering that persistent linear continuist history against which so many of us have railed over many years. As I see now more than a decade later, there is much work to do, especially at the level of the material image, embedded in the circuits of history, striated across formations of value, to disclose the potentiality of our future.

Living On

Hannah Arendt lives on in readings of *The Human Condition* that enlighten us to its remarkable contributions more than sixty years after its initial publication. Although I'm not an Arendt scholar, I've been taught by those who are about how fundamentally Arendt sought in this book to address precisely the relationship between freedom and attachment that I've wanted to pursue in this essay. In a reading that has become influential if not defining in the field of political theory, Roy T. Tsao emphasizes Arendt's Kantian injunction to define how we as human beings are able to *comprehend* basic kinds of continuity and change. Tsao shows us how, for Arendt, such comprehension comes through stories: "What makes it possible for human actions to cohere into stories, according to her, is their relation to a distinct, unique individual, whose own life is itself temporally bounded by birth and death. And whose stories are meaningful by virtue of the fact that their events occur within, and affect, an (always) already meaningful 'web of human relationships.'"[11] Which is to say that in order to enact one's story, one must both step into appearance, as Sylvia Rivera did upon that stage, and be recognized and comprehended, as that audience failed to do. In Arendt's language (added, as Tsao shows us, to the German edition of *The Human Condition*), "The risk of making an appearance as a 'someone' among others can be taken only by whoever is ready to move among others, to give out who one is, and to renounce the original foreignness of a newcomer born into the world."[12]

Sylvia Rivera's story didn't end on that fateful day in 1973, but the rest of her life was marked by the loss she experienced in that sea of booing gay men and lesbians. Andrea's story doesn't end with 2011 either: she eventually did come home to me and our single cat, Slash; when he died, we got two healthy boys and can now tell Phyllis, truthfully, that we have two cats (or, honestly, four cats, two of whom are dead). Since that May morning in 2011, however, our lives have not gotten "better": both of us have had cancer, mine advanced, and Andrea has had falls and emergency surgery and subsequent hospitalizations. Friends look at our lives and mutter things about Job.[13] Suffering continues.

However, what these monumental events miss is the repair we have made to our web of quiet attachment as we tend to those fragile infrastructures that make the long term a horizon that is still meaningful to us. I am learning new modes of both solitude and attachment as I go, living alone for the winters while Andrea escapes the cold for California. I travel alone or with friends; we entertain at home because Andrea can't really get into anyone else's house (or bathroom). We have home health-care aides, and they have become part of our extended support structure, just as the therapists, doctors, nurses, and caregivers have. When Andrea is gone, I watch TV and experiment with what its forms of relationality offer, in that ghost light of an evening. If I am still overcoded by loss and its sensations as I interact with new stories and imaginations, I am all the more appreciative for what they sustain in the long term.

NOTES

1 Tuan, *Space and Place*, 159.
2 See Stewart, *Ordinary Affects*; Berlant, *Cruel Optimism*; Cvetkovich, *An Archive of Feelings* and *Depression*.
3 Arendt, *The Human Condition*, 204.
4 Arendt, *The Human Condition*, 199.
5 On the translation of "Öffenlichkeit," see Negt and Kluge, *Public Sphere and Experience*, xi n1.
6 Weston, *Families We Choose*, 12.
7 Rivera, "Queens in Exile," 77.
8 Rivera, "Sylvia Rivera's Talk at LGMNY," 120.
9 Tourmaline, "Tourmaline on Transgender Storytelling."
10 Love, *Feeling Backward*, 3.
11 Tsao, "Arendt against Athens," 103.
12 Qtd. in Tsao, 104.
13 I tell them to read Antonio Negri, who learns something about suffering and resistance in his rereading of the Book of Job in *The Labor of Job*.

BIBLIOGRAPHY

Arendt, Hannah. *The Human Condition*. Chicago: University of Chicago Press, 1958.

Berlant, Lauren. *Cruel Optimism*. Durham, NC: Duke University Press, 2011.

Cvetkovich, Ann. *An Archive of Feelings: Trauma, Sexuality, and Lesbian Public Cultures*. Durham, NC: Duke University Press, 2003.

Cvetkovich, Ann. *Depression: A Public Feeling*. Durham, NC: Duke University Press, 2012.

Love, Heather. *Feeling Backward: Loss and the Politics of Queer History*. Cambridge, MA: Harvard University Press, 2007.

Negri, Antonio. *The Labor of Job: The Biblical Text as a Parable of Human Labor*. Durham, NC: Duke University Press, 2009.

Negt, Oskar, and Alexander Kluge. *Public Sphere and Experience: Toward an Analysis of the Bourgeois and Proletarian Public Sphere*. Translated by Peter Labanyi, Jamie Owen Daniel, and Assenka Oksiloff. Minneapolis: University of Minnesota Press, 1993.

Rivera, Sylvia. "Queens in Exile/The Forgotten Ones." In *Genderqueer: Voices from beyond the Sexual Binary*, edited by Joan Nestle, Clare Howell, and Riki Anne Wilchins, 67–85. New York: Alyson, 2002.

Rivera, Sylvia. "Sylvia Rivera's Talk at LCMNY, June 2011 Lesbian and Gay Community Services Center." *Centro Journal* 19, no. 1 (2007): 117–23.

Stewart, Kathleen. *Ordinary Affects*. Durham, NC: Duke University Press, 2007.

Tourmaline. "Tourmaline on Transgender Storytelling, David France, and the Netflix Marsha P. Johnson Documentary." *Teen Vogue*, October 11, 2017. www.teenvogue .com/story/reina-gossett-marsha-p-johnson-op-ed.

Tsao, Roy T. "Arendt against Athens: Rereading *The Human Condition*." *Political Theory* 30, no. 1 (2002): 97–123.

Tuan, Yi-Fu. *Space and Place: The Perspective of Experience*. Minneapolis: University of Minnesota Press, 1977.

Weston, Kath. *Families We Choose: Lesbians, Gays, Kinship*. New York: Columbia University Press, 1991.

Wilchins, Riki. "A Woman for Her Time." *Village Voice*, February 26, 2002. www.villagevoice.com/2002/02/26/a-woman-for-her-time.

3

UNHEALTHY ATTACHMENTS

Myalgic Encephalomyelitis/Chronic Fatigue
Syndrome and the Commitment to Endure

SALLY R. MUNT

Queer Feelings

"All of a sudden, I came over all queer." We all know how that feels, and what it doesn't usually indicate is a sudden and unexpected predilection for homosexuality. Queer sensations are usually allied to nausea, dizziness, confusion, and derealization, and they signify the abrupt onset of illness. Strange, disjunctive, or peculiar sensations that foretell dis-ease notify us of our abruptly changed physical materialities. We associate "queerness" with things not being normal, with disequilibrium, being "out of whack," "addled," or "off," and usually as a result of feeling queer, we take to our beds.

Feeling queer is a common synonym for the onset of illness; it echoes the paradigm of homosexuality as pathology. This queer feeling is experienced as something imposed, a disturbance in a steady state; in some intangible way it is about being covered by an invasive element that creates a milieu of discomfort or instability. It provokes retreat, introversion, and often infantilism as we retreat into our flannelette pajamas, switch on *The Golden Girls*, and sup soup. Feeling queer is a disruption of bodily order and control that provokes social withdrawal and a focus on our inner energies. Our focal point drills down into our body and its distressing malfunction.

Although "to be sick" usually involves a cartography of specific, Googleable symptoms depending on your diagnosis, we all have distinctive, ritualized, and rather idiosyncratic sick behaviors. When I am ill, I put on my beanie hat and eat coleslaw with cheddar cheese in a bowl. For many years, I used to wear my dad's pajamas, until they fell apart. Sickness has its own *dispositif*; in a kind of psychic splitting, self-loathing can make us draw back from others who are sick with the same diagnosis as ourselves, as though shame of inadequacy and imperfection is itself contagious.[1] Illness can be private, as sickness causes antisocial feelings; we preserve our psychological energy for own precious consumption and withdraw like a mollusk into a shell. Or it can propel us, needily, into disordered attachments as we cling to the imagined provision of others. In sickness-time, past and future recedes or interrupts, and we embody the present with more intensity, more awareness and focus. Functions like breathing, or the sensation of our skin, are gesticulating to consciousness in unusual patterns. Sensations become disrupted; organs start signaling in peculiar ways. *Dis-ease* is the formal name for feeling very queer, and "queer disability studies" is increasingly the name given to work that teases out the relation between this feeling of queerness and other experiences of class, gender, sexuality, race, and age.[2]

Health and illness are generally perceived to be mutually exclusive and stable, binary states, but clearly most of us move fluidly between one mode to the other. We are all ill, but for some of us, wellness is something that happens only occasionally. I have had myalgic encephalomyelitis (ME) for more than thirty years, most of my adult life. It is also known as chronic fatigue syndrome (CFS) and previously as postviral fatigue syndrome (although "fatigue" doesn't really seem to articulate these restrictive, diverse, and sometimes immobilizing symptoms accurately enough). I am using the acronym ME here because that was my initial diagnosis, and perhaps in spite of its biomedical origin, it is the term that feels most authentic.

For decades, ME has undergone a crisis of credibility and has been misread as a hysterical symptom, even a mass psychogenic disorder. Respected feminist historian Elaine Showalter, writing in 1997, named ME as indicative of the "crucible of virulent hysterias in our own time." She saw ME as an epidemiological cultural narrative or "hystory": "Patients learn about [such] diseases from the media, unconsciously develop the symptoms, and then attract media attention in an endless cycle." In her paradigm, ME is pathologically attention seeking. Showalter goes on to claim that patients "have no objective clinical signs of disease" and furthermore comments (dismissively) that "no-one has died from it" (despite the many suicides by sufferers who simply cannot endure anymore). Her analysis of ME as a case study of hysteria describes how, in 1996 on the UK television program *The Rantzen Report*, ME sufferers "*staged* a shouting match" between themselves and one respected Tory MP and medical columnist for the *Times*, who was arguing that it was a psychological condition symptomatic of depression and that audience members, "some in wheelchairs, *but most looking surprisingly fit*," were full of aggression. Her chapter relentlessly undermines patients' accounts, and her summary of the "plague" of hysteria infecting the 1990s is damaging to our "full humanity" by "distracting us from the *real* problems and crises of modern society [and] in undermining a respect for *evidence and truth*."[3] In Showalter's worldview, ME is "fake news" threatening the stability of Western liberal societies. (A position that is perhaps . . . a tiny bit hysterical in itself, wouldn't you say?)

My preferred label is "Icelandic disease," after when it appeared in 1948 in Akureyri, where it was thought to be a mild form of poliomyelitis. In the 1990s the popular media pejoratively labeled it "yuppie flu," and the consensus was, and remains, that it is a feigned illness deployed by maungy malingerers in order to manipulate and exploit precious medical resources and doctors' goodwill. It is perceived to be an excuse for chronic work avoiders, laggards. These beliefs persist, despite the World Health Organization classifying it as a brain, neurological, and central nervous system illness way back in 1969. An endemic disorder, ME appears in sporadic, episodic, and epidemic forms (as evidenced by the famous "outbreak" affecting nearly three hundred staff at the Royal Free Hospital in 1955, an outbreak that two psychiatrists in 1970 arrogantly declared to be an incidence of mass hysteria). The pathogenesis of ME is as yet unknown; it is described as "idiopathic," and prevalence estimates vary widely partly because diagnosis is inexact. Evidence-based studies of ME remain insufficient partly because of the diagnostic criteria being quite broad; the etiology isn't known, and ME is actually a "syndrome": a bunch of different but recognizably related symptoms with a core symptom of extreme fatigue. Research is uneven because orthodox medical practitioners persist in the belief that ME isn't real. Sufferers' doctors frequently respond with uncertainty, skepticism, and indeed open suspicion. Charlotte Blease, Havi Carel, and Keith Geraghty argue that there is "empirical evidence to substantiate the claim that patients with CFS/ME are indeed being negatively stereotyped in ways that unfairly deflate their credibility and that they also suffer disadvantage due to the lack of shared hermeneutical resources through which to frame and interpret their experiences."[4]

Until recently, the National Health Service (NHS) policy on ME was to concede that although it has a biological trigger, it can persist because of "abnormal illness beliefs" and dysfunctional somatizations that require cognitive behavioral therapy (CBT) and graded exercise therapy to "correct." Although this position is now discredited, ME is one of a group of illnesses that accrue patient blame and are widely judged to be self-inflicted.[5] Recently, Sarah Myhill made a pithy observation of ME that "it's mitochondria not hypochondria," as more science emerges and ME is looking more and more "legitimate" as a biological and specifically cellular aberration rather than poor stress management or "bad psychology."[6] Because ME is an inflammatory condition, the future is promising as medical research investigates anti-inflammatory treatments that are developing apace. Stanford University Medical School has recently argued that biomarkers for the severity of ME have now been discovered, which makes a simple diagnostic blood test foreseeable soon.[7]

I was diagnosed with ME in 1986, age twenty-six. In the previous term I had gone down to half my current body weight, was borderline anorexic, and was intensely lonely. I probably caught Epstein-Barr from my ex-girlfriend, and whereas she got better, I didn't. For the first couple of months I could hardly get out of bed. I would be half a mile away from home, and my legs would go from under me. Crying with fatigue, I would have to get a taxi to get back, which in those days involved struggling to find a public phone box. I was living on my own, so this crippling exhaustion was alarming. Not long after, I cared for my mum for five months while she died of esophageal cancer, so a heroic rallying was required. For a year, I lived on adrenaline, grief, and vegetarian ready-meals from Marks and Spencer. I grasped every straw for recovery, including injections of one thousand times the recommended daily allowance of vitamins, which is partly why I now also have chronic kidney disease caused by toxicity. I turned to complementary and alternative medicine and followed up every proposition for a cure. I chased every rainbow as I stumbled inexorably toward long-term disability. I never got better.

Having ME is quite a queer condition in itself. It is socially scorned, reviled, and derided; in fact, in terms of reputation, it is probably analogous to being a languid homosexual in the 1950s. The so-called cures are ineffective, it makes you a bit of a pariah, and really you are better off restricting your ME existence to shame, privacy, and secrecy. Just stay at home, sit quietly in a chair, and don't talk about it. (Why do you have to *push it down our throats?*) It exceeds diagnostic restraint, its effects truculently refusing strict categories of symptoms; it slithers away from its medical signifier. It causes aversion in those who suspect it to be contagious; they swerve away from you with their suspicion that there is something mental about it, something psychologically toxic. There is a discursive collapse between those who have ME and a quintessential victimhood. Just like no one likes a victim, no one likes you much if you have ME either. It is a queer, feminized plague in that it enforces passivity and dependency; it is the opposite of the virile masculine fantasies of the economically viable and productive neoliberal subject. At worst, ME can commit you to a lifetime of lying down or, at best, a life of drained efficiency, a mysterious malaise that is perceived to be akin to bloody-minded stubbornness. The fact that epidemiologically it affects women more than men enforces the cultural links among femininity, passivity, cryptic inscrutability, victimhood, and hysteria. It has yet to become accepted as a naturally occurring phenomenon; instead, it remains enigmatically suspicious.

The Problem with Shrinks

Having tried thousands of pounds' worth of alternative therapies in the 1980s, none of which made a penn'orth of difference, I concluded (along with most of the medical establishment) that my illness must be psychological, specifically what is called a functional disease, a "somatic conversion." So in 1994 I sank into psychoanalytic psychotherapy twice a week. I went to see John for sixteen years, who, with the exception of my cat companion Dora, has been my longest-term attachment. There was no cure to be found there either, but psychotherapy was transformative in other ways. The problem with crude psychoanalytical interpretations of illness is that symptoms are inevitably ascribed to the patient's (ill) will. The patient is at fault for stubbornly repressing their emotions (or perhaps not repressing them enough). Psychosomatic disorders are interpreted as a psychic cry for help, an attention-seeking neurosis. In psychoanalytic psychotherapy the assumption is that such hysterical maladies can be talked out. When people write about illness in the humanities, it is usually to allegorically describe an existential or symbolic crisis. This is not my experience, which is that this illness is not figurative but physical; it is intensely RL. From 2012 to 2014 I studied postgraduate medicine at medical school, specifically psychiatry, where I found that ME is still taught as a somatoform, or conversion disorder. Medically unexplained symptoms (MUS) was the catch-all category in the *Diagnostic and Statistical Manual of Mental Disorders, DSM-IV-TR* (2000) for somatoform disorders, but the more recent *DSM-5* (2013), replaced somatoform disorders with somatic symptom and related disorders, which was partly intended to address the previous implication that the patient wasn't medically sick. Several months after submitting this piece I found Christopher D. Ward's humane and grounded book, *Meanings of ME: Interpersonal and Social Dimensions of Chronic Fatigue*, in which he analyzes the history of diagnosis. Readers wishing to know more about the illness would be advised to start with this collection, in which Ward reminds us that "meanings, including those used by doctors, are arrived at discursively, through the contexts in which they operate. . . . Consequently, the way in which we speak . . . always participates in the creation of meaning rather than being an inert vehicle for objective interpretations."[8] He argues for a systemic perspective, or syndrome method, for understanding CFS/ME. Psychiatrists do love to grasp the MUS category and mine it for supposed psychosomatic jewels. With ME, the popular conviction that it is generated from a mental failing persists: only recently a member of my tai chi class asked me why I so frequently sit down and take rests when practicing the form. I explained it was because I have ME, to which she asserted that her friend was so incapacitated by ME that she could hardly lift a piece of paper, but when she went to psychotherapy, she got better immediately.

In terms of the recent scientific research, it seems as if ME is genuinely bloody-minded in that it turns out that the quality of the mitochondria in cells, the actual energy in your blood, may be its biological basis. Thus, the disorienting mental symptoms of ME might be caused by inflamed blood: an inflammatory response, which makes me reflect that I had a lot to get inflamed about.

The *Lebenswelt* (Lifeworld) of the Chronically Ill

My earliest memories consist entirely of being ill. I recall fragments: the weird, full feeling of having warmed Olbas Oil on a teaspoon trickled into my ear by my mother, as I yelled in pain. Screaming after I had poured boiling water down my scalded neck as I reached up to the kitchen table as a small toddler to grab a cup of tea. I remember the roughly enveloping, candy-striped bath towel I was wrapped in to travel to hospital and the stinky black tar the nurses painted on the burn. (My mother's dry comment, years later, was that she should never have left me alone with my dad, whom she accused of flirting with our young female lodger instead of paying attention to me.) Such injurious instances resulted in scars. I fell off a wall and split my leg open (scar); got bit in the cheek by a dog (scar); threw a dart at the dartboard and forgot to let go (scar); paddled in the black water of our four-foot-wide goldfish pond, which was filled with broken shells (scars); and once, when I went really high on our garden swing, the seat flipped over, and I came down on my face (ouch, big scar).

From the back end of every year onward, I spent my childhood at the GP's surgery in Moldgreen, coughing and wheezing my way through dozens of chest infections. Miserable, mardy, and nesh, I would be sat in the waiting room with the other drab, wool-clad patients, most of whom were chain-smoking, as was the norm in 1960s working-class Yorkshire. Winter blew straight in from the pages of a Brontë novel: we had chilblains on our split fingers, the wind really did howl ("direct from the Gorbals," as Mum would say), and I recall coming inside from the biting cold and standing with my bare, burning legs against the flames of the coal fire as they slowly turned mottled purple. This was no Munchausen's; it was Northern Grit. My six-weeks' premature, bruised, burned, infected, and marked little body emerged from childhood wounded, with weakened immunity, and anxious. I learned nippily about life's precarity, its unpredictability, and also of the necessity of tenacious survival. I learned how I mirrored my mother's vulnerabilities: "She was such a tiny scrap, we used to push her forward to the front of the fire as we used to worry that she wouldn't make it through the winter," observed my Auntie Mary. My grandfather was himself a small man because of childhood malnutrition. My genes were not right champion, as they say in Huddersfield.

Such wounds mutated into longer-term health concerns. In no particular order I have been diagnosed at one time or another with Barrett's esophagus (Mum herself died of throat cancer at the age of sixty-six), transient ischemic attacks (ministrokes), stress-induced chronic kidney disease, high blood pressure, folate deficiency anemia, ADHD, insomnia, asthma, moderate cognitive deficits, impaired visual recall, dyspraxia (the scars?), and a hearing impairment that was scornfully pronounced as being a "problem with your brain." I've endured pleurisy, dysentery, prolapsed fibroids, anal polyps, infective endocarditis, adult measles, shingles, a "sluggish" gall bladder, bird flu, swine flu, norovirus, bowel surgery, precancerous cervical cells, bronchial pneumonia, scarlet fever, and countless other disquieting things. I've been misdiagnosed with heart attacks twice. I suffer periodically from fickle bouts of anxiety and depression. I struggle to exercise, partly because of the illnesses and partly because of being on steroids and many other drugs for years. I'm overweight, a state of affairs I find daily startling, fundamentally, a perfidious insult. Such disclosures of infirmity are antithetical to the academic writing genre, which demands tropes of virility I am rarely capable of procuring or expressing.

Both my childhood friend Marie and I played on some of the most toxic fields in Europe, on Kilner Bank, Huddersfield, a mill town in West Yorkshire that since the Industrial Revolution until the 1968 Clean Air Act lay in a valley of permanent smog. Kilner Bank is a steep and high bank rising above Huddersfield Town Football Club, footed by two hugely polluting chemical plants that were weapons factories during the wars. Both Marie and I appear to have contracted the same neurotoxicity; we have both been diagnosed with ME, and she, like me, is chronically ill.

It's not cool to mither on about it. Friends will lecture me about doing more exercise; occasionally, their concern is microtinted with blame as they inelegantly hint that my afflictions are caused by the time I spend on the couch. I am ashamed by my corporeal failure of fatness, and it makes me defensive. The thing about chronic illness is that it is tiring, shaming, exposing, and indiscreet but also boring to all concerned, and lots find illness disgusting: it can evoke primitive unease. I've never once, in more than thirty years, had an extended conversation about what having ME means to me. I mention to people that "the ME isn't too good right now" in a strangled apology that discourages further questions. Despite being told seven years ago I am "legally disabled," I determinedly avoid thinking about it. I bought a pile of books in preparation for writing this very article, but I couldn't motivate myself to pick them up. They sat on my desk for months, hoping to inform me telepathically.[9] I don't include disability in my curricula; I'm in long-term denial, refusal, and intentional forgetting. I feel now that I am faking it, that not only are my illnesses fraudulent, my knowledge of illness is fraudulent too, and that no one, including me, will take me seriously. For the first time in my academic life then, in writing here, I am straining to focus on illness analytically because my purchase on it just keeps slipping from my dyspraxic grasp.[10]

Of course, I simultaneously self-monitor frantically in order to make chronicity intelligible and micromanage my activities in order to make ME's effects endurable. (I restrict activity in subtle, excusable ways in order to mitigate people's judgment.) I have had a lifetime, at sixty, to envy those alien, hard bodies that effortlessly shuck off the degradations of the flesh. I like to ruminate about what it might be like to be one of them, to be robust and well, to be able to actually *run*, and not to be tired all the time (or "TATT" as general practitioners write dismissively across the front of your medical notes in block caps). I frequently worry whether I am just a hypochondriac; I perform "wellness" without being really present, derealized, because I have a parallel sense of myself in suspension, waiting to lig i'bed. I am alarmed by multifarious symptoms (while conscious that if you focus too much on any part of the body, it will inevitably sensate). My body keeps prodding me with its damned neediness. Capricious symptoms intensify and degrade. As a disease, ME is very, very irritating, and I am chronically disappointed in myself. I feel defective. As a compensation, I tend to overwork.

An internal scan of one's organs is notoriously difficult to achieve other than when specific pain is present, unless you happen to be a Buddhist monk. Part of the mysterious threat of illness is its invisibility even to the person experiencing it. Chronic illness is also frequently invisible to others and therefore doesn't elicit recognition or concern. Sometimes I get so tired, and I really would like that seat on the bus or the comfy chair at a party, or to sit on a motorized airport cart to take me to the end of the interminable terminal. My ME is episodic, and when I'm in a relapse, my limbs can shake; my muscles misperform; I lose my balance; I can black out; my temperature regulation is erratic; I have constant aural hallucinations such as white noise, increased arousal, and vigilance; I mix up my words (linguistic aphasia); and my speech can be slurred or stuttering. After thirty years I can mostly hide all these symptoms in my attempt to pass as healthy. Being chronically ill also brings with it resilience, whether you like it or not.[11]

Disembodiment, Dis-ease, Disattachment, and Disassociation

I often used to joke that my body is just a trolley to get my brain around. This kind of splitting is common for those of us who have experienced an assault, particularly a childhood sexual assault, and it is a useful temporary strategy but not so advantageous in the long term. Cartesian dualism, and the mind/body split, have reinforced the idea that our minds control our bodies, being the superior partner of such symbiosis. (Indeed, it is plausible to view the feminine body as parasitic upon the noble, masculine mind.) Illness, or any insufficiency of the body, is frequently blamed on the mind's inadequacy and on our calculated, weak-willed indiscipline. Within the Christian legacy of somatophobia, it is expected that our minds regard with scrupulous moral authority our bodies. In medieval times we would scourge them in order to expiate sin. In Victorian times, extreme Protestantism decreed that the sinful body must be regulated purely by reason, its desires routinely denied. Within historically Christian cultures, the body has been subjected to a range of punishments, corrections, chastisements, castigations, and abysmal religious control. We understand from the Western Christian perspective that the body's sad perseverations are meaningless and to be ignored; we are exhorted instead to rise up and escape the warped limitations of the flesh. Body phobia remains intrinsic to Western cultural traditions, and the mortifications of the flesh remain far from medieval; they are omnipresent in contemporary diet regimes such as "clean" eating, in obsessive fitness routines, in fashion, in sexual denial and conservatism, and in plastic surgeries that culminate or articulate psychiatric dysmorphias.

The body, in contemporary Western cultures, is still to be disciplined and defeated. Note for example the current moral panic about the alleged crisis of obesity. Blame for this is laid largely on the residual poor, who are perceived to be the repository of addictions (whether alcohol, nonprescription or prescription drugs, tobacco, or sugar), people who cannot quench their noxious appetites. Rigorous physical discipline is still an elite, predominantly white, cultural value in Western societies, alongside the Victorian belief that bodily pleasure should be a reward for the correct application of the will. Within Western culture an unhealthy body is still openly regarded as the result of a *lack of commitment*, an implicit moral failure or indeed a psychological one. Throughout this logic, the contemporary political sickness of neoliberalism constructs the poor and disabled as malingerers and scroungers. The legacies of Christianity ensure that illness is the resultant failure of will, allied to the archaism of God's punishment. The shame of illness is directly proportional to the tyranny of individualism, as all dependency is regarded as toxic.

For the first two decades of my illness, I saw ME as a demonic invader, a parasitic enemy that I had to conquer and expunge through a commitment to analysis and the practice of disciplined reason. If only I could consciously unlock the right repressed emotion, my physical suffering would release. Illness should *mean* something cultural, moral, and profound. Susan Sontag asserted how unhelpful it is to think about illness in such metaphorical terms, charting how once tuberculosis, and now cancer, were seen as corrupted passions turned inward.[12] On her deathbed my mother told me that her esophageal cancer was her own fault because she had spent her life swallowing her anger. She got this nonsense from a friend who had recently moved to California; he had been reading Louise Hay's *You Can Heal Your Life* (1984), which was based on the naive simplifications of positive thinking.[13] Barbara Ehrenreich writes incisively about her own cancer in *Smile or Die* (2009). As a former cell biologist, she requested to see her own pathology slides, and observed the cancer cells, rather beautifully, as follows:

> I was impressed, against all rational self-interest, by the energy of these cellular conga-lines, their determination to move on out from the backwater of the breast to colonize lymph nodes, bone marrow, lungs and brain. These are, after all, the fanatics of Barbara-ness, the rebel cells that have realised that the genome they carry, the genetic essence of me in whatever deranged form has no further chance of normal reproduction in the postmenopausal body we share, so why not just start multiplying like bunnies and hope for a chance to break out?[14]

Later, she remarks that "cancer cells are not foreign," challenging the putative common sense of illness as something traitorous or corrupt that comes from outside (the allusion is quite racist, stressing as it does the necessity for hypervigilance toward an external threat).[15] Illness is not an invasion, bad karma, or God's punishment. Within folk narratives from ancient times to the present, illness is widely seen as retribution, so much so that we tend not to notice iconic examples—would Rochester remain a judicious match for Jane Eyre if his hubris hadn't been humbled by his blindness and incapacity?

The Gordian Knot of Mental Health and Physical Health

Research has found childhood trauma to be a predisposing risk factor in adults contracting ME.[16] As science unravels the knot between physical health and mental health—for example, in the exciting new research on the role that inflammation plays in the etiology of conditions as variable as cancer, schizophrenia, and ME—it seems a categorical error to insist on autonomous domains. "Mental" health conditions are seen to have genetic components; even behavioral conditions such as addiction or psychopathy have neurological evidence standing behind a diagnosis. Conversely, Ehrenreich reports that a meta-analysis of cancer-support groups found "no link" between positive emotions and recovery; thus, the mystery continues.[17]

A sick body can't be shaken off by a positive attitude. Physical sickness is culturally stigmatizing; in my front-stage performance I mainly try to pass as well, although my fatness rather undermines doleful attempts to join the normal people in my polished middle-class life. My fatness is classed; it betrays my father's fat, working-class family; it is a status embarrassment. Sometimes my sickness is visible, despite efforts to maintain bodily integrity. When the ME is erupting, my speech can stutter, my words simply elude, I can't find them, my hands tremble, I get very hot or very cold, I forget where I am supposed to be at what time, I get dizzy and can't manage the stairs because my balance is poor, and I fear falling down them. I want to sit down, I want to wee a lot as my kidneys are weak, my lazy eye kicks in, and occasionally I feel that I will black out. In relapse, which usually snatches several months out of every year, I would like to use a stick to support my walking, but I have never dared. (In 2020 I nearly died from COVID-19, and I began walking with a stick after I crossed that Rubicon.) I fear that people will imagine I am feigning illness in order to gain their sympathy. All this mess causes me mental distress and humiliation. When I am well, I pretend these things never happened. Fake.

In my workaholic life, I am also a cognitive psychotherapist. In working with refugees, I have learned that Western techniques of mental health treatment don't work so well for patients from other places. Direct questions about feelings and emotions mainly result in a polite deflection—"I am very fine, thank you"—which somewhat stymies clinical progress. Initially, the refugee client often presents with a list of physical problems and will wish to talk at length about these troubles (these can also and often do extend to discussions of extended family ailments, of their sister's diabetes, their mother's irregular heart, their father's arthritis, and so on). Long conversations about bad knees, or irregular sleep, or stiff necks must ensue. It is only *after* due attention has been paid to such physical ailments that nonsomatic feelings may come forward. Emotional distress becomes read *through* the body's disease. In Western traditions we imagine that our mental illness causes physical illness. In other cultures the physical problem is more imbricated, a gateway to understanding the person's emotional distress. So, to make things worse, the Gordian knot is culturally specific.

Illness and Capital

My daily life is configured by urgent questions because of ME: What shall I commit my energy to today? What can I leave and ignore? What resources need deploying? Energy is a currency, and my labor costs me. Being ill demands a range of sophisticated and strategic physiological and emotional responses. It requires commitment to acknowledge incapacity and to a dedicated care of the self. Illnesses are always already threatening a catastrophic escalation and demand monitoring. Illness requires physical and emotional labor, yet there is also a quota of real, practical labor demanded by illness: sourcing all the meds/supplements/healthy foods you read online that promise to alleviate some symptom or other (I take nearly thirty tablets a day). Fad (not food) shopping includes preparing/storing/cooking your expensive fresh ginger/green tea/quinoa/stewed blueberries with vegan kefir. Back from work and hauling yourself around miserably to cook "clean," when what you most crave is a big plate of oven chips and a tub of gourmet ice cream to share with the dogs. And of course you need pots of money: for the cranial osteopathy, the acupuncture, the psychotherapy, the taxis because you can't walk far, the expensive hotel rooms because you are such a bad sleeper, the online account at Holland & Barrett, the cleaner because you live with two dogs and four cats and the hairy dust kills your asthma, the organic supplies, the holidays/retreats, the Manuka honey. . . . Illness makes you poorer, as the statistics bear out.[18]

For many years I entertained fantasies of the perfect partner. I imagined that they would be sympathetic and meet me at the door with a green tea smoothie and a hot raw vegan banana hemp seed sushi slice.[19] (And not expect sex, for I'd be too tired.) One of my dear friends disabused me of this romance when she explained firmly that she hates her partner whenever he is ill and avoids him "like the plague." Illness does deal in a kind of relationship capital in that care is perceived to be due: it can be a kind of chip to be cashed in or a debt owed. When and if we marry, we make promises to love "through sickness and in health." Society disapproves if husbands abandon sick wives or take new lovers on the side. Care is obligatory, and the labor of care is indebted, or even indentured, if the sick one is a family member. Of course, women mainly perform this gendered labor of care. Nurses, the original handmaidens of wounded soldiers, can be hired to perform this care on behalf of others. Having said that, most of my lovers have totally decatastrophized the ME; one used to tell me, "If you are going to pass out, then stand over there where there's carpet."

Sick Methodologies

Audre Lorde challenged us about illness: "My silence had not protected me. Your silence will not protect you."[20] So how should this authorial voice go exactly? As a feminist writer, I follow the trend of personal criticism (so

Maoist!), as developed by Nancy K. Miller; her old comment about her father's penis disturbed me then and disturbs me now; it is a punctum of the genre.[21] In the 1990s, suddenly feminists all over the place were vomiting their dilemmas across the page. Later, life-history methods sneaked into a thousand research proposals. Then more recently still, autoethnography has become a thing. Skeptically, this urge to disclose seems so intimately bound up with the confessional cultural trends of psychotherapy, of individualism, of the cult of the self, to which I retain some ambivalence because it tends to benchmark the middle-class habitus.[22] I've deployed nuggets of my own life in print with indecision, shame, and anxiety. I've told anonymous readers things I haven't told my family. Admittedly, it was kind of therapeutic to throw out anecdotes willy-nilly and then to forget about them. But responding to a request from the editors of this volume to write something about commitment caused me to reflect on exactly what color of thread of commitment has endured throughout my sixty years, through changing lovers, houses, friends, cities, politics, animal companions, and fashions. My commitment to health was my conclusion or, rather perhaps, to my ill health, but I'm flummoxed by representing this accurately. Loosely, I've harnessed phenomenology to explain my experience of sickness, incapacity, and being unwell. Phenomenology, of the kind advanced by Maurice Merleau-Ponty, argues that the body is the site of all knowledge, perception, and being in the world. He defines this in *The Visible and the Invisible* as "indirect ontology": the ontology of the flesh, forcing us to recognize that consciousness (or "intellect") is cellular—in a nutshell, to have a thought, a neuron must fire.[23] Consciousness does not live in the brain but is distributed throughout the body, although we have yet to advance as far as the octopus, whose consciousness is so distributed that each arm is sentient.[24] I've always found it poignant that Merleau-Ponty died young, age fifty-three, of a stroke.[25]

Complaints versus Disorders

Despite illnesses being now categorized as "disorders," in my Northern childhood they were described as "complaints," something that alludes more directly to their vocality. A question used by older relatives—"What ails thee, lass?"—exhibited concern but also a working-class pragmatism reflecting the acceptance that most of those of a prewar generation remained perpetually ill. My parents grew up well before publicly funded health care, and their firstborn, Peter, died at birth because of lack of a doctor. Ailments and complaints are perhaps more kindly, tolerant designations than the scientific nomenclature of disorders. Before the NHS, British people were arguably more stoic through necessity because the population was in chronic discomfort and pain most of the time. Thus, enduring ailments and complaints formed part of everyday existence and were mundane. Victorians, of course, made maladies into performance art. Upper-class Victorian ladies and a few gentleman artists were said to suffer from neurasthenia, another syndrome that was restricted primarily to the alleged sensitivity of refined folk. Spinsters like myself were seen as peculiarly susceptible to "conditions." Freud thought that neurasthenia was caused by excessive masturbation. The cure for neurasthenia or hysteria was what my mum used to call the "rest cure," otherwise known as bed rest. For those perpetually and chronically tired, the idea of a rest cure distills all of our fantasies, although actually it is medically dangerous as it risks bedsores and thrombosis. Charlotte Perkins Gilman endured forced bed rest and used it in her short story "The Yellow Wallpaper" (1892), in which the protagonist, like the author, goes insane. (The bed-rest cure was trenchantly caricatured by Virginia Woolf in *Mrs. Dalloway* [1925].) As a disease, ME is taken to be the modern-day equivalent of neurasthenia, said to affect primarily neurotically underachieving or overachieving women. This seems to relate culturally to associating white femininity with pathology. In fact, community epidemiological research in Chicago found greatest prevalence among Black, Hispanic, and low-income social groups.[26]

As a cognitive behavioral psychotherapist also trained in psychiatry, now and then I muse about the diagnostic black hole of personality disorder. National Institute of Clinical Excellence guidelines, the proscriptory body of the British NHS, deem personality disorders to be untreatable, and indeed "PD" is the shoulder-shrugging acronym of mental health workers, the formal diagnosis that means informally that we think the patient is fucked.[27] There are those who argue ME to be indicative of a personality disorder: dependent, narcissistic, or even antisocial perhaps. In Arthur Frank's groundbreaking work *The Wounded Storyteller: Body, Illness, and Ethics*, he describes how people "surrender" to illness, implying defeat and referencing victim morphology.[28] Frank aside, these musings originate in the projections of the well, disturbed by a perennial sickness that they cannot cure. "Disordered" as a concept, from a queer perspective, is considered attractive. The romance of disordering is much vaunted in queer studies, but it is a very uncomfortable place to live. Over the years, queer studies' romantic mutterings about the disruptive outsider became really frustrating to me. Life, for most people, is a struggle, and economics is a bottom line; academics tend to keep discrete our absolute commitment to financial security and produce beautiful writing abstracted from the political economy of our material lives. This is a kind of privileged splitting in which thinking is valued as creative, more than doing, which is seen as mundane. Illness requires of us a sober materiality that regrounds our mind in/as the body.

Foucault and Subjectivity

The subjectivity of the sick has changed dramatically in the twenty-first century. For much of the West's history, medical care was the preserve of the rich, and the body was a mystery explicable only by the wisdom of folklore, poetry, religion, and farming. Most people were ill most of the time; lives were short and painful. Living to old age was exceptional, and half of the population died in childhood. Whereas sickness suffused everyone's existence, certain illness presentations were removed from society, for example the mad to the ship of fools or the lepers into colonies.[29] The earlier experience of illness was vastly different; as Pierre Bourdieu's unnamed "North African" woman states, people "went to bed and they died."[30] The science of medicine was restricted to the wealthiest men. It was not until the mid-twentieth century in the UK, when Ernest Bevan launched the NHS in Manchester on July 5, 1948, that limited medical care became accessible to the British poor, and illness became state-regulated. So far, so medical gaze, but changes in medical culture away from traditional subject/object hierarchies toward neoliberal presentations that an ill person is a consumer with choices has made ill health a confusing mirage.[31] Medical knowledge has been amateurized and arguably democratized by the epistemological rupture that was Dr. Google, and thus, for better or for worse, ill people's subjectivities are no longer so ignorant or so passive. If I am going for a hospital procedure, lo—I can watch it first on YouTube. Or I can self-diagnose on symptoms.webmd.com. I can join a support group online or browse a discussion with fellow sufferers. Ironically, this patient-based approach is happening at the same time that timely access to professional care is becoming increasingly restricted to those able to pay.

Following Foucault, what might be the biopolitics of ME? In Foucault's worldview, biopolitics and biopower work together with other, more explicit technologies of power to discipline the human subject.[32] In Foucauldian terms I am subjected to, and subjugated by, the academic labor market, my academic body is possessed by the machinic disciplines of the academic life— its rhythms, its regulatory clock time, its endless quantitative and qualitative measuring of my productivity—and of course I'm governed by the educational ideological state apparatus and its implicit power relations. Such rhythms operate in conjunction at the level of somatic experience, so my academic subjectivity clashes with the sick body; thus, cyclically, before every academic year in August, I get a relapse of the ME. Of course, there is the self-governance of illness through the monitoring, labeling, and performing of a specific diagnosis. There is also the fact of becoming a sick subject, an invalid, and the appropriation of an identity that will be ascribed to us whether we want it or not. Foucault describes biopolitics as nothing less than "the function of administering life" and the exercise of power to "put this life in order."[33] The requirements of illness bring this practice abruptly to consciousness.

Because biopower works from underneath, at the level of the *dispositif*, it contains the potential for resistance as the weft and weave of everyday existence erupts and flows. Power, as we know, is everywhere. Thus, being an invalid can be a form of committing passive resistance to forms of normativity, whether it is a refusal to work, to marry, to have sex, or to be conventionally productive. Yet strange things can happen: when I am working as a psychotherapist, despite feeling that I should cancel patients because I'm not up to it, there is also an unwritten rule that you show up no matter how rotten you feel. (As my clinical supervisor and ex-nurse, Catherine, says, "If you aren't ventilated, then you've got no excuse.") Because ME shreds my psychic boundaries, I'm usually more intuitive and kinder when I am sick—and thus often a better practitioner. Conversely, the repressed emotional load of patients can *make me sick*. I have discovered that ME makes visible emotional transactions so that they can pass more easily from their body into mine and that only when I am able to acknowledge the transference does the miasma lift. Illness *does things* with my unconscious, as emotions attach and detach in unpredictable ways. Once I saw a faith healer when I was significantly poorly with the ME. He moved his hand over my belly and said, "This black stuff is not yours," and immediately I felt a physical pop, and I was better. Illness can have a paranormal dimension, too. There's something about ME that evokes the paranormal—listen to this definition from Neville Millen: "a chimera-like medical anomaly, a variant illness entity that like the mythical creature is composed of a complex, and mysterious combination of parts which defy a clear description."[34]

Genealogies of Complaint

I come from generations of endurance, so I am hard to break. On the Munt side, my grandmother, Ethel, had eleven children, the youngest of whom was my father, Herbert. Dad was a short and round man. He was short, like all of his siblings, because when he was a child there wasn't enough food. When he was an adult, he liked to fill up his belly and slap it vigorously. He was a proud eater/shopper/provider who delighted in feeding his family up. Originally, the Munts were Swiss-German migrants; William, Alice, and their daughter Rose Allen were Anabaptists who were tortured and martyred for heresy in Colchester on August 2, 1557.[35] Foxe's *Book of Martyrs* describes how they were burned at the stake for malicious sedition, blasphemy, and perversion when they declared that the Catholic rituals "stunk."[36] From being stained-glass artists who built the magnificent St. Albans Cathedral, the Munts over time became working-class gravediggers and navvies who ventured north to Yorkshire during the building of the Great Railways (sixpence a grave). We Munts are distinctively resilient, proud, and stubborn.

On the Firth side, my maternal great-grandmother, Caroline, also had a lot of children, as poor people do, the oldest of whom was my grandfather, Albert Firth. When Albert was eleven, his father, a village bill poster, died, leaving Caroline destitute. She would walk the eight miles to Huddersfield market in order to pick up the rotten apples that the sellers threw on the ground. She would then walk the eight miles back to feed her children market scraps. They lived in a house with compacted earth floors, flour sacks for bedding, and no shoes. Caroline married again, to an alcoholic who beat her and the children and who eventually killed her, but at least they were not starving.

The Yorkshire winter is a season of endurance, even for those of us who grew up with the luxuries of coal fires, floorboards, and hot-water bottles at night. Albert married my grandmother, Annie Morton, a farmer's daughter who specialized in sheep and cattle droving, a hardy family business involving walking livestock long distances over the Yorkshire moors in all weathers. Annie and Albert were imprisoned for being conscientious objectors in World War I; they were pioneers who were spiritualists, socialists, vegetarians, and Esperantists. They cycled around Europe after the war, advocating world peace. They named my mother, Rosa, after Rosa Luxemburg, who was their much-admired contemporary. This is quite a radical pedigree for their descendants to honor. Two genealogies of stubborn idealists distill down into a certain kind of Northern endurance. Annie subsequently spent sixty years in the West Riding Lunatic Asylum, incarcerated (committed) by her husband when my mother was only four. Annie was a well-known medium who would lock herself away for hours generating spirit writing. Eventually this skill was diagnosed as paranoid schizophrenia. She died one month after my mother, in 1986, aged ninety-eight, which is quite a commitment to life, when you think about it, isn't it? Her husband, my grandfather, Albert, was not a nice man; he was a bully and a miser who died of syphilis in 1945. I have often wondered about what kinds of wounds those childhood beatings and starvation delivered to Albert, his wife, and his daughters. Despite and because of their struggles, both Annie and Albert clung to their strong ideals of social justice and fairness, but I think that life was not very fair to either of them in the end.

Sickness, Awareness, and Spirituality

The inward energy of sickness points us toward reflection and thus, for many, spirituality. I remember how, years ago, both Eve Kosofsky Sedgwick and Lynda Hart turned toward Buddhism after their cancer diagnoses. At first I was dismissive, then curious. As sickness nudges us toward mortality, the heart opens to more spiritual concerns; it needs it. The deception of academia is in its promise that theories can explain everything, and when we are younger, we rush around chasing that special theory that will make everything feel better. But life exceeds book learning, and academia is particularly feeble at providing insight into emotions (as feminists we have known this forever). Sickness makes you think about your wider existence and embodiment in ways that force you to raise your eyes from the page and blink.

When I was thirteen, despite being raised in the entirely reasonable, liberal, and calm Unitarian Church, I committed my life to Jesus and converted to evangelical Christianity. As a young woman, I entered a religious community, a rather special intentional group that was founded on the principles of 1970s counterculture. Post Green Community in Dorset was based on the belief and practice of social justice, emerging out of liberation theology and the Christian Left. In those days I read a lot of the Dutch theologian and Trappist monk Henri Nouwen. Delightfully, I didn't realize he was gay (who knew?!) until I researched his life just now. His writing wrangled with depression, loneliness (the gay shame subtext), and illness, issues that spoke to me as a young adult. Particularly, I drew comfort from contemplative books such as *The Wounded Healer* (1972), *Clowning in Rome* (1979), and *The Way of the Heart* (1981), works that proffered a view of humanity as essentially wounded, what was described in St. John of the Cross's poem in the sixteenth century as the "Dark Night of the Soul" (1577–79). The "Dark Night of the Soul" is understood to refer to the suffering wrought by the break in our union with God in the Christian mystical tradition that followed the fourteenth-century spiritual guide *The Cloud of Unknowing*. Nouwen, a contemporary mystic, writes about "experiential transcendence," which isn't the usual masculinist guff about escaping the reviled body but an internal state of suffering through which we are able to grasp the connectivity of all living things. This energy that Nouwen describes is similar to Buddha-nature and Hinduism/Vedanta, but is more likely influenced directly by another Christian theologian, Baruch Spinoza (in *The Ethics*): "There he touches the place where all people are revealed to him as equal and where compassion becomes a human possibility." Through Nouwen I realized as a young person that sickness, whether mental or physical, incites the sufferer's acute sensitivity to her connections because sickness raises our awareness of our attachment to life itself, to our dependence on others, and thus to the world around us. Following the logic of this revelation, Nouwen argued that to commit "revolution is better than suicide."[37] He was part of the movement that advocated a spiritual approach to social change, a sort of syncretic inward and external change, if you like, that produces intensity for life. Sometimes in my subsequent career I have found that academia's enforced secularism shuts down such thinking and feeling.

Thus, my attempt to tell a story of commitment and endurance lies more in the tradition of Protestant testimony, which here more authentically relates to my own specific cultural, religious, and spiritual histories. Testimony is often disorganized, playful, emotional, and intuitive as a method; it can include jokes, meandering comment, profundity, and piercing vignettes as it rolls spontaneously forward. Testimony as a form, or even a method, is quite messy; it takes the listener on a journey up and down and around, and shares an impression, remark, or disclosure. Testimony uses language iteratively and is a speech act grounded in feeling. Its purpose is to connect, to communicate with the heart as well as the head. Unlike academic discourse, in its tightly prescribed, empirical forms of objectivity, testimony can be an unreliable witness, for it poses subjective truth (but truths nonetheless). I am relying on testimony here, in spite of Blease, Carel, and Geraghty's findings that doctors routinely disbelieved and devalued the testimony of those suffering from CFS/ME and questioned their patients' moral character by assuming that they were deliberately malingering.[38] The authors deploy Miranda Fricker's concept of "epistemic injustice" to describe what ME patients' interaction is like with health/care.[39]

Mortality

Nessa Coyle talks about the "existential slap" that people get when they are told they are going to die.[40] In 2010, aged fifty, I was given a diagnosis of pre-senile dementia. These ephemeral little narratives of selfhood are one day all I will have left to record the life I have lived, as I suspect in my future lies an ocean of forgetting. My brother Richard Julian Munt died of complications arising from vascular dementia recently; he had it for ten years, and although his mind degenerated and he would lurch from perfect and acute political analysis to simple confusions and indeed psychotic episodes, he was still undeniably himself. His last words to me, when I stroked his face, were "fuck off." He wanted to be left in peace to die. Or did he? At the same time, he had waited, in his weakened state, to do this all week so that I could drive up from Brighton to Huddersfield and sit with him in his final hours, and moments beforehand his face had lit up when I had entered the room. Almost immediately relieved of the burden of dying alone, he went into a deep snoring sleep, but his eyes remained semi-open, as if checking that I was still there. I had the dementia diagnosis for five years before the neurologist said that he was probably mistaken: I could have memory and concentration loss because of a ministroke. He promptly discharged me because I wasn't making satisfactory progress speedily and effectively toward a full-blown Alzheimer's diagnosis, nor was I improving on my cognitive deficits either. Doctors really do like to see clear trajectories in their speciality, in one direction or another. But to return to our Richard: two weeks before he died, when he was lying in a hospital bed with shit under his fingernails, I was making casual conversation to cheer him up ("cheer him up"! He was dying FFS!!). I asked him what, in his life, was he most proud of. He thought for a minute, and then looking slightly amused and slightly embarrassed, he grinned and said, "You."

There's a Yorkshire saying—"There's nowt for getting old"—and certainly I'm not getting better; my *dasein* is interminably fragile. The vast majority of us will die from an illness, the body committing itself to death even as the mind refuses it, so in the end our body decides to shut herself down, cell by cell, organ by organ. It is our body, not our mind, which has this final say. We live with the potential for death every day, and death, of course, is the final detachment. Nevertheless, we cling to life doggedly and project forward a life energy that consistently embeds futurism in our hearts, living *as if*, on an optimistic promise of a perpetual long term. Ehrenreich calls it "existential courage."[41] The end is difficult to contemplate, yet the rapid growth of the Death Café movement suggests that without religion, we humans do need somewhere to talk about that severing we know is coming. Long-term illness pushes us unwillingly, perhaps inexorably, into a better awareness of impermanence and death, and a keen preoccupation with time. Furthermore, we know that trauma causes a sense of foreshortened future; illness (which can also be traumatic) causes anticipatory consciousness of more illness and a heightened alertness to death's certainty.[42] We are all marching toward death, some more speedily than others. Sometimes this can produce the drilling down of fatalism and a melancholic, clinging attachment to the thing (life) that we believe we have already lost and/or has been stolen prematurely. Temporal awareness can shift in queer ways so that illness on the one hand shortens life expectancy, while on the other induces a strong sense of limbo, of suspension. The pathologist Rudolf Virchow claimed in 1849 that "disease is nothing but life under altered conditions."[43] Illness can reconnect us to our life force through willful endurance. To escape melancholia, those of us with chronic illness can reconcile ourselves to time and learn to love the world "as it is." Chronic illness has bestowed on me a perverse optimism: I ceased to see ME as a malignant intruder, preferring instead to reach out to it as a companion state teaching me lessons of self-kindness. Out of a deep commitment to life's unfathomable and perpetually renewing energy can occasionally emerge a sense of wonder that we are here at all. Until we aren't. Right now, I do feel lucky. As E. M. Forster put it, only connect.

NOTES

I wish to thank Rose Richards of Stellenbosch University, South Africa, for very kindly reading and responding to an earlier draft.

1   Foucault, "The Confession of the Flesh," 194.

2   This critical tradition can be traced to the feminist intersectional work of Audre Lorde, especially *The Cancer Journals*. Important contributions to the literature on queer disability include McRuer, *Crip Theory*; Munson, *Stricken*; Mintz, *Unruly Bodies*; Kafer, *Feminist, Queer, Crip*; and Wood, *Criptiques*. For an analysis of how ethnicity might factor into the vectors of shame and social exclusion associated with disability, see Morris and Munt, "Classed Formations," and Munt, "Gay Shame."

3   Showalter, *Hystories*, 5, 6, 118, 128 (my emphasis), 206 (my emphasis).

4   Blease, Carel, and Geraghty, "Epistemic Injustice in Healthcare Encounters," 550.

5   Graded exercise therapy was adopted by the UK National Health Service (NHS) following the PACE (short for "pacing, graded activity, and cognitive behavior therapy, a randomized evaluation") trial. In 2016 the Cochrane Review of PACE concluded that the evidence for its success was compromised by poor data and that the evidence in support of clinical improvement was weak. Partly to blame has been the history in the UK of appropriating cognitive behavioral therapy (CBT) models in crude ways to substantiate government-driven ideological policy on work effectiveness. Cognitive behavioral therapy can help sufferers manage chronic illness but will not cure it. See "Government-Funded ME/CFS Trial 'One of Greatest Medical Scandals of 21st Century,'" ME Association, February 20, 2018, www.meassociation.org.uk/2018/02/government-funded-me-cfs-trial-one-of -greatest-medical-scandals-of-21st-century-20-february-2018.

6   Myhill, *Diagnosis and Treatment.*

7   See Bruce Goldman, "Researchers Identify Biomarkers Associated with Chronic Fatigue Syndrome Severity," Stanford Medicine News Center, July 31, 2017, http://med.stanford.edu/news/all-news/2017/07/researchers-id-biomarkers-associated-with-chronic-fatigue-syndrome.html.

8   Ward, *Meanings of* ME, 9.

9   After completing this article, something released, and I read Carel's excellent book, *Illness*, which develops the phenomenological approach much more meticulously.

10 Rose Richards, a scholar of chronic illness, commented as an informal reader of this paper: "Embodied experience and especially shame-filled or stigmatised experience/non-normative experience is very hard to articulate. The animality and emotionality are so much part of the experience, but so hard to capture." She recommended further reading in Drew Leder, *The Absent Body.*

11 Resilience was a shiny, aspirational quality that emerged from nineteenth-century Protestantism and then was recently polished up for reuse by neoliberalism, which particularly demands resilience from the poor. It also has a peculiarly British resonance, the "stiff upper lip" being a national pride. Resilience is seen as a public good, both in wartime and times of peace; no matter whatever private suffering might entail, or how our collective politics might be demolished, resilience is required and defeatism disapproved of. Thus, "mustn't complain" is a British mantra, this in spite of the paradox that complaining is a British obsession.

12 See Sontag, *Illness as Metaphor.*

13 For more on this matter see Peale, *The Power of Positive Thinking.*

14 Ehrenreich, *Smile or Die*, 18–19.

15 Ehrenreich, *Smile or Die*, 38.

16 Heim et al., "Early Adverse Experience and Risk for Chronic Fatigue Syndrome."

17 Coyne, Stefanek, and Palmer, "Psychotherapy and Survival," cited in Ehrenreich, *Smile or Die*, 37.

18 See, for example, the Papworth Trust's "Disability in the UK" report (2014). More recently, in 2017 the United Nations heavily criticized cuts to disability provision in the UK as part of its ongoing "austerity" program. See the House of Commons Library briefing paper "The UN Convention on the Rights of Persons with Disabilities: UK Implementation," House of Commons Library, November 18, 2020, http://researchbriefings.parliament.uk/ResearchBriefing/Summary/CBP-7367#fullreport.

19 I Googled /superfood recipe/, and this is the first thing that came up. Really! The second one was roasted garbanzo beans with sea salt and goji berries. You have to laugh.

20 Lorde, "The Transformation of Silence," 41.

21 See Miller, *Bequest and Betrayal.*

22 See Skeggs, *Class, Self, Culture.*

23 Merleau-Ponty, *The Visible and the Invisible.*

24 See Godfrey-Smith, *Other Minds.*

25 See Svenaeus, *The Hermeneutics of Medicine*.

26 Jason et al., "A Community-Based Study of Prolonged and Chronic Fatigue."

27 The National Institute of Clinical Excellence produces clinical guidelines and policies for the NHS. See www.nice.org.uk. In practice, many CBT therapists will willingly engage with a client with a diagnosis of PD, with the intention of working toward managing rather than curing the condition.

28 See Frank, *The Wounded Storyteller*.

29 See Foucault, *Madness and Civilization*.

30 Cited in Frank, *The Wounded Storyteller*, 5.

31 See Foucault, *The Birth of the Clinic*.

32 See Foucault, *Introduction*.

33 Foucault, *Introduction*, 138.

34 Millen, "Chronic-Fatigue Syndrome," 207.

35 Anabaptists believed that baptism should take place only when a person was old enough to make a choice for herself/himself. They were a Protestant sect that was an antecedent of Baptists, Quakers, and Mennonites.

36 See Foxe, *Book of Martyrs*, 275–76.

37 Nouwen, *The Wounded Healer*, 19, 20.

38 See Blease, Carel, and Geraghty, "Epistemic Injustice in Healthcare Encounters."

39 See Fricker, *Epistemic Injustice*.

40 Coyle, *The Existential Slap*.

41 Ehrenreich, *Smile or Die*, 6.

42 Ratcliffe, Ruddell, and Smith, "What Is a 'Sense of Foreshortened Future?,'" 9.

43 Virchow, *Die Einheitsbestrebungen in der wissenschlaftlichen Medezin*, 70.

BIBLIOGRAPHY

Blease, Charlotte, Havi Carel, and Keith Geraghty. "Epistemic Injustice in Healthcare Encounters: Evidence from Chronic Fatigue Syndrome." *Journal of Medical Ethics* 43 (2017): 549–57.

Carel, Havi. *Illness: The Cry of the Flesh*. Abingdon: Routledge, 2014.

Coyle, Nessa. "The Existential Slap—The Crisis of Disclosure." *International Journal of Palliative Nursing* 10, no. 11 (2013). https://doi.org/10.12968/ijpn.2004.10.11.17130.

Coyne, James C., Michael Stefanek, and Steven C. Palmer. "Psychotherapy and Survival in Cancer: The Conflict between Hope and Evidence." *Psychological Bulletin* 133, no. 3 (2007): 367–94.

Ehrenreich, Barbara. *Smile or Die: How Positive Thinking Fooled America and the World*. London: Granta, 2009.

Foucault, Michel. *The Birth of the Clinic: An Archeology of Medical Perception*. New York: Pantheon, 1973.

Foucault, Michel. "The Confession of the Flesh." In *Power/Knowledge: Selected Interviews and Other Writings 1972–1977*, translated and edited by Colin Gordon, 194–228. New York: Pantheon, 1980.

Foucault, Michel. *An Introduction*. Vol. 1 of *The History of Sexuality*. Translated by Robert Hurley. New York: Vintage, 1990.

Foucault, Michel. *Madness and Civilization: A History of Insanity in the Age of Reason.* Translated by Richard Howard. London: Vintage, 1988.

Foxe, John. *Book of Martyrs: Or, a History of the Lives, Sufferings and Triumphant Deaths of the Primitive.* Edited by Amos Blanchard. Originally published by N. G. Ellis, 1844. Reprinted in facsimile by Forgotten Books, 2015. Available online at Google Books.

Frank, Arthur. *The Wounded Storyteller: Body, Illness, and Ethics.* Chicago: University of Chicago Press, 1995.

Fricker, Miranda. *Epistemic Injustice: Power and the Ethics of Knowing.* Oxford: Oxford University Press, 2007.

Godfrey-Smith, Peter. *Other Minds: The Octopus and the Evolution of Intelligent Life.* London: William Collins, 2017.

Heim, Christine, Dieter Wagner, Elizabeth Maloney, et al. "Early Adverse Experience and Risk for Chronic Fatigue Syndrome." *Architecture of General Psychiatry* 63, no. 11 (2006): 1258–66.

Jason L. A., K. M. Jordan, J. A. Richman, et al. "A Community-Based Study of Prolonged and Chronic Fatigue." *Journal of Health Psychology* 4 (1999): 9–26.

Kafer, Alison. *Feminist, Queer, Crip.* Bloomington: Indiana University Press, 2013.

Leder, Drew. *The Absent Body.* Chicago: University of Chicago Press, 1990.

Lorde, Audre. *The Cancer Journals.* San Francisco: Aunt Lute Books, 1980.

Lorde, Audre. "The Transformation of Silence into Language and Action." In *Sister Outsider: Essays and Speeches*, 40–44. Berkeley: Crossing, 1984.

McRuer, Robert. *Crip Theory: Cultural Signs of Queerness and Disability.* New York: New York University Press, 2006.

Merleau-Ponty, Maurice. *The Visible and the Invisible.* Translated by Alphonso Lingis. Evanston: Northwestern University Press, 1968.

Millen, Neville. "Chronic-Fatigue Syndrome: A Sociological Perspective." In *Chronic Illness: New Perspectives and New Directions*, edited by Carmel Martin, Chris L. A. Peterson, Christine Walker, and Neville Millen, 206–20. Melbourne: Tertiary, 2003.

Miller, Nancy K. *Bequest and Betrayal: Memoirs of a Parent's Death.* Bloomington: Indiana University Press, 2000.

Mintz, Susannah B. *Unruly Bodies: Life Writing by Women with Disabilities.* Chapel Hill: University of North Carolina Press, 2007.

Morris, Charlotte, and Sally R. Munt. "Classed Formations of Shame in White, British Single Mothers." In "A Politics of Shame," edited by Tamara Shefer, Ronelle Carolissen, Viv Bozalek, and Sally R. Munt, special issue, *Feminism & Psychology* 29, no. 2 (2019): 231–49.

Munson, Peggy, ed. *Stricken: Voices from the Hidden Epidemic of Chronic Fatigue Syndrome.* New York: Haworth, 2000.

Munt, Sally R. "Gay Shame in a Geopolitical Context." *Cultural Studies* 33, no. 2 (2019): 223–48.

Myhill, Sarah. *Diagnosis and Treatment of Chronic Fatigue Syndrome and Myalgic Encephalitis: It's Mitochondria Not Hypochondria*, 2nd ed. White River Junction, VT: Chelsea Green, 2018.

Nouwen, Henri. *Clowning in Rome.* Garden City, NY: Image Books, 1979.

Nouwen, Henri. *The Way of the Heart*. London: Darton, Longman and Todd, 1981.

Nouwen, Henri. *The Wounded Healer*. London: Darton, Longman and Todd, 1972.

Peale, Norman Vincent. *The Power of Positive Thinking*. New York: Prentice-Hall, 1952.

Ratcliffe, Matthew, Mark Ruddell, and Benedict Smith. "What Is a 'Sense of Foreshortened Future?' A Phenomenological Study of Trauma, Trust, and Time." *Frontiers in Psychology* 5 (2014): 1–11.

Showalter, Elaine. *Hystories: Hysterical Epidemics and Modern Culture*. New York: Columbia University Press, 1997.

Skeggs, Beverley. *Class, Self, Culture*. London: Routledge, 2004.

Sontag, Susan. *Illness as Metaphor*. New York: Farrar, Straus and Giroux, 1978.

Svenaeus, Fredrik. *The Hermeneutics of Medicine and the Phenomenology of Health: Steps Towards a Philosophy of Medical Practice*. Dordrecht: Kluwer Academic, 2010.

Virchow, Rudolf. *Die Einheitsbestrebungen in der wissenschlaftlichen Medezin*. 1849. Translated by Knud Faber. *Nosography in Modern Internal Medicine*. New York: Paul B. Hoeber, 1923.

Ward, Christopher D., ed. *Meanings of ME: Interpersonal and Social Dimensions of Chronic Fatigue*. Basingstoke: Palgrave Macmillan, 2015.

Wood, Caitlin, ed. *Criptiques*. San Bernardino, CA: May Day, 2014.

4

A LIFETIME OF DRUGS

KANE RACE

FOR MY PARENTS

In the grounds of Sydney Hospital, behind the twisting boughs of a gingko tree, lie the offices of the Sydney Sexual Health Centre, where I first learned I had been infected with HIV.[1] It was 1996, the same year that the possibility of using combination therapy to "eradicate the virus" had been announced to the world with much fanfare and hype. It was no longer a death sentence but "a chronic manageable illness" predicated on lifelong treatment with heavy-duty pharmaceutical combinations. Taking charge of the virus—"hitting hard, hitting early"—was the order of the day. Useful as this tough-guy slogan was for shrugging off the psychosocial overtures of the counselor given the unenviable task of delivering me postdiagnosis support, I wasn't quite sure where it left me, also hit hard, hit early. What did it mean? How should I feel? How long do I have? *What just happened?*

I was twenty-five, in my final year of law school, trained to believe I had my *whole life ahead of me.* But with HIV infection so recently and dramatically converted to the enigmatic status of a nonevent, I found myself at a loss for words, unsure what to think. I can't remember feeling anything. Whatever recourse I might have once had to the melodramatic script of fatal diagnosis seemed to have been pulled from under my feet. The only script available for handling this situation positioned me as a biological citizen dependent on powerful combinations of antiretroviral medications: the new "drug cocktails," as they were called at the time. No longer facing a death sentence, I found myself confronted with a life-threatening illness that was said to demand an indefinite commitment to ongoing self-dosing with grueling antiretroviral drugs on a daily basis. The temporality of this long-term drug regime was particularly evasive, however, in the sense encapsulated by Ross Chambers when he describes antiretroviral drugs as "medications whose toxicity is able, for a time, to hold the virus at bay" (a deceptively simple formulation).[2] Withholding any approximation of how much time one had left, this was less a prognosis than a special sort of paradox that replaced the presumptive decade once invoked around HIV's progression with a great big question mark. On leaving the clinic, I made my way down the central avenue that cuts through Hyde Park toward the golden mile of Oxford Street in a state of mind so impassive it must have been a daze. The tree-lined avenue that arched before me was generous enough to extend some semblance of structure, shape, and purpose to a situation I couldn't begin to make sense of, let alone begin to know how to respond to, suspended as I was between optimism and desperation. This I what I remember most about that day: this positively meaningless *walk in the park.*

The Protease Moment

The Vancouver International AIDS Conference of 1996 is widely considered a hallmark event in the history of the HIV epidemic. Within a week of the conference, more than seventy-five thousand patients commenced combination antiviral therapy, hoping to reduce the rate of viral replication in their bloodstreams to undetectable levels.[3] The fact that 90 percent of the world's population of people living with HIV/AIDS (PLWHA) had no hope of accessing the expensive new drugs tempered universal enthusiasm for the new biomedical breakthroughs to some degree, redirecting activist energies toward grappling with the geopolitics of treatment access. But in wealthier countries, treatment advocates exhorted HIV-positive people to get with the pharmaceutical program by trying highly aggressive antiretroviral therapy (HAART).

It is difficult to convey the affective intensities—the mix of dogmatism and vacillation—that pervaded gay community discourses around new treatments at this time as medical knowledge morphed into community imperatives. In 1997 a man who had written to a PLWHA community newsletter expressing reservations about early initiation of HAART was met with a harsh rebuke from another reader:

> [The correspondent] is under a very serious misapprehension. He says that he has been HIV positive for four years and has "never been sick" [*sic*]. I guess he means he has never felt sick. The truth is that the virus is replicating voraciously and, as a direct consequence, is placing an enormous burden on his body's immune system. [He] is deluding himself if he thinks that being HIV positive is not cause to act immediately to attempt to suppress viral replication.[4]

Prominent HIV treatment advocates in Australia rallied around this purported "truth," describing plans to delay treatment as "crazy," "stupid," and even a "let-down to the community."[5] But considering the lack of clinical data on the long-term efficacy of these new pharmaceutical compounds at the time—not to mention their long-term safety—some clinicians were not so adamant about the imperatives of early intervention. Viral suppression had been demonstrated to be a remarkably accurate predictor of disease progression, but drugs can have unintended mechanisms of action and work through causal pathways that are independent of the disease process.[6] Thus, despite the intransigence of community advocates, it was precisely the length of this long-term commitment that eluded precise calculation or clinical certainty.

The possibility of suppressing the virus was received by some as an opportunity to return to a "normal" life with a new sense of energy, vitality, and agency.[7] In Western countries, sociologists began describing "the normalization of HIV."[8] Given the intense racial disparities that characterize health-care access in countries such as the United States, this normalization was predicated on structural factors that HIV service organizations were ill equipped to address. Even in countries with socialized health systems, viral management emerged for some as an onerous task, with medication manifesting as a sign of illness and a "constant reminder" of HIV status.[9]

The prospect of ongoing treatment posed difficulties for those already dealing with grief and loss who now found themselves having to consider the prospect of returning to work and reshaping relationships in the context of unexpected and uncertain futures.[10] A new sense of isolation began to characterize some people's experience of living with HIV, especially those who found themselves grappling with a range of noxious treatment side effects in their efforts to remain "undetectable." These ranged from serious complications such as liver damage, fat redistribution, diabetes, high cholesterol, and heart disease to mundane irritations such as nausea, fatigue, and persistent diarrhea: a cluster of symptoms succinctly characterized by one community educator as "low-level chronic ickiness."[11]

The conflicted nature of this situation produced tensions between different measures of health and well-being, as one of my research participants explained: "My feeling of well-being is shit-house. Um, really bad. Um, actual health—like going to the doctors—is fabulous. There's a nice contradiction for you. I feel awful, but my actual health is very, very good."[12] Here the word *health* refers to the results of his viral load test, which he uses to account for his persistence with treatment despite a range of distressing side effects. If antibody testing and CD4 counts created the historical possibility of being diagnosed as sick with HIV while feeling perfectly well, viral load testing created the possibility of being diagnosed as acceptably healthy while feeling or appearing otherwise.[13] Some treatment advocates tried to rationalize this situation by drawing analogies with gay men's enthusiasm for other kinds of drugs. In a community newspaper, HIV treatment advocate Martyn Goddard conceded that "these drugs have side-effects. People take ecstasy because they like the side-effects. HIV drugs are not like that. These are all serious, toxic chemicals. They're not as toxic as the virus though."[14] Perplexingly, Goddard's remarks classify the effects that consumers seek in ecstasy as "side effects." The passage appears to fumble on a major fault line that emerged for many people living with HIV at this time. The classification of drugs and drug effects as "therapeutic" and/or "toxic" appeared a somewhat arbitrary but indisputably ontopolitical determination with material consequences for patients, consumers, and practices of self-administration in general.

Whatever improvements in health and well-being became possible for those with the geopolitical, socioeconomic, and structural good fortune to have access to the powerful new pharmaceuticals, these new drug cocktails were also taken to spell a major problem for HIV prevention. Prevention specialists went into damage control: contrary to what the imagery of pharmaceutical advertisements might have consumers believe, living with a "chronic manageable illness" was "no picnic" and "hardly a walk in the park," they declared.[15] Countering glossy depictions of fresh-faced, smiling PLWHA engaged in healthy, active, sporting pursuits—"taking charge" of their disease—critics objected: "We don't think it's a sexy disease. It's not about climbing mountains. It's about IV poles, wheelchairs and pain."[16] In their bid to tackle increases in sexual risk taking among men who have sex with men, San Francisco's Stop AIDS Project even plastered confronting images of people suffering from some of the more gruesome side effects of protease inhibitors on bus shelters and restroom walls throughout the city as part of their "HIV Is No Picnic" campaign. The posters depicted PLWHA suffering night sweats, sporting distended abdomens and pronounced facial wasting, and sitting on the toilet with diarrhea.[17] The campaign illustrates how representations of the intimate experience of HIV infection were becoming hostage at this moment to the collective imperatives of public health and disease prevention.

As overblown and instrumental as these images appeared to anyone lucky enough to have been spared such complications, there was no doubt that the new treatments turned living with HIV into a different kind of problem. "Going the Distance"—an advertisement for Merck's new protease inhibitor—instructed consumers, "Focus on the rest of your life. Learn all you can about HIV therapy. Talk with your doctor. Stay informed and stay with the course. With viral load below the limit of detection and an increase in CD4 T-cells, it's easier to look forward to the future with confidence."[18] This passage describes treatment as a kind of marathon or high-endurance sport that requires commitment, focus, and the motivation to achieve one's personal best. But as Michael Flynn spelled out, the daily grind of treatment was not quite so blithe or glamorous: "We have all had to rearrange our daily living schedules to fit the drugs in at the right time and dosage. Our whole life is now regimented by our intake of drugs. Going out to dinner, meeting friends for a drink, staying away from home or partying all night long have now to be carefully planned like a military operation."[19] The disease may have transformed from an inevitable death sentence into a chronic manageable illness, but it was generally agreed that HIV infection was still a serious issue involving the dismal prospect of a *lifetime of drugs*.[20]

Personally, I was quite eager to sign on to the treatment bandwagon. However regimented these medical prescriptions, the idea of "taking charge" was irresistible. "The basis of optimism is sheer terror," Oscar Wilde once quipped, and this might as well serve as a description of what was going on for me.[21] My sense of the future was unstable enough to render nonsensical the idea of plugging away as a trainee solicitor in a law firm for five years (quite possibly the rest of my working life), so I applied for a job at the national HIV social research center. I was employed to research understandings and experiences of the new treatments among people living with HIV in the interests of "improving patient compliance." At the time I joined the center, most of its research team was working on questions of HIV prevention, busily devising statistical measures to scrutinize the pernicious effects of "treatment optimism," releasing their findings under titles as foreboding as "HIV Treatments Optimism Is Associated with Unprotected Anal Intercourse with Regular and Causal Partners among Australian Gay and Homosexually Active Men."[22] The dubious status of treatment optimism in my new workplace was not enough to derail my own optimistic attachment to the daily rigors of treatment, however. When interview participants tried to explain to me how they found the pills to be a "constant reminder" of HIV, all I could do was blink and stare, reassuring myself that I was "taking charge" and things would be OK and secretly wishing they would just get over it.

In order to be effective and prevent drug resistance, the new treatments were said to demand a very high level of "patient compliance." The question of "treatment readiness" was often framed in superconscientious terms: people were not ready to start treatment, so the maxim went, until they had "thought and talked it through and [were] ready to make the commitment to stick with it religiously."[23] Because the discourse on treatment adherence prominently foregrounded what Jack Halberstam has called the "normative scheduling of daily life," it might be understood to be "upheld by a middle-class logic of reproductive temporality."[24] But these pharmaceutical regimes lacked any of the self-surety associated with reproductive futurity, and there was nothing "natural" about some of the bodies they were producing. With their uneasy temporality, the new treatments seemed to demand a long-term commitment to "living in the moment," with each of these moments suspended on an arc of indefinite deferral. Sociologists working on the "normalization of AIDS" in Western countries conveyed some of the paradoxes of this predicament:

> The gain in time and the greater latitude to shape one's life face the challenge of also having to fill the same, i.e. having to normalize one's life, so to speak.... If [before 1996] maximum priority was attached to a search for ways to continue living, problems of living with and despite HIV and AIDS now have a far higher standing: a diagnosis of

HIV no longer appears to be tantamount to an early end of life. . . . Not all PWA are in a position to cope with this situation in adequate fashion and deal with the medicalization of their life: many have problems adhering to therapy and cannot handle the challenges of coping with the medicalization and normalization of their life, challenges that are, by nature, contradictory.[25]

If this "protease moment" presented the possibility of normalizing one's life, living "with and despite" a virulent pathogen nonetheless altered the experience of normality and normative temporality.[26] To achieve some chance of longevity, those affected had to incorporate into their everyday lives drug cocktails whose experimental, toxic, and indefinite outcomes prompted persistent personal and cultural anxieties. Moreover, sex did not seem to offer much critical resistance to this process of "normalization," notwithstanding the claims and investments of some queer critics.[27] Indeed, more typically sex emerged as an outcome or element in the effective restoration of normal life. As one review article on the topic discusses, HIV patients commonly report a loss of libido in the first stages of going into antiretroviral therapy, but "at thirty months on ART, many participants considered themselves as 'normal' and said that as 'normal people' one of their healthy functions was to have sexual desires. They also reported that drugs had increased their desire for sex, contrary to what many had mentioned at three and six months about the drugs having diminished their sexual desire."[28] Yet for every scientific article that problematizes sexual dysfunction among antiretroviral users in the name of health and medical normativity (and there are many), several more fret about the increased sexual behavior and erotogenic activity the new treatments were said to engender among this population.[29] These conflicting citations of normative health within different strands of sociomedical research might be taken to exemplify what Robyn Wiegman and Elizabeth Wilson describe as the "dispersed, consociating nature of normativity": its "dependencies, differentiations, clashes."[30]

Drug Cocktails

One of the most widely circulated accounts of the changing landscape of the epidemic at this time was a piece called "When Plagues End," written by prominent US homo-conservative Andrew Sullivan and appearing in the *New York Times* in 1996.[31] Combining descriptions of community events with personal anecdotes and reflection, Sullivan explores the promise of protease inhibitors for gay men of his class and generation, acknowledging the complications of treatment failure, the experience of toxic side effects, and the challenges associated with resuming a "normal life" alongside anxieties about a return to "unsafe sexual behaviour" caused by the "abatement of pressure" associated with the new treatments.[32] Less acknowledged is the sense in which Sullivan universalizes his own privileged experience (as a white man living in the United States with ready access to health insurance) as *the* experience of HIV/AIDS. As Phillip Brian Harper writes,

> If Sullivan can suggest that "most people in the middle of this plague" experience the development of protease inhibitors as a profound occurrence (indeed as the "end" of AIDS) while he simultaneously admits that "the vast majority of HIV-positive people in the world"—manifest in the United States principally as blacks and Latinos—will not have access to the new drugs and, indeed, will likely die, what can this mean but that, in Sullivan's conception, "most people in the middle of this plague" are not non-white or non-U.S. residents?[33]

For Sullivan, access to treatment is a given—the basis on which his narrative about the end of AIDS is staged. This ignores how the very prospect of accessing HIV-related services and care—from getting tested to the practice of regularly seeing doctors and taking medications—is premised on forms of racial privilege that mitigate not only poverty but also the material consequences of homophobia and HIV-related stigma, especially as experienced by dispossessed populations such as Black and Latino gay and bisexual men in the United States.[34]

Sullivan's fetishization of protease inhibitors as an unmediated factor in the end of AIDS soon gives way to another set of ruminations about another kind of "drug cocktail" doing the rounds among his peers and contemporaries (and perhaps just as fetishized). It is striking that a substantial portion of an essay devoted to gay men's cultural responses to the new HIV treatments concerns the seemingly unrelated topic of "the increasing numbers of circuit parties" catering to gay men of the time, all of which involve "the ecstatic drug-enhanced high of dance music." As Sullivan reports, "These events are made possible by a variety of chemicals: steroids, which began as therapy for men wasting from AIDS and recently spawned yet another growing sub-subculture of huge body builders; and psychotherapeutic designer drugs, primarily Ecstasy, which creates feelings of euphoria and emotional bonding, and ketamine, an animal anesthetic that disconnects the conscious thought process from the sensory body."[35] Although "on the surface the parties could be taken for a mass of men in superb shape merely enjoying an opportunity to let off steam," Sullivan advised that "underneath, masked by the drugs, there is an air of strain." He concludes that "these are not mass celebrations at the dawn of a new era, but raves built upon the need for amnesia."

"When Plagues End" went on to supply a narrative template for innumerable accounts of gay men's social and cultural responses to HIV medical developments in various different locations and contexts from the time it was published right up until the present. In this genre of HIV storytelling, concerns about the disinhibiting effects of treatment optimism invariably give way to breathless discussions about gay men's use of recreational drugs in a narrative formula that seems carefully designed to reprimand gay subjects for their reckless sexuality, complacency, and unbridled hedonism. A 1997 article titled "The Lethal Liberator" kicks things off in the *Guardian* by linking "the cocktail of protease inhibitors and other powerful pharmaceutical drugs" with "misplaced complacency" about safe sex.[36] However, the story's main focus is what it terms "the looming public health crisis" of methamphetamine abuse among gay men, a substance whose "disinhibitory effects" are said to make "users temporarily forget about safe sex."

A 1999 article in the *New York Times* is just one of many to repeat this formula: "With new drug therapies showing remarkable success in controlling HIV, some gay men have grown disturbingly complacent about safe sex in recent years."[37] Again, the main fixation of the story is what it frames as "another alarming trend," namely "the use of inhibition-relaxing drugs." The report goes on to cite anecdotal evidence from community groups that "much of the increase [in HIV infections] had been among young gay men and that many had become careless about sex while high on libido-enhancing drugs." Similarly in Australia in 2000, gay journalist Steve Dow attributed a small increase in HIV infections to gay men "partying on as though illicit drugs will make them forget the world outside, while prescription drugs will save them from the threat of the virus." Under the menacing title "Dancing with Death," Dow writes:

> Many will not be surprised. Recent surveys in Sydney and Melbourne have shown a greater incidence of sex without condoms. Health promoters believe it is not just casual unsafe sex, but problems with people getting into relationships and having unsafe sex before both partners are tested. . . . More to the point, however, a nexus has been found between drug use—ecstasy and speed, inextricably linked to the dance party circuit. Young gay men are taking risks because, like other

young men, they believe they are indestructible. In this case, however, gay men have had their minds altered by illicit drugs, and they assume the new protease inhibitor drug combinations will save them.[38]

Accounts such as these are typical of the time in their finger-wagging eagerness to attribute increases in sexual risk taking to the "misplaced optimism" they associate with various forms of prescribed and nonprescribed drug consumption. Where credible alternative explanations for new infections do make an appearance, they are typically subordinated to the narrative requirements of this cautionary tale about gay overstep and pharmacological overenthusiasm. "More to the point," Dow writes, "a nexus has been found between ecstasy and speed." As if this explained what, exactly? It is as if the only conceivable reason people might want to have sex without condoms at this time must involve some sort of drug impairment or pharmaceutical slippage.[39] Hit hard, hit early.

The most imaginative and capacious example of this genre I am aware of is an article titled "Higher and Higher: Drug Cocktails—Pleasures, Risks and Reasons" that appeared in 1999 in the *Village Voice*.[40] The piece introduces us to Dormil, an HIV-positive gay man who "takes four different AIDS medications, including AZT. For recreation, he goes to dance clubs where he gets high on a nocturnal medley of Ecstasy, Special K, and crystal methamphetamine." "It's therapeutic. It's a stress-reliever," Dormil is quoted as claiming. "It allows me to accept the fact of my disease and get on with my life." Dormil's main narrative function is to serve as a gateway informant, an individual case study devised to give a human face to a sensationalized scene of illicit activity and collective experimentation. The following passage cuts to the chase: "This weekend, and every weekend on dance floors across the city, thousands of teeth-grinding subjects like Dormil engage in an underground research project. Amid flashing lights and pounding music, untutored freelance pharmacologists conduct experiments on their own bodies to determine what happens when one consumes a bewildering array of pills and powders in the confined and humid setting of a nightclub. The results are not always pretty."[41] The article proceeds by reeling off a cautionary list of dangers and casualties associated with the polypharmaceutical mentality it takes as its main concern. As if testing the gullibility of readers, the article goes on to quote a "veteran drug dealer" who exclaims, "It's crazy! . . . The entire New York club scene revolves around drug cocktails."

To its credit, the story goes further than the standard moralistic fare, attributing the lack of reliable knowledge about the effects of various drug combinations to the dearth of clinical research on the interactions between pre-scribed medications and club drugs, which it names as an outcome of the "war on drugs." Polydrug use need not be synonymous with immoderation, the article concedes, for "some club patrons go to great lengths to figure out what each drug does individually and in combination." But the challenge of working out what to mix with what and when—replete with innumerable tricky questions about drugs' synergies, interactions, timing, and dosage—clearly demands careful planning in an exercise that is uncannily reminis-cent of the military operation that Flynn conceives in order to convey the regimented nature of antiretroviral treatment compliance.[42]

With its anxious but nonetheless productive focus on the complexities of drug effects, "Higher and Higher" repeatedly returns to the fuzzy distinction between therapeutic and recreational logics of drug consumption. Where some of the informants interviewed for the article attribute these "under-ground research experiments" to consumers' desires to escape from reality, others describe certain illicit combinations as capable of delivering other benefits when safely self-administered: "Disco polypharmacy involves risk. Nobody knows how safe some of these mixtures really are. Some say that not necessarily all combinations are bad for you—for instance, partygoers claim that swallowing Ecstasy followed by LSD (known as "candy flipping") can be extremely therapeutic."[43] Rather than concluding with another hapless indictment of gay men's complacency or reckless behavior, the article wraps up with a practical set of guidelines on "Doing Polydrugs Safely" complete with an informative "Polydrug Glossary."

In "Higher and Higher," Dormil's use of illicit substances is tentatively depicted as enabling him to normalize his life by accepting the fact of HIV disease. That is to say, chemical experimentation emerges as an activity that makes possible a long-term commitment to living "with and despite HIV."[44] Although Dormil's everyday life already teems with a veritable pharmaceuti-cal cornucopia on account of his HIV status, the various illicit drug cocktails he is said to depend upon appear to contribute to his ability to get on with a relatively normal life. This is a markedly different conception of what counts as normal (and its relation to illicit activity) than the reproachful narratives of pharmaceutically induced optimism that make up the mainstay of this ar-chive. Indeed, perhaps it is the normalization of experimental drug cocktails within the field of HIV treatment that precipitates a degree of systemic and discursive play around the variable taxonomies of pharmaco-activity and their contingent relations, historicity, and speculative possibilities. Drug use is encountered on the whole as a sphere of experimentation *and* normalization shot through with "differentiations, comparisons, valuations, attenuations, skirmishes."[45]

Against Pharmaceutical Amnesia

Another prominent voice in popular discourses of gay men's relation to HIV in North America at this time was that of HIV activist and community organizer Tony Valenzuela, one of the first gay porn stars to come out as HIV positive. With his naked arms wrapped around the dark mane of a horse that had clearly been chosen to accentuate his Mexican Italian features, Valenzuela first came to the attention of a wider public when he appeared on the cover of *POZ* magazine beneath the alluring headline "Tony Valenzuela and the boys who BAREBACK take you on a ride inside."[46] Extending and expanding upon his celebrity persona, Valenzuela's creative fiction provides insights into gay sex, HIV, and recreational drug use that are more self-reflexive than the standard fare encountered in gay journalism and health advocacy discourse. His 2004 short story, "The Day We Didn't Quite Manage to Smuggle Some K," tells the story of group of gay friends who travel to Tijuana to stock up on drugs for the White Party in Palm Springs, one of the circuit parties that Andrew Sullivan first brought to general public attention.[47] The narrator of the story describes the experience of living with HIV through the protease moment in terms that corroborate its queer temporality: "Being forced to think, over a prolonged period, that I might die sooner rather than later, was like dying over and over again, taking stock of my achievements, saying my goodbyes in a sentimentally overwrought imagination, until the notion sat with me, worn and familiar. Now, not dying was the resurrection, the survival day by day."[48] These remarks are followed immediately by a sequence of dialogue that conveys the appeal of the drug among a group of guys who have gone so far as traveling all the way to Mexico to scour veterinarian outlets in order to source it:

"I heard that ketamine produces 'near-death' hallucinations. No wonder I love it so much."

"I knew that already," Alex says . . .

"It's so obvious," I say, shaking my finger at a man holding a tree of glass wedding-cake crowns. "The drug that's made me intimate with death has helped me to reconcile it."[49]

Earlier in the story the narrator discusses the "solace" that he and his HIV-positive friends seek in recreational drugs. But where Sullivan's exposé attributed gay men's use of this "animal anesthetic that disconnects the conscious thought process from the sensory body" to a collective "need for amnesia," and where others point to a "desire for escape," Valenzuela's story rebukes such characterizations with deft precision:

> To call drugs an escape from HIV was, for us, the opposite of the truth. Getting high became a meditation and dialog on figuring things out. Shirtless and sweaty, in the midst of our other party-boy friends, we dropped E and snorted ketamine from tiny bumpers and screamed into each other's ears over the blast of disco: "Our generation has a different relationship to HIV!"; "AIDS prevention lies about the meaning of real sex!"; "Circuit parties are about survival as much as celebration!" The dance floor, the drug trips, and our friendship became a dark, lush terrain for this merciless self-awareness.[50]

I remember the burst of recognition I felt when I first read this passage and how well it captured aspects of my own experience of gay dance parties in the late 1990s. As with Dormil, who says his recreational drug use allows him "to accept the fact of my disease and get on with my life," in Valenzuela's account recreational drugs emerge as psychoactive elements in a process of collective self-experimentation that produces subjects who become capable of confronting and producing truths about living with HIV that might otherwise remain unbearable. Rather than blocking out the possibility of imminent death or operating as a mere anesthetic, these substances appear to emulate and magnify that apprehension precisely to discharge its terror.

In "Dosed," a short story published two years later, Valenzuela depicts a scene of home-based sex partying to explore how the drugs crystal meth and GHB may be used to remediate and recreate temporality, this time in the different setting of gay sexual encounters between men.[51] Dubbed PNP in North America and chemsex in the UK and Europe, the practice of using the internet to arrange drug-enhanced sex has been subject to recurring waves of moral panic in Western countries for more than two decades now.[52] In this scene of sexual activities, even the anticipation of certain cocktails of psychoactive drugs can interrupt what some queer critics term the logic of reproductive temporality.[53] As soon as the narrator of the story clinches a desirable hookup online, all he can think of is getting high on crystal meth: "I want to get twisted, gnarly high on Tina where I don't care about tomorrow and yesterday and time is reduced to an acute yen for body parts."[54] Here the appeal of crystal consists in how it allows the narrator to escape the pressures of the normative scheduling of everyday life.

As the narrative proceeds, however, things start to get more complicated. The storyteller describes the experience of sexual desire on crystal meth in the following terms: "On crystal, all that remains of me is my body with its moist orifices, ravenous as summer tornadoes. I am, otherwise, held in glorious suspension from the nuisance of the day's worries. I am erased of complicated history, like high school textbooks in the South. There is only lust here now, an empire of prurience whose frontier plots against the horizon: orgasm is defeat, is desire's drowning."[55] Insofar as this passage conveys a sense of escape from inconvenient histories that cast shadows on the present, it might be taken to reflect the "need for amnesia" that Sullivan discusses in "When Plagues End." But it also does something more or other than that: in particular, it evokes an experience of dilated temporality that resonates with the structure of feeling I earlier associated with the prospect of long-term HIV therapy beyond the protease moment. Crystal is invested in this scene with the specific value of enabling users to eroticize a suspended state of indefinite deferral. In other words, it enables the sexual subject to be "in the moment," where each moment gains its specific erotic charge by suspending users indefinitely on some intensified point in the normative arc of impending teleological resolution or climax. Here, the "long term" is effectively relocated from the scene of normative temporality to what Valenzuela characterizes as the "acute yen" of the moment. Rather than *escaping* the realities of HIV, being high on crystal seems to replicate and magnify a prehension that constitutes a temporal reality of HIV for those subject to this feeling, recreating it as a source of excitement, ongoing desirability, and desiring-continuity.

The vast and growing empirical literature on gay and HIV-positive experiences of crystal methamphetamine suggests that Valenzuela's account of the effects of this drug is far from idiosyncratic or isolated. "How to say this?" one participant asks in a 2006 qualitative study. "What I find on crystal, I kind of enter into a special space. A particularly sexual, sensual space" in which "every touch is enhanced."[56] Notably, this experience of a sensuously dilated temporality—of getting lost in the moment—is not confined to sexual activity for all users. In a 1997 study a self-identified transgender participant claims that "99 percent of drag queens who inject crystal use it to 'sketch on their face. They do their make-up, they tweak on their face': like I could get stuck in my bag, you know, stuck, for hours, in my bag—in my make-up bag. Just sitting, putting my make-up on. For hours. And keep putting it on. And leaving it on. Taking it off. Putting it back on." This is not the only thing crystal is good for, according to this informant. She describes how the drug makes a range of other activities she periodically engages in more possible, from walking to "cleaning the house until it's spotless."[57]

Some of the most careful studies of gay men's methamphetamine consumption reveal specific affordances of the drug among gay guys living with HIV. As one participant in a 2002 study puts it, "When I found out I was HIV+, I didn't know what was going to happen. I didn't know what to expect with HIV. I didn't know where I was going. But after I started using [crystal]—I started making some positive choices in my life. And actually I think I did some pretty good things. It helped me. I don't know how I would have ever got started again."[58] The drug's capacity to enhance energy, mood, focus, confidence, motivation, and sexuality becomes all the more significant in the context of a condition whose most commonly reported symptoms include fatigue, depression, anxiety, inability to concentrate, loss of libido, and lack of energy, focus, and motivation. The finding that HIV-positive people constitute the majority of gay male users of the drug starts to make sense, even from a therapeutic perspective.[59] This is unsurprising if one considers the use of this substance historically: clinicians and pharmacists prescribed methamphetamine as a treatment for depression for a good part of the twentieth century (1920–60).[60]

My purpose here is not simply to reduce the activity or meanings of this substance to the normatively acceptable frame of "self-medication" on the basis of its pharmacological properties. The protease moment invites us to go further and query the porous, arbitrary, and contingent nature of drug taxonomies more generally: the identification, coding, ranking, delegation, and prioritization of certain drug effects over those others deemed "side effects" or else "pleasure" (in which case their legitimacy comes into question, both normatively and, I think, perversely).[61] But I have also been trying to explore the queer resonances that appear to consociate between the practical logics of antiretroviral therapy and those that inform the use of certain illicit substances among a population that has been disproportionately affected by HIV since the beginning of the epidemic. Exhorted to persevere with the historically alarming side-effect profiles of early combination antiretroviral therapy—their toxicities, both known and unknown—in the name of a greater good, this subpopulation has had to grapple with the complex multiplicities of living with toxicity over the long term in both personal and collective efforts to normalize their day-to-day existence and realize their hopes of longevity. Through our collective experiments and "underground research projects" we have learned that some combinations of psychoactive drugs have the capacity to reproduce and constructively reenact some of the contingencies of living with the virus.

One source of appeal of some of the most popular recreational drug cocktails (such as ecstasy, ketamine, and crystal meth) in this analysis is their imputed capacity to magnify and discharge the distinctive temporalities of living with the protean experience of the virus and its treatment. Rather than escaping reality, recreational experiments with drug cocktails have helped some of us confront the difficult realities of a temporality whose prolongation is at once normatively desirable and precarious. Indeed, in a curious way drugs such as crystal meth (the use of which has been roundly condemned within gay-community HIV-prevention discourse) would appear to make good on the promise of restoring a sense of vitality, agency, confidence, and erotic possibility first associated with combination antiretroviral therapies when they initially became available in the West. The purported capacity of crystal meth to suspend temporality renders its use generically intelligible as a psychoactive substitute for "medications whose toxicity is able, for a time, to hold the virus at bay" (*pace* Chambers). But in an odd twist of fate, where pharmaceutical advertisements for protease inhibitors once depicted the dosing requirements of the new drug cocktails as a high-endurance sport that demanded of their consumers a commitment, focus, and stamina to "stay with the course" if they wanted to "look forward to the future with confidence," today the figure of the pharmaco-athletic gay man has become a source of moral panic as hundreds upon hundreds of scientific articles and media reports fret about the "72 hour drug-fuelled sex sessions" said to be sweeping the nation, and the "sexual marathons . . . among HIV-positive men who have sex with men" that researchers and commentators pin on the confidence, energy, stamina, and overactive sexuality that crystal meth is said to induce among this cohort.[62]

Of course, concern about the long-term psychological and bodily impacts of methamphetamine is warranted and understandable. My intention is certainly not to gloss over these potential harms. But it is surely revealing that one of the recurring tropes to feature prominently in this series of moral panics is the specter of gay men using drugs "in combination to facilitate sexual sessions lasting several hours or even days with multiple sexual partners."[63] In other words, it is precisely the prolonged and extravagant temporality of the sexual activities facilitated by the practice of experimenting with drug combinations that alarms moral commentators and incites condemnation, ultimately serving to produce these scenes of gay sex as excessive, deviant, and exceedingly problematic. Gay sex was never meant to last so long or be so uninhibited.[64]

Soon after receiving my HIV diagnosis I made an appointment with a general practitioner with years of specialist experience in HIV care and a loyal caseload of inner-city gays right in the middle of Darlinghurst. "Don't tell your parents" was the first piece of advice he offered me, followed shortly by a script for the antidepressants he suggested I go on. I remember finding both suggestions pretty outrageous. What did he know about my relationship with my parents or my general state of mind, for that matter, especially given the pains I had taken to present myself as unfazed and optimistic? I never filled that prescription, but I did hold off on telling my parents for some time. And though it irked me at the time, in retrospect I can see that my doctor's advice was well-intentioned. It was no doubt informed by years of clinical experience with traumatized patients whose pain stemmed as much from the drama of family rejection as the mere biological fact of HIV infection. With an HIV-positive boyfriend and friends and colleagues in the sector, I was fortunate enough to have access to a support network that made it possible to avoid a painful family drama during the early stages of learning how to live with this disease.

But living in constant fear of imminent exposure of a stigmatized, sexually humiliating condition takes its toll. Although I was relatively open about my status with friends and colleagues, my sexuality had already severely strained my relationship with my parents and family. It was only a matter of time before they discovered my dirty secret, I figured. In the narrative that dominated my parental imaginary, HIV operated as vindicating proof of sexual depravity: conclusive evidence of the wrongness of homosexuality and the foolish lifestyle I was leading. I imagined my parents' anger, disappointment, and deep shame on discovering that their only son had succumbed to the logical outcome of the homosexual lifestyle they had repeatedly warned me against. I had wasted my life, wasted everything, betrayed every hope they had invested in me. This apprehension of a wasted life filled me with a sense of impending catastrophe, the guilt-ridden intensities of which I felt most acutely—fittingly enough—while *getting wasted* on the dance floors of Sydney's party scene. Intensely conscious of the shameful disappointment I had become, I lived in constant fear of public humiliation and unwanted exposure at such events. In these spaces I often thought people were laughing at me—talking, whispering, pushing past me, pointing, smirking—as though everyone were in on some elaborate collective joke at my expense: a conspiratorial plot that singled me out for ridiculing attention. The dance floor sometimes struck me as a chaotic swarm of reckless figures who were not only oblivious to their wayward ways but manifestly out to get me. On more than one occasion, the partygoers around me grew devilish horns right before my eyes. It was a nightmare, a terrifying nightmare, that frequently recurred in such situations.

Over time I learned that the drugs I was using to party intensified whatever apprehensions and feelings I was experiencing with a force that was powerful enough to make those apprehensions a reality. This was true of both positive and negative apprehensions, affective states whose qualitative intensities could switch, without warning, according to circumstance. Psychoanalysts will squabble with psychopharmacologists over whether these psychotic episodes were caused by the recreational drugs I was consuming at the time or the intense sexual shame that the possibility of having my HIV status outed to my parents unwittingly provoked in me. Psychoanalysts would likely interpret the hellish apparitions I experienced on these occasions as drug-induced paranoid-schizoid delusional episodes stemming from the morbid fear of the social humiliation associated with the prospect of having my sexual turpitude exposed for all to see: the "I told you so" narrative of HIV infection I felt and projected so keenly.[65] But it is impossible for me to dissociate the sexualized nature of the guilt and shame I felt in relation to my HIV status from the stigmatized status of illicit drug use more generally.

Elsewhere I have discussed how the fear of a "wasted life" overwhelms popular conceptions of illicit drug use and its dangers in the neoliberal-aspirational parental imagination.[66] As a phrase of disdain, "What a waste!" is as familiar to gay men of my generation as it has been to many so-called junkies, a pejorative exclamation that takes its cue from normative determinations of what counts as a valuable or productive life, revealing the sexual, insidiously biopolitical nature of the economic investments that motivate and project it. As I have indicated, the regular use of drugs (both licit and illicit) was part and parcel of my sexuality and the practice of living with HIV in this time and location. For a time, there seemed to be no chance of escape from this wicked psychosocial alchemy.

At the risk of being dubbed a "freelance pharmacologist," what I can say now with some certainty is that these paranoid episodes were not an inevitable or intrinsic effect of these psychoactive substances, as pharmacological determinists would have it, but intensively conditioned by the historical social stigmatization and devaluation of homosexuality and illicit drug use. I base this claim less on any rigorous engagement with psychoanalytic theory than on more than a decade of disco-pharmacology: "underground research" involving careful experimentation with the relevant variables. These experiments have equipped me with a degree of intimate and practical expertise about their various combinatorial possibilities and affective contingencies.

It took me a decade to muster the courage to finally come out to my parents about my HIV status. My doing so was, importantly, not motivated by any sense of moral obligation, political valor, or hand-wringing guilt about having been dishonest with them: it was entirely in the interests of self-care that I came to this decision. Years of critical reflection about the enforced silence surrounding my condition and growing indignation about its deeply sexualized nature no doubt also played an important part in this process. Had I been diagnosed with cancer or diabetes or any other chronic illness, I would have shared the news with my family without hesitation. Moreover, I might have expected to receive the sort of care, sympathy, and support about my situation that conventionally emerges as an expectation and entitlement among family members insofar as such care and support is normatively considered one of the principal obligations of kinship. Whatever the case, I had nothing to lose: by this stage of my life, not only was I economically secure and socially independent enough to handle a bad response from them; I was also convinced that living in constant fear of humiliating exposure—of trying to remain socially as well as virologically undetectable—was having such corrosive effects on my mental well-being that I was already losing my mind. In this situation, telling my parents emerged as a risk worth taking, whatever the consequences.

As it happens, my parents' response was unexpectedly generous and immensely reassuring. "You poor bastard," my father said without the slightest hint of moral judgment. "What a terrible thing to live with, what a terrible accident." By 2006, the long-term effectiveness of antiretroviral therapy had been well enough established to make a new script for HIV disclosure normatively available. After thanking me for telling them (they acknowledged and conveyed their appreciation of my bravery in doing so), the discussion quickly turned to the topic of available treatments; they were eager to learn more about their effectiveness and my experience of them. Thank goodness for drugs; thank goodness for treatment optimism.

Today I regard this action as one of the best things I have ever done for my health and well-being. My paranoia gradually abated; an enormous weight had been lifted from my shoulders. What did it matter if my social life involved associating with a bunch of horned-up partygoers? With a mix of relief and just a whiff of disappointment, I came to realize that their horniness generally had nothing whatsoever to do with me. *Quelle surprise!* What a relief! But more to the point: What sort of self-absorbed, self-serving conceit had persuaded me to think otherwise? People had other things to worry about, better things to concern themselves with. There was no elaborate conspiracy against me. This was a disappointment I could live with.

Drugs for Life

In *Homosexual Desire*, Guy Hocquenghem argued (contra Freud) that paranoia illuminates the operations of homophobia rather than homosexuality.[67] In my own experience, the apprehension of homophobia has been inextricably bound up with HIV infection and the stigmatization of illicit drug use. But where I have had the rare good fortune of being able to come out to my family about my HIV status relatively painlessly—enabling me to move from a paranoid to a reparative position—the same opportunity cannot be taken for granted by a great many people living with HIV, especially those whose experiences of sexual stigma are compounded by race and class, and who also become all the more susceptible to the war on drugs on this basis. Those who are forced to hide these dimensions of their intimate experience have far less hope of accessing the care they need should they run into trouble. Dismantling these forms of enforced silence, stigma, and fears of exposure remains an urgent priority on this basis.

Of course, the consumption of a range of drugs has been a conspicuous part of gay world-making practices since the days of disco. But as I have argued, the emergence of combination antiretroviral therapy to treat HIV disease in 1996 brought a new kind of anxious attention to questions of drug use and the transformative possibilities associated with the experimental use of drug cocktails within and among this population. The moralistic tenor of the bulk of this discourse can be traced to cultural anxieties about the return of increasingly active expressions of gay sexuality at this point in the HIV epidemic, which sociomedical and public health discourses now pinned on the medical and recreational use of drugs. But the association of drug cocktails with the maintenance of "normal life" also made it possible to query a series of distinctions long deployed in the medicolegal classification of drugs: therapeutic/recreational, benign/toxic, medical/pleasurable, proven/experimental. The protease archive I have assembled here suggests that a more capacious perspective on experimental drug use might be possible—one that expands the bounds of normativity to incorporate a range of drug futures, such that the use of certain drugs currently deemed illicit and irrational emerges in alternative terms: as both intelligible and experimental.

When experimentality is foregrounded, a different story can be told about sex and drugs that is particularly pertinent for the age of biomedical prevention. This term refers to the present paradigm of HIV prevention, which is largely predicated on the repurposing of antiretroviral drugs to optimize their capacity to prevent HIV infection. Though rarely acknowledged, this is something gay men started experimenting with almost as soon as these drugs became available and the possibilities of viral suppression became apparent to them. Figuring that undetectable viral load could be taken to mean minimal risk of passing on the virus, some men began to change their sexual practices accordingly.[68]

Almost two decades later, the underground experiments of these "freelance pharmacologists" received the imprimatur that only *clinical* experiments are deemed capable of conferring. Their optimism, it turns out, was warranted. This has led to a high-profile overhaul and redesign of HIV-prevention services around the world to maximize the preventative capacities of these drugs ("the prevention revolution"). But the preceding labor of "freelance pharmacologists" is rarely acknowledged in official accounts of this moment. From the outset, our team at the national center was among the handful of researchers internationally who were prepared to take these underground experiments seriously enough to propose changes to the definition of safe sex. Other colleagues brought the same approach to the use of recreational drugs, arguing that attending to the "folk pharmacologies" circulating within gay dance culture might generate new concepts and practices of harm reduction.[69] Most scientists took what we approached as potential innovations in safe sex and harm reduction to be unprotected sex and substance abuse, plain and simple, effectively disqualifying the subcultural experiments in question.

Today, most of the drugs that gay men and their communities began experimenting with on the dance floors of the late millennium are being investigated for various "therapeutic" applications. Ecstasy, marijuana, LSD, and ketamine are among the drugs being tested for their use in addressing conditions such as post-traumatic stress disorder, anxiety, and depression in large-scale clinical trials. Of course, there are differences between clinical experiments and the collective, subcultural experiments that take place on dance floors. The former are far more controlled, have the luxury of quality control, and are randomized, documented, and closely monitored. But despite all these controlling measures, they miss something important. One only need imagine how the experience of taking ecstasy or ketamine would differ in the white padded cell of a clinic to the "flashing lights and pounding music" of a party or nightclub: all the contingencies, particularities, and historicity of a given night, those mediating conditions that Norman E. Zinberg once referred to as drug, set, and setting.[70] Perhaps clinical researchers have something more to learn from these underground research projects after all.

NOTES

1   This piece reworks and develops my previous work from "The Undetectable Crisis" and *Pleasure Consuming Medicine*.

2   Chambers, *Facing It*, 48.

3   Engel, *The Epidemic*, 246.

4   *Talkabout: The Newsletter of People Living with HIV/AIDS*, 9.

5   Dominic O'Grady, "AIDS Groups: Hit Early, Hit Hard," *Sydney Star Observer*, July 1996, 3; Martyn Goddard, "Half in Love with Easeful Death," *Sydney Star Observer*, May 1997, 8.

6   Pozniak, "Surrogacy in HIV-1 Clinical Trials."

7   Race, "The Undetectable Crisis," 178.

8   Rosenbrock et al., "The Normalization of AIDS."

9   Race, "The Undetectable Crisis," 178.

10 Bartos and McDonald, "HIV as Identity, Experience or Career"; Flowers, "Gay Men and HIV/AIDS Risk Management."

11 Race, "The Undetectable Crisis," 178.

12 Race, "The Undetectable Crisis," 183.

13 Navarre, "Fighting the Victim Label."

14 Martyn Goddard, "Time for a Nice Cold Shower," *Sydney Star Observer*, July 18, 1996, 10.

15 Lugliani, "Last Laughs." This trope of living with HIV endures well into the epidemic's third decade. See, for example, Cynthia Poindexter's *Handbook of HIV and Social Work*: "Living long term with HIV is possible, but it is not a walk in the park. Side effects of medication can range from serious to mere nuisance. Accepting a lifetime of popping pills on a regular and consistent basis can be challenging and tiresome" (108).

16 Laurie Garrett, "Eyeing an Ad Ban: Critics say HIV Drugs' Claims Paint Too Rosy a Picture," *Newsday*, March 13, 2001.

17 Stop AIDS Project, "HIV Is No Picnic" campaign, San Francisco, 2002.

18 Race, "The Undetectable Crisis," 181.

19 Flynn, "Compliance Ain't Easy," 214.

20 For example, a 1997 news report stated that "powerful drug combinations being taken by many people with AIDS do not eliminate the virus from the body, scientists have found—but neither does the virus develop resistance to the drugs in people who follow the dosage instructions. . . . The findings mean people who

benefit from the drug combination therapy cannot safely discontinue their medication, as had been hoped, and may need to stick with the costly treatment indefinitely." Denise Grady, "Survival Means Drugs for Life," *Sydney Morning Herald*, November 15, 1997, 28.

21 Wilde, *The Picture of Dorian Gray*, 54.

22 Van de Ven et al., "HIV Treatments Optimism."

23 Senterfitt, "The Message from Vancouver."

24 Halberstam, *In a Queer Time and Place*, 4–7.

25 Rosenbrock et al., "The Normalization of AIDS," 1617.

26 I further explore the impacts of the medical news broadcast during the 1996 International AIDS Conference in Vancouver in my essay "The Undetectable Crisis."

27 See, for example, Bersani, *Homos*; Edelman, *No Future*; and Berlant and Edelman, *Sex, or the Unbearable*.

28 Wamoyi et al., "Changes in Sexual Desires."

29 For a review of this literature, see Crum et al., "A Review of Hypogonadism and Erectile Dysfunction"; Elford, "Changing Patterns of Sexual Behaviour"; and Sullivan, Drake, and Sanchez, "Prevalence of Treatment Optimism-Related Risk Behavior."

30 Wiegman and Wilson, "Introduction: Antinormativity's Queer Conventions," 18, 15.

31 Andrew Sullivan, "When Plagues End: Notes on the Twilight of an Epidemic," *Independent*, February 16, 1997, www.independent.co.uk/arts-entertainment/when-plagues-end-notes-on-the-twilight-of-an-epidemic-1278905.html.

32 Sullivan characterizes this behavior as "manic," its practitioners "terrified by the thought that they might actually survive." See Sullivan, "When Plagues End."

33 Harper, *Private Affairs*, 93. See also Crimp, *Melancholia and Moralism*, 1–10.

34 See Millett et al., "Comparisons of Disparities"; Arnold, Rebchook, and Kegeles, "'Triply Cursed'"; and Van Doorn, "Between Hope and Abandonment."

35 Sullivan, "When Plagues End."

36 Frances Anderton, "The Lethal Liberator," *Guardian*, September 15, 1997.

37 Kevin Sack, "HIV Peril and Rising Drug Use," *New York Times*, January 29, 1999.

38 Steve Dow, "Dancing with Death," *The Age*, October 4, 2000.

39 I take the concept of "pharmaceutical slippage" from the work of Marsha Rosengarten, who presented a paper at the 2000 HIV/AIDS & Related Diseases Social Research Conference in Sydney with the title "Prophylactic Slippage." See, generally, Rosengarten, *HIV Interventions*.

40 Frank Owen, "Higher and Higher: Drug Cocktails—Pleasures, Risks and Reasons," *Village Voice*, July 20, 1999, www.villagevoice.com/1999/07/20/higher-and-higher.

41 Owen, "Higher and Higher."

42 Flynn, "Compliance Ain't Easy."

43 Owen, "Higher and Higher."

44 Owen, "Higher and Higher."

45 Wiegman and Wilson, "Introduction: Antinormativity's Queer Conventions," 18.

46 Cover page, *POZ*, February 1999.

47 Valenzuela, "The Day We Didn't Quite Manage to Smuggle Some K." A prepublication copy of this story was given to me by the author.

48 Valenzuela, "The Day We Didn't Quite Manage to Smuggle Some K."

49 Valenzuela, "The Day We Didn't Quite Manage to Smuggle Some K."

50 Valenzuela, "The Day We Didn't Quite Manage to Smuggle Some K."

51 Valenzuela, "Dosed." A prepublication copy of this story was given to me by the author.

52 See Race, *Pleasure Consuming Medicine*, chapter 9; Race, "Party and Play"; Race, *The Gay Science*, chapter 7; Gideonse, "Framing Samuel See"; Hakim, "The Rise of Chemsex"; and Kagan, *Positive Images*.

53 Halberstam, *In a Queer Time and Place*, and Edelman, *No Future*.

54 Valenzuela, "Dosed."

55 Valenzuela, "Dosed."

56 Isaiah Green and Halkitis, "Crystal Methamphetamine and Sexual Sociality," 323.

57 Reback, *The Social Construction of a Gay Drug*, 38.

58 Semple et al., "Motivations Associated with Methamphetamine Use," 153.

59 In recent Australian gay community samples, three times as many HIV-positive men report using crystal methamphetamine as HIV-negative and untested men. See Lea et al., "Methamphetamine Use among Gay and Bisexual Men in Australia," and Shoptaw, "Methamphetamine Use in Urban Gay and Bisexual Populations."

60 Rasmussen, *On Speed*.

61 See Race, *Pleasure Consuming Medicine*; and Keane, "Pleasure and Discipline."

62 Laura Mitchell, "The Rise of 'Chemsex': Craze Sees 72 Hour Drug-Fuelled Sex Sessions Sweep UK," *Daily Star*, December 13, 2015; Semple et al., "Sexual Marathons." See also Bourne et al., "The Chemsex Study." For a critical analysis of chemsex discourse, see Race, *The Gay Science*, chapter 7.

63 See McCall et al., "What Is Chemsex and Why Does It Matter?"

64 Critiques of the popular narrative that displays the AIDS crisis as a sexual morality tale can be found in Crimp, *Melancholia and Moralism*; Race, *Pleasure Consuming Medicine*; Race, *The Gay Science*; and Warner, *The Trouble with Normal*.

65 In his essay on the case of his patient Schreber, Freud claimed that "the strikingly prominent features in the causation of paranoia, especially among males, are *social humiliations and slights*. But if we go into the matter only a little more deeply, we shall be able to see that the really operative factor in these *social injuries* lies in the part played in them by the homosexual components of emotional life" (10, my italics). But Freud's theory that paranoid delusions emerge as a defense against latent homosexuality is slim on convincing explanatory detail and has been reasserted and contested since the time it was first published. See Freud, "Psychoanalytic Notes on an Autobiographical Account of a Case of Paranoia."

66 In neoliberal discourses of illicit substance use, the main problem associated with drug use is the threat that drugs are said to pose to the lives, dreams, and futures of middle-class aspirational subjects. See Race, *Pleasure Consuming Medicine*, chapter 3.

67 Hocquenghem, *Homosexual Desire*. See also Sedgwick, "Paranoid Reading and Reparative Reading," and Morrison, *The Explanation for Everything*, chapter 6.
68 Rosengarten, Race, and Kippax, "*Touch Wood*," and Kippax and Race, "Sustaining Safe Practice."
69 Southgate and Hopwood, "The Role of Folk Pharmacology"; Race, "The Use of Pleasure in Harm Reduction"; Race, *The Gay Science*, 10–19.
70 Zinberg, *Drug, Set, and Setting*.

BIBLIOGRAPHY

Arnold, Emily A., Gregory M. Rebchook, and Susan M. Kegeles. "'Triply Cursed': Racism, Homophobia and HIV-Related Stigma Are Barriers to Regular HIV Testing, Treatment Adherence and Disclosure among Young Black Gay Men." *Culture, Health & Sexuality* 16, no. 6 (2014): 710–22.

Bartos, Michael, and K. McDonald. "HIV as Identity, Experience or Career." *AIDS Care* 12, no. 3 (2000): 299–306.

Berlant, Lauren, and Lee Edelman. *Sex, or the Unbearable*. Durham, NC: Duke University Press, 2013.

Bersani, Leo. *Homos*. Cambridge, MA: Harvard University Press, 1995.

Bourne, A., D. Reid, F. Hickson, S. Torres Rueda, and P. Weatherburn. "The Chemsex Study: Drug Use in Sexual Settings among Gay and Bisexual Men in Lambeth, Southwark and Lewisham." Sigma Research, London School of Hygiene & Tropical Medicine, March 2014.

Chambers, Ross. *Facing It: AIDS Diaries and the Death of the Author*. Ann Arbor: University of Michigan Press, 2001.

Crimp, Douglas. *Melancholia and Moralism: Essays on AIDS and Queer Politics*. Cambridge, MA: MIT Press, 2004.

Crum, Nancy F., Kari J. Furtek, Patrick E. Olson, Christopher L. Amling, and Mark R. Wallace. "A Review of Hypogonadism and Erectile Dysfunction among HIV-Infected Men during the Pre- and Post-HAART Eras: Diagnosis, Pathogenesis, and Management." *AIDS Patient Care & STDS* 19, no. 10 (2005): 655–71.

Edelman, Lee. *No Future: Queer Theory and the Death Drive*. Durham, NC: Duke University Press, 2004.

Elford, Jonathan. "Changing Patterns of Sexual Behaviour in the Era of Highly Active Antiretroviral Therapy." *Current Opinion in Infectious Diseases* 19, no. 1 (2006): 26–32.

Engel, Jonathan. *The Epidemic: A Global History of AIDS*. New York: Smithsonian Books, 2006.

Flowers, Paul. "Gay Men and HIV/AIDS Risk Management." *Health* 5, no. 1 (2001): 50–75.

Flynn, Michael. "Compliance Ain't Easy." *Body Positive*, July 1997.

Freud, Sigmund. "Psychoanalytic Notes on an Autobiographical Account of a Case of Paranoia (Dementia Paranoides)." 1911. In *The Standard Edition of the Complete Psychological Works of Sigmund Freud*, vol. 12, translated and edited by James Strachey, 1–82. London: Hogarth, 1958.

Gideonse, Theodore. "Framing Samuel See: The Discursive Detritus of the Moral Panic over the 'Double Epidemic' of Methamphetamines and HIV among Gay Men." *International Journal of Drug Policy* 28 (2016): 98–105.

Hakim, Jamie. "The Rise of Chemsex: Queering Collective Intimacy in Neoliberal London." *Cultural Studies* 33, no. 2 (2019): 1–27.

Halberstam, Jack [Judith]. *In a Queer Time and Place: Transgender Bodies, Subcultural Lives.* New York: New York University Press, 2005.

Harper, Phillip Brian. *Private Affairs: Critical Ventures in the Culture of Social Relations.* New York: New York University Press, 1999.

Hocquenghem, Guy. *Homosexual Desire.* Durham, NC: Duke University Press, 1993.

Isaiah Green, Adam, and Perry N. Halkitis. "Crystal Methamphetamine and Sexual Sociality in an Urban Gay Subculture: An Elective Affinity." *Culture, Health & Sexuality* 8, no. 4 (2006): 317–33.

Kagan, Dion. *Positive Images: Gay Men and HIV/AIDS in the Culture of "Post Crisis."* London: I. B. Tauris, 2017.

Keane, Helen. "Pleasure and Discipline in the Uses of Ritalin." *International Journal of Drug Policy* 19, no. 5 (2008): 401–9.

Kippax, Susan, and Kane Race. "Sustaining Safe Practice: Twenty Years On." *Social Science & Medicine* 57, no. 1 (2003): 1–12.

Lea, Toby, Limin Mao, Max Hopwood, Garrett Prestage, Iryna Zablotska, John de Wit, and Martin Holt. "Methamphetamine Use among Gay and Bisexual Men in Australia: Trends in Recent and Regular Use from the Gay Community Periodic Surveys." *International Journal of Drug Policy* 29 (2016): 66–72.

Lugliani, Greg. "Last Laughs." *POZ*, October 1, 1997.

McCall, Hannah, Naomi Adams, David Mason, and Jamie Willis. "What Is Chemsex and Why Does It Matter?" *BMJ* (2015). https://doi.org/10.1136/bmj.h5790.

Millett, Gregorio A., John L. Peterson, Stephen A. Flores, Trevor A. Hart, William L. Jeffries IV, Patrick A. Wilson, Sean B. Rourke, et al. "Comparisons of Disparities and Risks of HIV Infection in Black and Other Men Who Have Sex with Men in Canada, UK, and USA: A Meta-analysis." *Lancet* 380, no. 9839 (2012): 341–48.

Morrison, Paul. *The Explanation for Everything: Essays on Sexual Subjectivity.* New York: New York University Press, 2001.

Navarre, Max. "Fighting the Victim Label." In *AIDS: Cultural Analysis, Cultural Activism*, edited by Douglas Crimp, 143–46. Cambridge, MA: MIT Press, 1987.

Poindexter, Cynthia. *Handbook of HIV and Social Work: Principles, Practice, and Populations.* Hoboken, NJ: Wiley, 2010.

Pozniak, Anton. "Surrogacy in HIV-1 Clinical Trials." *Lancet* 351, no. 9102 (1998): 536–37.

Race, Kane. *The Gay Science: Intimate Experiments with the Problem of HIV.* London: Routledge, 2018.

Race, Kane. "'Party and Play': Online Hook-Up Devices and the Emergence of PNP Practices among Gay Men." *Sexualities* 18, no. 3 (2015): 253–75.

Race, Kane. *Pleasure Consuming Medicine: The Queer Politics of Drugs.* Durham, NC: Duke University Press, 2009.

Race, Kane. "The Undetectable Crisis: Changing Technologies of Risk." *Sexualities* 4, no. 2 (2001): 167–89.

Race, Kane. "The Use of Pleasure in Harm Reduction: Perspectives from the History of Sexuality." *International Journal of Drug Policy* 19, no. 5 (2008): 417–23.

Rasmussen, Nicolas. *On Speed: The Many Lives of Amphetamine*. New York: New York University Press, 2008.

Reback, Cathy. *The Social Construction of a Gay Drug: Methamphetamine Use among Gay and Bisexual Males in Los Angeles*. Los Angeles: Van Ness House, 1997.

Rosenbrock, Rolf, Francoise Dubois-Arber, Martin Moers, Patrice Pinell, Doris Schaeffer, and Michel Setbon. "The Normalization of AIDS in Western European Countries." *Social Science & Medicine* 50, no. 11 (2000): 1607–29.

Rosengarten, Marsha. *HIV Interventions: Biomedicine and the Traffic between Information and Flesh*. Seattle: University of Washington Press, 2010.

Rosengarten, Marsha, Kane Race, and Susan Kippax. *"Touch Wood, Everything Will Be Ok": Gay Men's Understandings of Clinical Markers in Sexual Practice*. Sydney: National Centre in HIV Social Research, 2000.

Sedgwick, Eve Kosofsky. "Paranoid Reading and Reparative Reading; Or, You're So Paranoid, You Probably Think This Introduction Is about You." In *Novel Gazing: Queer Readings in Fiction*, edited by Eve Kosofsky Sedgwick, 1–37. Durham, NC: Duke University Press, 1997.

Semple, Shirley J., Thomas L. Patterson, and Igor Grant. "Motivations Associated with Methamphetamine Use among HIV Men Who Have Sex with Men." *Journal of Substance Abuse Treatment* 22, no. 3 (2002): 149–56.

Semple, Shirley J., Jim Zians, Steffanie A. Strathdee, and Thomas L. Patterson. "Sexual Marathons and Methamphetamine Use among HIV-Positive Men Who Have Sex with Men." *Archives of Sexual Behavior* 38, no. 4 (2009): 583–90.

Senterfitt, Walt. "The Message from Vancouver: The Hope Is Real and the (Reality) Check Is in the Mail." *Aegis*, August 1996.

Shoptaw, Steven. "Methamphetamine Use in Urban Gay and Bisexual Populations." *Topics in HIV Medicine* 14, no. 2 (2006): 84–87.

Southgate, Erica, and Max Hopwood. "The Role of Folk Pharmacology and Lay Experts in Harm Reduction: Sydney Gay Drug Using Networks." *International Journal of Drug Policy* 12, no. 4 (2001): 321–35.

Sullivan, Patrick S., Amy J. Drake, and Travis H. Sanchez. "Prevalence of Treatment Optimism–Related Risk Behavior and Associated Factors among Men Who Have Sex with Men in 11 States, 2000–2001." *AIDS and Behavior* 11, no. 1 (2007): 123–29.

Valenzuela, Tony. "The Day We Didn't Quite Manage to Smuggle Some K." *ZYZZYVA* 72 (Winter 2004).

Valenzuela, Tony. "Dosed." In *Inside Him: New Gay Erotica*, edited by Joel B. Tan, 31–42. San Francisco: Running Press, 2006.

Van de Ven, Paul, Patrick Rawstorne, Tamo Nakamura, June Crawford, and Susan Kippax. "HIV Treatments Optimism Is Associated with Unprotected Anal Intercourse with Regular and with Casual Partners among Australian Gay and Homosexually Active Men." *International Journal of STD & AIDS* 13, no. 3 (2002): 181–83.

Van Doorn, Niels. "Between Hope and Abandonment: Black Queer Collectivity and the Affective Labour of Biomedicalised HIV Prevention." *Culture, Health & Sexuality* 14, no. 7 (2012): 827–40.

Wamoyi, J., M. Mbonye, J. Seeley, J. Birungi, and S. Jaffar. "Changes in Sexual Desires and Behaviours of People Living with HIV after Initiation of ART: Implications for HIV Prevention and Health Promotion." *BMC Public Health* 11, no. 1 (2011): 633.

Warner, Michael. *The Trouble with Normal: Sex, Politics, and the Ethics of Queer Life.* Cambridge, MA: Harvard University Press, 2000.

Wiegman, Robyn, and Elizabeth A. Wilson. "Introduction: Antinormativity's Queer Conventions." *differences* 26, no. 1 (2015): 1–25.

Wilde, Oscar. *The Picture of Dorian Gray.* Mineola: Dover, 1993. First published 1891 by Ward, Lock.

Zinberg, Norman E. *Drug, Set, and Setting: The Basis for Controlled Intoxicant Use.* New Haven, CT: Yale University Press, 1984.

'Tis a human thing, love,
a holy thing, to love
what death has touched.
—YEHUDAH HALEVI,
"'Tis a Fearful Thing"

5

DEATH DO US PART

CARLA FRECCERO

Prelude

When I began this essay, in 2016, I had two dogs, not littermates, but the same breed, Basenji. According to Merriam-Webster, the etymology of the name may derive from the Lingala—the Bantu language used in parts of the Congo—*mbwa na basenji*, "dogs of the bushland people," dogs, that is, who were trained, after their ancient Libyan and Egyptian periods, as all-purpose hunting dogs by people in Central Africa and later referred to as "Congo dogs" and "Belgian Congo dogs." Their history is thus a colonial one; British travelers commented on (and photographed) the village dogs that accompanied hunter-gatherer communities in the Congo basin (especially the so-called African Pygmy peoples). Like many Africans in Europe, Basenjis died upon arrival from European diseases until, in 1936, a Mrs. Olivia Burns successfully imported and began to breed them in England. Their colonial travels follow those of nineteenth- and early twentieth-century European (mostly British) women who were breed fanciers and, during wartime Britain, liminal aristocratic figures with no role to play in the military atmosphere of the day. In the early 1940s Basenjis came directly from Africa to the United States, along with coffee and, in one case, baby gorillas. The 1950 movie *Goodbye, My Lady* sealed the fate of the breed as "popular," although that popularity was and is modest, relatively speaking. Basenji lovers tend to think it's because of the breed's ancient lineage, its prey drive, and its independence and intractability when it comes to the usual styles of training. Breed fanciers have won concessions from the American Kennel Club (AKC) to expand the foundation stock by continuing to bring African Basenjis into the European genetic pools. On the one hand, then, I inherit the colonial histories that are characteristic of many of the world's dog breeds; on the other hand, the living and active connection to African origins and people, along with the absence of visible European inscription (they look the same as their Congolese relatives), operates culturally as a kind of resistant material semiosis (or at least that is how I think of it sometimes). They are the living material sign of an unfinished story, often inscribed by the "African" and African-sounding names that most of the purebreds carry.

Mine were together from puppyhood, since Biko was born. Maji (Jato Zuri's Msemaji, destined for a prestigious show career) was six months old and living at the breeder's when Biko was born (Zuri's Biko, labeled "plain red dog #3" at birth, and destined for pet, not show, with a champion prize-winning father and a non–AKC-registered purebred mother, Isis). I saw Maji for the first time when I went to visit the puppy I had preordered. But . . . this isn't our life story.

I BEGAN THIS ESSAY before Maji, then Biko, died (six months apart) and perhaps, although it is difficult to remember now, in retrospect, before their irremediable decline. I learned that "hospice," insofar as I have come to understand it while engaged in "end-of-life" care for them (I cannot stand that expression, as though the end is why you are caring and as though the end of life is a place where any creature can live for long), is a strange borderland, perhaps a DMZ, between ferocious battles against disease and illness and the finality of making a decision to let die (or to kill, sometimes I think of it that way too). I learned that much of "owning" a domestic animal who is a companion and noninstrumentalized, as "pets" tend to be, challenged me early and late in the fifteen-year span that turned out to be their mortal lives. And that it is both "like" and not like raising a child or caring for an elder human, in part because of its chosen nature (as I contemplate the years of my elderhood given over, only somewhat voluntarily, to parental care). I would speak about this to every human considering joining his or her life to the life of a short-lived mammal: can you hold yourself and your wishes in abeyance when time slows down, when pain, patience, suffering, passion, and endurance, all those *patior* descendants, gather in one place to stand vigil over your life?

To commit: to throw together, to cast one's lot with, to trust oneself completely to, which is also to put in danger through an irrevocable preliminary act. The commitment I made lasted longer than my parents' marriage and had no yield that I can point to in the present, although somewhere Biko's children may still be in the world.

I loved these creatures in part for their beauty; I had shameless aesthetic investment in their sleek and muscular slender bodies, their shining red coats (people always said I colored my hair their color), that they cleaned themselves, their eloquent silence accompanied by intense regard, their regal bearing, their built-for-speed perfection. If there's a fully embodied equivalent of an ego ideal, they were it for me. Watching them run, when they were young, was breathtaking, even as it terrified me each time I tried to let them go the distance. Kind of like a mother watching her kid climb tall trees, or so I imagine. Freud suggested that people invest their kids with this kind of idealizing egoic aspiration, that, indeed, they reproduce in order to do this: to see in a mirror of themselves the potential fulfillment of what they aspired to but did not achieve. So I guess I could say that Biko and Maji were that, for me, on a physical plane. They were the perfect body I never had or would have. And they remained gorgeous to their deaths, in spite of the terrible things that were happening inside of them. And they had a face.

Emmanuel Levinas hesitantly accords dogs faces in an interview about the relevance of his philosophy to nonhuman beings.[1] For him, the interpretation goes, to be human is to confront another in a face-to-face encounter that makes an ethical demand first: the demand not to kill, a demand that is a responsibility toward the other, the other in all its alterity. It is an asymmetrical encounter too, occurring prior to the acknowledgment of two subjects facing each other and therefore, potentially, applies to the encounter with any mortal being that has a face. (Dogs are, of course, easy to confer the face-to-face encounter upon; thousands of years of coevolution have given them the capacity to be beings-for-human-others. It is an interesting question to ask whether we too have evolved that capacity.) I used to think that Basenjis were especially gifted with Levinasian faces because they do not bark. If many domestic dogs bark to get human attention, it is perhaps because we are lazy, distracted learners and we do not easily and readily confront the other (whatever other), requiring a far more strident demand than the naked face. However, Basenjis use their eyes, their faces, to get attention. If I was neglectful or distracted and Biko really wanted my attention, he would place his paw on my arm or leg and leave it there—often standing on his hind legs as I was sitting at my table or my desk—until I noticed. Maji, more often than not, would return resignedly to her bed and wait, unless it was a serious matter. I used to have to counsel visitors and new dog walkers to make an effort to go to her to greet her, because whereas Biko demanded a thorough and lavish greeting, Maji would trot up hopefully then, if the person wasn't quick enough, or if Biko was still commanding all the notice, she would trot back to her bed. She developed a strange "woof" she used rarely, upon the arrival of a male stranger at my door. For Maji, male strangers demanded my immediate and undivided attention, for they were untrustworthy, in her view. At other times, if their frustration grew too great, they made sure I suffered for having failed to attend, whether by ravaging my recycling bags or my garbage cans or, when they were young, my shoes, my phone, and the contents of my purse.

Over the course of time, they trained me to look them in the eyes and to pay attention. That is why, as well, I knew when they approached the end, for it was they who were distracted, gazing elsewhere, somewhere, reluctantly returning to me when I asked for their attention. I often wondered what absorbed them in those moments. I think Maji was measuring the progress of her illness; she had a way, throughout her life, of noticing her own health, whether it was in tasting her urine, drinking before a walk, or eating grass and dirt when she felt queasy. Biko I am less sure about; he never seemed to attend much to his creaturely needs, so riveted was he by others and the world. For him, it may have been misery or the mustering of all his life forces in the effort to breathe and to walk. I wonder this about other others too, misanthropically at the gym, where people wearing headphones move through space as though they were not surrounded by other people moving through space, oblivious to the community until someone taps them on the shoulder to command their notice. Then the startle reflex, the strange sudden apperception of another in the room. Where did you come from? Idiots, I think, you're in a gym full of other people. Other times, watching my father in the afternoon as he sits in the garden, half dozing, I wonder what inner worlds he is traversing. Is he remembering a past of his own, long before I was there to watch him? Does he feel grace? I suppose this is, as well, what lovers sometimes feel, so captivated and consumed by the other and yet forever distant from the other's inner world. I take to heart the Levinasian injunction, I am hostage to the stranger, I see the other, and in that moment my responsibility is infinite. I think Biko and Maji helped me remember this face-to-face, this awareness.

Awareness is not a Latinate word but one with Germanic roots (and of quite recent common usage): to be cautious, to be on guard, to take care, as of an object. We were aware of so many things, so much: the lizards, squirrels, rats! And the DEER!!, the CATS!! Then there were the sheep and the horses. The sheep inspired a special pleasure, perhaps lanolin is an attractor, but somehow the smell of sheep was irresistible and heady. Biko would grab mouthfuls of wool with such an excitement! And horses, well, they were the only other living creatures to still the dogs and inspire awe. Their cautious curiosity, face-to-face with a horse, their unsureness when a horse would incline his or her nose in a snorting inspection. Once, when I was living with Biko and Maji in New York City, we met a horse with narcolepsy (I'd like to mention that in my observation the humans in New York are somewhat less oblivious to living in community than the northern California gym-going counterparts I mentioned; they move through crowded communal space, and often their well-being depends on a certain awareness—not necessarily benign or compassionate or recognizant—of others). The (not) mounted policeman who was standing next to his horse in Washington Square Park took an interest in the dogs. This happens a lot; they seem exotic to people, relatively rare. As we watched Biko and Maji enact their strange dance of awe before the equine giant and began to talk about our companions, the policeman explained that his horse, if standing still and unmounted, would fall asleep and that he very often had to slap him (gently) to arouse him from slumber when it was time to move. He used the word: narcolepsy. And I remembered a lover of thirty years ago who would invariably fall asleep while we were driving. I once asked why, thinking that my driving was so good he must feel completely relaxed, and he replied that he was so terrified of being in a car that the only way to escape that terror was to fall asleep (here too I am reminded of a friend who would fall asleep during a lovers' quarrel, in the midst of "processing"—at the time I found this hilarious). I thought perhaps the horse was behaving similarly, having found that the only way to endure the noise and violence of the city he had to live in was to fall asleep at every opportunity, for peace. That is, in fact, how Maji endured her plane flights in a kennel in the cargo hold. She would curl up in her crate at one end of the journey, and when the other of us met her (at JFK or SFO), she would not have moved. She would still be curled up in that tight Basenji donut. The only way I knew she was terrified was that when she raised her head, her pupils were huge, eyes almost completely black as they stared out at me. Biko, on the other hand, tore up his bedding, chewed his plastic water and food dishes to bits, and bloodied his gums trying to break the bars of the crate with his teeth. I could hear him emerging from cargo from yards away, his high-pitched scream the sound of a child being beaten.

I make Biko sound like a foolish boy; in many ways he was, very outwardly focused, very attuned—lovingly so—to humans, and aggressive toward other male dogs. But when Biko began to fall ill, it was he who seemed to hasten the pace, countering my efforts to prolong his life by refusing his medications and, finally and successfully, refusing food. He wasted away. With Maji, it seemed more up and down, perhaps because her life force was never quite as extravagantly on display. She was stoic, assisting her keepers in their efforts to improve her health, while bearing silently any suffering she underwent. Except at the vet's. In those last two years we went to the specialist veterinary clinic at least every four to six weeks, and she was always frightened. She spent the entire time trying to escape, making small mewling sounds of distress, hiding herself under tables and chairs. And she would not find comfort in my arms or in the affectionate ministrations of some of the vet techs, which were false in any case, since they wanted to induce her docility for the various tests they were trying to conduct. She was never fooled by them, and I began to find their voices grating as well, sharing her profound mistrust of anyone who cooed or coaxed. Biko was a sucker for attention, and although he too eventually came to feel apprehension at the vet's, more often than not he made a point of greeting everyone, waiting patiently through the procedures, and climbing into my arms when he could not sustain his bravery. I cherished his sense that I was safety; I prized it above every other sign of affection he gave. Biko was universally admired for that quality of fortitude and courage in the face of strange medical procedures, his goodwill toward those who were conducting them, and his curiosity, his willingness to forgive.

Two years before she died, Maji began to have the first of her grand mal seizures. We were in New York City, it was three o'clock in the morning, my sister and I were sharing an apartment. She was manager at a veterinary clinic, fortunately for us. I had never seen a seizure before. Later, when I became a veteran of assisting the dogs through the seizures, I would come to understand them as less painful than they seemed. I have since heard them described as akin to running a marathon (I have never run a marathon), exhausting but not necessarily dangerous. It is nevertheless traumatic to witness. After her first seizure, Maji wove drunkenly through the apartment, blind, stumbling, crying for an hour. I took her outside in the cool night air, then brought her back. I came to learn she needed to cool down afterward—she would climb into the bathtub, curl up there, and go to sleep. The other difficult task during a grand mal (where one is trying to prevent the creature's rigid, seizing body from slamming hard against a surface, trying to protect her, that is, from getting hurt, while also avoiding the clenched jaw and teeth) is timing it. A seizure lasting four or more minutes is dangerous, for the body heats up uncontrollably during that time. But watching the seconds, then the minutes pass, was nearly impossible. Both dogs always stopped short of four minutes, and eventually we stockpiled Valium for them in case of such an emergency (that is how a continuing seizure is treated, with doses of Valium or something similar). I also read on listservs that offering vanilla ice cream helped to restore calories, cool them down, and, well, give them pleasure. They loved vanilla ice cream. When the neurologist prescribed leviteracetam (brand-name Keppra, used by epileptic humans to control seizures), Maji didn't have any more seizures. Her decline was through slow kidney failure and a tumor on her liver—probably not malignant—that grew so big as to displace her stomach and prevent her from eating. I often remember how her first MRI identified that tiny unremarkable benign tumor on her liver, but no brain tumor, which is what we feared the diagnosis would be, and how relieved I was. Had she had surgery then . . . but by the time her tumor grew to an obstructive size, she was too weak and unhappy to be subjected to a surgery that she might not have, in any case, survived.

Where Maji's seizures happened suddenly and seemingly without a trigger event, Biko always gave uncanny and monstrous warning. Right before his first, and many subsequent ones, his hackles went up and he bared his teeth, looking around as though at the approach of something threatening, and then shot rapidly along the hall, collapsing into the rigid shaking and foaming at the mouth of a grand mal. One time he lost all bowel control, but mostly both of them were not incontinent when the seizing happened. Unlike Maji, Biko's seizures, though managed for a while, broke through time and time again, exacerbated by the fact that he would not swallow the time-release capsules and fought with all his might the liquid syringes I plunged down his throat. For a year, I had a house streaked with sticky cherry-colored and flavored splash patterns (cherry-flavored: the liquid is supposed to be palatable to the human tongue). But he too died of slow kidney failure, and anorexia, which is what they call it in dogs, without the psycho-ideological baggage, although it may as well have the baggage attached, for his anorexia was by no means neutral. Now, retrospectively, I think it was his way of making me let go, but it may have been, instead, his way of going.

Except for some of the details, I imagine that anyone who has been involved in long-term medical and then palliative care finds these accounts familiar, if not what one wants to linger on in the contemplation of one's long-term commitment to a beloved. Chroniclers of the AIDS epidemic did linger on such detail, I remember, and helped many of us understand the way these bodily ministrations by friends and companions were both signs of love and political. Rebecca Brown's *The Gifts of the Body*, along with Douglas Crimp's work and numerous memoirs, is what educated me then, and writing this I think back to the ways these writers showed me what queer commitment was—loving in extremis.[2] They dwelled on the details of palliative care for a reason: for some, it was the first time their love was prematurely and agonizingly afforded the occasion of caring for the dying, and for many of those not accustomed to such caring-for, it is a shocking, disgusting, tender, and heartbreakingly slow, daily, hourly practice. Patience, suffering, endurance, *patior*—that passive Latin verb that is the paradigm of what Anne Dufourmantelle calls "the power of gentleness."[3]

It was during this time I also came to better understand some of the complexities of the medicalization of illness and dying. How do you know when you are trying to cure an illness and when you are trying "only" to offer comfort? When is chronic renal failure (CRF in the language of the listservs and medical shorthand) a disease, and when is it code for dying? I think those of us engaged in caring for dying others who are not human have some good fortune here in that we can determine whether or not to prolong the lives that are given to us to tend, and we can end those lives in wonderfully gentle and painless ways. But that doesn't mitigate what Lauren Berlant and others talk about under neoliberalism, the way it's on you to know what to do, the way, that is, the responsibility is yours (and so you must perforce become an expert), the way spending all that money is framed as a moral choice about your commitment to the beloved (thousands and thousands of dollars, no insurance).[4] Not to mention the ways you are told that your dietary choices for them have consequences, and nothing short of a total science of nutrition will suffice.

I did learn, thanks to the existence of some very important organizations and groups, K9Kidneys first and foremost. There, laypersons with extensive experience caring for (generations of) their kidney-impaired dogs share tips on diagnostics (how to read blood chemistry panels, especially blood urea nitrogen and creatinine levels), record keeping (I have an impressive spreadsheet of two years' worth of blood and urine tests), the latest drugs, foods low in phosphorous (bad for kidneys), foods that kidney-impaired dogs will find appetizing (kidney disease often results in inappetence because of acid reflux and other side effects of the filtration system malfunction), how to decide when enough is enough, how to assess the dog's well-being rather than following the numbers, and so on. Donna Haraway writes about such expertise in *When Species Meet*, and she is so right.[5] I had her in mind when I joined K9Kidneys and learned to respect a similarly grounded experiential wisdom as the kind she finds in the breeder/trainer world. And yes, they're mostly women writing and sharing. It is a rule never to tell an "owner" they have done something wrong or that they are making a bad choice. That can be irksome, but one quickly realizes why they practice this code of ethics and why they continually remind you that what they have to say is not medical expertise but loving, practical experience.

The community of others: many humans cared for Biko and Maji; I could not withdraw from wage laboring to provide hospice or other kinds of care, whether for them as young creatures or as elderly adults. There is no family medical leave or "parental" leave for nonhuman care. I do know, and am grateful, that my institution allows me to take time off to care for my parents, and I will need this benefit some time not too far in the future. Our community was primarily a community of college undergraduates and graduate students who answered my ads. We had an odd relationship; each of them forged deep and beautiful bonds with the dogs to which our human relationship was secondary. And yet it was strangely and acutely intimate: these (mostly, but not all, women) noted the minutiae of Biko and Maji's bowels, moods, wellness, energy, and appetite, and they recounted the amusing or startling adventures over the course of the day in the small but concentrated world of human-with-dog. They sent pictures too. And those who cared for them in their youth were not those who cared for them in their old age, given the time frame of higher education, an even shorter life span than the life span of medium-sized dogs. Toward the end, I reached out to all of them to see if they wanted to say good-bye. And they came, those who could bear witnessing the decline. I did not feel alone in my initial mourning, although I am in my grief.

I realized only recently that I was still grieving and that nothing has completely dissipated (except their smell, and the short red and white hairs I continued to find on my clothes, my Pilates mat, the blankets on my furniture, the backseat of my car long after their departure). I went to New York City in the summertime and found myself retracing all the walks we took the last time we lived there together, missing them acutely. At a barbeque, someone I know casually and mostly through social media greeted me by saying he was sorry for the loss of the dogs. I was startled, moved, grateful . . . and it hurt. Maji died on September 1, 2017, Biko on February 10 of 2018. I think of Ani DiFranco's lyric in "Bodily": "I'm trying to make new memories in cities where we fell in love."[6] This was the song that accompanied me, in the mid-2000s, when I had just split up with a human partner—an autumn romance, the last human one for me perhaps—and was spending months in New York City walking miles and miles with Ani in my head. My partner had grown up there. New York was also where my father was born. He was baptized ten minutes away from the Henry James movie-set apartment where he lived for many years while teaching at NYU. His Italian immigrant parents met in Greenwich Village, although by the time he lived in Manhattan they were in a remote high-rise in Flushing, unable (of course) to afford to live elsewhere. I stayed in my father's apartment while he was away. I spent an early period in New York City (in the 1950s) after my parents arrived from Germany, my English mother a new bride of a soldier returning from his Frankfurt posting during the Korean war into which he was drafted and thanks to which he later went on to receive a doctorate. She stayed in New York with my grandparents until my father finished his service, when we moved to Baltimore. There I had my first canine companion, who lost his life to the concerns of humans in that casual and brutal way we have of punishing, because he bit a child who was reaching to take away his food.

So there is a grief that is the grief of all the losses that come to visit one on the occasion of the most recent loss. And this loss is also a historical haunting in a city that was the site of so many painful migrations and displacements, both early in the century and late. I do not know how many of these losses inhabit me, but I know that some of them are historical (political, economic) and now, perhaps, also planetary. Bodily: the buildings and the bodies in the late 2000s, decaying, vacant, the waning liveliness of each an echo chamber and a living mirror. The work of mourning is endless, or so it seems in the dilated present.

I am visiting my oldest female friend to say goodbye to her canine companion, a big dog she got a few years after I got mine, the second of this breed, the first having died terribly young of a tumor and having been shared, as mine were, during a partner breakup. I have loved this dog since she was a puppy; she thinks of me as another kind of companion, not her mistress, as my friend is, but someone to play with, albeit more fragile than most of the other dogs. Whenever I visit, my friend talks to her dog about me; I've come to understand my friend's love for me through the ways she nourishes the bond between her dog and me. My friend is "straight" and married. There was once ample room in her life for the company of women, but that changes for married people, really for all long-term couples; one simply doesn't have the time or occasion to care as closely for those not attached by greater institutions—children, property, the state, the church—but by more intangible bonds. I understand well why early-modern friendships, in Alan Bray's account, were consecrated, commemorated with solemn acts and sacred objects; while filiation was a matter of state, sometimes of divine fiat, and thus a formal paradigm, and blood, though not definitive in its claim, was nevertheless ascendant, the bonds of friendship were transient, ephemeral, always subject to challenge unless cemented through some performative act or symbolic token.[7] Even contractualism has this loophole, which is why so many early-modern capitalist ventures kept things in the family. (One other formal attachment is ownership, the one most invoked in relation to nonhumans, and the one I have been skirting here because of its ethical impossibility as even a minimally coercive relation between living beings. Another is power of attorney or custody, both relations I veer away from as I do the prospect of a demented parent.) And so a space is made for this female friendship outside the marriage bond through the dog. I realize this as I mourn her imminent departure; I wonder how we, the friends, will affirm each other in the future and what claim I will stake that my friend might recognize and privilege. Yet lest I center my self and my love in this odd threesome, I also know that the relationship between those two is a friendship. They love each other as two female beings of different species, albeit of unequal rank. All these loves are queer, but they are not playful; their weight is considerable, sometimes unbearable. And it is precisely, intricately, absolutely in the bearing of them that I find one of the meanings of this word, *commitment*.

IN "THE POLITICS OF FRIENDSHIP," and in the book by the same name, Jacques Derrida remarks that "the great canonical meditations on friendship" emerge in a moment of loss and are linked to the experience of mourning.[8] He also writes that the "double exclusion" of the feminine in the classical friendship tradition (of friendship between women and friendship between a man and a woman) confers on this philosophical paradigm "the essential and essentially sublime figure of virile homosexuality," by which I always understood him to mean homosociality, since the lovers' radical inequality in ancient Greek pederasty could not achieve the lofty reciprocity demanded of friendship in the tradition.[9] As he explores the genealogy of classical friendship, Derrida muses that modernity brings with it new possibilities: incommensurability between friends and friendship across the lines of sex. He doesn't mention it, but ironically one of the most beautiful essays on friendship, in Derrida's opinion, Michel de Montaigne's (whose essay is indeed occasioned by the loss of his friend), sings the praises of the male friend while effacing the friendship with Marie de Gournay, a younger, "proto-feminist" colleague (perhaps an amanuensis, which would explain why he doesn't consider her a friend) who curated and published Montaigne's work after his death.[10]

Like Montaigne, whom he credits with creating a breach—introducing "heterology, asymmetry, and infinity"—in the tradition, Derrida had a cat, one of whose names was Sophia.[11] Both of them (Derrida "following" Montaigne here) introduce their feline companions in the context of autobiographical writing, inserting a differently valenced unknowingness into the Cartesian *cogito* with the phrase "qui suis-je?" ("Who am I?" and "Whom do I follow?"). Montaigne's feminine cat has agency, perhaps more than he does ("When I play with my cat, who knows if I am not a pastime to her more than she is to me?").[12] Derrida's (likewise feminine cat) watches him naked, padding through the house, but when he wonders who he is and who he is following, he makes explicit the abyssal heterological relations he detected implicitly in Montaigne's hymn to the friend by asking whether a cat might be, deep within the cat's eyes, his—the autobiographical I's—primary mirror, that reflection (with the aid of a psyche) that founds subjectivity in relation to an Other even before the subject can say "here I am."[13] Both men, in the notes of queer's rich dissonances, reach toward identification with and desire for an Other beyond the human, opening a path for a commingled animal subjectivity and sociality, and a new friendship tradition.

Both men also flirt with residual heterosexuality in their interspecific sociality. I suppose that's overdetermined when your companion is feline (and when male homosexuality sits in the murderous crosshairs of your culture), the very word fraught with centuries of feminine valorization and denigration. There is a lot of gender lore in the Basenji world too: they do better in different-sex pairs; dogs are goofy; bitches are . . . well, bitchy. I discovered a Freudian cliché about heterofemininity in my queer self, the fulfillment of a phallus-lacking woman's ambitious embodied aspirations in the possession of a son, although I recited to myself the ways that Biko was not human, not my child, not . . . mine. I fetishized his masculinity (he was not a "masculine" dog; I thought of him rather as a fey gay boy) through the possessive protectiveness (of me) conferred upon him by testosterone. I loved his balls (I understand why so many human men are reluctant to "cut" their intact male dogs). I reluctantly had him "neutered" at the age of two because others said he was dangerous intact. He did change then, no longer, at least in my impression, claiming me *in that way*, although his aggression did not. It was only much later in Maji's life that I had occasion to regret her hysterectomy because most of the physical manifestations of intactness seemed unpleasant to her (breeders detect a period of depression they call the blues after a bitch finishes her season, which in Basenjis is unusual in occurring only once a year and lasting a full month). But when I saw her sometimes taking responsibility for another dog, whether by disciplining (another friend's much bigger Labradoodle was thoroughly schooled into submission by Maji's growl, teeth hovering just over the Labradoodle's upturned throat) or by protecting, I felt sadness that she had never had puppies of her own.

Biko had sex with a bitch once, when he and she were puppies; a young man-woman couple brought their little girl to the beach while she was still fertile. Dogs go hormone-crazy around bitches in season; breeders often claim their dogs show better when the bitches are in "heat." Puppies don't really get the "tied" part of doggie sex (it must be so strange the first time, finding yourselves tied together, the effort to separate quite painful), so the man in the couple and I crouched together, each holding our own puppy while they finished the process (the semen sac gradually deflates). Puppies were born from this teenage coupling, and because Biko and the bitch were both purebred, their breeders/co-owners were happy and the story ended well. Maji never had sex with a dog, although she and Biko almost did during her first season. That's when I learned with astonishment how assiduously a bitch could court, repeatedly backing up into her dog to get him to mount her.

In these ways my gendered sexing haunted them or commingled with theirs, my identifications, desires, and kin networks entangled with them as sexed, gendered, and filiated, always haunted, as my imaginary is, by racial fantasies signaled by their Africanness (I'm thinking of *Fair Sex, Savage Dreams* here).[14] Their desires and pleasures, post-spay and post-neutering, were, like mine, sensual and embodied, if not sexual after the first year of their lives: food, especially treats, massages, sleep, the sun, other people. From sex to pleasure? Am I tracking here my trajectory or theirs? And was theirs, in their sudden hormonal subtraction, like mine in my more gradual one?

Who knew that I would understand what those feminist activists meant by "our bodies, our selves" through the becoming-together of two dogs and a human? Our bodies and our selves are continuous, coconstituted, and plural ("We are, constitutively, companion species," Haraway writes).[15] It's a worn-out cliché to say that nonhumans put humans in touch with their bodies, that they stand in for and repair the lack in human being introduced by so-called civilization. I've written about that in relation to racial ideologies of "carnivorous virility" and the prosthetic logic whereby dog-being supplements a perceived lost plenitude of masculine embodiment.[16] But the interspecific subjectivities and agencies of our commingled becoming fused us, perhaps reciprocally, in "the" body, that *pharmakon*, mortality's poison and its only life-giving condition (Circe, who changed humans into animals and back, was called *polypharmakos*—mistress of the magic of mortal becomings?). We lived bodily, queerly, the promise and commitment of the marriage vow "till death" that I always thought so morbid and so irredeemably imprisoning.

To commit is also to release, let go; send, throw, as when one commits ashes to the wind or a body to the ground. The day Maji died she was more lively than she had been of late. I wanted to wait; I felt rushed by the appointment we had made with the vet who was going to administer the drugs to kill her. I had just returned from being away; Maji had been several times to the ER so that she would not die while I was gone. The afternoon I spent with her was not enough. Her belly was misshapen by the tumor, and she was a little incontinent. When she finally settled down that afternoon, I took a picture. In the picture she looks so relaxed, so peaceful, so perfect, perhaps already dead, curled into the soft donut shape she always assumed when sleeping (see figure 5.1).

Later, she was moved and became agitated again. When someone opened the door, she alerted, as she always did, and as she did when the strange woman approached her to begin the dying process. Ever vigilant, always private, she died reluctantly surrounded by others. I had longer with Biko at the end. I wanted to taxidermy him (a strange colonial fantasy emerging?); he was my first, my most beautiful, my baby boy. The night before he died, I spent the evening watching television with the friend who had accompanied

FIGURE 5.1. Maji.

FIGURE 5.2. Biko.

me on the trip when I first brought Biko home at the age of eight or nine weeks. I have a photograph of him on the couch, resting against a pillow, gazing, I think, at me, but also elsewhere, not here (see figure 5.2). I think he is sad, or maybe in pain, and I think he wants to go. Whenever I look at this picture, I think of Roy Batty's dying soliloquy in *Blade Runner*.[17] He is holding a white dove; he is beautiful, and he is not human: "I've seen things you people wouldn't believe. . . . All those moments will be lost in time, like tears in rain. Time to die." I think too of the poem I return to like the synodic periods of the moon, Elizabeth Bishop's "One Art," and the rhythms of commitment that she, in her understated but chillingly absolute way, meters there.[18] She condenses memory, capacity, and the passage of time as though it were a piano lesson or a sort of scary skill to learn, like skydiving: "Then practice losing farther, losing faster: / places, and names, and where it was you meant / to travel. None of these will bring disaster." But in the typographical pause before the phrase that chokes me up (that intake of breath, that inaudible sob): "—Even losing you," and in the italicized imperative of the parenthetical command to the self that halts abruptly in a moment of hesitation, a moment of failure before yet another loss—"(*Write* it!)"—I conjure their ghosts.

NOTES

1   Levinas, "Interview."
2   Brown, *The Gifts of the Body*; Crimp, *Melancholia and Moralism*.
3   Dufourmantelle, *Power of Gentleness*.
4   Berlant, *Cruel Optimism*.
5   Haraway, *When Species Meet*, 95–132.
6   Ani DiFranco, "Bodily," *Educated Guess* (Righteous Babe Records, 2004).
7   Bray, *The Friend*.
8   Derrida, "The Politics of Friendship," 643; see also *The Politics of Friendship*.
9   Derrida, "The Politics of Friendship," 642.
10 Montaigne, "De L'Amitié" and "Of Friendship." For a discussion of Marie de Gournay and Montaigne, see Schachter, *Voluntary Servitude and the Erotics of Friendship*.
11 Derrida, "The Politics of Friendship," 644.
12 Montaigne, "Apologie de Raymond Sebond," 331. "Se jouer à" has a stronger meaning than being a pastime; it connotes meddling or fooling with.
13 Derrida, *The Animal That Therefore I Am*, 51.
14 Walton, *Fair Sex, Savage Dreams*.
15 Haraway, *The Companion Species Manifesto*, 2.
16 Freccero, "Carnivorous Virility, or Becoming-Dog."

17 *Blade Runner: The Final Cut*, dir. Ridley Scott (Warner Brothers, 2007, initial release 1982). Roy Batty, a replicant, was played by Rutger Hauer, who is reputed to have improvised the "Tears in Rain" monologue, also known as the C-Beams speech.
18 Bishop, "One Art."

BIBLIOGRAPHY

Berlant, Lauren. *Cruel Optimism*. Durham, NC: Duke University Press, 2011.

Bishop, Elizabeth. "One Art." In *The Complete Poems 1926–1979*. New York: Farrar, Straus and Giroux, 1979.

Bray, Alan. *The Friend*. Chicago: University of Chicago Press, 2006.

Brown, Rebecca. *The Gifts of the Body*. New York: Harper Perennial, 1995.

Crimp, Douglas. *Melancholia and Moralism: Essays on AIDS and Queer Politics*. Cambridge, MA: MIT Press, 2002.

Derrida, Jacques. "The Politics of Friendship." *Journal of Philosophy* 85, no. 11 (1988): 632–44.

Derrida, Jacques. *The Politics of Friendship*. Translated by George Collins. New York: Verso, 2006.

Derrida, Jacques. *The Animal That Therefore I Am*. Edited by Marie-Louise Mallet. Translated by David Willis. New York: Fordham University Press, 2008.

Dufourmantelle, Anne. *Power of Gentleness: Meditations on the Risk of Living*. Translated by Katherine Payne and Vincent Sallé. New York: Fordham University Press, 2018.

Freccero, Carla. "Carnivorous Virility, or Becoming-Dog." *Social Text* 29, no. 1 (2011): 177–95.

Haraway, Donna. *The Companion Species Manifesto: Dogs, People, and Significant Otherness*. Chicago: Prickly Paradigm, 2003.

Haraway, Donna. *When Species Meet*. Minneapolis: University of Minnesota Press, 2008.

Levinas, Emmanuel. "Interview." In *Animal Philosophy: Essential Readings in Continental Thought*, edited by Matthew Calarco and Peter Atterton, 49–50. London: Continuum, 2004.

Montaigne, Michel de. "Of Friendship." In *The Complete Essays of Montaigne*, translated by Donald Frame, 135–44. Stanford, CA: Stanford University Press, 1958. Reprinted in 1976.

Montaigne, Michel de. "Apologie de Raymond Sebond." In *Essais, Livre II*, edited by Alexandre Micha, 114–53. Paris: Garnier Flammarion, 1969.

Montaigne, Michel de. "De L'Amitié." In *Essais, Livre I*, edited by Alexandre Micha, 231–42. Paris: Garnier Flammarion, 1969.

Schachter, Marc D. *Voluntary Servitude and the Erotics of Friendship: From Classical Antiquity to Early Modern France*. New York: Ashgate, 2008.

Walton, Jean. *Fair Sex, Savage Dreams: Race, Psychoanalysis, Sexual Difference*. Durham, NC: Duke University Press, 2001.

6

NEVER BETTER

Queer Commitment Phobia in
Hanya Yanagihara's *A Little Life*

SCOTT HERRING

One of US marriage equality's "more profound benefits"—a phrase cited by retired Supreme Court senior associate justice Anthony Kennedy in his 2015 *Obergefell v. Hodges* majority opinion—is not solely more liberty but more sanity.[1] We can shrug off this assumption, but I query a warrant leading up to this landmark verdict: "psychological benefits" that advance longer life are a clear advantage of long-term relationality.[2] Though mentioned in both specialist and nonspecialist discourses, these linkages have largely gone unremarked in recent iterations of queer studies. Yet prior to the *Obergefell* verdict, researchers agreed that the psycho-physiological benefits of state-sanctioned same-sex coupling would match its legal returns. Late-modern marriage was thought to provide extensive health benefits (emotional, bio-medical, and psychotherapeutic) for both partners. For instance, one soci-ologist reported in 1973 that "data on psychological well-being uniformly indicate that the married, at least with regard to psychological variables, are better situated than the unmarried."[3] Tasked with addressing social ame-liorations that marriage would confer onto lesbians and gays, publications such as *American Journal of Public Health* and organizations such as the American Psychological Association agreed: like many lasting relations, they affirmed, same-sex marriage supposedly aids mental health, which aids longevity. This claim is an old saw not far removed from the shibboleth that one's associations should include intimates who "help them fight illness and depression, speed recovery, slow aging and prolong life."[4] Being married os-tensibly makes shared life for the better, given that "potential mental health benefits might incrementally accrue" over the days, weeks, and months of a long-term dyad.[5] "Good marriages," a Harvard Medical School affiliate opines, "promote health and longevity."[6]

I cook my introductory porridge just so because I want to mull over the implicit norms buttressing mental health claims for long-term partner-ships before, during, and after *Obergefell* via one recent case study, Hanya Yanagihara's novel *A Little Life* (2015). Coming in at 814 pages in paperback, her book is not easy to plot, but Yanagihara has offered a SparkNotes-type summary: "The reader would begin thinking it a fairly standard post-college New York City book . . . and then, as the story progressed, would sense it becoming something else, something unexpected."[7] True to this rundown, *A Little Life* starts off as a tale about "a foursome" of men—Jude St. Francis, Willem Ragnarsson, Malcolm Irvine, and Jean-Baptiste (JB) Marion—who achieve jaw-dropping professional prominence during their respective careers.[8] Gradually, their stories funnel into a tale of a twosome, Jude and Willem, who together negotiate the emotional and psychological legacy of Jude's sexual abuse while an orphaned child and young adult. Readers have questioned the novel's treatment of race and gender (one character wrongly considers Jude "post-sexual, post-racial, post-identity, post-past" [107]); its reliance on sex-trafficking panics; and its aesthetic sin of dipping into misery-literature conventions given that its lead character kills himself at age fifty-three after decades of self-harming.[9] Still, Yanagihara is correct. What begins as a tale of East Coast privilege morphs into "something un-expected" for an author who claims that she is "not sure there's a certain Asian-American aesthetic the way there is definitely a queer aesthetic"—to be precise, a damning account of late-modern therapeutic cultures and the relational norms of LGBTQ psychosocial well-being that inform a verdict such as *Obergefell*.[10]

I return later to how Yanagihara's deformation of the genre of misery lit aids this achievement, and I say from my start that previous writings leave me unlikely to defend elite queer men with multimillion-dollar homesteads in Tribeca. But I think that her book is astute at thinking athwart modern therapeutic ideals housed within lengthy marriages, friends forever, and years-long relations anchored in the helping professions. Tracking how Jude navigates these interlocking bonds over several unspecified decades, *A Little Life* spends hundreds of pages warping long-term commitment's hypothetical long-term allowances. In doing so it counters prescriptive benefits of enduring relationships, married or no, at the same time that it never outright dismisses long-term relationality. This, then, is my thesis: in the wake of its fictive homonormativities, the book negatively appraises long-term commitments when wedded to psychotherapeutic dictates. Yanagihara's is a life lesson that we need to commit to heart, and one, as I later discuss, that recent forays into queer mad studies have also been trying to teach us. This argument may seem counterintuitive to those who celebrate her book as an anthem to male friendship, alternative kinship, and intimate same-sex domesticity, but I believe that the last thing this novel affirms is marriage as a vessel for institutional directives toward long-term self-improvement. Although Jude is racially unspecified, it never lets you forget that queers of all colors and socioeconomic backgrounds still have to dodge—rather than embrace—institutionalized commitments of all sorts, about which its protagonist in particular and *A Little Life* in general remain positively phobic.

[I]

Why? Although I recognize that it can be insufficient to invoke authorial intention, Yanagihara offers some clues across several extended interviews published soon after *A Little Life*'s release, and I consider these remarks both valuable literary self-criticism and incisive queer-of-color theory. In one chat with *Kirkus*, "Yanagihara says . . . that the idea of getting married 'is one I personally find squirm-inducing. My friends and I just don't believe in it as an institution.'"[11] Talking to the *Guardian*, she promotes "a different kind of adulthood" that is centered on the "primacy of friendship."[12] A number of queer critics have made similar comments in the not-so-recent past, as did Michel Foucault in his 1981 *Gai Pied* interview "Friendship as a Way of Life."[13] Advocating for alternative modes of relational being in the wake of the *Obergefell* decision, Yanagihara also prioritizes long-standing nonmarried intimacies over state-recognized marriage relations, as does her novel. "As you got older," thinks Willem about Jude, "you realized that really, there were very few people you truly wanted to be around for more than a few days at a time, and yet here you were with someone you wanted to be around for years" (590). Refusing to dismiss the pleasures of lifelong affections, the novel does not reduce them in a marriage template. Yanagihara and her book instead cultivate a different mode of long-term interpersonal relations that does not cast the nonmarried as immature or the married as more psychologically developed.

A quarter through its plot, the novel formalizes Yanagihara's remarks in a pointed exchange between Malcolm's father and Willem. The latter worries that "the amount of time he spent with JB and Malcolm and, especially, Jude became evidence instead of his fundamental immaturity" (255). After Willem parts with his girlfriend, Philippa, "Mr. Irvine, hearing that they had broken up, shook his head (this had been at Flora's baby shower). 'You boys are really turning into a bunch of Peter Pans,' he said. 'Willem, what are you? Thirty-six? . . . Don't you think you guys should stop clinging to one another and get serious about adulthood?'" (256). Willem then expounds on his supposedly underdeveloped friendships in an interior monologue that mirrors Yanagihara's various interviews: "But how was one to be an adult? Was couplehood truly the only appropriate option (But then, a sole option was no option at all)" (256). Questioning hierarchies of maturity/immaturity and adult/youth, he asks of himself and, by extension, of the reader: "How was a friendship any more codependent than a relationship? Why was it admirable when you were twenty-seven but creepy when you were thirty-seven? Why wasn't friendship as good as a relationship? Why wasn't it even better? It was two people who remained together, day after day, bound . . . by the shared agreement to keep going, the mutual dedication to a union that could never be codified" (257). Shirking off the social stigma of prioritizing friends over married life in the prime of his adulthood, Willem emphasizes the emotional sustenance that nonmarried bonds offer. To repeat an observation made in this essay's introduction, the novel does not outright reject long-term commitments even though its narrative hinges on an antimarriage plot. It instead recognizes a relational hierarchy further congealed in the last third of the twentieth century that devalues friendship at the expense of marriage. The fact that Willem prods himself with these questions is historically telling in and of itself.

That said, whereas they commence as a critique of marriage's affective and relational limitations, Yanagihara's remarks sometimes shift into musings on proper mental health across late-modern relationality. In an *Electric Literature* interview headlined "A Stubborn Lack of Redemption," for instance, the conversation swerves from "friendship between two men" to what her interviewer terms "the limits of therapy."[14] When told, "You resist the comfortable narrative arc of abuse followed by healing," Yanagihara responds by saying that "one of things I wanted to do with this book is create a character who never gets better."[15] Yanagihara proposes that her "book is, obviously, a psychological book, but not one about psychology," but I think she undersells this interpretation. "I don't believe in it—talk therapy," she later declares. "One of the things that makes me most suspicious about the field is its insistence that life is always the answer . . . psychology, and psychiatry, insists that life is the meaning of life, so to speak; that if one can't be repaired, one can at least find a way to stay alive, to keep growing older."[16] Refusing to pathologize her main character, Yanagihara makes the convincing case that her book is not solely about extended friendships or extended lives but about how these lived relations must negotiate compulsions to long-term psychological betterment—compulsions that also mandate longevity for longevity's sake.[17] In tandem with her criticism of marriage as a developmental model of relationality, Yanagihara queries psychodynamic psychology's impulse to mature its subjects as they age over time thanks to whatever talking cure might be on hand.

As much as she slates the developmental norms of adulthood, then, Yanagihara is equally chary about any psychotherapeutic propulsion toward maturational development across late-modern life spans. She contends that she's "not convinced" by "the therapist's role to make one's life better, at least in some measure, through self-examination."[18] With this critique she also worries the presumptions of long-term psychodynamic psychotherapy (LTPP). She acknowledges that her remarks may overgeneralize as her criticism conflates schools of thought such as Freudian psychoanalysis, Kleinian and Winnicottian object relations theories, Kohutian self psychology, cognitive behavioral therapies, and feminist-oriented psychotherapies. Nevertheless, her disbelief centers on talk therapy, which can theoretically encompass any of these psychological practices and experientially occur across a lifetime.[19] Freud, after all, signaled talk therapy's elasticity in "Analysis Terminable and Interminable" (1937), where he laments "the inconveniently long duration of analytic treatment" at the same time that he delimits some of his therapies to "a few months."[20]

Although race and ethnicity go largely unannounced in these comments— the *Electric Literature* interview does address Yanagihara's status of writing as an Asian American female writer—it is also important to mark a longer history of reservation about the psychoanalytic and psychotherapeutic analytic on behalf of minority populations. Although JB states that "we don't know what race [Jude] is, we don't know anything about him" (107), Yanagihara's comments parallel critiques of the modern therapeutic function that historians such as Nayan Shah and Warwick Anderson have registered in their respective histories of Asian and Asian American communities and their fraught negotiations of colonial and imperial health imperatives. For example, Shah writes in *Contagious Divides* that "with the formation of contrasting categories of normal and deviant, medical therapy and public health instruction emphasized a repertoire of habits and civilizing norms to ensure health."[21] The *Electric Literature* interview confirms, widens, and updates this historical finding with careful attention to Yanagihara's commitment to lead characters whom she refuses to racially or ethnically disambiguate.

Arguing ethically for "giv[ing] a suicidal patient permission, as it were, to die," Yanagihara's fiction realizes these insights across race largely through her protagonist, Jude.[22] Her interview themes saturate *A Little Life* in terms of his characterological nondevelopment. Although a social worker promises a fifteen-year-old Jude a different future after years of horrific abuse, her prophecy proves false. Even after he partners with Willem, Jude gets caught in "a series of dreary patterns: sex, cutting, this, that" (783). "He has the sense, once again," after Willem dies in a motor-vehicle accident and Jude stops eating, "that his life is moving backward, that it is becoming smaller and smaller" (764). During and after these events he often refuses psychological treatment and kills himself soon after restarting therapy with his shrink, Dr. Loehmann. Confirming Yanagihara's interview comments, Jude's suicide answers a question that he asks of himself—"was his life even his to choose to live any longer?" (780). *A Little Life* thus confirms a dead-serious one-liner in Lauren Berlant's *Cruel Optimism*: "a fantasy from the middle of disrepair doesn't add up to repair."[23]

Interestingly, the novel's countertherapeutic stance applies not only to Jude's self-relation over fifty-three years of living but also to his ongoing institutional relationships within the helping professions as a queer crip. I have in mind Jude's encounters with his primary-care physician and friend, Andy, an orthopedic surgeon who exemplifies long-term care at its most literal. Until Jude tells Willem the details of his past life, Andy has the most intimate knowledge of Jude's cutting, past traumas, and suicidal ideations. He also fits well into the doctor-as-savior motif that the novel undermines, given his moralizing stance on Jude's noncompliance. One example: Andy laments Jude's "perplexing and

infuriating unwillingness to take proper care of himself, his maddening refusal to see a therapist, and his bizarre reluctance to take pain medication that
would probably improve his quality of life" (155). Another example: after Jude
again self-harms, Andy asserts his right to institutionalize him:

> "You're sick, Jude," he says, in a low, frantic voice. "You're crazy. This is
> crazy behavior. This is behavior that could and should get you locked
> away for years. You're sick, you're sick and you're crazy and you need
> help."
>
> "Don't you *dare* call me crazy," [Jude] yells, "don't you *dare*. I'm not,
> *I'm not*."
>
> . . . "You can't *legally* do that, Andy," he shouts, and everything spins
> before him. "I'll sue you for so much that you won't even—"
>
> "Better check your recent case law, *counselor*," Andy hisses back at
> him. "*Rodriguez versus Mehta*. Two years ago. If a patient who's been in-
> voluntarily committed attempts serious self-injury again, the patient's
> doctor has the right—no, the *obligation*—to inform the patient's part-
> ner or next of kin, whether that patient has fucking given consent or
> not." (580)

Rodriguez versus Mehta is a court case that Yanagihara invents (and racial-
izes with surnames that invoke, respectively, Latinx and South Asian populations). "Locked away for years" is likewise hyperbolic given the state of
New York's current inpatient rights. Yet it is hard not to read this exchange as
meta-commentary on therapeutic imperatives and the juridico-institutional
lattice that entangles both Jude and his doctor. Andy is by no means the
primary antagonist of *A Little Life*—Brother Luke and Dr. Traylor, who each
abuse a young Jude into his present state along with myriad other unnamed
men, share that title—but the text treats Andy's well-meaning intentions
with no small amount of reservation.

And for good reason: primary care may be one basis of their relationship,
but so too are Andy's repeated threats to commit Jude to a psychiatric ward.
To his credit, Andy may be invoking the state of New York's mandated legal
protocol under Article 9 of its Mental Hygiene Law. To his own credit, Jude
is terrified of Andy's legal power, given his physician's repeated references to
involuntary commitment: "'You can't do that,' he'd said, furious himself now,
although he knew Andy could: he had looked up the laws of involuntary
commitment in New York State, and they were not in his favor" (156). In
order to pressure Jude into compliance, Andy uses threats of institutionalization and talk therapy as a bargaining chip. He lashes out at Jude, yelling at

him that his "'utter refusal to listen to anyone about anything that concerns your health or well-being is either a pathological case of self-destructiveness or it's a huge fuck-you to the rest of us'" (157). However, Jude distrusts Andy's well-meaning push toward his well-being, insisting that "'there's something incredibly manipulative about you threatening to *commit* me whenever I disagree with you'" (157). Jude's logic is really not off base. This queer is rightly terrified of long-term commitment to the psychiatric ward for any number of unspecified years.

As I have also suggested, it doesn't get that much better for Jude with the aid of his long-term partner, Willem. Andy is initially central to this relationship as he goads Willem into facilitating Jude's self-improvement. At a chance meeting between the two, the good doctor informs Willem, "'If you do this, you should go in prepared to make some sort of commitment to him, and to being with him, because you're right: you're not going to be able to just fool around and then get out of it. . . . I don't think I'm betraying anything when I say that it's going to be very tough for him to be intimate with you, and you're going to have to be really patient with him'" (504). Andy offers Willem therapy-speak that imagines Jude's psychological improvement over an extended time frame precisely within the parameters of a long-term relational commitment. In tandem with the popularization of therapeutic discourses, he also casts Jude as a *commitment-phobe* when he describes his patient as someone who finds intimacy difficult, if not impossible. As an aside, I note the fairly recent historical novelty of this "pathological case": the term *commitment-phobe* was popularized in the United States thanks to Steven Carter and Julia Sokol's *Men Who Can't Love: How to Recognize a Commitmentphobic Man before He Breaks Your Heart* (1987). Earlier instances of this type appeared in Maxine Schnall's conservative and antifeminist treatise *Limits: A Search for New Values* (1981), which cites the term more than a half decade earlier in its criticism of "the commitmentphobia of the liberated lifestyle" that emerged during and after women's liberation movements.[24] For the purposes of my argument, this conversation about Jude's commitment phobia between his long-term physician and his long-term partner is where the "Peter Pan syndrome" disparaged by Malcolm's father overlaps with what the most recent edition of *Diagnostic and Statistical Manual of Mental Disorders* refers to as "avoidant personality disorder," whereby "interpersonal intimacy is often difficult."[25] Both psychopathological states appear to be relational aberrations that damper normative adult psychological well-being. Both manifest themselves in anxious discourses surrounding Jude's fears of intimacy.

True to Yanagihara's interview observations, however, *A Little Life* turns on a double meaning of commitment phobia: Jude's fears of interpersonal intimacy *and* his fears of institutionalization for not following standardized psychological protocol.[26] Although the novel confirms the ongoing psychophysiological effects of his sexual, mental, and physical abuse, it never wishes away Jude's commitment phobia regarding the psych ward. Unlike Andy, the novel is as interested in his terrors of psychiatric hospitalization and his fears of what Foucault referred to, rather abstractly, as "the apparatus of rectification."[27] Indeed, *A Little Life* figures Andy as a mouthpiece for a popular psychology that Yanagihara finds potentially harmful and deploys this physician as an exemplar of therapeutic banalities expounded by professional experts and late-modern American culture at large.

For a time, it appears as if Willem will function similarly, yet unlike Jude's physician, he eventually concludes that "he knew he would never be able to cure him" (647). Following Andy's advice, Willem initially longs to fix his lover. Like Andy, he wants Jude to do long-term therapy. At the start of their coupling his directives toward Jude uncannily parallel those of Andy: "'I either want you to voluntarily commit yourself, or I want you to start seeing Dr. Loehmann twice a week'" (606). Yet in the last third of the novel it becomes an unspoken rule that these two lovers, after years of shared life, will never go into couple therapy to make "their own unit" for the better (300). *A Little Life* is remarkably nonprescriptive about this decision. Jude remains the same; he and Willem do not seek out a talking cure; there is little if any joint investment in recovery. Theirs is instead a relational model informed by homonormative privilege yet untethered from social norms of psychotherapeutic betterment.

Fascinatingly, Willem's ruminations on his partner's refusal to heal also prompt him to expound on the deficits of his own psychotherapy. When he recounts his psychotherapy sessions, his point of view echoes Yanagihara's: "the sinister pedantry of therapy, its suggestion that life was somehow reparable, that there existed a societal norm and that the patient was being guided toward conforming to it" (644). This description is a skeleton key to understanding the novel's horizons of expectation. Long-term therapy, the novel argues through one of its major characters, can be as normative and unnecessary as it can be beneficial, and after one of his own sessions Willem admits that "the truth was, he didn't want Idriss to try to diagnose what was wrong with his relationship. He didn't want to be told how to repair it" (645). Notably, it is not exclusively Jude who refuses therapy, but also his partner who defies his own. Even as the novel features kind social workers (Ana), supportive psychotherapists (Idriss, Dr. Loehmann), and well-intentioned physicians (Andy) alongside sadistic psychiatrists (Dr. Traylor), it remains mistrustful of the overarching apparatus of psychology and its guiding principles of long-term amelioration. As such, *A Little Life* ironically confirms Freud's foundational observations on "unchangeable, fixed and rigid" patients who resist "analysis as a whole, and thus . . . recovery."[28] Freud found these incorrigibles here and there in clinical practice and especially among "very old people."[29] Yanagihara finds them in contemporary queer relations across the age spectrum.

To return to the interviews with which this section began: when asked if her book "was something of a manifesto for an alternative way of living as an adult," Yanagihara answered favorably. "It is a different version of adulthood," she confirmed and then described it as "one that is somehow considered childish in one sense, like something you pass through on the way to something else, whether that something is marriage or parenthood or whatever."[30] It is precisely these extended "whatever" relations to which I draw attention. Amid its critique of homonormative arrangements such as same-sex marriage and its confirmation of homonormative arrangements such as apolitical queer habitus, her contradictory novel questions developmental norms embedded within committed adult relations. Championing Willem and Jude's shared life, her narrative toys with long-term relational well-being only to undermine this ideal by its close. This is why, I believe, the penultimate chapter of *A Little Life* ends with a pitiless tease: "'Jude,' says Dr. Loehmann. 'You've come back.' He takes a breath. 'Yes,' he says. 'I've decided to stay'" (794). Two pages later we learn that Jude kills himself by injecting air into a vein. *A Little Life* refuses to commit to long-term healing even as it advances longish intimacies. Like Foucault in 1981, it offers the queerness of friendship—of nonmarried bonds—as a viable way of life. Unlike Foucault, it thinks to the side of this ideal and diagnoses the psychotherapeutic norms that barnacle onto this relation's more recent historical iterations.

[II]

I have largely addressed the novel's thematic content via Yanagihara's interpretive framings, but its formal strategies also confirm its antipsychotherapeutic stance. Indeed, my last example suggests that *A Little Life* is conscious of its rather experimental narrative techniques as it tantalizes its reader with an optimistic ending only to foreclose this possibility. Following Yanagihara's

lead, I have thus far interpreted *A Little Life* as a "psychological book"—
as psychological realism by a self-identified Asian American author—and
meta-references to realism certainly traverse this novel. Hammering home
its generic self-awareness, the novel mentions that Willem stars in a movie
titled *Henry & Edith* as "Henry James, at the beginning of his friendship
with Edith Wharton" (646).

Yet when we recall the novel's fictive citation of the *Rodriguez versus Mehta*
case, its fidelity to Jamesian verisimilitude is questionable as it repeatedly
extends beyond realistic conventions and into a "bizarre mix of *bildungsro-
man*, misery memoir, [Jonathan] Franzen-ish lit, and family saga."[31] Several
critics observed this hodgepodge, including Garth Greenwell, who found
that "it's clear that the book is after something other than strict realism,"
and Stephanie Hayes, who found the plot "psychologically unrealistic yet
often emotionally compelling."[32] Many reviewers read this as unintentional,
but Greenwell did not, and I believe that he is on to something, especially
when we consider that Yanagihara's previous novel, *The People in the Trees*,
uses magical realism to depict a Pacific islander population of Ivu'ivu "who
were living far beyond a normal lifespan: twenty, fifty, even a hundred years
longer" by eating a species of turtle that does not exist.[33] How this generic
mishmash further facilitates new iterations of long-term adult relations and
compounds the novel's guardedness regarding therapeutic psychology and
institutional commitment is this section's central concern.

A passing reference to a later twentieth-century movement in aesthetic
realism—photorealism—helps us accomplish this task. In the last eighth of
the novel, the narrator describes a painting that JB composes of Willem,
which "is by far the most sharply photorealistic painting JB has produced in
years, the colors rich and dense, the brushstrokes that made Willem's hair
feathery-fine" (769). Alluding to the postmodernist movement, the narrator
situates JB within an aesthetic tradition whereby "reality is made to look so
overpoweringly real as to make it pure illusion: through the basically magical means of point-for-point precisionist rendering the actual is portrayed
as being so real that it doesn't exist."[34] Photorealism (or superrealism) ap-
proximates reality so intimately that faux verisimilitude becomes its defining feature: "Photo Realism is not only unconcerned with realism, it is actively involved with artificiality."[35] Although its characters may literally and
figuratively appear to perform Jamesian modes of psychological interiority,
A Little Life also challenges them with a literary superrealism that may seem
Franzenian but is anything but. After all, there is no slow recovery of the
type that one often finds in *The Corrections* (2001), *Freedom* (2010), or *Purity*

(2015): no Enid Lambert who decides to take her older self in a new direction, no Patty Berglund who repairs her long-term relationship with Walter, no Purity Tyler who breaks free from generational cycles of familial conflict.

To their chagrin, many lay readers detected this superrealism and lamented that the novel seems incredible, commenting that character actions and even the novel's settings are too much of a stretch. Several critics likewise bewailed that there are no obvious allusions to discernible queer subculture, only one citation of AIDS, and no citation of 9/11.[36] Addressing "the issue of plausibility" and "the absence of any historical specificity," a *Bookanista* interviewer writes that "to say that Yanagihara lays it on thick is something of an understatement; one can't help but question whether such systemic and repetitive abuse could happen outside the confines of fiction." Yanagihara meets these complaints with simple agreement, as if they were the point but not the problem: "There are moments in the book when it's not believable exactly."[37]

Given that "Yanagihara's always been upfront about the novel's artificiality," how do the textual politics of this deliberately implausible superrealism relate to the novel's thematic concern with well-being over the long haul?[38] In *Electric Literature* Yanagihara speaks to this question, recalling that during the eighteen months she composed her experimental novel, "I tried to meld the psychological specificity of a naturalistic contemporary novel with the suspended-time quality of a fable."[39] In her theorization of *A Little Life*'s post-postmodern fabulation, there lies "a stubborn lack of redemption [given] that happiness, usually in the form of a marriage or a reunion, seems almost meaningless, an unsatisfying answer to outlandish feats of survival."[40] With this observation in mind, we see how her novel's calculated implausibility does not buoy but actually undermines psychological betterment. For hundreds of pages that record almost thirty years, the book tracks the flatness—the lack of self-examination—of men who do not grow emotionally sounder as they age. They instead appear in psychologically "suspended time" rather than headed for happier or emotionally healthier endings with their interpersonal psychological growth stalling out.

Faced with a novel filled with characters both entirely plausible and completely implausible, a literary scholar could claim with confidence that *A Little Life* inaugurates a genre of superreal psychological realism, or psychological unrealism, that inhabits yet stymies the contemporary genre of misery literature for queer ends. Popularized in the twenty-first century, misery literature typically focuses on the unconscionable damage done to a child or teenager, yet "the tale always ends in some form of escape or redemption" with "a happy ending."[41] Although it traffics in misery-lit conventions (as some reviewers noted), *A Little Life*'s formal innovations nonetheless torque the genre with its fantastic implausibility. In so doing it also refutes the historical genre of long-term psychological betterment as well as contemporary expectations for popular literature to advance self-improvement.[42] As its lead character undercuts psychological mandates of mental health care, *A Little Life* does the same for narratological and generic conventions of the psychological novel.

These generic manipulations are of further aesthetic interest—and of cultural note—not solely for queer lives after *Obergefell*, especially when we consider an even wider arc of LGBTQ social and literary history in the United States. However conservative its privileged habitus, the book's generic noncompliance, nonpsychological characterology, and unrealistic narrative strategies connect with iterations of queer and lesbian feminist US politics thanks to its formalized suspicion toward therapeutic well-being and ingrained queer fears over institutionalization. When Yanagihara states in a *TribLive* interview that "the book is not meant as any sort of therapy," there is a faint echo of what American studies scholar Abram J. Lewis, in a brilliant essay on queer antipsychiatry movements in the 1970s, refers to as "considerable skepticism about the redemptive power of psychiatric sanction" and its inclination to "elaborate rather than curtail the psychiatrization of human behavior."[43] Tracing "growth in antipsychiatric and 'mad pride' organizing" as well as "alternatives to normative rehabilitation" in the 1970s, he finds that lesbian feminists "often embraced dysfunction and maladaption, positing affective and cognitive deviance as central to lesbian experience."[44] *A Little Life*'s one percenters are their heirs as it launches its singular queer/of color mad character studies.

Stating this last claim is by no means to discount the good work done over the years by LGBTQ psychologists, counselors, or their allies. But it does help us comprehend how Jude's initial fears of *relational* queer commitment are inextricable from historically contiguous fears of *institutional* queer commitment that the novel aesthetically formalizes with its "bizarre" generic innovations. Despite its narrative's historical nonspecificity, *A Little Life* nonetheless embeds itself within an extended queer history of psychiatric policing that perhaps goes beyond the 1970s, given my earlier citation of Shah. In another intriguing bit of queer literary and social history that complements Lewis's findings, the twinned definitions of long-term commitment as relation and institutionalization that the novel underscores went hand in hand for some proto-queers in the turn-of-the-twentieth-century United States. I especially have in mind one ur-narrative of lesbian identity formation, the mental and criminal case of Alice Mitchell, an elite white southerner who murdered her lover Freda Ward in 1891, was found insane, and was committed to the Western Mental Health Institute, where she died in 1898. Both Mitchell and Ward longed for what we would now term a long-term commitment. "Please," Ward pleaded in an 1891 love letter to Mitchell, "be perfectly happy when you marry me, for I am true to you, and will always be forever."[45] Tragically, after Mitchell slashed Ward's throat, her lawyers convincingly argued for "commitment to the asylum with very little chance of eventual discharge," which Lisa Duggan annotates in her overview of this case as "a fate likely to amount to lifetime incarceration."[46]

Mitchell's institutional commitment and queer desire for marriage to Ward may seem an unnecessary historical detour, but consider the long fictional arc that connects Alice's queer little institutionalized life and Jude St. Francis's. The former, Duggan notes, became mythologized in modern sexological literatures and Western LGBTQ fiction as a deviant model for perhaps the most famous queer character in the twentieth century: Stephen Gordon in Radclyffe Hall's *The Well of Loneliness* (1928), a novel that both sanctifies and psychopathologizes its "abnormal" protagonist.[47] But also recall how queer commitment phobias—inseparable from queer fears of psychology and psychiatry—would later course through liberation-era literature such as Rita Mae Brown's *Rubyfruit Jungle* (1973). Coediting the 2000 collection *Take Out: Queer Writing from Asian Pacific America*, Yanagihara proves no stranger to the Western LGBTQ canon and its contemporary queer-of-color writings, and *A Little Life*'s psychological unrealism embeds itself within this literature that stretches back to Mitchell's long-term commitment to Ward and her long-term commitment in Tennessee. Like other fictions that precede it, the novel reconfirms that institutionalization fears have been at the heart of modern queer commitments as much as queer commitments are now at the heart of late-modern legal institutionalization.

To conclude: through the lens of twenty-first-century homonormativity, Yanagihara critiques long-standing therapeutic cultures of "psychic conformity."[48] In so doing *A Little Life* cautions contemporary queers across races, genders, and class divides that the mental well-being promised with longevity and legalized coupling may not be for all. Foreshadowing the *Obergefell* ruling, Jack Halberstam has noted that "we create longevity as the most desirable future. We applaud the pursuit of long life (under any circumstances) and pathologize modes of living that show little or no concern for longevity."[49] Some characters in the novel such as Harold confirm the object of Halberstam's criticism: "'Things get broken, and sometimes they get repaired, and in most cases, you realize that no matter what gets damaged, life rearranges itself to compensate for your loss, sometimes wonderfully'" (152–53). But most do not. I started my reading of Yanagihara's novel by citing her critiques of marriage equality that parallel many a queer theorist. I continued by showing how its manipulations of psychological realism and resistances to psychological discourses also align with longevity critiques—yet another normative mode of the long term. In lieu of the many societal norms that *Obergefell* legalized, *A Little Life* insists that psychological life doesn't always improve for queers. It shirks what Antonio Viego has called "the narcotizing effects of the notion of the Good."[50]

This novel asks us to think outside marriage with friendship alternatives, for sure. But the narrative also conjures other queer forms of relationality—if not long-term survival—with its antirepair and antirecovery stance that understandably and intentionally turns off some readers. A snake in the grass of LGBTQ mental health, the book is not titled *A Longer Life* for good reason: it presents a singular form of the long term over whatever may count for the long haul. Steeped in LGBTQ literary history and manipulating aesthetic genres from photorealism to misery literature, its unrealism finds that considerations of marriage or long-term relations as a developmental model for psychological well-being can turn themselves into social psychopathologies. Although I do not endorse wholesale the novel's positions on therapy—a Winnicottian in the American Midwest saved my psychic life twenty years ago—I nonetheless agree with its scrutiny of marriage as a boon to long-term wellness. I appreciate this novel as a tough read, and I find its insights motivating as we continue to explore "the complexity of normativity"—especially as longevity promises to further entwine with legalized marriage to become a technology of relational and psychological perfectability.[51]

Like Yanagihara, I am no longevity expert, nor am I that great at marriage. I know knotty questions remain about those of us who continue to survive or outlive the ones we love. This is why many of us walk for suicide-prevention awareness and staff hotlines for hours on end. But we should also attend to the resistances of unhealed queers like Jude. We should advocate something besides institutional commitment for maladaptive behaviors, even if that something has little personal profit and especially, contra Justice Kennedy, if it has less profound benefits.

1 *Obergefell v. Hodges*, 576 U.S. 644 (2015), available at https://supreme.justia.com /cases/federal/us/576/14-556.

2 Wright, LeBlanc, and Badgett, "Same-Sex Legal Marriage," 339.

3 Gove, "Sex, Marital Status, and Mortality," 45.

4 Tara Parker-Hope, "What Are Friends For? A Longer Life," *New York Times*, April 20, 2009, www.nytimes.com/2009/04/21/health/21well.html.

5 Wright, LeBlanc, and Badgett, "Same-Sex Legal Marriage," 345.

6 Harvard Health Publishing, "Marriage and Men's Health," 3.

7 Hanya Yanagihara, "How I Wrote My Novel: Hanya Yanagihara's *A Little Life*," *Vulture*, April 28, 2015, www.vulture.com/2015/04/how-hanya-yanagihara-wrote -a-little-life.html.

8 Yanagihara, *A Little Life*, 200. Page references to this novel will hereafter be given parenthetically in the text.

9 For these critiques, see Sean McCann, "'I'm So Sorry': *A Little Life* and the Socialism of the Rich," *Post45: Peer Reviewed*, http://post45.research.yale.edu /2016/06/im-so-sorry-a-little-life-and-the-socialism-of-the-rich; Alex Preston, "*A Little Life* by Hanya Yanagihara Review—Relentless Suffering," *Guardian*, August 18, 2015, on how the novel reads "stridently ahistorical"; Greenwell, "*A Little Life*," which observes that "HIV is conspicuously absent from the book's weirdly ahistorical New York City"; Michaud, "The Subversive Brilliance of 'A Little Life'"; and K. Thompson, "'A Little Life' and the Nature of Tragedy Porn," December 16, 2015, www.amazon.com/gp/customer-reviews/R1Q7YX3CA20NK8 /ref=cm_cr_arp_d_viewpnt?ie=UTF8&ASIN=0804172706#R1Q7YX3CA20NK8.

10 Yanagihara, "On Writing a Great, Gay Book," 59. Framing her aesthetic theoriza-tions as such, Yanagihara joins Lowe, "Heterogeneity," in the latter's call "to avoid this homogenizing of Asian Americans" (533); Chuh and Shimakawa, "Intro-duction," on "the eccentric perspective of the Asian diaspora" (7); and Espiritu, "Home, Borders, and Possibilities," on "complex personhood" (610).

11 Hanya Yanagihara, interview with Claiborne Smith, in "Best Books of 2015: Hanya Yanagihara," *Kirkus*, November 16, 2015, www.kirkusreviews.com/features /hanya-yanagihara.

12 Tim Adams, "Hanya Yanagihara: 'I Wanted Everything Turned Up a Little Too High,'" *Guardian*, July 26, 2015, www.theguardian.com/books/2015/jul/26/hanya -yanagihara-i-wanted-everything-turned-up-a-little-too-high-interview-a-little-life.

13 See Warner, *The Trouble with Normal*; Franke, *Wedlocked*; Eng, *The Feeling of Kinship*; and Foucault, "Friendship as a Way of Life."

14 Adalena Kavanagh, "A Stubborn Lack of Redemption: An Interview with Hanya Yanagihara, Author of *A Little Life*," *Electric Literature*, May 21, 2015, https:// electricliterature.com/a-stubborn-lack-of-redemption-an-interview-with-hanya -yanagihara-author-of-a-little-life-c6b7523d0b9f.

15 Kavanagh, "A Stubborn Lack of Redemption." Framed as such, this novel partici-pates in and departs from a queer Asian American literary tradition that Stephen Hong Sohn refers to as "the *survival plot*" (*Inscrutable Belongings*, 65). For a discussion of the plotting of modern/ist queer betterment, see Matz, *Modernist*

Time Ecology. For a psychoanalytically oriented rumination on Asian American suicides that incorporates the literature of Monique Truong, see Eng and Han, *Racial Melancholia, Racial Dissociation*.

16 Kavanagh, "A Stubborn Lack of Redemption." In a complementary interview, Yanagihara contends that her novel charts "the realization that we really can't be saved, that the idea of being saved itself is sort of a false conceit" (Trisha Ping, "Interviews: Hanya Yanagihara," *BookPage*, March 2015, https://bookpage.com /interviews/17890-hanya-yanagihara#.W8i-h2hKiUk).

17 Her novel is thus a fellow traveler to Piepzna-Samarasinha's *Care Work*, which argues for thinking beyond any "ableist model of cure" (231) and wonders "what might happen if I and we experimented with the dichotomy of fixed or failed" (236).

18 Kavanagh, "A Stubborn Lack of Redemption."

19 Late-modern psychotherapeutic practice has sometimes truncated this time line. Whereas one practitioner, Joseph D. Lichtenberg, in *"The Talking Cure,"* finds that "six years is probably the average time for a successful analysis, but *many* successful analyses take longer" (60), other publications, such as Alpert and Bowman's *Be Fearless: Change Your Life in 28 Days*, promise much quicker fixes.

20 Freud, "Analysis Terminable and Interminable," 234, 216.

21 Shah, *Contagious Divides*, 46. See also Anderson, Jenson, and Keller, *Unconscious Dominions*, and Anderson, *Colonial Pathologies*.

22 Kavanagh, "A Stubborn Lack of Redemption."

23 Berlant, *Cruel Optimism*, 266.

24 Schnall, *Limits*, 157.

25 American Psychiatric Association, "Avoidant Personality Disorder," 673.

26 Given this insight, it is hard not to read the novel as a literary counterpart to ongoing debates over institutionalization in works such as Miller and Hanson, *Committed*; Szasz, *Coercion as Cure*; and Saks, *Refusing Care*, which argues that "we risk forcing treatment" with regards to "upsettingly deviant" acts such as self-injury (76).

27 Foucault, *Abnormal*, 328.

28 Freud, "Analysis Terminable and Interminable," 242, 239. See also Rose, "Something Amiss," on "obdurancy (another form of militancy), the mind's best defense against any demand that it might transform itself" (394).

29 Freud, "Analysis Terminable and Interminable," 242.

30 Lucy Scholes, "Hanya Yanagihara: Among Friends," *Bookanista*, September 16, 2015, http://bookanista.com/hanya-yanagihara.

31 Danhartland, "'People Don't Change': Hanya Yanagihara's *A Little Life*," *Story and the Truth*, January 22, 2016, https://thestoryandthetruth.wordpress.com/2016/01 /22/people-dont-change.

32 Greenwell, "*A Little Life*"; Hayes, "Man Booker Shortlist 2015."

33 Yanagihara, *The People in the Trees*, 12.

34 Henry, "The Real Thing," 11.

35 Dyckes, "The Photo as Subject," 152.

36 See Michaud, "The Subversive Brilliance," but also note Yanagihara's passing comment that "the worst years of New York's AIDS crisis was a flowering of

friendship" and "in that way the book was inspired by a part of gay history," in "On Writing a Great, Gay Book" (61).

37   Scholes, "Hanya Yanagihara: Among Friends."

38   Scholes, "Hanya Yanagihara: Among Friends."

39   Kavanagh, "A Stubborn Lack of Redemption."

40   Kavanagh, "A Stubborn Lack of Redemption."

41   Esther Addley, "So Bad It's Good," *Guardian*, June 15, 2007, www.theguardian .com/society/2007/jun/15/childrensservices.biography. For more on misery-literature conventions, see Bates, "'Misery Loves Company,'" and Twitchell, "Dave Eggers's *What Is the What*."

42   Preston, "*A Little Life*," also mentions "her unwillingness to embrace the approved message that we get from Dave Pelzer et al.," with "Pelzer et al." referring to an originating author of this genre. See also Aubry, *Reading as Therapy*, on his claim that "in subsequent decades, American fiction seemed to be even more focused on the individual mind as psychological realism became the predominant literary mode, gradually supplanting naturalism, modernism, and postmodernism" (27).

43   Rege Behe, "Author Still Surprised by Reaction to 'A Little Life,'" *TribLive*, March 29, 2016, http://triblive.com/aande/books/10197810-74/book-yanagihara -says; Lewis, "'We Are Certain of Our Own Insanity,'" 84, 87. See also Kunzel, "Queer History, Mad History, and the Politics of Health"; Staub, "Radical"; Cvetkovich, "Sexual Trauma/Queer Memory"; Huffer, *Mad for Foucault*, on "Foucauldian archiveologies of nonwhite, non-European, non-Western sexualities" (183); Pickens, *Black Madness*; and Curtis et al., *Mad Pride*. For a counter to these claims, see Powers, *No One Cares about Crazy People*.

44   Lewis, "'We Are Certain of Our Own Insanity,'" 100, 105, 106.

45   Freda Ward letter to Alice Mitchell, July 11, 1891, qtd. in Duggan, *Sapphic Slashers*, 214.

46   Duggan, *Sapphic Slashers*, 89, 90.

47   Duggan, *Sapphic Slashers*, 119; Hall, *The Well of Loneliness*, 391.

48   Lewis, "A Mad Fight," 115.

49   Halberstam, *In a Queer Time and Place*, 152.

50   Viego, "The Madness of Curing," 155. See also Puar, "Prognosis Time" and *The Right to Maim*; Berlant, "Do You Intend to Die"; Kim, *Curative Violence*; and Freeman, "Hopeless Cases."

51   Wiegman, "Eve's Triangles," 66.

BIBLIOGRAPHY

Alpert, Jonathan, and Alisa Bowman. *Be Fearless: Change Your Life in 28 Days*. New York: Center Street, 2012.

American Psychiatric Association. "Avoidant Personality Disorder." In *Diagnostic and Statistical Manual of Mental Disorders*, 5th ed., 672–75. Washington, DC: American Psychiatric Publishing, 2013.

Anderson, Warwick. *Colonial Pathologies: American Tropical Medicine, Race, and Hygiene in the Philippines*. Durham, NC: Duke University Press, 2006.

Anderson, Warwick, Deborah Jenson, and Richard C. Keller, eds. *Unconscious Dominions: Psychoanalysis, Colonial Trauma, and Global Sovereignties*. Durham, NC: Duke University Press, 2011.

Aubry, Timothy. *Reading as Therapy: What Contemporary Fiction Does for Middle-Class Americans*. Iowa City: University of Iowa Press, 2011.

Bates, Victoria. "'Misery Loves Company': Sexual Trauma, Psychoanalysis, and the Market for Misery." *Journal of Medical Humanities* 33 (2012): 61–81.

Berlant, Lauren. *Cruel Optimism*. Durham, NC: Duke University Press, 2011.

Berlant, Lauren. "Do You Intend to Die: Lauren Berlant on Intimacy after Suicide." *King's Review*, March 4, 2015. www.kingsreview.co.uk/essays/do-you-intend-to-die-lauren-berlant-on-intimacy-after-suicide.

Chuh, Kandice, and Karen Shimakawa. "Introduction: Mapping Studies in the Asian Diaspora." In *Orientations: Mapping Studies in the Asian Diaspora*, edited by Kandice Chuh and Karen Shimakawa, 1–23. Durham, NC: Duke University Press, 2001.

Curtis, Ted, Robert Dellar, Esther Leslie, and Ben Watson, eds. *Mad Pride: A Celebration of Mad Culture*. London: Spare Change, 2000.

Cvetkovich, Ann. "Sexual Trauma/Queer Memory: Incest, Lesbianism, and Therapeutic Culture." *GLQ* 2, no. 4 (1995): 351–77.

Duggan, Lisa. *Sapphic Slashers: Sex, Violence, and American Modernity*. Durham, NC: Duke University Press, 2000.

Dyckes, William. "The Photo as Subject: The Paintings and Drawings of Chuck Close." In *Super Realism*, edited by Gregory Battcock, 145–62. New York: Dutton, 1975.

Eng, David L. *The Feeling of Kinship: Queer Liberalism and the Racialization of Intimacy*. Durham, NC: Duke University Press, 2010.

Eng, David L., and Shinhee Han. *Racial Melancholia, Racial Dissociation: On the Social and Psychic Lives of Asian Americans*. Durham, NC: Duke University Press, 2018.

Espiritu, Yến Lê. "Home, Borders, and Possibilities." In *Asian American Studies Now: A Critical Reader*, edited by Jean Yu-wen Shen Wu and Thomas C. Chen, 603–21. New Brunswick, NJ: Rutgers University Press, 2010.

Foucault, Michel. *Abnormal: Lectures at the Collège de France, 1974–1975*. Edited by Valerio Marchetti and Antonella Salomoni. Translated by Graham Burchell. New York: Picador, 2003.

Foucault, Michel. "Friendship as a Way of Life." Translated by John Johnston. In *Essential Works of Foucault, 1954–1984*. Vol. 1, *Ethics: Subjectivity and Truth*, edited by Paul Rabinow, 135–40. New York: New Press, 1997.

Franke, Katherine. *Wedlocked: The Perils of Marriage Equality*. New York: New York University Press, 2015.

Freeman, Elizabeth. "Hopeless Cases: Queer Chronicities and Gertrude Stein's 'Melanctha.'" *Journal of Homosexuality* 63, no. 3 (2016): 329–48.

Freud, Sigmund. "Analysis Terminable and Interminable." In *The Standard Edition of the Complete Psychological Works of Sigmund Freud*, vol. 23, translated and edited by James Strachey, 216–53. 1937; repr., London: Hogarth, 1964.

Gove, Walter R. "Sex, Marital Status, and Mortality." *American Journal of Sociology* 79, no. 1 (1973): 45–67.

Greenwell, Garth. "*A Little Life*: The Great Gay Novel Might Be Here." *Atlantic*, May 31, 2015.

Halberstam, Jack [Judith]. *In a Queer Time and Place: Transgender Bodies, Subcultural Lives*. New York: New York University Press, 2005.

Hall, Radclyffe. *The Well of Loneliness*. London: Vintage Classics, 2016.

Harvard Health Publishing. "Marriage and Men's Health." *Harvard Men's Health Watch* 14, no. 12 (2010): 1–3.

Hayes, Stephanie. "Man Booker Shortlist 2015: Hanya Yanagihara's *A Little Life*." *Atlantic*, September 15, 2015. www.theatlantic.com/entertainment/archive/2015/09/a-little-life-hanya-yanagihara-man-booker-2015-shortlist/405385.

Henry, Gerrit. "The Real Thing." In *Super Realism: A Critical Anthology*, edited by Gregory Battcock, 3–20. New York: Dutton, 1975.

Huffer, Lynne. *Mad for Foucault: Rethinking the Foundations of Queer Theory*. New York: Columbia University Press, 2009.

Kim, Eunjung. *Curative Violence: Rehabilitating Disability, Gender, and Sexuality in Modern Korea*. Durham, NC: Duke University Press, 2017.

Kunzel, Regina. "Queer History, Mad History, and the Politics of Health." *American Quarterly* 69, no. 2 (2017): 315–19.

Lewis, Abram J. "'We Are Certain of Our Own Insanity': Antipsychiatry and the Gay Liberation Movement, 1968–1980." *Journal of the History of Sexuality* 25, no. 1 (2016): 83–113.

Lewis, Bradley. "A Mad Fight: Psychiatry and Disability Activism." In *The Disability Studies Reader*, 4th ed., edited by Lennard J. Davis, 115–31. New York: Routledge, 2013.

Lichtenberg, Joseph D. "*The Talking Cure*": *A Descriptive Guide to Psychoanalysis*. New York: Routledge, 2012.

Lowe, Lisa. "Heterogeneity, Hybridity, Multiplicity: Marking Asian American Differences." In *Contemporary Asian America: A Multidisciplinary Reader*, edited by Min Zhou and Anthony C. Ocampo, 531–53. New York: New York University Press, 2016.

Matz, Jesse. *Modernist Time Ecology*. Baltimore: Johns Hopkins University Press, 2018.

Michaud, Jon. "The Subversive Brilliance of 'A Little Life.'" *New Yorker*, April 28, 2015.

Miller, Dinah, and Annette Hanson. *Committed: The Battle over Involuntary Psychiatric Care*. Baltimore: Johns Hopkins University Press, 2016.

Pickens, Therí Alyce. *Black Madness :: Mad Blackness*. Durham, NC: Duke University Press, 2019.

Piepzna-Samarasinha, Leah Lakshmi. *Care Work: Dreaming Disability Justice*. Vancouver: Arsenal Pulp, 2018.

Powers, Ron. *No One Cares about Crazy People: The Chaos and Heartbreak of Mental Health in America*. New York: Hachette, 2017.

Puar, Jasbir K. "Prognosis Time: Towards a Geopolitics of Affect, Debility, and Capacity." *Women & Performance* 19, no. 2 (2009): 161–72.

Puar, Jasbir K. *The Right to Maim: Debility, Capacity, Disability*. Durham, NC: Duke University Press, 2017.

Rose, Jacqueline. "Something Amiss." In *Clinical Encounters in Sexuality: Psychoanalytic Practice and Queer Theory*, edited by Noreen Giffney and Eve Watson, 391–96. Brooklyn: Punctum, 2017.

Saks, Elyn R. *Refusing Care: Forced Treatment and the Rights of the Mentally Ill*. Chicago: University of Chicago Press, 2002.

Schnall, Maxine. *Limits: A Search for New Values*. New York: C. N. Potter, 1981.

Shah, Nayan. *Contagious Divides: Epidemics and Race in San Francisco's Chinatown*. Berkeley: University of California Press, 2001.

Sohn, Stephen Hong. *Inscrutable Belongings: Queer Asian North American Fiction*. Stanford, CA: Stanford University Press, 2018.

Staub, Michael E. "Radical." In *Rethinking Therapeutic Culture*, edited by Timothy Aubry and Trysh Travis, 96–107. Chicago: University of Chicago Press, 2015.

Szasz, Thomas. *Coercion as Cure: A Critical History of Psychiatry*. New Brunswick, NJ: Transaction, 2007.

Twitchell, Elizabeth. "Dave Eggers's *What Is the What*: Fictionalizing Trauma in the Era of Misery Lit." *American Literature* 83, no. 3 (2011): 621–48.

Viego, Antonio. "The Madness of Curing." *Feminist Formations* 25, no. 3 (2013): 154–59.

Warner, Michael. *The Trouble with Normal: Sex, Politics, and the Ethics of Queer Life*. New York: Free Press, 1999.

Wiegman, Robyn. "Eve's Triangles, or Queer Studies Beside Itself." *differences* 26, no. 1 (2015): 48–73.

Wright, Richard G., Allen J. LeBlanc, and M. V. Lee Badgett. "Same-Sex Legal Marriage and Psychological Well-Being: Findings from the California Health Interview Survey." *American Journal of Public Health* 103, no. 2 (2013): 339–46.

Yanagihara, Hanya. *A Little Life*. New York: Anchor, 2015.

Yanagihara, Hanya. "On Writing a Great, Gay Book: Garth Greenwell and Hanya Yanagihara in Conversation." Interview by Garth Greenwell. *Hello Mr.* 8 (2016): 57–70.

Yanagihara, Hanya. *The People in the Trees*. New York: Doubleday, 2013.

1

RACE, INCARCERATION, AND THE COMMITMENT TO VOLUNTEER

AMY JAMGOCHIAN

In Barry Jenkins's 2017 film, *Moonlight*, Chiron, aka "Little," the physically and emotionally vulnerable young Black boy at the center of the first two acts of the film, later emerges from prison as "Black," a muscle-bound adult drug dealer still longing for romance with his high school one-night stand. In this Oscar-winning representation, prison is the sexless lacuna where a sweet Black teen becomes a yearning gangster, newly marked by race in name and body but yet to be marked as gay. Although popular culture abounds in representations of prison as a space of predatory or pathological sex, *Moonlight* makes gay male sex virtually unimaginable, both inside the unrepresented gap of Chiron's prison sentence, which falls between the second and third acts, and the postprison outside world, where muscular Black bodies that might otherwise threaten white audiences are swaddled in melancholy feeling. The film's chaste and aesthetically pleasing representation of Chiron's sexuality succumbs to the American prerequisite that Black bodies be desirable yet harmless. Adhering to this racialized norm, *Moonlight* consents to the loss of sexual personhood that it implies.

This representational bargain can also be observed in racialized enactments of prison volunteerism, which, like Jenkins's film, are also marked by romantic impulses to fantasy and disavowal around incarceration that play out on both institutional and personal levels. To ask that *Moonlight* follow its queer protagonist to prison is to expect too much of the film's already overdetermined rhetorical endeavor.[1] However, finding queerness in prison encounters does not require attending to acts between prisoners, but rather to the queer difference created within and throughout interdictions on prison relationality, particularly as this difference relates to the troubled issue of white witnessing of Black trauma and the structures of fantasy that ensue. Prison, as *Moonlight* so efficiently demonstrates, is frequently hidden from mainstream attention, an elision compounded by the fact that its wards have limited interactions with outsiders. Prison is thus a limit case in the degradation and abuse of people of color in the United States, a reality that white people seldom know how to address even as we volubly deplore it. As many have demonstrated, the sentencing laws that disproportionately confine people of color between prison walls carry on the legacy of slavery in America, rescinding freedoms, forcing labor, and degrading whole populations for often indeterminate periods, sometimes entire lifetimes.[2] Meanwhile, prison, specifically San Quentin State Prison, the carceral setting I am familiar with in my role as a college administrator, also attracts armies of mostly white volunteers who are committed to service toward incarcerated people, the majority of whom are people of color.

From the perspective of someone not employed by the prison but charged with running a college program inside its walls, San Quentin sets a stage for a specific and fraught form of American witness at the same time as it unwittingly makes available a possible queer reframing of the same encounter. For an outsider to see the traumatic reality of prison, which manifests a persistence of cruelty and dehumanization that white Americans have benefited from for centuries, is to have an opportunity to forgo the usual recourse to ignorance, denial, and minimization. Yet "seeing" is difficult inasmuch as the observation of racialized violence, even on an institutional scale, continues to be filtered through the sediment of history and fantasy. As part of my work within the University Prison Project, a nonprofit that provides free junior-college–level education to prisoners, I spend time in prison regularly and routinely encounter tragedy in the shade of housing units that lock up eight hundred men in miniscule shared cells, such as the student whose son had died the month before at the hands of police or the student whose family couldn't afford to pay for his young grandson's funeral. Learning in passing about monumental adversity is a regular occurrence, and I can attest to the conflicted feelings that it can provoke around advantage and its obligations. There is also the accompanying human difficulty of witnessing trauma in a situation in which natural-feeling responses to distress, such as touch or tears, are forbidden under the explicit regimes of depersonalization and deprivation that enfold prison encounters across race and other unbridgeable differences.

Entering a prison as an outsider and engaging with prisoners works through this racialized terrain in ways that are both novel and foreshortened. In her ethnographically based study of bonds between prisoners and prison staff at San Quentin, Nicole Lindahl has persuasively argued that, contrary to the many correctional rules in place to police against it, the prison presents "an environment hyper-conducive to intimacy."[3] Lindahl's research concerns employed prison staff rather than the volunteer population, which often holds deep ideological opposition to the system of corrections and its mandated codes of conduct. This distinction is important to keep in mind because, as Lindahl notes, prisoners and the staff employed to run prisons in the United States are demographically identical in terms of race and class: working-class whites and people of color guard the same. Elsewhere, Joe Lockard makes the case that the working class in America is for all intents and purposes the "prison class," whether locked in its cells or guarding its grounds.[4] However, prison volunteers present a stark demographic contrast to both prisoners and prison staff and also present a different relational pattern than the intimacy-regulation dialectic that Lindahl documents.

To be clear, on first and final impressions San Quentin can feel like the straightest environment in America. There is a strong culture of heterosexual masculinism, or rather many different strains of it, all of which take on the coloration of the environment. Whatever path taken, striving to be a "grown-ass man" is a near-universal goal, such that an incarcerated student in our program refers to the prison as "man camp." Inside San Quentin, homophobia appears like a 1980s parody of itself. In this context it comes as no surprise that I have yet to meet any prisoner who publicly identifies as gay. This outward-facing denial may also make sense of why, to date, queer theory's chief engagements with the carceral tend to have to do with a commitment to abolitionist politics rather than with lived experiences of sexuality in prison.[5] Yet as the crystallization of the workings of panoptic and disciplinary power, prison sexuality and its long-term reverberations have also been seen as quintessentially queer.[6]

No amount of time spent working inside a prison will allow a free person to know the experience of being held involuntarily in such institutions. Nor do race and class distinctions erode over time spent among demographics different from one's own. I am concerned here not with how prisoners experience or work through rules about sexuality and the relational, but rather with the rules themselves and the productive, unpredictable, and unevenly risky ways that outsider interactions cut across them. An oversized portion of the American imaginary of men's prisons involves crude conjectures about hierarchies established through anal rape. There is the erroneous assumption that if sexual assault is prevalent in prison (and studies suggest it is), then prisoners are the perpetrators, not prison staff (a belief that belies fact), the idea that prisoner victims deserve rape if they don't manage to avoid it, and the fantasy that many in prison are "gay for the stay."[7] What is true is that more than 2.3 million people in America are imprisoned in physical environments and regimes that lend themselves to sexual degradation if not out-and-out assault. Exploring prison rules about relationships is therefore also useful for understanding the racialized violence and play of power at the core of American thinking about sex and sexuality in general.

Regulations

Prisoner-volunteer relationships are bound by a series of formal regulations as well as by the informal culture of the prison. Although my knowledge about other prisons is limited to descriptions provided by our students and prison staff, I understand that San Quentin is atypical as California prisons go in the warmth of exchanges between prisoners and nonprisoners inside its gates. Prisoners and free people greet one another, ask "How are you?" and know one another's names. Officers address prisoners by name rather than as "inmate." However, the relaxed atmosphere relative to other prisons is counterbalanced by state rules governing prisoner-nonprisoner intimacy. According to the California Department of Corrections and Rehabilitation (CDCR) Code of Regulations, "Employees must not engage in undue familiarity with inmates, parolees, or the family and friends of inmates or parolees," nor "discuss their personal affairs with any inmate or parolee."[8]

Although these rules address CDCR employees, they are also used to regulate volunteers, though to different effect. In either case, the adjective *undue* introduces opacity to the already fraught notion of *familiarity*. How is *undue* defined, and what are its parameters? What does it mean to be familiar with another person? How familiar is too familiar? Although the fact that these questions are impossible to answer supports arbitrary displays of power, there are several standard and concrete rules and norms that structure the ban on overfamiliarity inside the prison: staff and volunteers in the prison must not be family, friends, or lovers of any prisoners there; personal items such as letters, photographs, gifts, or food may not be exchanged; and physical contact between prisoners and nonprisoners is forbidden, although at San Quentin this prohibition does not include handshakes, fist bumps, or high fives, all of which are regularly transacted between staff, inmates, and volunteers.

Other kinds of body language are subject to more panoptic inspection. In general, there must not be any appearance of intimacy in interpersonal behaviors, for excessive attachment is thought to create a space for manipulation. In one episode of *Ear Hustle*, a podcast produced inside San Quentin, incarcerated host Earlonne Woods cautions his cohost, volunteer Nigel Poor, that "there's no crying in prison."[9] This unofficial but nevertheless critical interdiction also falls on volunteers, who would be under high suspicion if they were seen to tear up because of the appearance it would create of an emotional connection. Such rules and norms are policed formally by officers and informally through innuendo and gossip. Either form of reporting, citation or rumor, can create consequences for both prisoners and the volunteer programs that rely upon the goodwill of the prison administration to continue their work inside.

As if the result of a long-running dystopian experiment in voiding the social contract, US prisons are skilled in regulating against interpersonal empathy and erecting barriers between prisoners and staff, although the intense energy put into policing these interdictions indicates that there are near-constant lapses. In order to preserve the college program's place in San Quentin, one of my duties is to train volunteer faculty in maintaining distance between themselves and prisoners. The pitfalls and challenges that I confront are quite different from those that the prison faces in training and supervising its staff. Whereas the rhetorical modus operandi of corrections has to do with installing the distinction between prisoner and nonprisoner through dehumanization practices that depict the prisoner as bad, manipulative, and a danger to others, the abiding presumption of those who volunteer for a program that provides free college education to prisoners is not only that prisoners are human and thus deserving of education and other basic citizenship and human rights but moreover that the putative badness of the incarcerated person is more a measure of social inequities and failures than of individual depravity. This is the split world that I have to navigate on behalf of volunteers who often think of themselves as separate from the carceral system but are thus free to affectively project into a space they cannot understand.

The most immediate official rationale for the ban on overfamiliarity is to prevent nonprisoners from providing prisoners with contraband such as drugs, cell phones, or escape paraphernalia. Every recent prison escape attempt in the United States has been enabled in some manner or another by materials from an outsider, whether an officer, an administrator, a service provider, a visitor, or a volunteer. In line with this evidence, there is a presumption that, if allowed to thrive, emotional closeness may eventually compel a nonprisoner to provide illegal assistance to a prisoner either volitionally or by coercion. For the purposes of our college program, however, my primary concern is the safety of our incarcerated students and the ongoing delivery of the college program, both of which could be at risk in a variety of both material and visceral ways should a volunteer breach, intentionally or not, rules against overfamiliarity. This presents a challenge for organizations and their staff, who must teach and administer rules that they and their volunteers often ideologically oppose in order to maintain their program's precarious place inside the prison.

Much as the reasoning may differ, our program is engaged in a similar project to the prison system, namely compelling human actors to behave according to sometimes inhumane prescriptions. San Quentin's volunteer guide cautions: "BE FIRM, SET LIMITS, AND AVOID OVERFAMILIARITY— Don't discuss personal matters with inmates. Inmates may push you until you say 'stop.' How hard and how far they push will depend on how hard and how far you allow them to push. If an inmate makes an improper advance, handle it appropriately. If you are unable to do so, notify your sponsor."[10] Positioning incarcerated people as manipulators, a standard gambit of correctional rhetoric, these instructions suggest that volunteers must treat all words and actions of prisoners as potential trickery, as ploys that are perhaps part of a "long game." In such a view, any attempt at human connection is a deceitful endeavor to "push" the volunteer into inappropriate conduct. Relying on the volunteer's fear of being fooled or taken advantage of, and the retributive fantasies that so often follow such fears, this type of warning works—when it does—to install a defensive projection onto the person of the prisoner. For the prison system in general, control and discipline are often approached through invoking fear. Not only is there a belief that this tactic is necessary to prevent unwanted behaviors, but it also perpetrates the idea that prisons are full of scheming criminals, a clichéd stereotype that further rationalizes and justifies the work that prison staff do in containing and punishing incarcerated people. It also serves to draw a firm line between prisoner and outsider. But when one views incarcerated people and volunteers as mutually human, that line can be more difficult, if not impossible, to discern.

Happily, the Prison University Project does most of its volunteer training apart from the prison, which allows some degree of critique if not outright circumvention of prison-mandated modes of interaction. Whereas San Quentin runs occasional information and training sessions about prison regulations, volunteers are selected, prepared, and supervised chiefly by the outside organization with which they work. One of the most vital, if seemingly mundane, parts of my training of volunteers involves the directives we must follow about attire. To start, there are certain relatively benign rules about color: volunteers' clothing must not resemble in color that of prisoners or of officers so that all categories of person are visually distinguishable at all times. Skin should be covered; shoes should be comfortable. Additionally, clothing must not be tight, transparent, or otherwise "suggestive." From the start of my work inside the prison, I took the clothing rules seriously, so it was only when walking in with a woman volunteer whose clothing was tighter than I would have allowed myself that I had the chance to experience the very different reactions she got from both officers and men on the yard. Although there was nothing explicitly inappropriate or out-of-bounds, I had the sense of seas parting as we walked toward the education area. In that moment some previously suppressed thought appeared, unbidden, in my mind: "Why don't *I* get that reaction?" My own identifications would belie it, but it turns out I appreciate the cultural capital that the performance of femininity generates in a yard full of men. In relating this story to new volunteers, I ask them to consider the often ingrained and sometimes unexpected communicative appeals that drive so many of our sartorial decisions. Women in particular are enculturated to try to be sexually attractive on a day-to-day basis and, however one interprets or obeys that injunction, to expect a set of reactions to our physical presence. Many of our decisions and actions lie beneath conscious awareness, cordoned off from conscious agency or choice by their very routine and historical character, but within the netherworld of prison, in which agency and choice are systemically removed, it is crucial to make the unconscious patent or at least attempt to do so.

Like the prison staff charged with overseeing institutional regulations, I work to compel volunteers to dress according to CDCR rules. Instead of invoking fear, I appeal to commonplace understandings of social reality and their magnification in the prison environment. I also reiterate the risk to students of being suspected of association with a sexily dressed or flirtatious-seeming woman. Any behavior attracting an officer's suspicion—or another student's—could send the putative offender to administrative segregation, which would force the student to miss class and potentially get transferred to another prison, among other possibilities. What starts as a confession of naïveté about unconscious motivations turns into a cautionary tale about unspoken communications and consequences. I ask volunteers to think through their performance of self in order to present inside the prison as a relatively desexualized educational professional.

Another subset of CDCR rules that is pertinent to our program has to do with permitted materials. Our program strives to offer college courses identical to what students would encounter on the outside and consistent with the freedom of speech that college education traditionally stands for, yet we are subject to interdictions about representation in the prison system as well, some of which pertain to obscenity. Most immediately, images of nudity or sexual acts are considered "obscene" and thus contraband.[11] Although some prison officers have complained that displays of pornographic images contribute to a hostile work environment, a grievance that has increased with the addition of more female employees within traditionally male-dominated institutions, the notion of obscenity is generally connected to a fear of criminal violence rather than to a more general cultural disparagement of women. This can be seen in the CDCR's "Centralized List of Disapproved Publications." In this document, hundreds of pornographic titles are listed, alongside books about fairies, tattoos, native Mexican languages, and hand-to-hand combat, among fourteen other pages of titles on various topics. Although it is obvious why an instructional text on combat could be an item of concern in a prison, it takes longer to decode other categories of proscription. Concerns about fairies, tattoos, and native Mexican languages, as it turns out, follow a similar rationale: all are associated with "security threat groups," otherwise known as gangs, with their all-too-real association with violence in prisons. The antigang "safety-and-security" rationale sheds light on the interdiction on sexual "obscenity" as well: to the CDCR's collective mind, sexual arousal might trigger predatory behavior in a prisoner, regardless of the nature of the prisoner's crime. This is primarily a concern with images, but also with potentially incendiary texts, so we instruct volunteers to submit texts to us to photocopy before distributing them to students. Once again, this rationale is designed to ensure the safety and well-being of our students, for whom the possession of banned material could have serious implications.

On the side of correctional philosophy and practice, pseudoscientific biological theories of crime, literalist ideas about the effects of representation, probably racist notions of sexually predacious behavior, and the custom of a sexist culture to blame women for crimes against them are all brought to bear on the prison's practices of censorship and social control. More than merely preventing access to contraband, the rules against access to representations of sexuality mount an ideological monolith that prison staff are expected to defend and enforce. For their part, volunteers must not awaken the specter of predatory criminal sexual desire by dress or demeanor or any other relational infringement. Although I could mount a theoretical critique of these CDCR codes and their underlying rationales, I nonetheless take very seriously my role in inculcating volunteers into obedience of these strictures. To do so, I suggest an alternative understanding: we are engaging in practices whose initial codification reeks of dehumanization and cruelty in order to further other forms of humanization within the prison system. At the same time, I also stress how the all-too-human acts, symbols, and representations that we are banned from conveying are themselves implicated in abuses of power that are not as easy to discern as the prison rules suggest. In an institutional world where intrinsic depravity and violence are assumed, it is easy for nonprisoners to deny the ways in which we are all implicated in the form of power that prison symbolizes. Such denial can mean that volunteers, who bring other expectations and forms of thinking to their relationships with incarcerated people, tacitly infringe rules in ways that place those people at risk.

A final element in CDCR interdictions has to do with sexual relations with prisoners, which are all but impossible in the cramped and crowded spaces in which our volunteers teach and tutor, but which nevertheless are enough of a concern that I bring this subject up in every training session. Here too, I balance the CDCR interpretation against our own understanding of the importance of compliance. Sexual acts are technically illegal in prison in California, as in all other areas in the United States. The 2003 Prison Rape Elimination Act (PREA), which "mandat[es] zero tolerance toward all forms of sexual abuse and sexual harassment," expressly includes relations between custody staff and prisoners as matters of legal concern.[12] The issue here is abuse of power: because prisoners are physically trapped and subject to manifold forms of control of their bodies—of their time, of their labor, of their diet, of their location from one hour to the next—they are not in a position to fairly consent to sex with individuals who hold rights over their bodies. Correctional thinking also assumes the converse: that sexual relations between prisoners and prison staff could lead to the prisoner having "undue" influence over the nonprisoner. Central to both concerns is an acknowledgment of uneven power relationships and the exploitation, sexual or otherwise, that can result.

According to Title 15, "Inmates are specifically excluded in laws, which remove legal restraints from acts between consenting adults."[13] Correspondingly, and no matter how many condoms are made available in prison, to the eye of corrections, prisoners cannot consent to sex, even among one another, being wholly stripped of the capacity to consent to begin with.[14] While this statutory lack of the right to speak for their own bodies contributes to their infantilization, if not their utter dehumanization, the removal of consent can also be seen as placing protections on potential victims within a complex environment of interpersonal distrust and with great potential for physical danger. In prison, the incarcerated person's body is not truly his or her own in either a legal or a practical sense. In this proleptic perspective, all sex in prison is coercion because uneven power relationships are acknowledged for the abuses to which they are prone. If the state must carry through the infantilization of its wards, then it also has to work to protect those who cannot protect themselves, in a concise demonstration of the paradoxical and ultimately damaging sequelae of institutionalization.

Whereas volunteers might in principle agree with the idea that anything leading to or involving sexual relations with an incarcerated person would invariably involve a power disproportion, that calculus can often be thrown out in the face of desire. My approach is to acknowledge that love can happen without warning: certainly, enough relationships have been born of volunteer programs in prisons that I would be foolish to imagine that I could influence this eventuality. However for the prisoners' safety as well as for durability of any future equitable relationship, the volunteer who falls in love must recuse himself or herself from the program and is advised to wait before pursuing an intimate connection with a prison student. Although this is no different from guidelines that apply in other teaching contexts, volunteers hearing this at their initial training may balk at the suggestion that they would ever fall prey to such feelings. All I can hope is that the caution will take seed before the volunteers enter the prison environment and are swept away by the complex and layered dynamics of relating to short- and long-term prisoners whose experience of duration and futurity is shaped not only by the power differentials between freedom and incarceration but also by race and its institutionalization both within the prison and beyond it.

In inducting volunteers into this collection of rules, I am navigating the vast realm of contradictions that make up correctional philosophy as it defines and redefines the purpose of prison. The inconsistencies and incoherence around prohibitions on sexual activity between prisoners would seem of a piece with other arrays of meanings around this form of punishment in the twenty-first century: prison is understood alternately as recompense for criminal damage, penitence for sins, deprivation of cherished freedoms ostensibly designed to cause regret, rehabilitation, or redemption of the criminal mentality, to name just a few ways the idea is mobilized. To forbid sexual material and activities locates desire and sexual acts as tokens of value in America, which the incarcerated person is theoretically stripped of to pay for his or her crime, or to be made to regret it, and the prison system is at liberty to a certain degree to create and enforce these rules apart from state or federal legislation or from the prisoner's sentence. Alternately, the state may intervene with its own concerns. Thus, a network of institutions with incompatible dictates hems the carceral subject in all the more tightly. If our program is to survive within this mesh of power effects, then volunteers who are intent on combating the prison-industrial complex need to understand the limitations that constrain our particular form of intervention. This pragmatism frequently butts up against the idealism of much social justice activism in the United States, which often evinces desires to discard the master's tools over and against the notion that there is no exterior to power.

In all, state and CDCR legal and administrative rules for prisoners' social and sexual relations simultaneously acknowledge abuses based in power differences and justify parallel abuses as attempts at addressing their consequence. This rhetorical lack of interest in consistency or realism recalls *Moonlight*'s spectacular jump cut across the time of incarceration, a leap that leaves the hero improbably nonsexual, a figure of fantasy rather than history. The prison matrix is much like the school that brings together Chiron and his teenage crush only to have them turn on each other. The school and the prison, like the world of street crime into which the character Black graduates, are all institutions in which the ephemeral signs of intimacy must be policed and self-policed in order to maintain one's safety in a structurally unsafe world. Whether free or incarcerated, many people of color know that lesson from childhood on, but the majority of the volunteers who walk into San Quentin have a lifetime of inhabiting the contradictory desires and inequalities of contemporary America on the other side.

Disavowal

Volunteers are a regular feature of prison life at San Quentin. They enter the prison in the hundreds each week. The recent upswing in prison volunteerism reflects the fact that progressives across America are increasingly appalled at the crisis of mass incarceration. On a scale that has not been evident since the era of civil rights, white liberals are feeling the weight of their privilege, their own unearned good fortune in contrast to other groups, juxtaposed with the suffering that those inequities cause people of color. It is with such conscious impetuses that many begin prison work. Not all volunteers are white, but volunteerism at San Quentin bears out trends observable in volunteerism in the United States more generally: more women are volunteers than men, and more white people volunteer than other ethnicities. Although the ethnic breakdown of San Quentin's prison population is not available in the public domain, the self-reported ethnic breakdown of incarcerated students with the Prison University Project in 2017 was 50 percent African American, 14 percent White, 10 percent Hispanic, 7 percent Asian, and 19 percent Other. Given the racial disparities and the intense and often unconscious desires that feed the principled liberal commitment to donate labor to the prison cause, it is critical to train prison volunteers to recognize their own motivations and the risk they pose to the prisoners they wish to assist.

As one who spends a great deal of time in prison, I am very mindful that the temptation to transgress the rules of familiarity regularly asserts itself. The humanity of incarcerated people juxtaposed with the degradation of the prison environment is so palpable that flirtation might seem like a gift, an opportunity for the prisoner to feel pleasure and the agency of desire, if only briefly. Moreover, there is the pleasure of the volunteer to take into account: the environment of prison can be an ego stroke to volunteers anywhere on the gender spectrum. It is hard not to enjoy interactions with people who are glad to see you, interested in you, and volubly grateful for your presence. The intoxication of appreciation can make it easy to lose sight of the overfamiliarity rules, especially in a situation where recognizing the equal humanity of an incarcerated person can seem an ethical stance. As I caution volunteers, however, the relationship between volunteer and prisoner is never unproblematically human-to-human, equal-to-equal, as long as one is able to leave and the other remains locked in, as long as the prisoner's safety and well-being are at risk from actions the volunteer might take without personal endangerment to self, as long as the volunteer has the power to make decisions that affect prisoners or that can influence the prison's decisions. In this context there is a fine line between humanizing and exploitation, between kindness and cruelty or taunting. The gap in perceived meaning of any action or communication can be profound: what for the volunteer might be felt as a momentary engagement could for the incarcerated person be the only connection they have had with another person in years, such is their condition of emotional deprivation and extreme limitation of options. Such experiential disproportions are a feature of all interactions, but in the face of such profound disparities, intensive deliberation and constant self-awareness are required to ethically navigate this world. However, confidence in the transparency of motive is often misplaced in the arena of race, which, like sexuality, is subject to dynamics of social shame and abjection, and the fetishizations and disavowals that accompany those feelings.

Attempting an ethical response in this context is all the more troubled by the ethnic disparities that mark many prison interactions and the lifeways that precede them. We know that white people in America who were brought up middle class or wealthy have typically had very little exposure to people of color, particularly African Americans. This is compounded in California, which is only 6.5 percent Black and, like much of America, is largely made up of unofficially racially segregated neighborhoods, made separate by virtue of socioeconomic realities and "white flight." This is the same America in which people of color are statistically poorer, more frequently incarcerated, far more likely to be shot by police, subject to unfair treatment in the school system, and in many other ways systematically oppressed, whereas white people are, comparatively speaking, immune to such constant societal ills. White liberals are well aware of these realities and are often eager to demonstrate to themselves and others that they condemn structural racism, that they like and respect people of color.

For some of these volunteers, to be accepted, relied on, or loved by people of color is perhaps to be personally absolved of racism. Certainly at the structural level there is an element of dark tourism to white volunteers' work, as many are experiencing Black and Brown people in the majority for the first time and are frankly curious not only about prison but also about the cultures that much of white America alternately shuns and idealizes. There is a tradition of theoretical critique from Freud and Marx to Lacan and Žižek that links such vacillation to disavowal as a negative force, a perverse mechanism, supported by fetishism, through which people avoid confronting loss or lack while at the same time necessarily acknowledging it to a certain degree. Freud's idiosyncratic but fertile example and imagined origin of fetishism has to do with the moment that the boy realizes his mother has no penis.[15] This recognition is too much of a wound to the boy's narcissism for him to fully accept this seeming blatant evidence of castration, so he disavows that catastrophic possibility by unconsciously understanding her penis to be elsewhere, such as her foot, which is the beginning of eventual fetishism.

Disavowal and fetishism are close partners: a reality can be disavowed—at the same time consciously understood and unconsciously denied—by virtue of the force of desire, which creates a substitute or metaphor for the denied object. Disavowal is seen in much contemporary theory as an unconscious support of capitalism, racism, and phallocentrism. For Homi Bhabha, for instance, the scene of racial fetishism is a disavowal founded in traumatic response on the part of a white person to the loss of the idea of white superiority.[16] The fetishistic response that Bhabha posits is a fixation on stereotypes of difference—as with the fetish object of the foot for Freud, racial stereotypes operate as a more anodyne substitute for the lost alternative of racial superiority.

The fetish of the virile Black man, both threatening and compelling, has abounded in the popular white imagination since the time of slavery, but this racialized and sexualized stereotype, and its psychic and social utility, are compounded in many ways by the contemporary carceral aftermath. In a context of a generally held national fantasy of Black men as sexually predatory animals, the fact that the volunteer need not commit to association with the incarcerated person other than in the discrete hours of volunteering and the fact that the prisoner is trapped and restrained in movement means friendliness or flirtation in this situation can feel safe. Exploitation and abuse of power are, in a sense, already taking place when a volunteer enters the prison, whether or not she or he considers contravening the rules. As Foucault reminds us, such disciplinary traps have their corollaries in everyday life outside prison, where intersections of race, gender, and sexuality are also at play. As much as we aspire to the norm of equality, abuses of power within relationships are rampant in the United States outside of prison as well as inside, and just as subject to disavowal.

Yet, like many of the theorists of disavowal, I have come to believe there is a positive side to this psychic mechanism. For Freud, disavowal can play a productive role in traumatic grief when the mourning subject is able to simultaneously recognize the death and nevertheless, on another register, not accept it. In *Coldness and Cruelty*, Deleuze is even more sanguine about disavowal's possible effects: "Disavowal should perhaps be understood as the point of departure of an operation that consists neither in negating nor even destroying, but rather in radically contesting the validity of that which is: it suspends belief in and neutralizes the given in such a way that a new horizon opens up beyond the given and in place of it."[17] Although disavowal involves the same refusal of "that which is" that others understand as its core, for Deleuze refusal also marks disavowal's promise: it is an imaginative procedure whereby neither reality nor reality's negation are paramount but rather takes issue with the terms of engagement altogether in the attempt to forge a new relationship to given terms. As in the Lacanian tradition, disavowal still represents lack of power over representation, but it also has the potential to yield a creative engagement with given signification. In much of the psychoanalytic tradition, this fetishistic substitution and creativity have been labeled "perverse" in a negative sense, yet in a more queer (or Laplanchian) tradition, what is perversion but another word for sexuality, desire, pleasure?

Another way to put this is that it may well be part of the problem that even almost half a century after Nancy Friday accounted for and defended women's rape fantasies, in many activist circles fantasy is still relegated to the realm of abuse. Take, for example, the 2014 protest at kink.com's Armory office, where the pornography production company hosted a "Prison Love Party." Protesters' projected slogans read: "There is no Prison in Queer Paradise" and "There is nothing sexy about prison."[18] Although unconscious fantasies can be toxic, in Freud and Deleuze's understandings of the workings of fetishism and disavowal there is also the possibility for fantasy and fetishism to be reparative and even potentially transformative. The notion that one could or should legislate others' fantasies performs the very same authoritarianism that progressives in the United States decry. A fetish party is hardly the solution to American racism and mass incarceration, but viewing the "Prison Love Party" as a necessarily wrongheaded revelry in the abuses of the prison-industrial complex rules out the possibility that a sexual fantasy-based preoccupation with one of the most influential drivers of racial inequality in America could represent a reparative gesture within the terms of a perverse social contract rather than its willful denial.

Prison is without doubt traumatic: it is a place of extreme deprivation, violence, and overt racism in which America warehouses whole populations of already systematically disenfranchised people. Prisoners are cordoned off from others in elaborate ways through prison rules and state laws. To encounter prison and to accede to its rules, even as a free person, is to enter a symbolic economy of loss, to which disavowal may be one possible response. It would be unreasonable to deny the idea that disavowal can operate destructively. At times it does further racism and other insidious realities, but it is also within disavowal's perverse remit to bring the carceral and the queer together. Just as the contemporary LGBT movement seems mired in a commitment to the twin homonationalist forces of marriage and militarization, so too is the US punishment system enmeshed in regulations that operate through restriction, delimitation, and deprivation. Both cases include an attempt to fend off specters of the predatory—the pervert, the terrorist, the criminal, the convict—and to deny normative America's implication in the production of these feared figures.

How might disavowal work alternately to address this constellation of dangers? Recall that disavowal and its partner activity, fetishism, might operate as a productive force within their capacity to aid a person in grieving the ungrievable, to help the sufferer develop a different and more survivable narrative of loss. In the face of a reality too traumatic to accept, disavowal uses the fetish as a pleasurable stand-in for that which is lost. As such, disavowal is a possible way to endure grim realities through imaginative transformation. The dehumanizing rules governing interpersonal relations in prison are a case in point. Lost to all parties in these regulations are necessary facets of existence: touch, everyday signs and signals of emotional connection and affection, and avowals of relational commitment to others. In the face of this inhuman negation, the nonprisoner who wants to avoid either championing the rules or breaking them might turn to the substitutive faculty of fetishism as a third way, a positive negation that offers a new form for that which is lacking that allows one to endure the lack and that forges even something akin to pleasure—or radical transformation—in its loss. The object of fetishism need not be a stereotype of difference that permits cruelty; it could be an object that functions to combat cruelty. Some responses that feel natural, that feel innately human, may through disavowal and fetishism be called into question, urging one to rethink, for example, crying in the face of another person's trauma.

Although it is not a written rule that one may not cry in prison, it is seen as important that the nonprisoner avoid crying, to avoid the appearance of coercion in relationships with incarcerated people. Yet as the prohibition implies, tears can be a prime signifier of affective connection, particularly when one is confronted with an emotionally moving reality being suffered by another person. Such scenes of witnessing trauma can contribute to what is known as "secondary trauma," but little remarked upon in discussions of this phenomenon are the situations of vast socioeconomic disparity and imbalance of privilege this scene of witness frequently arises from. That a person in one's midst is suffering is compounded with the knowledge that this is a form of suffering that whiteness and affluence and other vagaries of history have effectively inured the onlooker from, whatever their intent. Crying also comes with cultural weight. In many Black communities, white women in particular have a reputation for crying as a defense mechanism against the possibility of our own racism, as a way of proclaiming victimization to avoid taking responsibility. Working toward an alternate response, then, can operate not only as a way of following prison rules, but also as a pledge to confront one's position of privilege through positing a different narrative of one's own reaction to another person's hardship.

How might one express an interpersonal connection and a response to another's suffering without co-opting that suffering, without disowning the inevitable and very real power differential? The fetish here might involve the nameless affect occasioned by witnessing another's trauma unflinchingly, being available to listen, and indeed not crying or appearing to break in the face of it. Instead of claiming the place of feeling as a way to unsee one's own cultural advantages and complicity, one might take on the role of the listener who affirms the reality of the unfairness and sorrows at hand. It would seem irreverent to appeal to the "pleasure" of such a moment, but to be trusted with the burden-lifting act of witnessing can invoke something akin to joy.

It may not be possible to train people in this form of racial witness. If anything, it must be modeled. Volunteers should have the opportunity to talk through the ongoing process of encountering their own fantasies and projections. They require, that is, a similar kind of listening witness while they are coming to understand their own place in the everyday traumas they are beholding and unwittingly benefiting from. On a larger scale, disavowal might be the delicate operation of accepting one's inevitable entrapment in the webs of ideology where we all find ourselves by virtue of being born into interweaved and violent histories, but at the same time refusing normative responses to this entrapment, insisting on different metaphors and language, and bearing witness to the traumas we are faced with every day in lived experiences of racial difference.

As if following *Moonlight*'s glaring disavowal of prison sexuality, I have declined to approach queer sex directly in this essay. Instead of pressing into representation sex between prisoners of color, I am imagining that queerness is not a narrowly defined matter of sexual preference or identity or even non-normativity but is rather an ethic of relationality that refuses the fear-based disavowals and stereotypes that make up contemporary relational reality. This would be an ethic that works to become aware of race-based hierarchies and abuses of power, that learns about everyday manifestations of them, and then imaginatively produces metaphorical substitutions and relational forms that invoke a queer manner of joy. That this political affect might be born inside prison walls is a testament to the hope-giving ironies of traumatic disavowal, which in this case declines to ache for a pure moment before or beyond the reach of fantasy or power relationships and instead transforms their terms.

NOTES

1   Rinaldo Walcott has recently suggested that questioning *Moonlight*'s many representational bargains is "not an attempt to steal cinematic joy in the filmic text but to begin to figure the stakes of representing Black queer masculinities as more complex and multivalent than any one film might offer at this time." See "*Moonlight*'s Necessary Company," 341.

2   See, for example, Ava DuVernay's Netflix documentary *13th*; Alexander, *The New Jim Crow*; and Davis, *Abolition Democracy*, *Are Prisons Obsolete?*, and *The Meaning of Freedom*.

3   Lindahl, "Intimacy, Manipulation, and the Maintenance of Social Boundaries at San Quentin Prison."

4   Lockard, "Prison Writing Education."

5   With notable exceptions: Kunzel, *Criminal Intimacy*, and Dillon, *Fugitive Life*.

6   See, for instance, Stanley and Smith, *Captive Genders*.

7   See Bruenig, "Why Americans Don't Care about Prison Rape," and Peter Wagner and Bernadette Rabuy, "Mass Incarceration: The Whole Pie 2017," *Prison Policy Initiative*, March 14, 2017, www.prisonpolicy.org/reports/pie2017.html.

8   California Department of Corrections and Rehabilitation, Code of Regulations, Division 3 "Adult Institutions, Programs, and Parole," Title 15 "Crime Prevention and Corrections," Subchapter 5, Article 2, Section 3400, www.cdcr.ca.gov /Regulations/Adult_Operations/docs/Title15_2017.pdf.

9   Nigel Poor and Earlonne Woods, episode 10, "Getting a Date," *Ear Hustle*, podcast, October 25, 2017, www.earhustlesq.com/episodes/2017/10/25/getting-a-date.

10   *San Quentin Volunteer Handbook*, 6.

11   Quoting the now-standard "Miller test" for obscenity, the California Penal Code defines *obscene* as "matter, taken as a whole, that to the average person, applying contemporary statewide standards, appeals to the prurient interest, that, taken as a whole, depicts or describes sexual conduct in a patently offensive way, and that, taken as a whole, lacks serious literary, artistic, political, or scientific value." CDCR Code of Regulations, Division 3, Title 9, Chapter 7.5, Section 311, Subdivision (a).

12   Prison Rape Elimination Act 2003, Prison and Jail Standards, Prevention Planning 115.11, www.prearesourcecenter.org/training-technical-assistance/prea-101 /prisons-and-jail-standards.

13 CDCR Code of Regulations, Division 3, Title 15, Chapter 1, Article 1, Section 3007.

14 The notion that prisoners cannot consent also holds true in rules about sex between prisoners, which is likewise disallowed. In spite of the prohibition, it is an open secret that such sex occurs inasmuch that it is acknowledged as a hazard to health. Since 2015, California law has stipulated that condoms must be made available in all correctional institutions, in spite of sex being technically barred. Even masturbation is not permitted, with the rationale that any such act could be construed as a public display and thus lewd exposure. As one ruling on this matter reasons, "Prisoners have no cognizable right to sexual privacy in a jail cell." In this impressive tautology, the state disallows the right to privacy because it has provided the prisoner no privacy.

15 Freud, "Fetishism."

16 Bhabha, "The Other Question."

17 Deleuze, *Masochism*, 31.

18 See Daniel Hirsch, "Protest at Kink.com Leads to Three Arrests," *Mission Local*, June 30, 2014, https://missionlocal.org/2014/06/268484.

BIBLIOGRAPHY

Alexander, Michelle. *The New Jim Crow: Mass Incarceration in the Age of Colorblindness*. New York: New Press, 2010.

Bhabha, Homi. "The Other Question: Difference, Discrimination and the Discourses of Colonialism." *Screen* 24, no. 6 (1983): 18–36.

Bruenig, Elizabeth Stoker. "Why Americans Don't Care about Prison Rape." *Nation*, March 2, 2015. www.thenation.com/article/why-americans-dont-care-about-prison-rape.

Davis, Angela. *Abolition Democracy: Beyond Prisons, Torture, and Empire*. New York: Seven Stories, 2005.

Davis, Angela. *Are Prisons Obsolete?* New York: Seven Stories, 2003.

Davis, Angela. *The Meaning of Freedom: And Other Difficult Dialogues*. San Francisco: City Lights Books, 2012.

Deleuze, Gilles. *Masochism: Coldness and Cruelty & Venus in Furs*. Translated by Jean McNeil and Aude Willm. New York: Zone, 1991.

Dillon, Stephen. *Fugitive Life: The Queer Politics of the Prison State*. Durham, NC: Duke University Press, 2018.

DuVernay, Ava, dir. *13th*. Netflix, 2016. www.netflix.com/au/title/80091741.

Freud, Sigmund. "Fetishism." In *The Standard Edition of the Complete Psychological Works of Sigmund Freud*, vol. 21, edited by James Strachey, 149–57. London: Hogarth, 1971.

Kunzel, Regina. *Criminal Intimacy: Prison and the Uneven History of Modern American Sexuality*. Chicago: University of Chicago Press, 2008.

Lindahl, Nicole. "Intimacy, Manipulation, and the Maintenance of Social Boundaries at San Quentin Prison." Institute for the Study of Societal Issues Fellows Working Papers Series, University of California, Berkeley, 2011. https://escholarship.org/uc/item/15w491vk.

Lockard, Joe. "Prison Writing Education and US Working-Class Consciousness." In *Prison Pedagogies: Learning and Teaching with Imprisoned Writers*, edited by Joe Lockard and Sherry Rankins-Robertson, 11–31. Syracuse, NY: Syracuse University Press, 2018.

Stanley, Eric A., and Nat Smith, eds. *Captive Genders: Trans Embodiment and the Prison Industrial Complex*. Oakland: AK, 2015.

Walcott, Rinaldo. "*Moonlight*'s Necessary Company." GLQ 25, no. 2 (2019): 337–41.

8

THE COLOR OF KINSHIP

Race, Biology, and Queer Reproduction

JAYA KEANEY

On a muggy June afternoon in 2016, I interview David in the lounge room of his inner-city terrace. We sit side by side on an enormous leather couch as he recounts how he and his husband, another white gay man, conceived their biracial son with the labor of a commercial surrogate and a commercial egg donor in India. As we talk, I face a floor-to-ceiling ebony bookshelf that seems close to sagging with the weight of dozens of neatly posed family photographs of the men, their son, Cameron, and extended family and friends.

When I ask David how he tells people about his son's origins, he describes an upcoming kindergarten project. As part of the curriculum, Cameron's class will chart their collective heritage on a large world map. In preparation for this task, Cameron's fathers have been asked to provide information about where their son is from. "We ask that you think about where your family has originated," the form instructs, "rather than just writing down where they are born." After discussion with the teacher, David and his husband list their backgrounds as "American" and "Australian." They exclude the Indian backgrounds of the egg donor and surrogate. As Cameron's teacher advised, "People are born all over the world, but that doesn't necessarily make their heritage from the country they were born." David tells me that six-year-old Cameron "is very proud of his story." He then adds, "He is a child born from pure love."

IN HIS FIELD-DEFINING TEXT *Cruising Utopia*, the late Cuban American cultural critic José Esteban Muñoz engages the utopian possibilities of a queer political project. Honing attention on the racialized and sexualized reproductive formations that delimit our ability to imagine queer lives outside the business as usual of white national orders, Muñoz offers a notion of queer futurity as a practice of forging other worlds and refusing to reproduce more of the same. Against the dominant horizon of white reproductive futurity, Muñoz imagines a "'not-yet' where queer youths of color actually get to grow up."[1] In this essay, rather than track the thriving of a current generation of queer youth, I take up the implications of Muñoz's queer utopianism for an increasingly common racialized and queered figure of contemporary childhood: the child of same-sex parents who is conceived through assisted conception. With the gay and lesbian baby boom of the 2000s behind us, the recent legalization of gay marriage has formally institutionalized the already settled social genre of the gay-parented family. Although the numbers of gay-parented families are on the rise, the forms of those families are changing with reference to an assisted-reproduction industry that pushes would-be parents away from adoption, fostering, and coparenting toward surrogacy and donor-assisted conception, practices that are often centered on the nuclear grammar of "a child of one's own." Because of the transnational structure of assisted-reproduction markets, many of the queer families brought into being through such practices comprise a white parent or parents and "gaybies" of color.

The significant uptake of assisted reproduction by queers demands that we approach the queer family as a scene of racialized commitment. Under what conditions, and within what visions of kinship, do children of color like David's son Cameron grow up? In the family narratives I consider here, queer parents manage or, more commonly, efface racial difference by centering their reproductive origin stories on children born from love. According to many of the parents I interviewed in the course of my research, love is all it takes for queer families to stay the course. In these accounts, racial difference is cast as insignificant or peripheral to the feeling of belonging in a family. This discourse is consistent with a decades-long strategy in queer activist movements of promoting choice as the defining quality of queer intimate forms. No longer constrained by our families of origin, we are "families of choice." But although this strategy has spurred rich vernaculars for making intelligible queer attachments that reject biological imperatives, the racializing and nationalist implications of such a discourse have been less substantially addressed.

This critical neglect is partly a result of the way in which important traditions of queer theory preemptively cast marriage and reproduction as normative projects entwined with the state. Second only to marriage, child rearing is considered to be among the prevailing heteronorms that, even when given a same-sex makeover, continue to structure the life course around heteronormative generational rhythms that render other teleologies of cultural reproduction unthinkable.[2] In response to the disciplinary function of reproductive futurity, many queer theorists have reveled instead in the queerness of antisociality or the possibility of a world beyond the symbolic order of the Child.[3] But while the uppercase figure of the Child has been a generative spark for queer theory, the everyday life of children and their fleshy creation are less frequently considered to be fertile sites for queer critique.

Exploring queer reproduction from the vantage point of the everyday makes visible the intimate processes whereby queerness, race, and reproduction are assembled and lived out in increasingly common scenes of queer kin making. In charting how some queer families encounter race in their reproductive lives, we gain insight into how the study of the particular can shift established theories of queer intimacy and duration. As Heather Love establishes in her work on the "queer ordinary," emphasizing the plurality of the normal as something that is enacted in daily practices draws all of us, critics included, onto the same enmeshed social plane.[4] Certainly, the same-sex parents described here dwell in the promise and muck of the procreative long term, and it is from this position that they negotiate the "racial ephemera" associated with surrogacy and other reproductive technologies.[5]

In order to trace the racialized commitment of queer families out to public discourses of queerness, race, and nation, the archive mined here is a series of interviews conducted with same-sex parents who used or were using the reproductive technologies of gamete donation and surrogacy to conceive children. Many of these families are multiracial, with parents of a different race from their children. Although a substantial literature on assisted reproduction and queer family making has positioned race matching—the process through which intending parents prioritize ethnic resemblance in gamete donor selection—as the norm, this study contravenes this, with a significant number of parents rejecting the imperative to match race.[6]

The interview data were collected in the form of open-ended narrative interviews conducted in urban cities in Australia between 2016 and 2017. This process is best phrased as collaborative storying, or what Jennifer Mason and Katherine Davies call "creative interview encounters" in which "multiple vocabularies" are in play across verbal, gestural, and affective domains.[7] As a queer, mixed-race woman of color, my embodied experiences of interpellation by informants emerged as a powerful factor in studying racialization across affective vocabularies. More than once, I found myself plunged into shock, biting back rage or swallowing tears in response to my participants' stories and questions about my race. While I veiled these responses, they reverberated around the conversation and indelibly shaped my understanding of how my informants allowed for or denied the everyday reality of racism in the lives of their children of color.

Love Makes a Family

Love has proved to be a salient political technology in the recent transnational campaigns for gay marriage. In 2017 an Australian campaign followed on the heels of the juggernaut United States campaign launched by several LGBTIQA+ organizations, including the Human Rights Campaign and the Civil Marriage Collaborative. "Love Is Love" became the rallying cry in the lead-up to the 2017 voluntary postal survey that polled Australian citizens on whether same-sex marriage should be introduced into law. Spread across billboards and the facades of countless houses, printed on a run of colorful promotional T-shirts by Australian fashion designer Gorman, and scrawled in marker across placards and bodies, "Love Is Love" was a magnetic and effective campaign slogan. As a tautology, "Love Is Love" also turns attention to the role of repetition and temporal ricochet in discourse formation, gesturing implicitly to genealogies through which its referent—queer coupledom—is recognizable.

The emphasis on love is intelligible through a long history of mobilization around alternative families. Queer discourses centered on love as a means to reimagine kinship notably appeared in the 1980s. Kath Weston documents the emergence of this discourse in *Families We Choose*, her landmark ethnography of the affinity bonds formed between queer people and their children in the Bay Area of San Francisco in the 1980s and 1990s. Weston argues that queer families do not reject the terms of biological kinship outright but rather reappropriate the established vernacular to transform kinship beyond nuclear, heterosexual terms. Love, rather than the political anger or outrage central to other activist campaigns, emerged as a lever in reappropriation strategies that brought queers out of the shadow of antifamily rhetoric and into the family fold.[8] A notable flash point was the centering of the phrase "love makes a family" at the second Gay and Lesbian March on Washington in 1987, where it functioned as a defense against the virulent "family values" rhetoric of the Christian far right, and the lack of durable legal or social protections for queer parenting claims.[9]

In the 1980s, that is, love offered a through line between the ideological opposition of choice versus blood that queer people navigated when staging their kinship claims.[10] By the second march on Washington, gay messaging on this point had taken on a new edge. As Weston recalls,

> The sign at the 1987 Gay and Lesbian March on Washington read: "Love makes a family—nothing more, nothing less." From the stage, speakers arguing for domestic partner benefits and gay people's right to parent repeatedly invoked love as both the necessary *and the sufficient* criterion for defining kinship. Grounding kinship in love deemphasized distinctions between erotic and non-erotic relations while bringing friends, lovers, and children together under a single concept. As such, love offered a symbol well suited to carry the nuances of identity and unity so central to kinship in the United States, yet circumvent the procreative assumption embedded in symbols like heterosexual intercourse and blood ties.[11]

It is not that the call to love negates "the procreative assumption" but that it redefines family against the narrow vertical criterion of reproductivity by allowing friendship, erotic histories, and community building to register as reproductive forms. Amid the vast destruction wrought by the AIDS crisis and the reality or threat of queer parents' loss of custodial rights, love offered a vital platform for articulating the power of alternative social forms. Speaking of queer activist organizing around AIDS, Cindy Patton describes the discourse of love in this era as "a state of durable and transportable respect, not a government- or church-sanctified union," a statement that also points to the capacity of the concept to jump across national borders and contexts.[12]

Today, however, prominent love discourses do not stage oppositional claims but instead seek identity-based state recognition for marriage and child rearing. These discourses and the recognitions they seek are overwhelmingly yoked to nuclear forms of family. The phrase "love makes a family," once a slogan for queer community making, is now emblazoned on merchandise that marks both the increasing banality of queer families and the consolidation of the gayby into a discursive entity.[13] In the decades since the 1980s, "love" of this kind has shifted from a counterdiscourse to a settled regime of truth that delimits the bounds of family. As in the past, the discourse of love is still used to articulate the significance of the bonds between queer parents and children, but now it is also used to legitimate conception across biotechnological domains that differently expand and retract notions of queer kinship.

"Love makes a family" discourse is increasingly used to express the legitimacy of nonbiological parenthood in the assisted-reproduction field, a domain that otherwise gets nailed down in the hard language of transnational legislation and biotechnology. As the Australian advocacy body the Victorian Assisted Reproductive Treatment Authority (VARTA) writes in a recent document on donor conception,

> There is no right or wrong way to talk to children about their donor origins but it may be helpful to consider some of the strategies suggested by experts in the field. In addition to making sure that the tone of the story is positive, framing it around "how we built our family" rather than "how you were conceived" may help to reinforce the donor-conceived person's place in the family. A narrative of donor conception based on the idea of "family building" or "love makes a family" can also be useful for different types of families, such as heterosexual couples, single mothers or lesbian and gay couples.[14]

Here, the explanatory framework of love in the context of assisted reproduction is self-evident: it is expansive enough to encompass family diversity and universalizing enough to group diverse families together, exfoliating queer difference within a broader desexualized cohort. But this universalizing discourse is not the same as the queer community-making discourse that it supersedes.

VARTA's rendition of "love makes a family" exemplifies what Jenny Gunnarsson Payne describes as an emerging "grammar of reproductive intent" in constructions of parenthood. Emerging with the rise in commercial surrogacy practice, which rapidly outpaced the development of robust legal regulation, this grammar constructs parenthood as a relation of intent and reproductive effort rather than genetic or gestational ties.[15] In the interviews

I conducted, combined appeals to love and voluntary choice were used to evoke an affective bond between parents and child that existed prior to conception and the involvement of reproductive technicians or laborers. Time and again, this discourse of choice and intent overlapped with counterclaims about the power and validity of queer family-making efforts and legacies that were also premised on love. In this sense, the mainstreaming of assisted conception and its discourses of parental intent reframes queer experiments in creating intimate collectivities that exceed the nuclear as aspirations to universalism. It also places sexual subjectivity and family formation in the domain of voluntarism, a place that is no longer constrained by rote biological dictums such as the biogenetic transmission of race.

Gay and lesbian discourses of reproductive intent often seek to emphasize the added value of deliberative conception journeys, particularly in response to suggestions that such methods of family formation are onerous, deromanticized, or less "natural." As Robert Pralat writes, "a popular argument in support of lesbian and gay parenting is that, because of the necessity of planning for parenthood among same-sex couples, resulting children are always wanted and parents are additionally prepared to take care of their offspring."[16] This was indeed the case for Timothy, who emphasized the significance of choice in enhancing the value of his family ties. Speaking of the great lengths and expense to which he and his partner went in conceiving their child with an egg donor and a surrogate in the United States, Timothy said that "we are very cognizant of the fact that we didn't do it in the back seat of a Barina after three Bacardi Breezers. Ours was a long process, and a very, very expensive process to get there, so we had to put a lot of thought into it."

One implication of Timothy's statement is that families of choice are to be valued for their conscious or informed mobilization of biological factors in reproduction, as opposed to the conjured figure of the reproductively reckless girl in the back of a Holden Barina, a car as déclassé as the RTDs she is said to have drunk. Timothy implies that financial effort and transnational mobility frame his actions as the result of careful deliberation, rather than accidental hedonism. As Pralat notes, gays and lesbians often invoke the trope of not having a child "by accident" to highlight the way that heteronormativity renders straight conceptions "immune from scrutiny," whereas queer family-making efforts face significant cultural surveillance and moral judgment.[17] Yet Timothy also reveals how the families-of-choice discourse can stigmatize working-class mothers and other actors who are seen as not having the capacity to make concerted reproductive choices. As Timothy's invocation of stereotype makes clear, the grammar of reproductive intent is heavily encoded with social class, where values of preplanning, responsibility, and wealth reinforce middle-class notions of stability and life-course expectations. As Don Romesburg writes of his own privilege in navigating the adoption system, "Transracially adopting white gay couples get framed as families that *can* choose because we appear to *deserve* choice. We get contrasted with families divided by foster care and adoption, who have supposedly failed to make the right choices to such an extent that choosing is no longer an option."[18] The queer discourse of reproductive intent can thus reinforce classed notions of responsibility and autonomy that inflect dominant constructions of citizenship, with material consequences for working-class and racialized families. "Love makes a family" discourse stages citizenship claims on the basis of freely chosen, unencumbered intimate associations that are available to some but denied others.

Elizabeth Povinelli argues in *The Empire of Love* that love has always functioned as a fundamental mode of recognition within settler societies.[19] Indeed, she argues, to be without love, and the recognition that follows it, "is to risk being dehumanized and subject to all the harms of the dehumanizing practices of modernity."[20] For Povinelli, the operation of intimacy in liberal states is centrally built on the binary of freedom and constraint. It is through this opposition that kinship and, subsequently, citizenship, are made intelligible.[21] Povinelli casts this as a contest between the "autological" and "genealogical" imaginaries that organize liberal notions of citizenship and accordant distribution of material resources. Autological society, according to Povinelli, engages "discourses, practices, and fantasies about self-making, self-sovereignty and the value of individual freedom associated with the Enlightenment project of contractual constitutional democracy and capitalism." Genealogical society, by contrast, engages "discourses, practices, and fantasies about social constraints placed on the autological subject by various kinds of inheritances." These are not discrete categories but rather coconstitutive channels through which different intimate arrangements come into view. As the "citational field" against which diverse socialities become visible, they are the predominant lens for apprehending difference.[22] Through this dominant bifocal lens, diverse kinship ontologies are reduced to differences between autology and genealogy, between individual self making and cultural tradition. In settler states this reduction process serves to justify the slow death of indigenous people and lifeworlds under colonization by stigmatizing indigenous kinships as trapped in genealogy, and thus illiberal and antimodern.[23]

In contemporary "love makes a family" discourse, queer subjects are constituted through their ability to humanize themselves through freely choosing love. As the global success of the marriage-equality movement attests, the cause of humanization is advanced and legitimated in intelligible genealogical shapes that are autologically engineered: the monogamous couple and their chosen child are recognized as the proper domain in which love can be freely given. Against these paradigmatic subjects of intimate love, we have the ephemeral, pleasure-centered, autological socialities created by practices of cruising and public sex as documented by foundational queer theorists and historians.[24] In the liberal imaginary that Povinelli scopes out, these queer subjects provide the "nightmare version of the modern unattached self."[25] Under the liberal order, the autological experience of intimate love must culminate in a genealogical plot that serves to reproduce the state. Queer families may be families of choice, but only some queer choices are recognized as the autonomous enactments definitive of citizenship in a liberal political terrain. Certainly, in the interviews I conducted, many queer families conceived through assisted reproduction performed an autological narrative by phrasing their reproductive decisions as concerted choices, voluntary or contractual arrangements that they deliberately pursued in order to plot a genealogical story.

What kind of ground does such an autological premise pave for the everyday racialized kinship practices of queer families? Racial descent is typically understood through genealogical models—as a biological inheritance derived from parents—but queer families made through reproductive technologies challenge this logic. In loosening the transmission of race, a child's racial identity formation emerges as a more open question, particularly if it differs from their parents' racial identity. The queer autological discourse of love as a reproductive substance in its own right readily frames race within rhetorics of choice and privacy. David Eng calls this dynamic the "racialization of intimacy," wherein a queer movement grounded in liberal premises "does not resist, but abets, the forgetting of race and the denial of racial difference."[26] For my informants, such a process is newly bound up with the technical affordances of gamete donation and surrogacy that enable nuclear family building beyond cultural or racial ties.

Queer Origins

In the ethnographic vignette with which I opened this chapter, David's Cameron is cast as a "child born from pure love," voicing the dream that emotion could replace biology as reproductive substance. David and his husband are loving, paternal progenitors of their son who are assisted in their intimate aims by the commercial reproductive industry. As Sharmila Rudrappa writes of the Indian surrogacy industry, the discourse of intent is the crucial bedrock on which the economies of surrogacy are stabilized: "Such language allows [the parents] to believe that this baby was always meant to be and always had a place in their hearts prior to even its birth. And once the infant is born, they can walk away with a child that has no social history, and whose origin story begins not with the surrogate mother but with their intentions."[27] If the legacy of decades of activism around love and queer kinship can be heard in David's story, the long-held fantasy that queer love could, of its own accord, make a child is now underwritten by the technology and labor of a transnational assisted-reproduction market. Yet these technological and reproductive laborers are cauterized from the imagined and material family space. Though central to their son's prehistory, the egg donor and surrogate slip away from the family story of parental heritage; they are absent from the primal scene in which familial identity is crafted.

When a child is of a different race from their parents, the redaction of reproductive history can also cauterize racial difference. In narrating an origin story based in love, David rehearses what for many queer families is a banal fact: clearly, the salient field of belonging is the daily labor of parenting young children, which far outweighs the one-off reproductive labors of biological donors and surrogates. In foregrounding the fathers' white American and white Australian ethnic backgrounds as the relevant family heritage, the racialized labor of their Indian egg donor and surrogate and the resultant race of their child are cut ambiguously adrift. This strategy can minimize a child's racial difference itself by constructing it as background, part of the biological leaf litter through which the queer family emerges. The queer nuclear family, by extension, can become a raceless space joined by love rather than the racializing mechanics of biological reproduction.

One of my informants, Stuart, tied his choice of nonwhite egg donors to the central task of creating a good origin story for his daughters. He and his partner are white gay men who conceived their daughters via egg donation and surrogacy. After they could not find any friends or family to act as altruistic surrogates in Australia, the two men turned to what was the global hub for surrogacy at the time: India. They conceived their first mixed-race daughter, Samantha, using an Indian commercial egg donor based in Mumbai and the labor of an Indian commercial surrogate. By the time they wanted to have their second child, though, India was closing as a viable option after global pressure to regulate the industry led the Indian government in 2016 to pass a ban on gay and unmarried couples accessing surrogacy. So

Stuart and his spouse went to Thailand and had their second daughter by commissioning a Thai egg donor and Thai surrogate.

In selecting Thai and Indian egg donors, Stuart and his partner contravene the widespread presumption in many assisted-reproduction markets that parents will "race match." Stuart explained this decision as directly wrapped up with the task of creating a positive queer family origin story for his children:

> Their story is already complex enough, you know. I have two dads, I was born in India through surrogacy and egg donor. I think for us, we thought it was more straightforward to say I have brown skin because I was born in India. . . . Whereas friends of hers that are of a similar age that used South African donors don't know they were born in India and they're four and a half. To me, I prefer to have that transparency with my child.

For Stuart, Indian and Thai egg donors allow for greater parental transparency because they actively compel the conditions of disclosure: the fact of assisted conception is evident in the physical body of the child, through visible racial difference between fathers and children. Stuart directly intervenes into the way that clinical industry norms enshrine a model of relatedness that centers racial resemblance and passing, assumptions that he critiques in his deliberate queer multiracial family making. Here, the use of nonwhite egg donors performs a coming out of sorts, ameliorating the possible harms of secrecy by mapping the child's assisted-conception story explicitly on their body as a method of giving the child direct ownership of that story.

Stuart's reproductive decisions are impelled by an ethic of transparency and openness that values clear communication about a child's origins. The story emerges as an important axis in what Joshua Gamson calls the "heightened sense of storytelling" that characterizes families conceived through assisted reproduction, who often face pressure to tell good stories as a social and legal safeguard.[28] This storytelling is a crucible of racialization through the way a child's race is positioned in terms of the happy ending of the queer family scene. In Stuart's case, selecting Thai and Indian donors is important because it fosters healthy communication and a strong family unit. This selection does not necessarily lead to any further racialized engagement. In this instance, the fathers "made a very conscious decision not to make a fake link" to Indian or Thai culture, because as white Australian fathers, they felt that kind of cultural engagement would be "false" and at the same time risk undermining the truth of their own family unit: "We didn't want to force a culture onto them that is not their family's. . . . Their family unit is the most important to them, I think."

Transparency is a central ethic for Stuart, a quality that is braided into a color-blind portrait of relatedness. In his understanding, race is a univocal visual epistemology. Color does the work of openness simply by appearing as itself, serving the declarative function of announcing the origin story of donor conception and surrogated birth. Race is primarily a static bodily trait that has little broader significance and is detached from, say, minority culture or community. Stuart's personalized narrative reflects broader discourses of racialization that are pervasive in the assisted-reproduction industry, where race is exclusively constructed as genetic: a biological and heritable quality that comes from gametes. Intending parents are compelled to select race through the donor, a process enabled by the routine cataloging of donors by race, phenotype, and personality traits. According to Daisy Deomampo, the broadening availability of gamete donation has "precipitated a return to ideas of genetic and racial essentialism, in which sperm and egg donor profiles are scrutinized for certain traits, with the promise of inheritable phenotypic and skin color characteristics."[29] Certainly, Stuart selects egg donors with the presumption that they will confer easily readable race to his daughters, which becomes, in turn, a resource for family storytelling as well as a biological statement of fact.

Rendering a child's race in color-blind terms reinforces family ties that are otherwise considered socially vulnerable. It affirms the status of queer parents as real parents in the face of enduring constructions of family as biological and heterosexual. This can hold particular significance for parents who do not share a genetic link with their child, as was the case for another of my informants. Amy identifies as white with a Russian grandmother, and with her partner Janice, who is Maltese, conceived a child with sperm from a Peruvian Australian donor. Janice leaned toward an "embrace" of Peruvian culture in their family, but Amy was less keen: "I don't want to necessarily over-identify it. I think it's important for her to know who she is and where she comes from, but I don't know I'd go so far as to read Peruvian books or stories or culture. I would definitely make sure she knows where Peru is in the world and what language they speak and that sort of stuff, but I don't think I'd start cooking Peruvian food or need to go there." Amy understood Janice's relative openness to Peruvian culture as bound up with her secure maternal role as the birth and genetic mother, in contrast to her own need to build a relationship after birth. "It's about us, about the parents," she said.

"That's really ultimately what makes me her parent is being there and doing that. . . . [Peruvian culture] is the donor, not the parent. We're the parents, so therefore it's all about us now."

Amy's description of motherhood as a practice resonates with queer understandings of kinship as formed through loving labor that congeals into a relation over time. But when a child's race is understood as a biological-cultural inheritance from the donor, it has nowhere to go in a family space defined by voluntarism and kinship, crafted by doing, not by biology. In white-parented multiracial families, the decision to foreground the parents' heritage as the basis of family culture is by default a decision to foreground whiteness. In a 2011 interview-based study of twenty sets of gay and heterosexual parents who pursued Indian surrogacy, Rudrappa identifies that although parents who choose Indian donor eggs and surrogates may appear to resist dominant white family forms, in practice they reinforce them through casting Indian surrogates and donors as peripheral to white genetic paternity. In such surrogacy family stories, "The Indian origins of the surrogated babies are racial ephemera absorbed into the familial lineage."[30] For my informants, however, this absorption is inseparably linked to the pressure to reinforce a queer family unit and foreground queer family ties as the primary zone of shared marginality.

Rudrappa's concept of "racial ephemera" might be usefully extended out from specific family stories to the broader discursive terrain of contemporary queer citizenship in which my informants' narratives take root. In positioning surrogates and donors of color as peripheral resources to a central process driven by love, queer conception stories can embed on a micro scale the broader temporality of "beyond" that marks the relationship between queer movements and public discussion of race. For Eng, this beyondness manifests most clearly in strategies that frame queer rights as the latest iteration of civil rights demands that have their political origins in calls for racial equality or the removal of social distinctions. In my informants' narratives, consigning a child's race to a prior moment of consumer selection that results in a queer family obscures the vital textures of racial difference that continue to animate family life and that are inseparable from a queer family identity. As Eng writes, "The logic of queer liberalism in our colorblind moment works to oppose a politics of intersectionality, resisting any acknowledgment of the ways in which sexuality and race are constituted in relation to one another, each often serving to articulate, subsume, and frame the others' legibility in the social domain."[31]

Eng's notion is key to understanding how a narrative of queer origins can sideline consideration of racial difference even when those differences are freely chosen, as in the cases under discussion. The queer discourse of "love makes a family," which seeks to establish parental validity and the distinctive value of nonbiological kinship, subsumes race by sidelining reproductive laborers of color. This gesture also risks rendering illegible the ongoing role of race as a persistent structure for ordering everyday kinship relations between parents and children. In Stuart's case, for example, the positing of cross-racial gamete selection as bound up with queer ethics but detached from racialized social risk frames cross-racial intimacy as a settled social genre, a matter of personal reproductive choice. Casting racial difference as the settled prehistory of the queer family depoliticizes race by cutting it off from the ongoing reality of both personal intimacy and institutional racism.

Origin stories of children "born from love" can thus draw procreation into the realm of queer love and free choice while simultaneously investing the genealogical plot with the capacity to harmonize racial difference. For Robyn Wiegman, reproductive technologies signal a new era in racialized citizenship in the United States that she calls "multiracial kinship," as distinct from the more established "interracial kinship." In separating reproduction and sex, Wiegman argues, reproductive technologies disarticulate race "from the material lineage of coercion and cultural disavowal that has governed, quite literally, interracial sex and reproduction in the United States."[32] Reproductive technologies offer the possibility of cross-racial kinship without interracial sex, that fleshy specter of colonial coercion. These technologies thus offer ample ground for reforming racial transmission, typically considered a matter of biological ties, within logics of choice, autonomy, and self-realization.

Such a reformulation of racial transmission coincides with the shift in queer public discourse away from families of choice toward procreative genealogical plots. As Patton has argued of the post-AIDS era, sex and love, two fixtures of early queer activism, have now been tacked onto the nation.[33] The advent and availability of reproductive technologies deepen the prospect of a sanitized queer subject who reproduces without sex, a formation deeply compatible with broader discourses of race as an elective identification, not a space of interracial coercion. In establishing love as the primary reproductive matrix, queer family discourse offers agentic and deracializing love as the engine for something as rigid and racializing as the family tree. In this desexualized dynamic, race—specifically, racialized reproductive labor—is alienated from a story of autonomous queer family creation.

Despite the recurring construction of race as a prehistory among my informants, race featured again and again as a "live texture" in their daily lives.[34] The experience of queer multiracial families is characterized by hypervisibility, which means they must frequently navigate public curiosity. Many of my informants relayed experiences where strangers puzzled over their children's ambiguous racial appearances by asking questions about conception, a strategy that seeks to "place the person in a web of racialized kinship."[35] Yet in relaying such unsolicited inquiries, parents consciously framed the child's race in overwhelmingly positive terms, keeping the language of voluntarism and choice on center stage even in a situation that speaks to unequal racial prerogatives, such as who is entitled to ask about racialized kinship and who must do the answering. Such encounters attest to the seamless compatibility of the families-of-choice rhetoric with the color-blind protocols of multiculturalism that officially dominate Australian culture.

Several informants described experiences where strangers commented on their child's racial visibility. The parents' responses ranged from celebratory to minimizing, either casting race as "irrelevant," as Stuart did, or commenting on their child's beautiful skin and features, as in Juz and Ella's description of their daughter and her cosmetically "ideal line." Amy also identified with other positive aspects of her daughter's dark skin: "I think lucky little thing, she's not going to have my skin that burns." Very rarely did any parent acknowledge that the hypervisibility of their children in contrast to others reflects a larger landscape of racial inequality.[36]

When parents did subject such racializing questioning to reflection, they typically did so through the lens of heteronormativity. For example, Christine described how people frequently assume she is the genetic mother of her biracial Chinese and Anglo Celtic baby. "People love to ask his ethnicity," she said. "People love to ask, 'What nationality is the father?' That's what they ask me because they assume that I'm the mother—because I hang out with him and he calls me Mama. So they assume that I gave birth to him, and they just want to know what the other half is." Christine accurately captures the deep and inextricable heteronormativity of race as a system for ordering bodies into biological lineages. Yet in casting such an experience as heteronormative, another vital element may be too quickly sidelined. That is, the fact that such exchanges are sparked by the initial interpellation of their children's bodies as out of place in a racial schema where whiteness functions as "a background to social action" such that people of color always stand out.[37] This disjunctive interpellation will structure the experiences of children of color wherever they go, whether or not they are seen with their white parent or parents.

For Eng, celebratory and color-blind framings of race are characteristic of the "new global family." Eng argues that "unlike prior histories of sexual or racial passing" that inscribe the epistemology of the closet, the new order "seems to be less about the problem of detecting a hidden sexual or racial trait than about our collective refusal to see difference in the face of it."[38] For my informants, the erasure of racial difference is not, or not only, about avowing the "truth" of kinship. It is also about the refusal of race as mattering to reproduction, as if reproduction stood outside the institutionalized inequalities that attach to other matters of public concern.

Stuart offered a particularly troubling example of the refusal to see difference when he described his four-year-old daughter Samantha's relationship to her brown skin. Briefly abandoning the discourse of love for something more hard-nosed, Stuart speaks the blunt and obvious truth of his daughter's body: "She knows she has brown skin; she's no fool." Yet he did not acknowledge that this bodily reality may be bound to racialization at any other social level. Stuart explained that although his daughter is aware of her racial difference and is able to relate this to her conception story, the meaning she attaches to it has shifted throughout her young life. "For a while," he said, "she thought she was brown because she ate too much chocolate." Told as a joke, the innocent story nonetheless exemplifies the uneven burden of color blindness. Brown skin is an ornamentation that does not penetrate the field of identity but remains in need of explication or fantasy. Whiteness is the unmarked norm here, with brown skin the deviation and potential blight of a child's self-understanding.

Even in this arresting example, it is clear that "race as accessory" is not the totality of experience for the racialized subject, however young. Stuart added a little later in the interview that Samantha "sometimes speaks in a pretend language." When asked what she is doing, he went on, she responds with "I'm speaking in my language. I'm speaking Indian." When I ask if he thinks she is making a cultural distinction between herself and her parents, Stuart answers, "Yeah, of her own." Despite the evidence that his young daughter experiences her difference in ways she can already articulate, Stuart holds to the belief that for now, fostering a primary investment in immediate family is the best way to nurture his daughter's identity and self-confidence as she grows.

The question of the child's interpellation as different was put off into the future by many of the parents I interviewed. As Janice and Amy said of their daughter Mika, "We don't know how she'll identify." This openness seemed to reflect a queer ethic of wanting to give children autonomy in forging their own affinities and orientations. Unlike the discourse of the closet, the idea of racial identity as an open question ultimately casts the child as the privileged subject of multiculturalism, as a subject who is empowered to self-racialize. Claudia Castañeda critiques a similar dynamic in the context of transracial adoption and the assimilationist framework that she sees it engaging: "Insofar as the child has a racial identity (as opposed to racial makeup), the child nevertheless exercises a liberal 'choice,' such that the child is ultimately self-racializing. Once individualized and detached from a community and shared identity, furthermore, this child can be 'loved' as an 'other' that is . . . no longer 'racially hostile' or 'culturally different.'"[39] The desire to leave a child's identity open relies on a liberal logic whereby the child no longer has a link to a racial or cultural group by virtue of birth. Although a racial makeup is supposedly conferred biologically through gamete selection, the chain of essentialism ends here, with no necessary link between genetic race and cultural belonging. Cultural assimilation is cast as a loving act concordant with Ahmed's description of multiculturalism as "an imperative to love difference" that "works to construct a national ideal that others" (namely, those who insist that difference matters) "fail."[40] Thus, the discourse of self-racialization can work in the service of queer parental space by evacuating the domain of biological-racial inheritance—or what Povinelli would call genealogy—and rendering race a cosmetic accessory to be freely chosen amid all the other elective choices that constitute queer family ties.

It is important to note that this liberal, self-racializing position is available only to some subjects, namely those who are sufficiently able to transcend the uglier constraints of race. Notably, all of the children of color in my study were mixed race with part-white heritage. As Ralina Joseph writes, mixed-race subjects are increasingly used to symbolize the multicultural nation and its fantasy of assimilation and the ultimate dissolution of race. These "exceptional multiracials" are, she writes, "the ultimate 'floating signifiers.'" Such mixed-race bodies can be "de-raced or e-raced" in pursuit of a postracial dynamic wherein race is a selectable commodity, as it is in the assisted-reproduction industry with its routinized categorization of gamete donors by race and phenotype.[41] For Stuart, a mixed-race appearance would mean that people "don't know where that child's from," an ambiguity that would aid family recognition through minimizing the interruptive effect of a racial heritage that is more readily categorizable. David similarly understood his child's ambiguous mixed-race appearance as an attractive quality.

"When I look at you," he said to me, "I wouldn't think that your mother was born in India," as if racial ambiguity was a social asset without negative consequence, unlike other forms of racial demarcation.

I remember feeling deeply uneasy at this moment in the interview. In the tape I can hear tension in my voice. Sitting on David's luxe leather lounge, I was called on to affirm my own body as "less raced" than that of other people of color—my mother, perhaps—so as to confirm our shared commitment to the thriving of queer kinship. David found in my body evidence of the color blindness that I sought to narrativize, a situation that seemed to reduce me to the level of his child, someone who experiences constant racial hailing paired with the refusal of its significance. For a few dilated moments, I was left with nothing to say.

David's commentary on my body also drew to the surface my strong seam of identification with the mixed-race gaybies I met, something that, consciously or not, directed the research from early on. Celebration, fetishistic commentary, and minimization have always been fixtures of my experience of racialization, a routinized gaslighting in a national domain where multiculturalism is pursued as policy if not practice. In my interviews I was struck by the way that queer parenting discourses of love and choice frequently echo the affective tenor of the multicultural discourse central to my experience of racial interpellation and erasure. Perhaps the starkest manifestation of my informants' minimizing of race is their explicit rejection of racism as relevant to their children's lives. Rather than understanding racism as a social structure, the families I spoke with tended to define racism narrowly, as exceptional negative speech acts that occur outside the family home. In my early interviews I did not ask about racism outright. I have come to understand my reticence as braided into the broader dynamic of effacement where queer love—both in its familial forms and in the conviviality established between researcher and researched—takes shape as a happy object. Race, by contrast, is a decidedly unhappy object even in postracial frameworks. To raise race in interviews, especially interviews with white people, was to risk becoming a feminist killjoy as described by Ahmed, someone who "spoils" the happiness of others because she refuses the double narrative of color-blind harmony and the idea that queer parenting is an antidote to racism.[42]

When racism was acknowledged in my interviews, it was most commonly imagined as something as unremarkable as schoolyard bullying. Emma and Simone considered racism as no more damaging than other banal and universal social slights: "Every kid is going to get bullied one way or another." Timothy thought of racism as akin to being teased because "you may have red hair . . . or you may be overweight, or too skinny." He explicitly offered love as the solution to such taunting: "It's true there are some horrible people in the world, but they're going to be horrible no matter what your family history is. . . . So you just have to make sure you give lots of love to your kids, teach them to love themselves, teach them to love others. If you get those things right, really everything else is just your own fears and anxieties." Here, racism is an isolated event imagined as radically exterior to the family or to, say, the selection processes engaged in reproductive markets. It is exceptional, not structural. Hence, the best safeguard against racism is love, the very substance through which queer families are brought into being and the public index of queer civil belonging today.

Something about the gayby of color does not allow racism to stick. Among my informants, the issue of racism was either denied relevance or deflected by raising the issue of queerphobia. When I asked David about the potential for racism in Cameron's life, he answered that "I probably think about him being discriminated against because he has gay parents, more than him being discriminated against because of the egg donor that helped us have a family." For Juz and Ella, a similar question about how their daughter might navigate identity formation in a white family was quickly placed within a broader field of "the identity thing of having same-sex parents" and "the identity thing of having one parent who's Aussie and one who's English."

A similar dynamic played out in a more extended way with Janice and Amy. When I asked them if sadness caused by racism is something they considered in Eva's life, the mothers quickly refocused the conversation on queerphobia as the salient concern. As Janice said, "I think for me it's more about you know, how she's going to go with two mums. How her peers will treat her not coming from your standard mum-dad family. Racism isn't something that we're too sort of concerned about." Amy concurred: "I don't actually think it had crossed my mind that there would be." On tape, this exchange is followed by a few moments of uncomfortable silence before I introduce a new question about diversity in Eva's playgroup. I remember this point in the interview. I was torn between wanting to move things along and give them an "out" and wanting to dwell in the moment of discomfort and give pause for collective thinking.

In hindsight, the blunt effacement of race and the lack of a vocabulary to discuss intimate racism with progressive, color-blind queer people still make me uncomfortable. Because racism is conceived as a possible interruption to queer family solidity, it was frequently backgrounded in favor of considering queerphobia, an experience that draws parents and child together.

Suzanne Lenon and OmiSoore H. Dryden identify such narratives of "homoinnocence" as endemic to gay communities more broadly. Discussions of racism, colonization, and empire among gay people, they observe, "are often framed as extraneous to the authentic, 'real' questions of the insider-outsider status of sexual minorities, where the privileged positioning of injury (re)articulates and further solidifies a heterosexual-homosexual binary."[43] Although my informants considered queer family love both miraculous and ordinary, racism was rendered out of place in the intimate domain and the settled joy of queer domestic diversity, where racial makeup is construed as a cosmetic trait not necessarily bound up with identity formation.

IMPLICIT IN THE QUEER family discourse engaged by my informants is the dream that something other than identity might organize our affiliations and generate vital energy for change. This dream pulses in the folds of their universalizing narratives as they invest love with the ability to rise above sharp, segregationist lines of difference and empower their children with pride in their queer origins. In these family stories, love is invested with the promise of guaranteeing happiness within a queer family refuge that will stay the course. Love speaks to considered and deliberate kin creation, with the assisted-reproduction market lending itself to the creative force of queer intentionality.

Love discourse is a pervasive feature of the social field of intimacy. It has proved hugely effective in conferring civil recognition for queer families, albeit on deeply prescriptive terms. But as a primary tool for rendering confrontations with difference inside queer families, the discourse of love can deracialize kinship on ground already tilled by liberal multiculturalism. Such discourse freely centers chosen love as the key criterion for liberal recognition, just as it constructs race and racialization as objects that find their proper home not in public discussions of structural racism but in the private domain, in voluntarism and assumptions of autonomy. The transnational market of assisted conception seamlessly reinforces such formulations by positioning race as one selective consideration among many in the customization of children.

In attempting to transcend heterosexist definitions of family by emphasizing love over biology, queer discourse as it is lived rather than theorized can lean heavily on broader constructions of reproduction and intimate recognition that have a deracializing universalism at their heart. In the narrative framing of children as "born from pure love," queerness is remade into a vertical kinship system in which the shared familial inheritance involves queer traditions of choice, self making, and creativity that may be hard to distinguish from their neoliberal counterparts. Simultaneously, the characteristic verticality of race is flattened into a horizontal resource to be managed by the child rather than shared as a collective responsibility. The insistence on love represents a powerful rejection of rote biological dictums about what constitutes a family, but displacing race in favor of intergenerational queer affinity fails to grapple with the racial politics of assisted reproduction, which continues to play out on both autological and genealogical axes.

A final irony is that love, of all things, should be called upon as the durable basis of queer kinship discourse and claims for recognition. Love, it seems to me, is the occasion not of our conscious and intentional affiliation but of our interpermeation with systems that are not of our own making. Although the vulnerable and transformative thrust of love may be interior to the experience of queer conception and familial attachment, it often drops out of the outward-facing discourse that crafts queer parenting as the bedrock of a futurity premised on color-blind harmony. Love might still be a fertile resource for remaking kinship in a queer vein, but only if it is conceived as a channel for transformation through relation and a processual reckoning with racialization rather than the guarantee of a deracialized happy ending in which all bodies and labors, including the bodies and labors of surrogates, are factored the same.

NOTES

1 Muñoz, *Cruising Utopia*, 95–96.

2 See, in particular, Edelman, *No Future*; Eng, *The Feeling of Kinship*; Puar, *Terrorist Assemblages*; Halberstam, *The Queer Art of Failure*.

3 Chief among these is Edelman, *No Future*. Further are the proponents of what has been called the "antisocial thesis."

4 Love, "Doing Being Deviant," 91–93.

5 Sharmila Rudrappa coins the concept "racial ephemera" in her exploration of how Indianness is constructed among Western parents who commission Indian surrogates and egg donors. I extend her concept to explore racialization in both queer family narratives and queer movement genealogies. See Rudrappa, "Reconsiderations of Race," 209–21.

6 For an analysis of the queer multiracial family as an emergent figure made possible by the assisted-reproduction industries, see Keaney, "The Queer Multiracial Family as Figuration."

7 See Mason and Davies, "Experimenting with Qualitative Methods."

8 Weston, *Families We Choose*, 26–28.

9 Briggs, *How All Politics Became Reproductive Politics*, 149–56.

10   Weston, *Families We Choose*, 26–28.

11   Weston, *Families We Choose*, 107.

12   Patton, "On Me, Not in Me," 356.

13   Hosking, Mulholland, and Baird, "We Are Doing Just Fine."

14   VARTA, "Why, When and How to Tell Children about Donor Conception: A Review of the Literature," The Victorian Assisted Reproductive Treatment Authority, January 2014, 7. www.varta.org.au/resources/research-and-publications/why-when-and-how-tell-children-about-donor-conception.

15   Payne, "Autonomy in Altruistic Surrogacy," 74.

16   Pralat, "Parenthood as Intended," 4.

17   Pralat, "Parenthood as Indented," 12.

18   Romesburg, "Where She Comes From," 9.

19   Povinelli, *The Empire of Love*.

20   Povinelli, "Notes on Gridlock," 228.

21   Povinelli defines liberalism as a "moving target," not a firm referent but a historical formation of practices, discourses, philosophies, and mythologies that reinforce its power as a cited ideology while affording it sustaining flexibility. She traces this moving target from the projects and power relations of European empire and its accordant political philosophies to the contradictions evident within contemporary systems of affective governance. See Povinelli, *The Empire of Love*, 13–14.

22   Povinelli, *The Empire of Love*, 3–4, 37.

23   Berlant, "Slow Death (Sovereignty, Obesity, Lateral Agency)," 754.

24   See, for example, Delany, *Times Square Red, Times Square Blue*, and Berlant and Warner, "Sex in Public."

25   Povinelli, *The Empire of Love*, 101.

26   Eng, *The Feeling of Kinship*, 4.

27   Rudrappa, "What to Expect When You're Expecting," 300.

28   Gamson, *Modern Families*, 207–8.

29   Deomampo, *Transnational Reproduction*, 101.

30   Rudrappa, "Reconsiderations of Race," 221.

31   Eng, *The Feeling of Kinship*, 3.

32   Wiegman, "Intimate Publics," 869.

33   Patton, "On Me, Not in Me," 370.

34   Stewart, *Ordinary Affects*, 107.

35   Wade, *Race, Ethnicity, and Nation*, 8.

36   Transracial-adoption scholars have observed a similar dynamic, where adoptive parents tend to minimize their children's racial difference, with significant harm inflicted on the children's identity formation as a result. See Romesburg, "Where She Comes From," 6. See also Samuels, "Being Raised by White People," and Vonk, Lee, and Crolley-Simic, "Cultural Socialization Practices."

37   Ahmed, "A Phenomenology of Whiteness," 149.

38   Eng, *The Feeling of Kinship*, 2.

39   Castañeda, *Figurations*, 92.

40   Ahmed, *The Cultural Politics of Emotion*, 133.

41   Joseph, *Transcending Blackness*, 26.

42 Ahmed, *The Promise of Happiness*, 65.
43 Lenon and Dryden, "Introduction," 9.

BIBLIOGRAPHY

Ahmed, Sara. *The Cultural Politics of Emotion*. Edinburgh: Edinburgh University Press, 2004.

Ahmed, Sara. "A Phenomenology of Whiteness." *Feminist Theory* 8, no. 2 (2007): 149–68.

Ahmed, Sara. *The Promise of Happiness*. Durham, NC: Duke University Press, 2010.

Berlant, Lauren. "Slow Death (Sovereignty, Obesity, Lateral Agency)." *Critical Inquiry* 33, no. 4 (2007): 754–80.

Berlant, Lauren, and Michael Warner. "Sex in Public." *Critical Inquiry* 24, no. 2 (1998): 547–66.

Briggs, Laura. *How All Politics Became Reproductive Politics: From Welfare Reform to Foreclosure to Trump*. Berkeley: University of California Press, 2017.

Castañeda, Claudia. *Figurations: Child, Bodies, Worlds*. Durham, NC: Duke University Press, 2002.

Delany, Samuel R. *Times Square Red, Times Square Blue*. New York: New York University Press, 1999.

Deomampo, Daisy. *Transnational Reproduction: Race, Kinship, and Commercial Surrogacy in India*. New York: New York University Press, 2016.

Edelman, Lee. *No Future: Queer Theory and the Death Drive*. Durham, NC: Duke University Press, 2004.

Eng, David L. *The Feeling of Kinship: Queer Liberalism and the Racialization of Intimacy*. Durham, NC: Duke University Press, 2010.

Gamson, Joshua. *Modern Families: Stories of Extraordinary Journeys to Kinship*. New York: New York University Press, 2015.

Halberstam, Jack [Judith]. *The Queer Art of Failure*. Durham, NC: Duke University Press, 2011.

Hosking, Gipsy, Monique Mulholland, and Barbara Baird. "'We Are Doing Just Fine': The Children of Australian Gay and Lesbian Parents Speak Out." *Journal of GLBT Family Studies* 11, no. 4 (2014): 1–24.

Joseph, Ralina L. *Transcending Blackness: From the New Millennium Mulatta to the Exceptional Multiracial*. Durham, NC: Duke University Press, 2013.

Keaney, Jaya. "The Queer Multiracial Family as Figuration." In *The Reproductive Industry: Intimate Experiences and Global Processes*, edited by Vera Mackie, Sarah Ferber, and Nicola Marks, 79–96. Lanham, MD: Lexington, 2019.

Lenon, Suzanne, and OmiSoore H. Dryden. "Introduction: Interventions, Iterations, and Interrogations That Disturb the (Homo)Nation." In *Disrupting Queer Inclusion: Canadian Homonationalisms and the Politics of Belonging*, edited by OmiSoore H. Dryden and Suzanne Lenon, 3–18. Vancouver: UBC Press.

Love, Heather. "Doing Being Deviant: Deviance Studies, Description, and the Queer Ordinary." *differences* 26, no. 1 (2015): 74–95.

Mason, Jennifer, and Katherine Davies. "Experimenting with Qualitative Methods: Researching Family Resemblance." In *Understanding Social Research: Thinking Cre-*

atively about Method, edited by Jennifer Mason and Angela Dale, 33–48. London: Sage, 2011.

Muñoz, José Esteban. *Cruising Utopia: The Then and There of Queer Futurity*. New York: New York University Press, 2009.

Patton, Cindy. "'On Me, Not in Me': Locating Affect in Nationalism after AIDS." *Theory, Culture & Society* 15, nos. 3–4 (1998): 355–73.

Payne, Jenny Gunnarsson. "Autonomy in Altruistic Surrogacy: Conflicting Kinship Grammars and Intentional Multilineal Kinship." *Reproductive Biomedicine Online* 7 (November 2018): 66–75.

Povinelli, Elizabeth A. *The Empire of Love: Toward a Theory of Intimacy, Genealogy, and Carnality*. Durham, NC: Duke University Press, 2006.

Povinelli, Elizabeth A. "Notes on Gridlock: Genealogy, Intimacy, Sexuality." *Public Culture* 14, no. 1 (2002): 215–38.

Pralat, Robert. "Parenthood as Intended: Reproductive Responsibility, Moral Judgments, and Having Children 'by Accident.'" *Sociological Review* 68, no. 1 (2019): 161–76.

Puar, Jasbir K. *Terrorist Assemblages: Homonationalism in Queer Times*. Durham, NC: Duke University Press, 2007.

Romesburg, Don. "Where She Comes From: Locating Queer Transracial Adoption." *QED* 1, no. 3 (2014): 1–29.

Rudrappa, Sharmila. "Reconsiderations of Race: Commissioning Parents and Transnational Surrogacy in India." In *Reconsidering Race: Social Science Perspectives on Racial Categories in the Age of Genomics*, edited by Kazuko Suzuki and Diego A. von Vacano, 209–21. Oxford: Oxford University Press, 2018.

Rudrappa, Sharmila. "What to Expect When You're Expecting: The Affective Economies of Consuming Surrogacy in India." *Positions: Asia Critique* 24, no. 1 (2016): 281–302.

Samuels, Gina Miranda. "Being Raised by White People: Navigating Racial Difference among Adopted Multiracial Adults." *Journal of Marriage and Family* 71 (2009): 80–94.

Stewart, Kathleen. *Ordinary Affects*. Durham, NC: Duke University Press, 2007.

Vonk, Elizabeth M., Jaegoo Lee, and Josie Crolley-Simic. "Cultural Socialization Practices in Domestic and International Transracial Adoption." *Adoption Quarterly* 13, nos. 3–4 (2010): 227–47.

Wade, Peter, ed. *Race, Ethnicity, and Nation: Perspectives from Kinship and Genetics*. New York: Berghahn, 2007.

Weston, Kath. *Families We Choose: Lesbians, Gays, Kinship*. New York: Columbia University Press, 1991.

Wiegman, Robyn. "Intimate Publics: Race, Property, and Personhood." *American Literature* 74, no. 4 (2002): 859–85.

9

TOWARD A POLITICAL ECONOMY
OF THE LONG TERM

LISA ADKINS AND MARYANNE DEVER

Introduction

This chapter seeks to situate the issue of long-term same-sex commitments in the changing dynamics of financial obligations in households. In so doing, it seeks to build toward a political economy of long-term commitment (or long termism). This political economy complicates and muddles the axiomatic reading of long-term same-sex commitments found in critical queer and sexuality studies, namely that such commitments—and especially shared household financial obligations—are expressions of the domestication of gay and lesbian lives and of homonormativity. As is well rehearsed in critical queer and sexuality studies, homonormativity is understood as a sexual politics whose foundation was built in the 1990s through alliances between conservative elements of gay and lesbian organizations and the then-ascendant third way politics. This alliance, in turn, is understood to have opened up a set of exclusionary benefits and rights for gays and lesbians—and especially for same-sex couples—who live lives or aspire to live lives that approximate to existing heteronormative orders. However, what this chapter will suggest is that this account of homonormativity consistently fails to take into account the ways in which finance capital and the state in the current era have activated long-term financial commitments and obligations within couples as part of strategies to promote financial expansion and asset-based welfare across the whole population. In turn, such strategies must be understood in terms of the central role of the household in the financial system and the configuring of household assets as resources to fund life.

Therefore, the intervention of this chapter is that rather than as an expression of a particular form of conservative and regressive sexual politics, long termism might be better understood as a political-economic phenomenon specific to the current era: the outcome of a set of policy and legal interventions that seeks to activate the uptake of financial obligations. Understood in this way, long termism emerges less as an effect of a set of unfolding benefits and rights for specific same-sex couples from which a range of other sexual dissidents are excluded, and more as the effect of a policy regime that seeks to maximize the capacities of whole populations and especially of households constituted as financial units.

To build this intervention, the chapter focuses on the case of Australia and especially on the bundle of rights and obligations given over to same-sex couples following a 2006 national inquiry into discrimination in the areas of financial and employment benefits. For critical queer and sexuality scholars, these rights and obligations would doubtless be located as prime exemplars of the operations of homonormativity because, at face value, they appear to give privileges and benefits to wage-earning, home-owning, mortgage-paying, and superannuation-investing cisgender same-sex couples to the exclusion of poor, unemployed, unwaged, non-asset-owning sexual minorities. However, we will show how these rights and obligations, now codified in an array of institutional practices—including the guarantees of superannuation companies and the client assessments performed by welfare agencies—are ones that give shape to and activate a particular same-sex household: one comprising a couple defined by their financial obligations and commitments to each other who will make use of their assets to provision their own welfare.

We will show how the very same sets of rights and obligations operate in regard to the poor, the unwaged, the wageless, and the unemployed—indeed, how the bundle of rights and obligations given over to same-sex couples seeks to activate these same capacities in the nonwage-earning, welfare-dependent same-sex couple. To begin, it is necessary that we briefly map debates in critical queer and sexuality studies on the homonormative.

Homonormative Times

The political historian Lisa Duggan has described homonormativity as the sexual politics of the neoliberal era.[1] Emergent from the 1990s onward, and operating as a key component of third way politics, homonormativity, Duggan argues, is a "politics that does not contest dominant heteronormative assumptions and institutions but upholds and sustains them while promising the possibility of a demobilized gay constituency and a privatized, depoliticized gay culture anchored in domesticity and consumption."[2] She is careful to make clear that homonormativity in no way parallels heteronormativity, especially inasmuch as the latter concerns a range of embedded and durable institutional structures that supports its reproduction. Her point instead is that in the neoliberal era, sexual politics has taken a distinctive turn in which long-term, committed, monogamous, domesticated, and propertied (especially home-owning) relationships are desired not only by portions of the gay and lesbian community but also by the state.[3]

The role of the state in the promulgation of homonormativity is evidenced, so the story tends to go, in the swath of rights-based and equalities-based legal and policy changes that have taken place across advanced liberal societies over the past thirty years. These include the passing of a range of antidiscrimination laws, the legal recognition of same-sex relationships, the passing of same-sex marriage legislation, the granting of certain reproductive rights to same-sex couples, the passing of same-sex partnership adoption legislation, and the extension, in particular circumstances, of immigration rights to same-sex couples. Although these liberalizing, rights- and equalities-based measures have actively been lobbied for by reformist (and well-resourced) LGBT organizations—and gay marriage now stands as the acceptable face of sexual minoritarianism—they are routinely located by critical queer and sexuality scholars as deleterious on at least two counts.

First, it is argued that these measures have reduced LGBTIQ struggles to a narrow liberal agenda of equalities and rights and in so doing have not only obscured more radical and progressive LGBTIQ political agendas, especially those seeking a redistribution of resources, but have also worked toward rendering such agendas and politics anachronistic.[4] In other words, these measures have worked toward a process of the delegitimization of progressive LGBTIQ political agendas and have done so in an era where inequalities, especially those based on wealth, are rapidly intensifying.[5] Indeed, critical queer and sexuality scholars regularly point out that at our current juncture the state is paradoxically seeking to extend certain protections to particular sections of the LGBTIQ community while at the same time—via ongoing welfare reform and the continuing promotion of asset-based welfare—abandoning those sections of that same community who are out of work, in work but impoverished, imprisoned, disabled, homeless, and/or reliant on state benefits for survival.[6]

Second, and as this implies, such measures are widely understood to be actively contributing to fault lines and inequalities within LGBTIQ populations. Through the provision of special legal statuses and certain rights, measures such as same-sex marriage and antidiscrimination legislation for same-sex partners incentivize and privilege certain LGBTIQ sexual relationships, especially the committed, cohabiting, private, propertied couple, to the exclusion of those relationships (and identities) that necessarily fall outside of this framework. In so doing they not only authorize those LGBTIQ relationships that approximate and comply with established state-sanctioned sexual norms, but further embed the institution of marriage and with it the conjugal couple as central to the regulation of sexuality and to the allocation and distribution of resources.[7] The set of rights- and equalities-based liberalizing measures have then both extended and intensified the biopolitical functions of the state and have set in play a new hierarchical ordering of the LGBTIQ population.

For Craig Willse and Dean Spade, the agendas of the gay and lesbian organizations that have lobbied for such rights and benefits (and which, not coincidentally for them, are characteristically led by wealthy, white, and educated gay men and lesbians) are symptomatic of this new ordering. These agendas, they write, focus on the "rights of people with occupational, educational, gender and race privilege and marginalize or ignore the struggles of transgender people, queer and trans people of color, and queer and trans poor people." These organizations, they observe, "have fought for the rights of gays and lesbians to pass their apartments on to one another and to rent or buy property without facing discrimination, but have provided no assistance to queer and trans people struggling in blatantly homophobic and transphobic homeless shelter systems and . . . in the criminal justice system."[8] Their point here is that these agendas are exclusionary and have focused on shoring up and extending the privilege of the already advantaged.

Nowhere, they argue, is this dynamic seen more clearly than in the gay-marriage or marriage-equality agenda—that is, in the demand for state-legislated same-sex marriage on the grounds that marriage is a right that should not be denied to same-sex couples. This shoring up and extension of privilege is the case because marriage instigates, allocates, and distributes resources via the rights that it guarantees. These resources include access to property (via mechanisms such as inheritance law) and employment-based marital benefits such as spousal access to employment-based health care and other forms of employment protection, including employment-based super-annuation and pension schemes. Willse and Spade point out that in a context where employment has become increasingly precarious and intermittent, and where the costs and risks of employment are increasingly being transferred from employers and the state to contingently employed wage laborers, such rights and benefits apply to a shrinking minority of the LGBTIQ population.[9] Moreover, focusing on access to such rights and benefits entirely puts to one side the aggregate reduction in full-time jobs with benefits attached to them as well as the structural discrimination in labor markets operating against queer and trans workers.[10] Strategies focusing on access to employment-based benefits and rights therefore ignore a key dynamic of the contemporary era, namely the opening up of vast class-based inequalities fueled in part by the transformation of wage labor. In this context, they argue, seeking out marital employment benefits for same-sex couples amounts not only to the pursuit of benefits for already advantaged members of the LGBTIQ population but also to the backing and fueling of inequalities within that population via the distribution of additional resources to the already advantaged.

For Willse and Spade, then, the extension of rights and benefits to certain sections of the LGBTIQ population represents a regressive movement in regard to the allocation and distribution of resources and is fueling socioeconomic inequalities within that population via this distribution. Same-sex marriage and its rights- and equalities-based bedfellows therefore concern "the formation of populations with access to life resources, and populations without such resources."[11] Though not necessarily expressed in the same theoretical register, the sentiment that special legal statuses and rights granted to certain sections of the LGBTIQ community in the name of equality are contributing to inequalities is echoed across critical queer and sexuality studies. In her analysis of same-sex reproductive law, and especially the same-sex legal parenthood rights arising from the UK's Human

Fertilisation and Embryology Act 2008, Eliza Garwood, for example, has argued that such legislation prioritizes those in civil partnerships or who are married and does so especially for long-term, committed, and monogamous relationships.[12] In so doing, same-sex reproductive law not only actively divides LGBTIQ populations into those deserving and undeserving of assisted-reproductive technology but also allocates resources and access to services on this basis. Moreover, in extending the possibilities of legal parenthood to stable, monogamous, committed, cisgender same-sex couples, same-sex reproductive law contributes to the incorporation of same-sex couples and their children into the provisions of family and inheritance law, including the rules of intestacy. Thus, such laws establish kinship lines for the transmission and distribution of property. They establish same-sex couples and their children as property-bearing and property-transmitting families, but they do so by excluding other LGBTIQ relationships and intimate forms from these provisions.

A further example of how the extension of rights and benefits to certain sections of the LGBTIQ population has been understood as regressive can be found in research on shifting immigration regimes. For example, Nan Seuffert has analyzed a set of apparently paradoxical shifts in immigration law and policy in New Zealand. On the one hand, policies and laws governing immigration have increasingly restricted migration by tightening residency requirements—especially in regard to race (via, for instance, increasing English-language requirements for those from non–English-speaking countries)—such that migration is increasingly (and significantly) whitened. Simultaneously, the introduction of a partnership policy has meant that residency requirements for same-sex couples have progressively loosened to align with those required of heterosexual couples. Although at face value these two processes might appear to be contradictory, Seuffert argues that they should be understood in terms of the operations of homonormativity. Same-sex couples who most easily meet the immigration and residency criteria are those whose countries of origin are comparably advanced liberal states that also recognize same-sex relationships according to an assimilative model and who, moreover, live together in "long-term stable, monogamous, property owning relationships sharing domestic chores." This is so not least because immigration criteria recognize the legal unions, marriages, and partnerships of same-sex couples from a limited number of other advanced liberal societies and require that same-sex relationships are genuine and stable, exclusive, and likely to endure. Immigration policy requires that the latter are to be verified by way of documentary proof of the "duration of the relationship, the existence, nature and extent of the partners' common residence, the degree of financial dependence or interdependence, the common ownership, use and acquisition of property, the degree of commitment of the partners to a shared life, children, the performance of common household duties by the partners, and the reputation and public aspects of the relationship." Thus, to fulfill the "genuine and stable" criteria, same-sex would-be immigrants must demonstrate that their relationships are long-term, domesticated, exclusive, and property bearing (and, importantly, amenable to documentation and certification). That these criteria are exclusionary is obvious: they not only favor and benefit the property bearing and the domesticated, but inasmuch as they operate alongside racialized immigration criteria, they also favor same-sex couples from other advanced liberal states "who are white, middle class and part of the 'new neo-liberal sexual politics' of a domesticated, de-politicised, privatised gay constituency."[13] In short, what Seuffert shows in her analysis is how equalities-based immigration law and policy favor certain same-sex couples over others and gives resources (rights to immigration and residency) to certain sections of the LGBTIQ population and denies these re-sources to those whose lives do not meet the standards of homonormativity.

The Financial Era

What is clear from these analyses is that long termism, especially long-term commitments around the financing of a privately funded present and future, is widely located as part of the political formation of homonormativity in which the distribution of life resources is at stake. In this observation re-garding the distribution of life resources, and especially the bifurcation of populations in regard to this distribution, scholarship on homonormativ-ity aligns with broader scholarship on neoliberalism. The latter has under-scored that neoliberalism has ushered in a new politics of existence whereby, rather than being protected, those who are unable to fund their own lives are progressively being abandoned and rendered disposable by the state.[14] Thus, just as scholarship on neoliberalism observes that it has heralded a new poli-tics of life, scholars on homonormativity observe that this politics is actively transforming and dividing LGBTIQ populations and is paradoxically doing so under the banners of equality and justice.

Yet the body of scholarship on homonormativity, as well as much of the broader scholarship on the political formation of neoliberalism in which homonormativity is nestled, tends to ignore a critical process that operates as a coterminous backdrop to many of the developments that these bodies of scholarship describe. This is the expansion of finance, and especially the emergence of finance from the 1970s onward as the key source of economic growth (or, as it is sometimes termed, financialization). As a number of political economists and finance studies scholars have documented, rather than operating as an ephemeral or superstructural phenomenon, the ascendance of finance has been supported and enabled by a range of long-lived policy, infrastructural, and institutional shifts.[15] This includes the floating of currencies and interest rates; the development of markets for asset-backed financial securities; the transformation of central banks into market-making institutions via monetary policy; the transformation and vast expansion of markets for consumer finance, including the development of new consumer finance products; and the range of policies—from those that have opened up mortgage financing to more and more people to those that have decreased the provision of social housing—that has supported increasing rates of home ownership. It has also involved a ratcheting up—again, by institutional and policy means—of the capacities of populations, and especially the capacities of households, both to shoulder and to service debt alongside an associated transformation of life into a financial proposition, such that education, health, housing, and other fundamentals of existence are all to be accessed and maintained through financial means. In their totality, these transformations have occasioned an unprecedented penetration of finance into daily life or, as Randy Martin describes it, a financialization of daily life.[16]

It would, however, be an error simply to maintain that for households the main implication of finance-led growth is that daily life and the mechanics of social reproduction have just become more or increasingly defined by finance. This is because in the financial era households have themselves undergone a process of transformation. In the postwar Keynesian era the household was the key site for the reproduction of labor power, and it fueled the capacity of capital to extract surplus value from human labor. In the current post-Keynesian financial era, however, the household serves instead as the anchor of the financial system.[17] It does so by acting as a source of contracted payments, including mortgage and household bill payments. On an everyday level, households make payments to secure subsistence, but these payments flow to finance capital and make up asset-backed securities, which are then traded on finance markets. Rather than acting as a privileged site for the reproduction of labor power, in the financial era households have become deeply implicated in the production of profits for finance capital by serving as a source of safe assets. This latter development has been made particularly explicit in the aftermath of the financial crisis of 2007–2008. Since the crisis, central banks have maintained record low interest rates. In 2016 the Reserve Bank of Australia, for example, set interest rates at a record low cash rate of 1.5 percent, and it has subsequently reduced this rate to an even lower 1 percent. As well as encouraging more consumer borrowing, in holding such low rates central banks ensure that payments on mortgages are both affordable and maintainable for households. Such central bank policy is therefore ensuring that the payments that act as the asset base for financial securities continue to flow from households to finance capital. Central bank policy is, in other words, safeguarding and guaranteeing financial capital's key asset base.

What is critical in this set of arrangements is that whole populations have been actively sought by both financial capital and the state to perform this anchoring role.[18] In this regard, the financial era departs from the exclusionary logics of Keynesianism, a departure that could not be more obvious than in its policy regimes. Whereas, for example, employment policy in the Keynesian era supported full male employment and female financial dependency, in the financial era employment policy is based on an adult worker model. Here, via employment policy and social security legislation, all adults—no matter what their circumstances—are incorporated into the wage-labor imperative.[19] And whereas in the Keynesian era it was typically only male workers who could access mortgage and other forms of consumer financing—not least because debt loading and schedules of repayment were calculated with reference to the wage rates and working lives of men and especially of white male workers in receipt of the family wage—in the financial era, backed by monetary policy, mortgage securitization, and the associated growth of secondary mortgage markets, mortgage financing is expansionary and includes those groups historically excluded by such calculative practices.[20] Thus, in the financial era, mortgage borrowing has been "democratized" and is no longer based on the presumption of the white heteronormative family household.[21] As Melinda Cooper has put it in regard to the US case, these shifts have "allowed unprecedented numbers of previously marginal borrowers (women, African Americans, Latinos) and non-normative households (single-mothers and those living in other non-normative arrangements) to aspire to home ownership."[22] In concert with these destandardizing measures, the financial era has also seen the rapid expansion of limits on consumer borrowing. Where mortgage calculations were previously based on the assumption that the male wage was the primary or only income source for a household, from the 1990s onward these calculations have come to be based on the possible future incomes of households, and especially the possible future incomes of cohabiting joint mortgage holders.[23]

As this analysis implies, these policy shifts have had major implications for the structuring and ordering of households. Rather than a household ordered to reproduce labor power and held in place by specific employment policies, social security legislation and policy, consumer financing practices, and banking policies, the ideal household of the financial era is one that is optimal for the provisioning of payments to finance capital. This is a household in which all adults are working (or are in preparation for working) and that manages its typically volatile (and repressed) wages both to leverage debt (such as mortgage debt) and to make timely payments on that debt as well as other contractual household payments (such as bill payments). This is also a household that necessarily shoulders and manages financial risk as a condition of its existence. Indeed, in the context of the winding back of a Keynesian state that sought to protect its populations and shouldered the costs and risks of such protection (through, for instance, collective forms of insurance), this is a household that itself shoulders the costs and risks of the whole of life—from housing through education to health care—and provisions its own welfare, primarily through the mechanisms of finance. In line with its Keynesian antecedent, this household is then one that is actively shaped and held in place by specific policies and institutional mechanisms. These include the aforementioned monetary policies, employment policies and labor law (which have progressively repressed wages and rendered working contracts contingent and precarious), social security policy and legislation (which demands that whole adult populations are working and that private assets such as superannuation are used to fund life), and consumer finance and banking practices that have both maximized the borrowing capacities of households and extended consumer borrowing to the previously excluded. Critically, in the financial era there is, then, a radical complicity between the state and finance capital, with both seeking a household that shoulders the costs and risks of life through finance and, in so doing, continuously expands the horizons of accumulation through finance.

Same-Sex Entitlements in Australia

It is against this background that many of the developments located by critical queer and sexuality theorists as being part of the apparatus of homonormativity—such as the passing of a range of antidiscrimination laws and the legal recognition of same-sex relationships—should be set. This is so not least because these are measures that target the LGBTIQ population to ensure that they are fully activated and calibrated to shoulder risk and debt and to fund their whole lifetimes. They are measures that are, in other words, transforming LGBTIQ lives from lives organized through the exclusionary logics of Keynesianism into lives now organized by the inclusionary and expansionary logics of the financial era. As such, it is critical to understand that these measures that work toward such activation and calibration are not simply or straightforwardly exclusionary, as theorists of the homonormative suggest. Rather, these measures represent attempts to enroll LGBTIQ populations into the wider project of the private funding of the whole of life. Thus, it is not—as many critical queer and sexuality theorists suggest—the already privileged or the already advantaged who are the primary targets of these measures, but also the poor, the impoverished, the aspiring migrants, the out of work, and the homeless. However, this whole of population enrollment becomes apparent only when the totality of antidiscrimination measures is taken into account. In this respect, analysis needs to extend beyond the effects of antidiscrimination measures in regard to property, income, inheritance, mortgages, and superannuation to include the effects of the same legislation on welfare benefits (such as unemployment and housing benefit payments) via changes to social security legislation. In what follows we illustrate the necessity of such an approach by considering a specific instance of the extension of rights and benefits to same-sex couples in Australia.

Despite the presence of a hostile federal government led by conservative prime minister John Howard, by 2006 all Australian states and territories had "introduced comprehensive de facto relationship status for same-sex couples."[24] Nevertheless, significant discrimination against same-sex couples continued across a number of key domains and specifically in federal government legislation. In 2007, following an audit of federal laws and a national inquiry held across 2006 (involving public hearings, community forums, and 680 written submissions from interested individuals and organizations), the Human Rights and Equal Opportunity Commission of Australia (HREOC) recommended that the federal government amend laws that discriminated against same-sex couples in the area of financial and work-related entitlements and benefits.[25] These recommendations were contained in a 448-page report titled *Same-Sex: Same Entitlements*.[26] In the report the commission laid out how same-sex couples in Australia "experience systematic discrimination on a daily basis" and do so because they are "denied basic financial and work-related entitlements which opposite-sex couples and their families take for granted" (9).

The report documented how this discrimination was operating in "the most ordinary areas of everyday life" (16), including workers' compensation payments, tax benefits, social security benefits, health care subsidies, family law, migration law, superannuation entitlements, and other employment-related benefits, including housing allowances, loans, health insurance, and education. It documented how "same-sex couples and families get fewer leave entitlements, less workers' compensation, fewer tax concessions, fewer veterans' entitlements, fewer health care subsidies, less superannuation and pay more for residential aged care than opposite-sex couples in the same circumstances" (16). The report identified how this was the result of discriminatory federal laws that "breach the rights of same-sex couples" (10). Indeed, the report identified and cataloged fifty-eight federal laws that "breach the International Covenant on Civil and Political Rights" (10).

The report spelled out how this discrimination turned on specific definitions of the couple in existing federal laws. Same-sex couples, the report set out, "are denied . . . basic financial and work-related entitlements because they are excluded from the definitions describing a couple. . . . Federal law after federal law defines a 'partner' or a 'member of a couple' or a 'spouse' or a 'de facto spouse' as a person of the opposite sex" (16). In the area of employment benefits, for example, the report cataloged the operation of restrictive definitions of the couple in workplace awards, collective agreements, and labor legislation such as the Workplace Relations Act 1996. The latter defines a "de facto spouse" of an employee as "a person of the opposite sex to the employee who lives with the employee as the employee's husband or wife on a genuine domestic basis although not legally married to the employee."[27] The report also documented how same-sex partners are excluded from definitions of "immediate family" in the same legislation.

These kinds of definitions, the report made clear, operate to ensure that same-sex couples do not enjoy the same employment conditions as opposite-sex couples. In particular, such definitions have the effect of denying same-sex couples rights to statutory leave entitlements (such as employee leave to care for a same-sex partner if they are sick), travel entitlements (allowing an employee to travel with their same-sex partner), work visa categories (allowing a same-sex partner of a primary visa applicant to accompany them to Australia), and employment allowances (which help to support an employee's same-sex partner). The report recommended amendments to workplace agreement and federal legislation definitions of the couple "so they are inclusive, rather than exclusive, of same-sex couples and families" (137). The report outlined that the commission's preferred approach for bringing equality to same-sex couples in the area of employment benefits and entitlements is to "retain the current terminology used in federal legislation . . . [and to] redefine the terms in the legislation to include same-sex couples (for example, redefine 'spouse' to include a 'de facto partner'), [and to] insert new definitions of 'de facto relationship' and 'de facto partner' which include same-sex couples" (137).

Similarly, for the case of tax and superannuation (including superannuation tax law), the report documented how definitions of the couple exclude same-sex couples from specific entitlements and benefits that are available to opposite-sex couples. For example, it outlined how Australian tax and superannuation legislation defines a spouse as "a person who, although not legally married to the person, lives with the person on a genuine domestic basis as the person's husband or wife" (64) and how some superannuation legislation defines a marital relationship: "a person had a marital relationship with another person at a particular time if the person ordinarily lived with that other person as that other person's husband or wife on a permanent and bona fide domestic basis at that time" (65). The report documented how these restrictive definitions of the couple had deleterious effects for same-sex couples not least because superannuation scheme members in a same-sex relationship could not nominate their partner as their beneficiary of death benefit transfers either in the form of a lump sum or as a reversionary pension. Because of this discrimination, same-sex couples have previously needed to distribute such superannuation benefits to their surviving partners through estates, a distribution that attracts high rates of tax. The report noted that in 2004 private superannuation schemes introduced a category of "interdependency relationship" that "opened the door for same-sex partners to qualify as a 'dependant'" (293). However, the report detailed that establishing such interdependency is onerous and requires far more evidence than that required for opposite-sex couples. Moreover, it showed how the interdependency category emphasizes a carer over a couple role. Thus, even where it did (at least implicitly) recognize same-sex couples, superannuation definitions held that same-sex couples and same-sex relationships were somehow of a different quality and order from their opposite-sex counterparts. In light of these forms of discrimination, the report found that "same-sex couples are worse off than opposite-sex couples because the definitions in superannuation and associated taxation legislation fail to treat same-sex couples and families in the same way as opposite-sex couples and families" (306).

Based on the commission's findings, the report recommended that the federal parliament should enact omnibus amendments to existing legislation to end the discriminatory treatment of same-sex couples in regard to financial and work-related entitlements. As already mentioned, it identified and listed fifty-eight federal laws that were exclusionary and discriminatory, and recommended that definitions of couples in such laws be amended. In August 2007 the minority Australian Democrats Party moved to put into law the recommendations from the HREOC report, but the Howard government used its majority in the Senate to block these moves. It was only after a change of federal government in December 2007 that action was taken with a newly commissioned audit identifying further areas of discrimination beyond the fifty-eight listed in the HREOC report. The new federal attorney-general, Robert McLelland, announced in April 2008 that the Rudd government would legislate to make the amendments identified in *Same-Sex: Same Entitlements* along with twenty-six others. It did so via a series of bills, including the Same-Sex Relationships (Equal Treatment in Commonwealth Laws—Superannuation) Bill 2008 and the Same-Sex Relationships (Equal Treatment in Commonwealth Laws—General Law Reform) Bill 2008. Commenting on the passing of the superannuation bill, the then human rights commissioner, Graeme Innes, said that "members of same-sex couples now have the security of knowing that their partners will inherit their superannuation savings."[28]

The Costs of Inclusion

Inasmuch as these reforms have provisioned rights and benefits to the employed, the superannuated, the asset owning, and the coupled, the set of legal changes associated with *Same-Sex: Same Entitlements* might be regarded as paradigmatic of the extension of rights that critical queer and sexuality scholars have located as being at the very heart of homonormativity. This set of legislative changes might, in other words, easily be understood as part of the process that is contributing to the opening out of fault lines and inequalities within LGBTIQ populations. This is so on a number of counts. First, these legislative changes privilege and prioritize long-term, cisgender same-sex couples and exclude those members of the LGBTIQ community whose lives, relationships, and identities fall outside the parameters of a couple relationship. Second, they appear to address the already advantaged—for instance, those in waged work whose employment has a string of benefits attached to it, including travel allowances and superannuation. Third, these legislative changes actively distribute resources (such as employment and superannuation benefits) and do so for those living in couple relationships. The legislative changes associated with *Same-Sex: Same Entitlements* could then easily be understood as mechanisms that distribute resources to the already privileged and fuel inequalities between the in work and out of work, the asset rich and the asset poor, the propertied and the unpropertied.

But to interpret these legislative changes in this way would be to neglect the fundamental reworking and redefinition of same-sex relationships at play within them and how this aligns with the wider logics of the financial era. For it is not the case that these changes prioritize and provision benefits only to the same-sex couple. In addition, they define and classify same-sex couples in a particular way, namely as couples who are bound together by financial assets and financial obligations. More than this, these legislative changes activate the very capacities required for such a binding. For example, they have activated the capacities of asset transfer and receipt within same-sex couples. Nowhere is this clearer than in the case of superannuation, where, as a consequence of the legislative changes, same-sex partners have become legal beneficiaries of superannuation benefits. And it is worth pointing out that in the case of Australia this transfer is consequential. Australian labor law requires *all* workers to be members of superannuation schemes and—as the *Same-Sex: Same Entitlements* report recognized—in the Australian context "superannuation is usually a person's largest asset apart from the home" (285). It is not, then, simply that the legislative changes have provided for the distributed resources to same-sex couples and the transfer of them within such couples, but that they have constituted same-sex couples as financial units.

This transfer is by no means insignificant in a context where asset-based welfare—a form of welfare in which households are required to mobilize the income-generating capacities of any assets they hold to provide for their own welfare provisioning and social reproduction—has been pursued by advanced liberal states for the past thirty years or more via policies that promote asset ownership. Here, the income-generating capacities of assets such as superannuation replace dependence on state-provisioned forms of welfare such as retirement pensions. Indeed, inasmuch as the set of rights-based legislative changes put in play by *Same-Sex: Same Entitlements* enables transfers of income-generating assets between same-sex partners, and hence enables the same-sex household to continue to provision for itself privately after the death of one partner, they may be precisely regarded as part of the bundle of policies that have promoted asset-based welfare. In fact, they should be understood as a set of legislative changes designed to enroll same-sex couples into the project of asset-based welfare, and especially as extending the socio-legal basis for this form of private welfare provisioning. That they do so in regard to couples is also of no surprise, for it is the long-term coupled household that is at the very heart of both asset-based welfare policies and the expansion of finance, whether that be via the promotion of homeownership, the extension of mortgage borrowing to those previously excluded from home loans, or the introduction of compulsory superannuation for all workers. Indeed, and inasmuch as the rights-based legislative changes prompted by *Same-Sex: Same Entitlements* focus on the couple and the financial commitments and obligations of partners in such couples to each other, they should be regarded as actively promoting this form of long-term coupled household.

That this change does not simply concern the already advantaged is made explicit when one considers that the very same set of processes is an issue for the asset poor, the unemployed, the out of work, the impoverished, and especially those in receipt of welfare. *Same-Sex: Same Entitlements* laid out in some detail how same-sex partners were not recognized as partners or as members of couples in existing Australian social security legislation. The report highlighted how "a person who has a same-sex partner will be treated as a single person for social security purposes" (198). This, the report noted, "can have either a positive or negative impact on the type and rate of payments a person is eligible to receive because of the way income and assets tests are administered. . . . Either way it is clear that same-sex couples are treated differently to opposite-sex couples" (198). In light of this element of discrimination, the report recommended an amendment to the definition of "the couple" in the Social Security Act to include same-sex couples. This amendment came into effect in 2009 following the passing of the Same-Sex Relationships (Equal Treatment in Commonwealth Laws—General Law Reform) Bill 2008.

One immediate outcome of this reform was that any member of a same-sex couple who was in receipt of welfare payments (such as unemployment benefit payments) was compelled to register their relationship with Australia's welfare agency, Centrelink. Indeed, Centrelink ran a public information campaign—"Couples Are Couples"—regarding this change, with newspaper and television advertisements alongside widely circulated free postcards detailing how same-sex couples had new rights and how these rights bore new obligations (see figure 9.1). One postcard read: "COUPLES ARE COUPLES. If you're a couple at home, you're now a couple at Centrelink." The text on the reverse of the card read: "New laws mean couples have to tell Centrelink about their relationship from 1 July 2009. Changes to the law mean Centrelink will recognise same-sex relationships from 1 July 2009. Centrelink customers

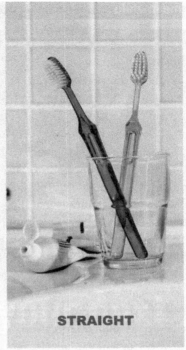

GAY

STRAIGHT

COUPLES ARE COUPLES. If you're a couple at home, you're now a couple at Centrelink.

Changes to the law mean Centrelink will recognise same-sex relationships from 1 July 2009. Centrelink customers who are living in a same-sex de facto relationship will be recognised as partnered and assessed in the same way as opposite-sex couples.

If you are a member of a same-sex couple, declare your relationship to Centrelink by 1 July 2009, to ensure you receive the correct payment. Because couples are couples.

To declare your relationship or find out what the changes mean for you contact 13 6280 or visit a Centrelink Customer Service Centre.
www.australia.gov.au/samesexreforms

Australian Government

Centrelink
giving you options

Authorised by the Australian Government, Capital Hill, Canberra.

CLSSGP1/2

FIGURE 9.1. Centrelink campaign postcard, "Couples Are Couples," 2009. Reproduced with permission from the Australian Government Department of Human Services.

who are living in a same-sex de facto relationship will be recognised as part-nered and assessed in the same way as opposite-sex couples."[29]

As this suggests, at stake in the shift in legislation was not simply an ob-ligation on the part of same-sex couples to declare their relationships (with any failure to do so resulting in the accumulation of social security debt, compulsory repayment, and even prosecution) but also new forms of benefit assessment by Centrelink in terms of that couple status. From July 1, 2009, onward, members of same-sex couples were to be assessed not as separate singles, the way that they had been prior to the legislative change, but as part of a cohabiting couple. As a consequence, members of same-sex couples became subject to different kinds of assessment and administrative rules. In practice, this change meant that in any application for welfare support, the incomes of both members of the couple were taken into account when cal-culating entitlements. The immediate effect of this legislative change was that welfare payments to many members of same-sex couples were reduced or canceled (for instance, in cases where only one partner was in employment).[30] This was because existing Centrelink assessment criteria for coupled relation-ships assumed these relationships to be based on cohabitation, financial in-terdependence, and enduring financial commitments.[31] Thus, much like the amendments to superannuation legislation, the shift in social security law produced a same-sex couple defined in terms of their financial obligations and commitments to each other. For both the employed and unemployed, asset rich and asset poor, the legislative changes associated with *Same-Sex: Same Entitlements* therefore had at their very core the actualization of same-sex couples defined in terms of these commitments and obligations.

Much commentary in Australia on the shifts in social security legislation overlooked this critical conjunction and instead connected the reform to the welfare state's long history of prurient surveillance, sexual regulation, and the stigmatization of poverty.[32] Much attention was focused, for example, on the compulsory requirement for individuals to "out" themselves to the gov-ernment agency responsible for welfare payments.[33] In so doing, many com-mentators entirely sidelined how the social security reform, when placed in the context of the totality of the legislative changes associated with *Same-Sex: Same Entitlements*, contributed to shifting the socio-legal status of *all* same-sex couples to one defined in terms of long-term financial obligation and commitment. For welfare-dependent same-sex couples, the reductions in payments were the obvious face of this change, but their same-sex couple status had been secured via their status as financially interdependent. This is a couple that allows the state to shift its risk by reducing its welfare bill. Like their asset-rich counterparts, this is a couple crafted by policy and other institutional mechanisms to sit at the heart of the twinned projects of financial expansion and asset-based welfare.

Long Termism as Finance Capital's Guarantee

In this chapter, by focusing on a specific instance of the extension of rights and benefits to same-sex couples in Australia, we have suggested that in their assumption that such rights and benefits are exclusionary, theorists of the homonormative have missed a critical dimension of the dynamics at stake in such extensions—namely, how the latter have reworked definitions of *all* same-sex couples (be they asset rich, asset poor, in work, or out of work) as long-term cohabiting units who are bound together by financial commitments and obligations, and who will privately provision for themselves in the present and the future. The changes to legislation we have described for the Australian context do allocate resources to the already privileged. Thus, employed, asset-owning, and superannuated same-sex couples have gained in financial terms from changes to definitions of the couple that the legislative reform has delivered. In this respect, the extension of rights and benefits to same-sex couples discussed above does result in a new distribution of resources, but not because the poor, the unemployed, and underemployed are excluded from such rights and benefits. On the contrary, the very same set of legislative changes extends to cohabiting same-sex couples who lack such assets and who may, for example, depend on welfare. These latter couples have typically experienced a loss of income in the wake of the changes, but this is evidence of their *inclusion* rather than of their exclusion.[34] We have suggested that this inclusion can be understood only by taking into account the accord between the expansion of finance and the project of asset-based welfare. What we highlight via our analysis is the emergence of couples as household units held together by financial obligations and commitments and a long termism that finds its expression in those very commitments.

In highlighting this, the analysis presented in this chapter raises the broader question of the relationship between the state and finance capital. We have characterized this relationship as one of radical complicity, with both the state and finance capital seeking a household that shoulders the costs and risks of life through finance, thereby continuously expanding the horizons of accumulation through finance. The interconnections between finance capital and the state are very often highlighted by drawing attention to how the functions of the state, for instance the operations of fiscal policy, are increasingly governed by the principles of market-based finance; how the architectures of finance are embedded in the state; and how states are increasingly beholden to finance markets and financial institutions through the pricing, grading, and dealing of government bonds.[35] But in this chapter we have been concerned less with the capture of the functions and financing of the state by finance capital and more with how the state's governance of populations through social policy and legal measures is working in accord with finance capital to both activate and guarantee the key asset base for finance—namely, households with long-term financial obligations and commitments. In this sense, our analysis adds fuel to the observation that the lines between political interventions and the expansion and operations of finance are very often blurred and inseparable.[36] What is clear, though, is that through the management of populations the state is not operating outside of or against finance, but actively actualizing and extending its operations. It is also clear that to enable a full analysis of how the distribution of life chances and inequalities are shifting within LGBTIQ populations, and to capture the dynamics of these distributions, analyses of homonormativity must broaden their gaze to situate rights-extending and rights-giving legislative change as part of a broader policy regime that has sought to activate and promote asset ownership, long-term financial commitments, and asset-based welfare across whole populations.

Understanding such change in this way opens up the opportunity to think about inequalities within LGBTIQ populations in more relevant registers than those foregrounded in existing identity-based readings of the homonormative. As we have stressed, any such inequalities are not the outcome of a logic of inclusion and exclusion. Rather, the twinned projects of financial expansion and asset-based welfare are ones that have attempted to enroll whole populations. It is, as we have stressed, through these general dynamics of enrollment that new social fault lines have emerged. Thus, the consequence of defining all same-sex couples as cohabiting units bound together by financial commitments and obligations who privately provision for themselves has been financial gains for some and losses for others.

NOTES

1   Duggan, "The New Homonormativity" and *The Twilight of Equality?*
2   Duggan, "The New Homonomativity," 179.
3   See also Butler, "Is Kinship Always Already Heterosexual?," and Reddy, *Freedom with Violence.*
4   Duggan, "The New Homonormativity."
5   See, for example, Piketty, *Capital in the Twenty-First Century.*

6   See, for example, Ludwig, "Desiring Neoliberalism," and Willse and Spade, "Freedom in a Regulatory State?"

7   Willse and Spade, "Freedom in a Regulatory State?"

8   Willse and Spade, "Freedom in a Regulatory State?," 317–18.

9   See, for example, Hacker, *The Great Risk Shift*, and Standing, *The Precariat*.

10 See, for example, Irving, "Future Investments."

11 Willse and Spade, "Freedom in a Regulatory State?," 324.

12 Garwood, "Reproducing the Homonormative Family."

13 Seuffert, "Same-Sex Immigration," 131, 142.

14 See, for example, Giroux, "Violence, Katrina, and the Biopolitics of Disposability"; Povinelli, *Economies of Abandonment*; and Tadiar, "Life-Times of Disposability within Global Neoliberalism."

15 See, for example, Mehrling, *Fischer Black*; Panitch and Gindin, "Finance and American Empire"; and Konings, "Rethinking Neoliberalism and the Crisis."

16 Martin, *Financialization of Daily Life*.

17 Bryan and Rafferty, *Risking Together*; and Bryan, Rafferty, and Tinel, "Households at the Frontiers of Monetary Development."

18 Adkins, *The Time of Money*.

19 Adkins, "Out of Work or Out of Time?"

20 See Federici, "From Commoning to Debt." For an account of the phaseout of structural discrimination in the US home mortgage market, especially in regard to gender and race, see Cooper, "The Strategy of Default."

21 This is not to suggest that the terms and conditions of such inclusion are not themselves problematic. In the case of the United States, for example, Black and Latinx borrowers have been consistently found to be offered higher-cost and higher-risk mortgages than similarly situated white borrowers. See, for example, Steil et al., "The Social Structure of Mortgage Discrimination." This is one outcome of assessments of creditworthiness via the technology of credit scoring. Although the uptake of the latter has seen a move away from exclusionary borrowing practices informed by hierarchies of social attribution, credit scoring inscribes hierarchies of risk. See, for example, Poon, "From New Deal Institutions to Capital Markets."

22 Cooper, "The Strategy of Default," 83.

23 See Adkins, "Speculative Futures in the Time of Debt," and Aalbers, *The Financialization of Housing*.

24 Graycar and Millbank, "From Functional Family to Spinster Sisters," 122. For an account of the Howard government's position on recognition of same-sex relationships, see Willett, "Howard and the Homos."

25 HREOC was renamed the Human Rights Commission in 2008.

26 HREOC, *Same-Sex: Same Entitlements*. Page references to this report will be given parenthetically in the text.

27 Workplace Relations Act 1996, 9. Available online at www.airc.gov.au/legislation/wra.htm.

28 Human Rights Commission, "Finally, Same Rights to Super Savings for Same-Sex Couples."

29 Reproduced from a blog post by Jeremy Sear, "Sex Tax for the Poor Now Applies to Gay Couples Too," April 8, 2009, https://anonymouslefty.wordpress.com/2009/04/08/equality-in-being-screwed-over.

30 For example, on 2007 rates, single individuals on a Newstart payment received a maximum fortnightly payment of AU$424.30 compared to AU$382.80 for an individual in a partnered relationship. Centrelink, *A Guide to Australian Government Payments 20 March–30 June 2007* (2007), 16. Cited in Tranter, Sleep, and Stannard, "The Cohabitation Rule."

31 The Australian federal government's *Social Security Guide* (Version 1.257, released August 12, 2019) Section 2.2.5.10 "Determining a De Facto Relationship" contains the following: "It is likely most couples in a de facto relationship will be *financially intertwined* in some way" (emphasis added). https://guides.dss.gov.au/guide-social-security-law/2/2/5/10.

32 See, for example, Sleep, "Sex-Snooping."

33 See, for example, Law, "A Gay Old Time."

34 This double dynamic of income losses and gains should be understood as contributing to the widening inequalities of the current era.

35 See, for example, Bryant and Spies-Butcher, "Bringing Finance inside the State," and Gabor and Ban, "Banking in Bonds" and "Europe's Toxic Twins."

36 See Mirowski, *Never Let a Serious Crisis Go to Waste.*

BIBLIOGRAPHY

Aalbers, Manuel B. *The Financialization of Housing: A Political Economy Approach.* London: Routledge, 2016.

Adkins, Lisa. "Out of Work or Out of Time? Rethinking Labour after the Financial Crisis." *South Atlantic Quarterly* 111, no. 4 (2012): 621–41.

Adkins, Lisa. "Speculative Futures in the Time of Debt." *Sociological Review* 65, no. 3 (2017): 448–62.

Adkins, Lisa. *The Time of Money.* Stanford, CA: Stanford University Press, 2018.

Australian Government. *Guides to Social Policy Law: Social Security Guide.* Version 1.257, released August 12, 2019. https://guides.dss.gov.au/guide-social-security-law.

Bryan, Dick, and Mike Rafferty. *Risking Together: How Finance Is Dominating Everyday Life in Australia.* Sydney: Sydney University Press, 2018.

Bryan, Dick, Mike Rafferty, and Bruno Tinel. "Households at the Frontiers of Monetary Development." *Behemoth* 9, no. 2 (2016): 46–58.

Bryant, Gareth, and Ben Spies-Butcher. "Bringing Finance inside the State: How Income-Contingent Loans Blur the Boundaries between Debt and Tax." *Environment and Planning A: Economy and Space* (March 2018): 1–19.

Butler, Judith. "Is Kinship Always Already Heterosexual?" *differences* 13, no. 1 (2002): 14–44.

Cooper, Melinda. *Family Values: Between Neoliberalism and the New Social Conservatism.* New York: Zed, 2017.

Cooper, Melinda. "The Strategy of Default: Liquid Foundations in the House of Finance." *Polygraph* 23/24 (2013): 79–96.

Duggan, Lisa. "The New Homonormativity: The Sexual Politics of Neoliberalism." In *Materializing Democracy: Toward a Revitalized Cultural Politics*, edited by Russ Castronovo and Dana D. Nelson, 175–94. Durham, NC: Duke University Press, 2002.

Duggan, Lisa. *The Twilight of Equality?: Neoliberalism, Cultural Politics, and the Attack on Democracy*. Boston: Beacon, 2003.

Federici, Silvia. "From Commoning to Debt: Financialization, Microcredit, and the Changing Architecture of Capital Accumulation." *South Atlantic Quarterly* 113, no. 2 (2014): 231–44.

Gabor, Daniela, and Cornel Ban. "Banking in Bonds: The New Links between States and Markets." *Journal of Common Market Studies* 54, no. 3 (2016): 617–35.

Gabor, Daniela, and Cornel Ban. "Europe's Toxic Twins: Government Debt in Financialized Times." In *The Routledge Companion to Banking Regulation and Reform*, edited by Ismail Ertürk and Daniela Gabor, 134–48. London: Routledge, 2017.

Garwood, Eliza. "Reproducing the Homonormative Family: Neoliberalism, Queer Theory, and Same-Sex Reproductive Law." *Journal of International Women's Studies* 17, no. 2 (2016): 5–17.

Giroux, Henri. "Violence, Katrina, and the Biopolitics of Disposability." *Theory, Culture & Society* 24, nos. 7–8 (2007): 305–9.

Graycar, Reg, and Jenni Millbank. "From Functional Family to Spinster Sisters: Australia's Distinctive Path to Relationship Recognition." *Journal of Law & Policy* 24, no. 121 (2007): 121–64.

Hacker, Jacob S. *The Great Risk Shift: The New Economic Insecurity and the Decline of the American Dream*. Oxford: Oxford University Press, 2006.

Human Rights and Equal Opportunity Commission. *Same-Sex: Same Entitlements*. Sydney: HREOC, 2007.

Human Rights Commission. "Finally, Same Rights to Super Savings for Same-Sex Couples." Human Rights Commission Media Release, November 27, 2008. www .humanrights.gov.au/news/media-releases/2008-media-release-finally-same-rights -super-savings-same-sex-couples.

Irving, Dan. "Future Investments: Gender Transition as a Socio-Economic Event." In *The Post-Fordist Sexual Contract: Working and Living in Contingency*, edited by Lisa Adkins and Maryanne Dever, 31–48. Basingstoke: Palgrave Macmillan, 2016.

Konings, Martijn. "Rethinking Neoliberalism and the Crisis: Beyond the Reregulation Agenda." In *The Great Credit Crash*, edited by Martijn Konings, 3–30. London: Verso, 2010.

Law, Benjamin. "A Gay Old Time." *Monthly*, July 2009, 19–20.

Ludwig, Gundula. "Desiring Neoliberalism." *Sexuality Research and Social Policy* 13, no. 4 (2016): 417–27.

Martin, Randy. *Financialization of Daily Life*. Philadelphia: Temple University Press, 2002.

Mehrling, Perry. *Fischer Black and the Revolutionary Idea of Finance*. Hoboken, NJ: Wiley, 2005.

Mirowski, Philip. *Never Let a Serious Crisis Go to Waste: How Neoliberalism Survived the Financial Meltdown*. London: Verso, 2013.

Panitich, Leo, and Sam Gindin. "Finance and American Empire." *Socialist Register* 41 (2005): 46–81.

Piketty, Thomas. *Capital in the Twenty-First Century*. Cambridge, MA: Harvard University Press, 2014.

Poon, Martha. "From New Deal Institutions to Capital Markets: Commercial Consumer Risk Scores and the Making of Subprime Mortgage Finance." *Accounting, Organizations, and Society* 34 (2009): 654–74.

Povinelli, Elizabeth A. *Economies of Abandonment: Social Belonging and Endurance in Late Liberalism*. Durham, NC: Duke University Press, 2011.

Reddy, Chandan. *Freedom with Violence: Race, Sexuality, and the US State*. Durham, NC: Duke University Press, 2011.

Seuffert, Nan. "Same-Sex Immigration: Domestication and Homonormativity." In *Changing Contours of Domestic Life, Family, and Law: Caring and Sharing*, edited by Anne Bottomley and Simone Wong, 131–50. Portland, OR: Hart, 2009.

Sleep, Lyndal. "Sex-Snooping in Australian Social Welfare Provision: The Case of Section 4 (3) Surveillance." PhD thesis, Griffith University, 2016.

Standing, Guy. *The Precariat: The New Dangerous Class*. London: Bloomsbury, 2011.

Steil, Justin P., Len Albright, Jacob S. Rugh, and Douglas S. Massey. "The Social Structure of Mortgage Discrimination." *Housing Studies* 33, no. 4 (2017): 1–18. 10.1080/02673037.2017.1390076.

Tadiar, Neferti X. M. "Life-Times of Disposability within Global Neoliberalism." *Social Text* 31, no. 2 (2013): 19–48.

Tranter, Kieran, Lyndal Sleep, and John Stannard. "The Cohabitation Rule: Indeterminacy and Oppression in Australian Social Security Law." *Melbourne University Law Review* 32, no. 3 (2008): 698–738.

Willett, Graham. "Howard and the Homos." *Social Movement Studies* 9, no. 2 (2010): 187–99.

Willse, Craig, and Dean Spade. "Freedom in a Regulatory State?: Lawrence, Marriage and Biopolitics." *Widener Law Review* 307 (2005): 309–29.

10

SERIAL COMMITMENT, OR, 100 WAYS TO LEAVE YOUR LOVER

ANNAMARIE JAGOSE AND LEE WALLACE

Act One: Performing Repetition

It has long been recognized in performance studies that one of its enabling contradictions is the ephemerality of its object, which does not persist beyond the simultaneity of the now. As performance studies founder Richard Schechner puts it, "One of the chief jobs challenging performance scholars is the making of a vocabulary and methodology that deal with performance in its immediacy and evanescence."[1] In particular, the fleeting quality at the definitional heart of performance means that it cannot be reenacted or captured by other media systems without loss. Precisely because of its temporary quality and resistance to descriptive and technological capture, feminist and queer—and importantly queer-feminist—artists have often been drawn to performance as a form that speaks to the general ephemerality of experience and, more particularly, to the shared experience of being at the same time both visible and invisible, recognized, even fetishized, while also disregarded as irrelevant to normative social forms that therefore claim for themselves a sheen of timelessness, inevitability, permanence, and longevity.[2]

Certainly, the idea that femininity is a social performance whereas masculinity simply sets the coordinates for the social explains why so many classic melodramas turn on the figure of the actress, such as Joseph L. Mankiewicz's *All About Eve* (1950), Douglas Sirk's *Imitation of Life* (1959), Ingmar Bergman's *Persona* (1966), and John Cassavetes's *Opening Night* (1977). Inspired by the latter, Anna Breckon and Nat Randall have cocreated *The Second Woman*, which was originally developed for Melbourne's Next Wave Festival in 2016, then subsequently performed by Randall at Hobart's Dark Mofo and Sydney's Liveworks Festival of Experimental Art, both in 2017, and the 2018 Perth Festival.

It is testimony to *The Second Woman*'s near perfection as performance that there can be no possibility of a plot spoiler. The high-concept premise of the piece is broadly touted in the promotional materials designed to attract its audience: "In an epic endurance performance, Nat Randall repeats a single scene inspired by the John Cassavetes' American meta-theatrical drama *Opening Night*. One hundred times over a twenty-four-hour period, Randall performs over and over a scene between a man and a woman in a relationship that has lost its creativity, romance, and vitality."[3] It is also no secret to anyone turning up that Randall will perform opposite one hundred publicly solicited men in a scene that will be simultaneously remediated to the audience on a big screen via a live camera feed. But to say that *The Second Woman* recasts the performance hierarchies at work in the cinematic convention of telling real-seeming stories about putting on a show—something Cassavetes's film is also thought to do—scarcely captures the mediatized originality of the Breckon-Randall piece.[4] The screen takes up half the performance space, the other half given over to the transparent square room in which the action unfolds. Seven fixed and moving cameras capture Randall and the different men she plays against in close-up and medium takes that are real-time edited backstage in a strictly predetermined sequence so that every iteration of the scene is cinematically more or less the same, except for what the actors bring to it. Which is everything.

In superficial ways, the dramatic conceit is simple. A woman in a room (see figure 10.1) is joined by a man. There is something unfinished between them that needs talking out. They have a drink and share the takeaway noodles he

FIGURE 10.1. Nat Randall in *The Second Woman*, Carriageworks, Sydney.

has brought. She puts on some music. They dance, then break away from each other. The man leaves. Repeat. Repeat. Repeat. It is the repetition that rivets. Across the course of twenty-four hours, this scene of repair and estrangement plays out a hundred times with a hundred different men. Played by Randall in a cinematically iconic red dress and blonde wig that pays homage to Gena Rowlands's *Opening Night* character, the woman, named Virginia in the script but nameless on stage, remains the same but becomes progressively more exhausted across the demanding twenty-four-hour cycle as the men keep coming at her freshly with their conflicting demands and brute physicality.[5]

The men are acting too, of course, having been recruited to the performance by an open call and the promise of a modest payment that becomes part of the staged scene, the gesture with which they are dismissed from the set. Composed chiefly from lines taken from the play that appears in

Cassavetes's film, which are creatively resequenced and sometimes reassigned from male to female lead, Breckon's pared-back script and stage direction puts both figures tightly, at times awkwardly, through their paces but also leaves just enough room for improvisation such that each man can imprint his persona on the scene. The effect is fascinating as man after man is caught out performing a version of masculinity that folds under pressure and reveals something unintended but not, it turns out again and again, wholly unexpected: something brought to light by the experimental conditions of the live scene and its relentless unfolding in real time.

The liveness of *The Second Woman* also imprints on the audience members, who, unlike Randall, are free to come and go during the performance, which we saw in the cavernous space of Bay 20, Carriageworks, Sydney. Having arrived for the Friday 6 p.m. opening with the intention of peeling away after an hour or two, we were among the many members of the audience who found themselves caught in a compulsive cycle of wanting to see one more and then one more enactment of the eight-minute scene, whose increasing familiarity made the minute differences within and between each individual performance twang with significance.

It turns out we are not endurance types ourselves, requiring a minimum eight-hour sleep for steady daytime functioning, so shortly before ten we extracted ourselves with the promise to return as soon as we woke in the morning, a plan that was literally put into play when one of us stirred at three and misread the time as six. By the time the error was discovered, we were already up and dressed and committed to returning. Although the requisite hundred men had been signed up for staged slots across the twenty-four hours of the performance, it seems that reliable men can be hard to find at 3:30 a.m. And so it was that Breckon came out into the sparse audience and asked us if we would be prepared to stand in for two of the missing men. Yes and no, we said without conferring, the simultaneity effect magnified by the dreamlike state we had maintained in the silent car hurtling across an empty city. Thus, in an instant, we became two women queerly separated by the social performance of masculinity, a not uncommon phenomenon for lesbians of our generation, although still not quite what we thought we were in for when we fell out of bed (see figure 10.2).

For a member of the audience, the gauze screens that demarcate the illuminated red box of the set bring to mind the set of a David Lynch film, perhaps *Blue Velvet* (1986) or *Mulholland Dr.* (2001), another melodrama about actresses in rooms that fail to observe coherently the rules of continuity.[6] But as one of us found, from the unexpected perspective of an erstwhile man who

FIGURE 10.2. Annamarie Jagose as one of the Martys in *The Second Woman*, Carriageworks, Sydney.

has walked the lonely corridor from the stage manager's silent countdown to the single door that opens into the diegetic world of *The Second Woman*, the gauze intensifies the performance encounter. It muffles the presence of the audience and filters out the nonbinary crew roaming the perimeter of the room like cyborgs—half-human, half-camera—under the direction of EO Gill.

The Second Woman is a very different experience when you move beyond the relative safety of being in the audience. You approach Randall, who is standing looking out the window, whisper your actual name to reset the action, kiss the back of her neck, and trickily clasp her left hand with your right. And all that before you deliver your first line:

MARTY
I'm sorry I was so crude to you.
You shocked me.

Crude was an unfamiliar word to deliver in that context, and there was another challenge ahead in the run-on line taken near verbatim from *Opening Night*, where it is delivered on stage by Cassavetes as the camera fastens on Joan Blondell's aging face:

```
                    MARTY
    OK. You are capable. You
    are capable and you are pretty and
    you are wonderful and you are
    talented and you are great
    and outstanding and . . .
```

Though wanting to be faithful to the script, even in a scene that had the whiff of infidelity, the feminist that persisted inside the assigned male role couldn't help but substitute "beautiful" for "pretty" as the cameras rolled.

Although resisting preset scripts is familiar work to many women, whatever their orientation, it can still come as a surprise to many men, including those clustered backstage nervously going through their lines as if what they said, or how they said it, could determine the course of onstage events. It does not seem to cross their minds that Randall and Breckon's genius ensures that the space inside the box is owned by the half-cut blonde tottering around on heels that eventually make her ankles swell to the point where she can no longer kick her shoes off as she did in the first twelve hours of the performance. "It didn't go like I expected," said one man returning backstage after exiting the red room, cash in hand. "Acting is really hard."

It is also really hard, it turns out, to be left in the audience to watch your female partner, ostensibly a man but in no way different from the woman you were just sleeping with, break up with another translucently beautiful woman in a staged mise-en-scène that is amplified by fractionally delayed screen projection and whatever else your subconscious brings to the split scene. The first half of the scene repurposes lines from Rowlands's on-screen performance against her director husband that underscore the rote nature of the situation and the one-sided drinking that adds to its emotional imbalance:

```
Marty looks at Virginia with a big smile before he
leans in and kisses her. Virginia, dissatisfied with
his response, throws her drink back in one gulp and
stares into her empty glass.

She walks toward the bar. She pours herself another
drink.

                  VIRGINIA
    What a mess I am. I'm begging
    again.
```

The reformulated script that everyone is playing to continues to specify sufficient stage business and dialogue to indicate the well-worn back-and-forth of coupled familiarity and complaint, although it does not specify tone, which is left to each Marty to provide:

Marty takes the chopsticks and food out of the paper bag and begins to eat.

Virginia walks back to the table and trips subtly on the carpet.

Virginia sits and watches Marty eat and eventually gets her food out. The lines are delivered while eating.

> VIRGINIA
> You know, I don't care if you don't think that I am beautiful anymore.

> MARTY
> I do.

> VIRGINIA
> Well, you don't think that I am funny.

> MARTY
> You are hysterical.

> VIRGINIA
> Well, you don't think that I am capable. That's what I want to be, I just want to be capable.

> MARTY
> OK. You are capable. You are capable and you are pretty and you are wonderful and you are talented and you are great and outstanding and . . .

> VIRGINIA
> And I love you.

> MARTY
> And you love me.

Virginia tips her food over the table. Marty sits and watches her. Virginia swills back the remains of her drink. She gets up.

How Randall tips her food is up to her, and many self-absorbed Martys who miss the cue embedded in "And I love you" end up wearing the noodles.

It turns out that, for all their differences of age and ethnicity and the way in which they eat when watched by an audience of three hundred, most Martys are unable to bring any compassion to the scene even when it is clear they have walked into the room intending to show that this Marty is not like the others. As the reputation of the piece has grown, and more of the responders to the call-out understand the governing conceit, so too has the sense that this is something a good actor can ace. Given the script in advance, as they are, many of the amateur actors and the occasional professional who rocks up seem confident they can beat Randall at her game. It is a very rare Marty who intuits that the scene is not really his to begin with. It belongs to Randall and the queer-identified crew of camera operators, lighting and sound technicians, digital editors, and backstage Marty wranglers who keep the whole thing rolling in three roughly eight-hour shifts. Randall alone goes the distance. Four to five Martys an hour, each of them bringing their needs and indifference into her space for eight minutes at a time, and then a further four spent cleaning up after them: picking vermicelli off the floor, putting the empty glasses on the drinks trolley, resuming her place at the window until the next Marty makes his entrance. After the first eight iterations of the scene, and thereafter at two-hour intervals, she rolls the trolley out the door into the deep, black no-man's-land between stage and backstage. Ten minutes later, we hear the trolley rattling back before the door opens and a recoiffed Virginia rolls in, the bottles of booze replenished. Randall takes her mark and gazes out as she waits for the next Marty to come in.

The ten-minute break is in line with Australian occupational health and safety regulations. Backstage, Randall's minder massages her and lets her vent about the Martys who grope. Even with regular stipulated breaks the performance is physically crushing, and as the hours tick by, the audience begins to wince each time Virginia trips on the carpet or yet another Marty takes hold of her. The script specifies that after the food is tipped the manhandling begins in earnest:

```
Virginia walks to the stereo, presses play on the
cassette deck, and turns up the volume. She stands
facing the back wall and closes her eyes. Marty lets
her stand there for a moment. Marty gets up from the
table and walks towards Virginia. He comes up behind
her and wraps his arms around her and holds her
tight.

Virginia slumps into Marty's arms.
```

The next sequence is a slight struggle / sloppy
dance.

Marty tries to keep Virginia on her feet. Virginia
starts holding and grabbing at Marty's face. Marty
finally lets go of Virginia after a minute of the
struggle/dance and she drops to the floor.

Marty takes a seat on the sofa chair.

Virginia composes herself, stands up and turns the
music off.

> VIRGINIA
> I think you should leave Marty.

Like most things presented in the format required of writing for theater or screen, this reads flatly to the eye and comes alive only in performance. Once the music starts—diegetically associated with the stereo that sits against the back wall of the red room but arriving with the full decibel force of the venue's professional sound system—wild crosscut editing takes off in rhythm with the funk riffs and falsetto lyrics of Aura's "Taste of Love," a track both unknown and oddly familiar. The cinematic force of the scene begins to dominate as the levels of dramatic agitation rise until Randall's woman collapses like Lana Turner in Frank O'Hara's poem, quietly resetting the scene for whatever resolution this Marty can wring from whichever final lines he chooses.[7]

> MARTY
> (Choose your final line)
>
> I love you./ I never loved you.

The split was about fifty-fifty, or at least it was among the Martys we saw at Carriageworks, a mix of men, mostly straight with the occasional gay man or butch lesbian thrown in. Some fluffed their lines, others took liberties with the script as if it asked them to improvise, but every once in a blue moon someone would seem so sweet and unguarded in performance it made you cry.

In the world premiere of *The Second Woman*, at the Australian Centre for the Moving Image in Melbourne, the last man to play Marty was Randall's father, who is in his late sixties and, although still fit, has Parkinson's disease. A walking lesson in pain and endurance, he was paid to go away like all the rest. In Hobart, at the Salamanca Arts Centre, the configuration of the venue meant that the paid-off Martys had to exit through the audience, many taking high fives along the way as if it were their show after all. In that performance the final Marty was played by Breckon, whose unexpected arrival in her physically broken girlfriend's scene threw out the carefully gauged balance between the scripted and the unscripted so that the couple struggle/dance became real. The next iteration of *The Second Woman*, in November 2018, will be different again. It will be staged at the National Kaohsiung Center for the Arts in Taiwan. Breckon and Randall will direct, but in order to stay with the principle of open local recruiting, the performance will be in Chinese. As Virginia they have cast Zhi-Ying Zhu, whose breakthrough role was in Ang Lee's *Lust, Caution* (2007), another script about the durability of attachment and its masochistic profile. And so it goes. Repeat, repeat, repeat.

Fifty bucks is all we have to show for the late-night lesson in serial melodrama administered by Randall and Breckon because the rest is lost to the ephemeral nature of performance. In case any readers are thinking of answering future calls to participate, know this: yes, this endurance piece is about heterosexual scenarios that seem ingrained, but it is also about queer patterns of displacement and deferral, some of which can fall very close to home. Recycling the title of the play within *Opening Night*, *The Second Woman* subtly captures "the particular quality of twiceness" that Schechner attributes to performance. As some theorists—and many queers—know, in this tangled system of social enactment and psychic projection, gender is also "twice-behaved behavior," for men as for women.[8] At this historical point in time when in Australia, as in many other liberal jurisdictions, gays and lesbians are newly transacting marriage vows—the textbook example of a performative utterance—*The Second Woman* is a reminder that the public/ private performance of intimacy undoes us all. One of the things that strikes us about *The Second Woman* in the context of gay marriage—the Sydney performance we attended across October 20–21, 2018, was in the middle of the Australian Marriage Law Postal Survey plebiscite—is that it brings out the element of repetition in attachment of any kind, including theoretical critical attachments, such as our own.

Act Two: Repeating Ourselves

There are serial lesbians like there are serial killers.[9] We are two of them. Our seriality has taken a particular form: we repeat ourselves and each other, most typically in writing but also in life. Although we have been involved in formal academic collaboration with each other, most notably in joint publications on teaching and research pedagogy, there are also more informal creative alliances between our traditional and nontraditional research initiatives and their sources in our personal relationship. *In Translation* (1994) is a roman à clef, a fictionalization of the circumstances in which we first came together and then, briefly, apart.[10] Archival research into the English missionary Reverend William Yate, who was embroiled in a same-sex sexual scandal in the 1830s Australian and New Zealand colonies, which substantially informed a chapter in *Sexual Encounters: Pacific Texts, Modern Sexualities*, was also the inspiration for the multi-prizewinning novel *Slow Water*, both published in 2003.[11] To date, this mutual indebtedness has been signaled through the usual scholarly protocol of footnotes and references, with the addition of more oblique personal thanks in other paratextual matter such as dedications and acknowledgments, all of which constitute what Kate Lilley would call our "scholarly coming out" as a lesbian academic couple.[12] More recently, however, in our academic work we have each individually engaged an autotheoretical perspective as a means of extending our methodological and critical reach. In an inventive instance of what Anna Poletti, following Eve Sedgwick, has dubbed the "queer periperformative," one of us has recently contributed an essay to a special issue of GLQ on the ontology of the couple that toggles between a standard scholarly address and an auto-ethnographic inquiry into our joint raising of a dog.[13] The other is currently completing a manuscript on gay marriage as remarriage, which is both a theoretical intervention in same-sex marriage debates and a book-length meditation on our experience of serial reattachment across the nearly three decades we have been together.[14]

In feminist and queer studies there have been some field-transforming contributions that have taken nontraditional formats or melded traditional and nontraditional formats, many of which deploy the personal to rethink the political or social.[15] The one that comes immediately to mind in this context is *Living with His Camera*, a couple collaboration between literary theorist Jane Gallop and art photographer Dick Blau, whose professional creative work captures candid images of Gallop and their children going about their domestic lives. A selection of these photographs, many of which record the passive-aggressive resistances internal to intimate relationships, provides the occasion for Gallop to revisit three key theorists of photography: Susan Sontag, Roland Barthes, and Pierre Bourdieu. In the introduction to her book, Gallop makes an argument for cohabitation as methodology, a line of thought that is brought about by the fact that although she and Blau are not married, the photographic evidence says otherwise. Their ongoing relationship is "actually and explicitly" an attempt to differ from the clichés of married domestic life, but Gallop and Blau repeatedly "discover to our horror and amusement that we 'look like' the worst conjugal stereotypes." Whereas she admits her attraction to the "grand old synthesis" of marriage as "the figure for merger, union, two melting into one," Gallop considers cohabitation "a better figure for the irreducible doubleness of this book" and its attempt to balance the personal and the professional, the photographic and the textual. "Keeping the center double," she writes, is central to "the long-term project of cohabitation" and the writing that arises in its vicinity.[16]

Gallop draws attention to how heterosexual couples visually imprint in the world as married even when they are not, but we have argued that the opposite is true for homosexual couples—even couples like Sontag and Annie Leibovitz, whose relation to photography and its theorization is as lived out as Gallop and Blau's—because historically their relation to domestic conjugality is less socially patent, or has been until recently.[17] As a result of this strained relationship to visibility and domesticity, the field of gay and lesbian studies and its offshoots in subcultural studies sit squarely on the assumption that queer forms of intimacy escape conventional methods of quantitative and qualitative data capture.[18] A lot of theoretical energy, including some of our own, has been spent unraveling the methodological problem posed by the ephemerality of gay and lesbian history, yet we now find ourselves in a moment in which the political advent of same-sex marriage is sought, won, and celebrated as a measure of social and emotional advancement for all. In this sense, the success of marriage equality has made a failure of our queer theoretical home.[19]

In order to unravel what is at stake in this all-too-familiar slide between intimate companionship and collective belonging, lubricated by the slippery idea that the quality of the former is a measure of the health of the latter, we follow Gallop in taking the couple as both research object and research tool. Or so we like to think. In reality, we are presently enjoying—perhaps one of us more than the other—the disinhibition that comes with writing in the couple-collective voice. This is not a voice that is often heard in queer theoretical circles, which have long been skeptical of the normative force of the couple formation or, as Michael Cobb puts it, "the painful, standardizing culture of couple control." Cobb is reacting against the ubiquitous valorization of the couple form, which he likens to totalitarianism in its advancement of the "rhetorics and politics of connection" and its implicit denigration and suspicion of the singleton and others who willfully stand outside the social domain of coupled intimacy.[20] As support for Cobb's point that couple totalitarianism thrives on the fear of loneliness, we point to the *Marie Claire* headline—"Love Wins!"—that appeared on January 8, 2018, the first day that same-sex marriages were legally performed in Australia and a mere two months after the results of the postal plebiscite were more soberly announced by Australia's chief statistician.

Although the popular tendency is to read the legalization of same-sex marriage as a victory for social progressivism, expert opinion is more likely to consider it in relation to the instrumental rationalisms associated with neoliberalism. Couple longevity, we are told from all points of the disciplinary compass, is an incontestable good insofar as the durability of intimate relationships between individuals is generally recognized as generating benefits that accrue to everyone, regardless of their class, ethnicity, or sexuality. Psychologically, it has been mapped to higher levels of individual happiness.[21] Socially, it has been associated with domestic stability and the thriving of children.[22] Economically, it has been shown to rest more lightly on the state purse than its alternatives.[23] The legal incorporation of same-sex couples into a framework where the success of coupled life is thought to support the success of the commonweal prompts us to look anew at the committed long-term couple as a popularly idealized—and critically deidealized—form from which both individual and general cultural benefits are said to devolve.

Calls for long-termism can be found everywhere. Reading the *Sydney Morning Herald* together one morning, as couples do, our small interpretative community neatly sundered by our divergent commitments to old and new media (tabloid and tablet), two items connected with our thinking about the long term. They were both associated with September 2018's spill of the Australian prime minister (the fourth in eight years to be deposed by internal party vote), a political sideshow we glancingly engage with the superiority common to Kiwis who live in Australia but remain attached to the New Zealand national imaginary, particularly as it pertains to the step-by-step setting of a country to rights in the wake of settler colonialism. The first item covered a Twitter meme of a mocked-up environmentally friendly shopping bag riffing on New South Wales's recent prohibition on the giving away of single-use plastic bags at supermarkets. A simple black on white affair, the sans-serif slogan read "Ban the Single Use Prime Minister." No hyphen. The appeal of this graphic attack on disposable politicians and the parties who trash them meant that not only did the meme go viral but also that the response was so keen it became an actual bag overnight, in production with more than four hundred preorders taken in thirty-six hours.[24] The second was a think piece from the director of the Australian Futures Project, "a non-profit, non-partisan organization dedicated to ending short-termism in Australia," which denounced the spoiled brattism of Australian culture in both its elite and demotic forms before launching into a familiar lament about how "vested interests cynically pursue their narrow benefit at the expense of society" while "much of the media has lost its attention span and rigour."[25] Rolling selfish greed and attention-deficit disorder into a single diagnostic, short-termism derives from economic theory, where it denotes fiscal concentration on short-term outcomes and objectives for immediate profit at the expense of long-term goals and security. Strongly associated with financial institutions and thought to be the root cause of the 2008 global financial crisis, short-termism is now applied more generally to any kind of institution or endeavor that seems governed by present-tense individualized results rather than future-oriented investments and the deferral of personal profit in favor of collective gain.

The social institution of marriage, particularly in the era of gay marriage, is sometimes thought to be weakened by short-termism or the idea that folk now enter marriage for a good time, not necessarily for a long time. Rather than celebrate or dismiss the value of marriage, either straight or gay, it is the supposed connection between long-term intimate companionship and collective thriving that requires testing, especially as psy-professionals have now begun to adopt the counterargument that marriage is best conceived as a finite, rather than permanently binding, contract that should be voided as soon as it ceases to serve either partner.[26] But although queer theory has a long history of thinking through alternatives to the dynastic family of birth through which social value is inherited and transmitted, most notably in accounts of families of choice or what Eve Sedgwick, following the Thatcher government's condemnation of "pretended" gay-affirmative families, reclaimed as the extended pretended family, discussions around marriage have been less inventive.[27] Whether queers are for it or against it, there is remarkably little theoretical interest in what marriage is beyond an instrument of the state and even less interest in how the history of marriage—understood as the affective framework of long-term partnering—might have evolved in sync with the history of homosexuality.[28]

In the topsy-turvy world in which we now live, same-sex marriage is more likely to appear as the epitome of the marriage ideal than clapped-out forms of heterosexual alliance. Consider, for instance, Bruce Miller's straight-to-streaming television adaptation of Margaret Atwood's 1985 dystopian novel, *The Handmaid's Tale*, and its complex affective replication of the marriage plot around a central female narrator who is handmaiden, lover, and wife to three different men in a highly recognizable but low-fertility future world in which reproduction has been fully instrumentalized.[29] In this factional world, in which state ideology simultaneously idealizes marriage and deidealizes sexuality, it is notable that both are made available for reidealization via association with a specifically lesbian marriage scene, which takes place in Season Two as an improvised deathbed ceremony conducted in the bleak light of the postnuclear labor camp to which dissident and no-longer-fertile women are sent. It is precisely this process of same-sex reidealization that we wish to investigate in the vicinity of long-term coupled intimacy—not least because we think we might be implicated in it.

The advent of marriage equality in Australia, as elsewhere, provides a timely framework in which to address questions around the affective bases of social belonging and what counts as a publicly valued attachment or way of being in the world. No doubt because of our own disciplinary and relationship history, we are drawn to case studies of coupled intimacy that blend the autobiographical and the fictional and that invoke seriality, repetition, and rupture in order to problematize the emotional stability and social consolidation typically attributed to long-term relationships when apprehended from outside. Inside is another story. "Everything changes," wrote Gertrude Stein speaking for herself, but especially for us, about the mystery of attachment. Stein then zeroes in on the feeling of expansion and contraction familiar to anyone who has ever attached to anything, whether they have wanted to or not: "I had never had any life with dogs and now I had more life with dogs than with any one."[30] The dogs in question are Basket I and Basket II, the consecutive white standard poodles that came into the domestic lives of Stein and Alice B. Toklas in 1929 and 1938 respectively. But the sentiment also attaches to us and our relation, shared and separate, to our miniature black poodle, Farley, whose serial nature registers most subtly in her physical and nominal likeness to dark and curly Farley Granger, the actor Alfred Hitchcock repeatedly cast in roles that derived their charge from his queer legibility on screen and who died in 2011, the year our Farley was conceived.[31]

The point here is not about canine attachment specifically but rather about the transferable nature of attachment, something that is more easily observed in our attachments to nonhuman companions whose lifetimes are measured in scales radically different from our own. For attachments are not steady-state phenomenon. They exist in time. And the time they exist in is not the time of the state, as the proponents for and against marriage presume, nor the time of the family and reproductive futurity in which we take our place in a continuously unspooling genealogy that predates and postdates us, nor even the time or hit of the ecstatic in which selves are said to be erased, but in the time of dailiness and repetition: the interstitial space where intricate, individual habits and life trajectories mesh with intricate, impersonal, superstructural systems. Cultural studies often refers to this repeated encounter between institution and person, between structure and agency, between constraint and choice, as the time of everyday life. However, it is important to understand that everyday life is not on the side of the individual and against the rationalized system but rather comes into being as the expression of a tension between these two orders.[32] The "starting point for the everyday," write Alice Kaplan and Kristin Ross, "is neither the intentional subject dear to humanistic thinking nor the determining paradigms that bracket lived experience" but "is situated somewhere in the rift opened up between the subjective, phenomenological, sensory apparatus of the individual and reified institutions," including, we would add, the reified institution of marriage experienced less as an apparatus of the state than as the day-in, day-out banality of coupled attachment to domestic routine.[33]

In this ordinary register, coupled attachment unfolds as a series of everyday enchantments and disenchantments that make up a life lived together in the diurnal rhythms of night and day and all the unfinished and inconclusive patterns in which they immerse us. These everyday patterns are both disrupted and confirmed by the novel aesthetic pull of *The Second Woman*, which was enough to lift us from sleep and propel us through the night like sleepwalkers. The genre for this kind of attachment, we would argue, is not marriage but remarriage, understood less as a commitment than an inclination toward perpetual reattachment and the welcome incorporation of change into what is recognizably continuous, if not the same. Our practical training in this way of attaching to the world is reflected in Farley's everyday behaviors. Although she has been diagnosed with anxiety and has the serotonin reuptake inhibitors to prove it, Farley has never manifested any form of separation anxiety except when, after knowing only our collective dailiness, our temporary estrangement meant she briefly went into joint custody. Typically, Farley manages changes in circumstance, such as the arrival of strangers in the house, via a transitional object, a ragged piece of green polar fleece that is a permanent feature of her—which is to say our—domestic world, constantly gnawed through and regularly replaced by an exactly similar one, bought from Spotlight at $9.99 the meter. Although we initially worried that Farley would balk at the substitution of a different, if near identical, thing for the one object in the world that was hers to love and abuse from the moment we removed her from her litter, her passion for each blanket in turn has proved our best lesson in serial attachment as a means of holding steady our place in the world. Repeat, repeat, repeat.

Act Three: Repeating Repetition

With a collaborative history spanning ten films from 1963 to 1984, Cassavetes and Rowlands repeatedly typecast themselves as the husband and wife team they were. Frequently estranged on film, but united in its script development and production, Cassavetes and Rowlands might be considered the first couple of American independent cinema, a genre that is usually measured by the distance it maintains from studio production protocols and the melodramatic clichés of Hollywood, many of which center on the heterosexual couple. Anticipating our own line of thinking, Charles Warren has linked Cassavetes's interest in human relationality with Stanley Cavell's contemporaneous account of the Hollywood melodrama of the unknown woman and its more upbeat counterpart, the Hollywood comedy of remarriage, an idea Cavell derives from a clutch of highly scripted Hollywood studio movies whose key protagonists were estranged married couples whom the events of the film would reunite.[34] In their final film together, *Love Streams*, shot in their own house and described by Warren as a "compendium" of their previous nine collaborations, Cassavetes and Rowlands play brother and sister, a narrative conceit that confirms Cavell's counterintuitive observation that in order to see the institution of marriage for what it really is, you sometimes need to remove what it is often mistaken for, namely heterosexuality or, even more commonly, family.[35] Considering the universal absence of children in the original Hollywood comedies of remarriage, Cavell is led down a queerly compelling path: "One might take its immediate function to be that of purifying the discussion, or the possibility of divorce, which would be swamped by the presence of children. But what this means, on my view of these comedies, is that the absence of children further purifies the discussion of marriage. The direct implication is that while marriage may remain the authorization for having children, children are not an authentication of marriage."[36] Cavell reads these dialogue-driven films in institutional and sociological context, claiming that they constitute an ongoing philosophical conversation about the nature of marriage once it has been desacralized by the middle-class acceptance of divorce. Although he is obsessed with the narrative idiosyncrasies of each of the seven films he considers to be the epitome of the remarriage subgenre, a deeply selective personal canon that he rereads multiple times across his long career, he also places these Hollywood movies within a longer philosophical debate about marriage that stretches from John Milton, a well-known apologist for divorce, to Stein, who is not usually counted among leading theorists of marriage.[37] Cavell arrives at Stein through thinking about Leo McCarey's *The Awful Truth*, a film in which the divorcing couple share custody of their dog, Mr. Smith, a situation that keeps open the possibility of their reattachment, a plot point that Farley can attest to in the nonfictional realm of our double (or should that be triple?) autobiography.

Canine connections aside, it is the internal rhythm of McCarey's film that recommends Stein to Cavell. *The Awful Truth* departs from the other six classical remarriage comedies in eschewing comic high points or standout scenes in favor of a narration that rocks between day and night, night and day, thereby keeping open the possibility of an erotic reawakening that is domestic rather than ceremonial in quality. Rather than, say, the remarriage festivities that end George Cukor's *The Philadelphia Story* or the way that Cukor's *Adam's Rib* tests marriage in court, McCarey keeps audience attention tethered to the possibility of the small but significant matter of two people going to bed together as they have many times before. As we have elsewhere said, "Cavell persuasively argues that whereas classical comedy promises the redemption of festival as represented in the succession of the seasons, modern remarriage comedy promises the redemption of dailiness and 'the acceptance of human relatedness, as the acceptance of repetition' in the everyday."[38] Although Cavell traces this idea of a "metaphysics of repetition" to Søren Kierkegaard's study of marriage—tellingly titled *Repetition*—and Friedrich Nietzsche's notion of the "heightening" of time expressed as "*Hochzeit*"—the German term for marriage—he is ultimately led to Stein's *The Making of Americans*, which he prefers to summon through the dramatic machinery of memory rather than literal citation:

> She speaks, I seem to recall, to the effect that the knowledge of others depends upon an appreciation of their repeatings (which is what we are, which is what we have to offer). This knowing of others as knowing what they are always saying and believing and doing would, naturally, be Stein's description of, or direction for, how her reader is to know her own most famous manner of writing, the hallmark of which is its repeatings. The application of this thought here is the suggestion that marriage is an emblem of the knowledge of others not solely because of its implication of reciprocity but because it implies a devotion in repetition, to dailiness.[39]

Cavell's recollection of Stein suggests that marriage practiced in this lesbian way—as remarriage with no necessary relation to formal celebration or sanctification but with every relation to the repetition embedded in the everyday—will be the making of us all, or at least those of us who are predisposed to refind happiness in the repetitive and reciprocal experience of dailiness rather than seeking outbreaks of happiness in what is otherwise experienced as dull routine.[40]

We think of this as lesbian remarriage. And we are not the only ones. As evidence that there is an emergent school of thinking about modern marriage as a lesbian practice, we point to Lillian Faderman's foundational account of Boston marriages and Sharon Marcus's brilliant reframing of nineteenth-century relationships between women as models for modern heterosexual marriage rather than the other way around. But remarriage is not easy, not for anyone. Attachments cannot be willed into being, any more than they can be willed away. For us to reattach took a whole new city and a whole new genre of repetition. The city was Berlin, the very capital of German reunification, where we arrived on sabbatical in 2015 to take up residence in the formerly proletarian suburb of Wedding. So far, so auspicious. The genre was electronic dance music (a diverse swath of music styles now regularly homogenized via the initialism EDM), and its two subsets techno and house, as experienced in the vast concrete underworld of Berghain, where the famously erratic door staff never once turned us away, seeming to understand instinctively that their dance floor needed two middle-aged lesbians almost as much as we needed it. Specifically, it was in the enchanted precincts of the Panorama Bar, where the only indication that another Berlin night has passed into day involves the momentary opening of window shutters in time with an ecstatically uplifted rhythm, that we perfected what Robert Fink has elsewhere called the "pursuit of repetition-driven ecstasy," an aim broadly supported by the industrial cultures of reproduction that constitute postmodernism, particularly its sonic landscape.[41]

In his dazzling book on American minimal music as a cultural practice that bridges high and low aesthetic forms, Fink gives a compelling account of the parallel emergence of two musical genres in the mid-seventies: one, the minimalist compositions associated with Philip Glass and Steve Reich, and the other, the "avant-disco" experiments of Giorgio Moroder and Arthur Russell that eventually led to the emergence of electronic dance music.[42] The subsequent rise of EDM across the eighties and nineties is often linked to the psychoactive effects associated with the use of methylenedioxymethamphetamine (MDMA), also known as ecstasy, itemized by the National Institute on

Drug Abuse as "increased extroversion, emotional warmth, empathy toward others and a willingness to discuss emotionally charged memories."[43] Although they come wrapped in the would-be off-putting language of clinical neuropsychology, these intoxicating effects would not be out of place in the Shakespearean romances that are the precedents to Cavell's comedies of remarriage. Here, likewise, the candidates for remarriage are required to set aside their waking inhibitions in order to dance, sing, or play with each other like children in order to overcome the strictly internal obstacles that beset their relationships. For instance, the rules of erotic connection that apply in the drug-fueled underworld of *A Midsummer Night's Dream* are convincingly repurposed in *The Philadelphia Story*, a film in which Katharine Hepburn and Cary Grant play an estranged couple whose reunification is dependent on the magical elixir of champagne that drunkenly compels the morally superior ex-wife to a nocturnal interlude of increased extroversion, emotional warmth, and irrational empathy toward a man who is neither her ex-husband nor her husband-to-be. Occurring on the eve of her second marriage, these out-of-character experiences are what ultimately allow her and her ex-husband to slip the emotionally charged memories that keep them apart and set the stage for remarriage as the bringing back together of two people who were never really separated. As Cavell points out, the quick-witted couple dialogue that is bandied back and forth between Grant and Hepburn confirms not just their compatibility but their inability to "*feel* themselves divorced" because the conversation they share with each other and no one else "is continuous with the conversation that constituted their marriage."[44] We know this failing well, as an effect of both speech and writing: never married and never divorced, no matter how hard we tried our collective hand at both.

Fortunately for us, the rules of remarriage that apply in Cavell's Hollywood comedies also apply in the benign setting of Berghain, where strangers, including the recently estranged, can be brought together anew as if in the grip of a love potion that allows "one to begin again, free of obligation and of the memory of compromise."[45] In the amnesia-inducing aerie of the Panorama Bar, our coupled connection was frequently remixed by resident DJ Tama Sumo (aka Kirsten Egert), who did not stop short of spinning up to three vinyl records at a time to build a distinctive sound from improvised combinations of disco and Afrobeats, and on one memorable night handed off to her wife DJ Lakuti (aka Lerato Khathi). Consistent with the remarriage plot, our Berghain narrative involved setbacks and obstacles, including a panic attack that required the hand-in-hand crossing of the downstairs techno floor, with its counterpoint soundscape of mechanically repeated noise calling to mind Jacques Attali's extraordinarily bleak account of repetitive society.[46] First appearing in French in 1977, the year the *Saturday Night Fever* soundtrack mainstreamed disco, Attali's political economy of music points to the endlessly repeatable sound object as "a harbinger of mass cultural suicide." Though acknowledging that "the painful thrill of the media sublime has more than a little self-abnegating death drive in it," Fink effectively counters Attali's condemnation of synthesized sound loopings with a more sympathetic take on "ambient repetition as a form of homeostatic *mood regulation*," which might include the generation of equilibrium across the social field of a dance floor or a couple in distress.[47]

Resisting the dystopian cast of Attali's account of repetitive music, Fink argues for "the presence in minimalist music of both Eros and Thanatos, of dialectical entrainment to desire as well as libidinal liberation from it, never forgetting that these lofty psychoanalytic terms are just metaphors for the bodily effects of material social constructions." As an example of the sound culture of Eros or desire, Fink gives Moroder's extended remix of Donna Summer's "Love to Love You Baby," which creatively combines two teleological drives across a seventeen-minute sonic arc. One drive is sublimated into its repetitively systematic musical structure; the other drive is made "boldly and transgressively explicit" in the second half of the track when Summer's vocal line is dropped in favor of a "complex, syncopated, additive pattern of intakes and moans" that simulates orgasm. As an example of the sound culture of Thanatos or the death instinct, Fink gives us Summer and Moroder's follow-up single, "I Feel Love," which abandons the human drive to climax in favor of "cold computerized repetition" and points to the emergence of machine-based techno.[48]

Although we collectively lack any of the musical training that Fink brings to his task, his division of sonic repetition into two types more or less corresponds to our apprehension of the two sound cultures that characterize Berghain. One is the culture of Eros, where repetition is in the service of desire as heard and embodied in the relatively intimate space of the Panorama Bar, where the human voice still holds affective sway in sampled disco vocals that minimally sustain couple identification. The other is the culture of Thanatos, where the mood regulation served by repetition is more mechanical than human, as heard and embodied in the cavernous dimensions of the main techno dance floor with its eighteen-meter-high ceiling and viewing gallery that looks down on a thousand machine-driven bodies in nonstop movement that is hard to call as either peak or plateau.[49]

Although it would be very easy to gender the distinction between these two cultures of repetition—house and techno—as the distinction between a personalized lesbian sound and an impersonal gay noise, we instead draw attention to the way in which it is the movement between the personal and the impersonal that is at the heart of Berghain's pleasures. At the risk of repeating ourselves yet another time, in this doubled perspective sexual reattachment is based in the recognition that the personal and the impersonal are seamed together in ways that are

> less a bind than a bond, less an impasse than a way of cohabiting—beyond domesticating logics—a shared circumstance. This is not to prettify the paradigm, to suggest some easier occupancy of modern regimes of sexuality and their simultaneous promise to cherish and obliterate one's sense of self. Rather, it is to draw on the doubled meanings of "bond," the capacity of this single word to describe both conditions of loathsome subjection and ardent attachment, in order to stress, in an entirely unapocalyptic tone, the inextricable entanglement of modern sex in personalizing and impersonalizing technologies of the self.[50]

So for us the industrial-scale impersonal allure of Berghain, which has no mirrors or reflective surfaces and where a photographic prohibition is rigorously enforced, is continuous with the everyday urban magic of the M10, the bright yellow disco-tram that runs continuously from Friedrichshain to Wedding. No matter what time of the day or night we departed, the M10 would reliably pull up within minutes and take us home to our personal repeatings. Of such things are worlds remade.

NOTES

The authors acknowledge the support of the Australian Research Council which funded the larger project of which this is a part (DP 190101539).

1 Schechner, *Between Theater and Anthropology*, 50.

2 Theoretically formative accounts of feminist and queer performance can be found in Phelan, *Unmarked*, and Muñoz, *Disidentifications*.

3 *The Second Woman*, Performing Lines, www.performinglines.org.au/projects/the -second-woman. Although Breckon and Randall exercise some control over the promotional material that circulates in the vicinity of the performance, a sense of the discordant performance and reception life of the piece can be gained from the 2017 Australian Broadcasting Commission documentary *Behind The Second Woman*, available at the time of writing to stream on ABC iView, at https://iview .abc.net.au/show/behind-the-second-woman.

4 For a discussion of *Opening Night* and the way it "establishes a wholly unconventional relationship of the spectator to the action both of the film and the play within it," see King, "Free Indirect Affect in Cassavetes' *Opening Night* and *Faces*," 106.

5 Since the time of writing, *The Second Woman* has been performed three times internationally with locally cast performers, first Zhi-Ying Zhu at the National Kaohsiung Center for the Arts, Taiwan, November 2–3, 2018; then Laara Sadiq at BRAVE Festival, Toronto, July 20–21, 2019; and most recently with Alia Shawkat at BAM Fisher, Brooklyn, October 18–19, 2019.

6 For further discussion of *Mulholland Dr.* as an engagement with discontinuous space, see Wallace, *Lesbianism, Cinema, Space*, 99–116.

7 O'Hara, "Poem (Lana Turner Has Collapsed!)," 64.

8 Schechner, *Between Theater and Anthropology*, 51, 52.

9 For an account of the historical origins of the lesbian-love-murder nexus and its repetition across different bandwidths of medical, legal, and popular culture, see Duggan, *Sapphic Slashers*. For a more general diagnostic of the role of seriality in modern "wound culture," see Seltzer, *Serial Killers*, which explores the violence done to representation by technological relay. For a more benign take on lesbian seriality and its theoretical profile, see Jagose and Wallace, "Dicktation."

10 Jagose, *In Translation*.

11 Wallace, *Sexual Encounters*; Jagose, *Slow Water*.

12 Lilley, "Lesbian Professor," 81.

13 Poletti, "Periperformative Life Narrative"; Jagose, "Anthropomorphism, Normativity, and the Couple."

14 Wallace, *Reattachment Theory*.

15 Consider the following queer studies classics, for example, whose classicism derives from their capacity to engage the autoethnographic without breaking theoretical cover: Miller, *Bringing Out Roland Barthes*; Koestenbaum, *Jackie under My Skin*; Sedgwick, *A Dialogue on Love*; and Lord, *The Summer of Her Baldness*.

16 Gallop, *Living with His Camera*, 5, 18.

17 For further discussion of homosexuality's inability to register a domesticated form of intimacy, see Wallace, "Sontag's Late Lesbianism" and "Queer Chattels and Fixtures."

18 Wallace, "Outside History."

19 For a pop-cultural anthem that captures the ambivalence felt by many about the success of gay marriage, we nominate Loretta Lynn's original honky-tonk recording of Johnny Mullins's "Success" (Decca, 1962) and its subsequent covers, particularly those by Elvis Costello (F-Beat, 1981) and Sinéad O'Connor (Chrysalis, 1992).

20 Cobb, *Single*, 192, 21.

21 Robles et al., "Marital Quality and Health." For further discussion of this point, see Herring, this volume.

22 Proulx, Helms, and Buehler, "Marital Quality and Personal Well-Being"; Cummings and Davies, *Marital Conflict and Children*.

23 "Australian Budget Fact Sheet: Stronger Relationships, 2014"; Hewitt, "Marriage Breakdown in Australia."

24 Cara Waters, "Bagging Single-Use Prime Ministers," *Sydney Morning Herald*, August 28, 2018, 11.

25 Ralph Ashton, "Australia Is Behaving Like a Spoiled Brat," *Sydney Morning Herald*, August 28, 2018, 18.

26 Exemplary of this trend in the marriage-counseling literature is Esther Perel, best-selling author of *Mating in Captivity: Unlocking Erotic Intelligence* and *The State of Affairs: Rethinking Infidelity*. Perel is now paired on the celebrity book circuit with Laura Kipnis, author of *Against Love: A Polemic*, which stridently argues against long-term commitment pursued at the cost of happiness. As readers will know, *Against Love* is a boiled-down version of the compelling Marxist argument first put forward by Kipnis in *Critical Inquiry* under the title "Adultery." Kipnis's work features significantly in Wallace, *Reattachment Theory*.

27 Weston, *Families We Choose*; Sedgwick, *Tendencies*, 71.

28 A notable exception to this rule is Marcus, *Between Women*.

29 Miller, *The Handmaid's Tale*.

30 Stein, *Everybody's Autobiography*, 49.

31 Human Farley Granger was already third in a line of Farley Grangers and refused to change his name even when Samuel Goldwyn pressed him to adopt a stage name. Granger with Calhoun, *Include Me Out*, 17.

32 For further discussion of the interlocking of the personal and impersonal, see Jagose, "Media and Everyday Life."

33 Kaplan and Ross, "Introduction," 3. For an Australian takedown of the French origins of the defense of the everyday, see Morris, "Banality in Cultural Studies."

34 Warren, "Cavell, Altman, and Cassavetes." See also Cavell, *Pursuits of Happiness* and *Contesting Tears*.

35 Warren, "Cavell, Altman, and Cassavetes," 15.

36 Cavell, *Pursuits of Happiness*, 58. The seven remarriage films Cavell considers are, in the order in which he discusses them, *The Lady Eve* (Preston Sturges, 1941), *It Happened One Night* (Frank Capra, 1934), *Bringing Up Baby* (Howard Hawks, 1938), *The Philadelphia Story* (George Cukor, 1940), *His Girl Friday* (Howard Hawks, 1940), *Adam's Rib* (George Cukor, 1949), and *The Awful Truth* (Leo McCarey, 1937).

37 Stein is becoming better known as a practitioner of marriage thanks to Edward Einhorn's play *The Marriage of Alice B. Toklas by Gertrude Stein*, which premiered at the HERE Arts Center, New York, in May 2017.

38 See the discussion of Andrew Haigh's *45 Years* and its indebtedness to Eric Rohmer's *A Tale of Winter* and Shakespeare's *A Winter's Tale* in Wallace, *Reattachment Theory*, 177–78.

39 Cavell, *Pursuits of Happiness*, 241.

40 For a compelling gloss on Stein's understanding of people as "fundamentally rhythmic" and its relation to wider accounts of the habitual and the chronic as a problem for both a modern biopolitics that valorizes life-enhancing choices and a queer theory that valorizes transgression and rupture, see Freeman, "Hopeless Cases," 337.

41 Fink, *Repeating Ourselves*, 26.

42 Fink, *Repeating Ourselves*, 27. For another influential account of the role of music technology in the formation of club cultures, see Thornton, *Club Cultures*. Against

a field that has tended to value the technical production of music over its popular consumption, Margie Borschke has more recently argued for the mutually informing relationship that exists between live DJs and their dance-floor audiences in *This Is Not a Remix*.

43   As described on the US National Institute for Drug Abuse (NIDA) website: www .drugabuse.gov/publications/research-reports/mdma-ecstasy-abuse/what-are -effects-mdma.

44   Cavell, *Pursuits of Happiness*, 151.

45   Cavell, *Pursuits of Happiness*, 31.

46   Attali, *Noise*.

47   Fink, *Repeating Ourselves*, 7, 11.

48   Fink, *Repeating Ourselves*, 6–7, 60–61.

49   Our description deliberately recalls Richard Dyer's account of disco as "a form of music that denies the centrality of the phallus while at the same time refusing the non-physicality which such a denial has hitherto implied." Dyer, "In Defence of Disco," 22.

50   Jagose, *Orgasmology*, 105.

BIBLIOGRAPHY

Attali, Jacques. *Noise: The Political Economy of Music*. Translated by Brian Massumi. Minneapolis: University of Minnesota Press, 1985.

Australian Broadcasting Commission. *Behind The Second Woman*. Directed by Olivia Rousset. 2017.

"Australian Budget Fact Sheet: Stronger Relationships, 2014." www.dss.gov.au.

Borschke, Margie. *This Is Not a Remix: Piracy, Authenticity, and Popular Music*. London: Bloomsbury, 2017.

Breckon, Anna, and Nat Randall. *The Second Woman*. 2016. www.performinglines.org .au/projects/the-second-woman.

Cavell, Stanley. *Contesting Tears: The Hollywood Melodrama of the Unknown Woman*. Chicago: University of Chicago Press, 1996.

Cavell, Stanley. *Pursuits of Happiness: The Hollywood Comedy of Remarriage*. Cambridge, MA: Harvard University Press, 1981.

Cobb, Michael. *Single: Arguments for the Uncoupled*. New York: New York University Press, 2012.

Cummings, E. Mark, and Patrick T. Davies. *Marital Conflict and Children: An Emotional Security Perspective*. New York: Guilford, 2010.

Duggan, Lisa. *Sapphic Slashers: Sex, Violence, and American Modernity*. Durham, NC: Duke University Press, 2000.

Dyer, Richard. "In Defence of Disco." *Gay Left* 8 (1979): 20–23.

Fink, Robert. *Repeating Ourselves: American Minimal Music as Cultural Practice*. Berkeley: University of California Press, 2005.

Freeman, Elizabeth. "Hopeless Cases: Queer Chronicities and Gertrude Stein's 'Melanctha.'" *Journal of Homosexuality* 63, no. 3 (2016): 329–48.

Gallop, Jane. *Living with His Camera*. Photographs by Dick Blau. Durham, NC: Duke University Press, 2003.

Granger, Farley, with Robert Calhoun. *Include Me Out: My Life from Goldwyn to Broadway*. New York: St. Martin's Griffin, 2008.

Hewitt, Belinda. "Marriage Breakdown in Australia: Social Correlates, Gender, and Initiator Status." Social Policy Research Paper 35. Canberra: Department of Families, Housing, Community Services and Indigenous Affairs, 2008.

Jagose, Annamarie. "Anthropomorphism, Normativity, and the Couple: A Queer Studies/Human-Animal Studies Mash-Up." In "The Ontology of the Couple," edited by S. Pearl Brilmyer, Filippo Trentin, and Zairong Xiang, special issue, GLQ 25, no. 2 (2019): 315–35.

Jagose, Annamarie. *In Translation*. Wellington: Victoria University Press, 1994.

Jagose, Annamarie. "Media and Everyday Life." In *Media Studies in Aotearoa/New Zealand*, edited by Luke Goode and Nabeel Zuberi, 46–57. Auckland: Pearson Education, 2004.

Jagose, Annamarie. *Orgasmology*. Durham, NC: Duke University Press, 2013.

Jagose, Annamarie. *Slow Water*. Wellington: Victoria University Press, 2003.

Jagose, Annamarie, and Lee Wallace. "Dicktation: Autotheory in the Coupled Voice." In "Autotheory Theory," edited by Robyn Wiegman, special issue, *Arizona Quarterly* 76, no. 1 (2020): 109–39.

Kaplan, Alice, and Kristin Ross. "Introduction." In "Everyday Life," special issue, *Yale French Studies* 73 (1987): 1–4.

King, Homay. "Free Indirect Affect in Cassavetes' *Opening Night* and *Faces*." *Camera Obscura* 19, no. 2 (2004): 104–39.

Kipnis, Laura. "Adultery." *Critical Inquiry* 24, no. 2 (1998): 289–327.

Kipnis, Laura. *Against Love: A Polemic*. New York: Pantheon, 2003.

Koestenbaum, Wayne. *Jackie under My Skin: Interpreting an Icon*. New York: Farrar, Straus and Giroux, 1995.

Lilley, Kate. "Lesbian Professor." *Australian Feminist Studies* 11, no. 23 (1996): 81–88.

Lord, Catherine. *The Summer of Her Baldness: A Cancer Improvisation*. Austin: University of Texas Press, 2004.

Marcus, Sharon. *Between Women: Friendship, Desire, and Marriage in Victorian England*. Princeton, NJ: Princeton University Press, 2007.

Miller, Bruce, dir. *The Handmaid's Tale*. MGM Television, 2017–. Available to stream on Hulu.

Miller, D. A. *Bringing Out Roland Barthes*. Berkeley: University of California Press, 1992.

Morris, Meaghan. "Banality in Cultural Studies." *Discourse* 10, no. 2 (1988): 3–29.

Muñoz, José Esteban. *Disidentifications: Queers of Color and the Performance of Politics*. Minneapolis: University of Minnesota Press, 1999.

O'Hara, Frank. "Poem (Lana Turner Has Collapsed!)." In *Lunch Poems*, 64. San Francisco: City Lights Books, 1964.

Perel, Esther. *Mating in Captivity: Unlocking Erotic Intelligence*. New York: HarperCollins, 2012.

Perel, Esther. *The State of Affairs: Rethinking Infidelity*. New York: HarperCollins, 2017.

Phelan, Peggy. *Unmarked: The Politics of Performance*. New York: Routledge, 1993.

Poletti, Anna. "Periperformative Life Narrative: Queer Collages." *GLQ* 22, no. 3 (2016): 359–79.

Proulx, Christine, Heather Helms, and Cheryl Buehler. "Marital Quality and Personal Well-Being: A Meta-analysis." *Journal of Marriage and Family* 69, no. 3 (2007): 576–93.

Robles, Theodore, Richard Slatcher, Joseph Tombrello, and Meghan McGinn. "Marital Quality and Health: A Meta-analytic Review." *Psychological Bulletin* 140, no. 1 (2014): 140–87.

Schechner, Richard. *Between Theater and Anthropology*. Philadelphia: University of Pennsylvania Press, 1985.

Sedgwick, Eve Kosofsky. *A Dialogue on Love*. Boston: Beacon, 2000.

Sedgwick, Eve Kosofsky. *Tendencies*. Durham, NC: Duke University Press, 1993.

Seltzer, Mark. *Serial Killers: Death and Life in America's Wound Culture*. London: Routledge, 1998.

Stein, Gertrude. *Everybody's Autobiography*. New York: Random House, 1937.

Thornton, Sarah. *Club Cultures: Music, Media, and Subcultural Capital*. Middletown, CT: Wesleyan University Press, 1995.

Wallace, Lee. *Lesbianism, Cinema, Space: The Sexual Life of Apartments*. New York: Routledge, 2009.

Wallace, Lee. "Outside History: Same-Sex Sexuality and the Colonial Archive." In *Embodiments of Cultural Encounters*, edited by Sebastian Jobs and Gesa Mackenthun, 61–74. Munster: Waxmann Verlag, 2011.

Wallace, Lee. "Queer Chattels and Fixtures: Photography and Materiality in the Homes of Frank Sargeson and Patrick White." In *Domestic Imaginaries: Navigating the Home in Global Literary and Visual Cultures*, edited by Bex Harper and Hollie Price, 191–209. London: Palgrave Macmillan, 2017.

Wallace, Lee. *Reattachment Theory: Queer Cinema of Remarriage*. Durham, NC: Duke University Press, 2020.

Wallace, Lee. *Sexual Encounters: Pacific Texts, Modern Sexualities*. Ithaca, NY: Cornell University Press, 2003.

Wallace, Lee. "Sontag's Late Lesbianism: Sexuality, Photography, Celebrity." *Celebrity Studies* 6, no. 2 (2015): 206–18.

Warren, Charles. "Cavell, Altman, and Cassavetes." *Film International* 4, no. 4 (2006): 14–20.

Weston, Kath. *Families We Choose: Lesbians, Gays, Kinship*. New York: Columbia University Press, 1991.

11

THE LONG RUN

HEATHER LOVE

Since dinosaurs roamed the Earth, marriage has been the most significant thing that can take place in the life of two human individuals. So runs the US Supreme Court decision to grant same-sex couples the right to legally marry. In the words of Justice Kennedy, "From their beginning to the most recent page, the annals of human history reveal the transcendent importance of marriage."[1] The combination of tautology and overcompensation (for not having perhaps read every word of the annals . . .) recalls the puffed-up opening of a weak undergraduate paper.[2] The majority opinion continues: "The lifelong union of a man and a woman has always promised nobility and dignity to all persons without regard to their station in life." The work of such an argument is to immortalize companionate marriage, attributing values of dignity, equality, and reciprocity to an institution that was, in many phases, not at all concerned with them. It is also to brazenly deny, while pointing to, the exclusions of the institution of marriage, which throughout its history flatly denied or made a mockery of unions depending on the participants' "station in life."[3] Kennedy praises the quasi-magical properties of marriage, for instance the fact that it turns two people into one. But the argument turns on the claim to longevity, which is repeated with minor variations throughout the decision: "The centrality of marriage to the human condition makes it unsurprising that the institution has existed for millennia and across civilizations. Since the dawn of history, marriage has transformed strangers into relatives, binding families and societies together." The conclusion of Kennedy's opinion strikes this note again, supporting a view of marriage as sacred rather than temporal: "No union is more profound than marriage, for it embodies the highest ideals of love, fidelity, devotion, sacrifice, and family. In forming a marital union, two people become something greater than once they were. As some of the petitioners in these cases demonstrate, marriage embodies a love that may endure even past death" (28).[4]

Obergefell v. Hodges is all about the long run: it backdates marriage to the dawn of time and postdates it to the afterlife. By emphasizing the timelessness and universality of the institution, Kennedy increases the stakes of the argument for inclusion. In arguing that marriage is and has always been the most important social bond, Kennedy suggests that the right to marry defines us as human: for this reason, no other arrangement will suffice. At the same time, this argument serves to quiet fears that the expansion of marriage rights to same-sex couples will destabilize the institution. By insisting on the stability of marriage across its history—by insisting that it has no history—Kennedy makes it clear that the absorption of same-sex couples into marriage law will not weaken the institution in the slightest. To the contrary, the expansion of marriage will only extend its reign. As conservative proponents of gay marriage have argued, the effect of legalizing same-sex unions is to stabilize couples, families, and society itself.[5] Kennedy suggests that this accommodation will be agreeable to both the petitioners in this case and to society at large, and that it is in fact the intent of the petitioners to honor marriage and to share in its transcendence and timelessness. "Were their intent to demean the revered idea and reality of marriage," Kennedy writes, "the petitioners' claims would be of a different order. But that is neither their purpose nor their submission. To the contrary, it is the enduring importance of marriage that underlies the petitioners' contentions.

This, they say, is their whole point. Far from seeking to devalue marriage, the petitioners seek it for themselves because of their respect—and need—for its privileges and responsibilities. And their immutable nature dictates that same-sex marriage is their only real path to this profound commitment."

By extending access to "one of civilization's oldest institutions," *Obergefell* promises to bring stability and longevity to relations understood to be episodic and inconsequential. But to gain eternity by hitching your wagon to marriage can be understood as a rather poor bargain, given the radical changes that the institution has undergone, its variability across cultures, and its fragility in the present. The denial that the institution is variable or vulnerable is so often repeated, and in so many forms, that it can be understood as a primary rather than an incidental aim of the decision. The repeated claim that it is eternal is bolstered by citations, for instance of Confucius, who "taught that marriage lies at the foundation of government," and of Cicero, "who wrote, 'The first bond of society is marriage; next, children, and then the family.'" More generally, Kennedy asserts, "There are untold references to the beauty of marriage in religious and philosophical texts spanning time, cultures, and faiths, as well as in art and literature and all their forms." He adds a caveat: "It is fair and necessary to say that these references were based on the understanding that marriage is a union between two persons of the opposite sex." The acknowledgment that historical claims for the beauty and transcendence of marriage described the unions of men and women does not undermine the justification for same-sex marriage; instead, it points to the high stakes for all parties in bringing gay couples under the eternalizing aegis of marriage.

One might, of course, have cited other precedents. There is a body of literature, art, and philosophy with equally deep and wide roots that places marriage in a rather different light. In place of Confucius, one might cite Aristotle, who sees not marriage but elite male friendship as the foundation of government. Although Cicero sees marriage and family as *primary* social bonds, it is friendship that is understood as *exemplary*. In "On Friendship, or Laelius," he writes, "Now friendship may be thus defined: *a complete accord on all subjects human and divine, joined with mutual good will and affection.* And with the exception of wisdom, I am inclined to think nothing better than this has been given to man by the immortal gods." Friendship is a gift from the gods to virtuous men for their enjoyment and use: "Turn which way you please, you will find it at hand. It is everywhere; and yet never out of place, never unwelcome. Fire and water themselves, to use a common expression, are not of more universal use than friendship." Friendship for Cicero is elemental and pervasive. And although natural bonds may come first, their primacy does not make them more stable than the bonds of friendship: "If you don't see the virtue of friendship and harmony, you may learn it by observing the effects of quarrels and feuds. Was any family ever so well established, any State so firmly settled, as to be beyond the reach of utter destruction from animosities and factions? This may teach you the immense advantage of friendship."[6]

The long and idealizing tradition of writing about friendship stakes its claims on the superiority of willed to natural bonds, of male-male relations to those involving women and children, and to the bonds of comrades to those motivated by erotic attraction or the necessity of procreation. Montaigne relates the elevation of friendship to the denigration of marriage, linking both to the moral inferiority of women: "You cannot compare friendship with the passion men feel for women" but proceeds to do just that:

> As for marriage ... it is a bargain struck for other purposes; within it you soon have to unsnarl hundreds of extraneous tangled ends, which are enough to break the thread of a living passion and to trouble its course, whereas in friendship there is no traffic or commerce but with itself. In addition, women are in truth not normally capable of responding to such familiarity and mutual confidence as sustain that holy bond of friendship, nor do their souls seem firm enough to withstand the clasp of a knot so lasting and so tightly drawn. And indeed ... if it were possible to fashion such a relationship, willing and free, in which not only the souls had this full enjoyment but in which the bodies too shared in the union—where the whole human being was involved—it is certain that the loving-friendship would be more full and more abundant. But there is no example yet of woman attaining to it and by the common agreement of the Ancient schools of philosophy she is excluded from it.[7]

The natural inferiority of women, assumed by the Ancients and the Moderns, makes both marriage and the possibility of friendship with women secondary to the friendship between men. But Montaigne nonetheless sees this as an aspiration flickering on the horizon of historical possibility. Montaigne fantasizes about the possibility of a relation that would involve both body and mind. Women are not capable of such a fully realized relationship, but engaging in such relations with other men involves risks: at the beginning of the following paragraph, Montaigne distinguishes such relations from the "alternative licence of the Greeks," which is "rightly abhorrent to our manners."[8] Montaigne's attempt to thread the needle suggests the difficulty of establishing a transhistorical basis for marriage as the highest form of human relation. It is also a reminder that the possibility of companionate marriage has haunted the literature of friendship. In this framework, gay marriage does look like the fulfillment of a deep human aspiration, but it is an aspiration informed as much by the fantasy of ideal friendship as it is by the fantasy of perfect romantic fulfillment.

Obergefell pitches the legalization of same-sex marriage as an opportunity to share out the resources of heterosexual marriage. Yet the fantasy it articulates recalls Montaigne's wish that the dignity, stability, and universality of friendship might serve to transform and idealize marriage. In this sense we might understand the *Obergefell* decision not as a gift extended to precarious queer subjects but as an infusion of new energy into a dying institution. The affirmations that marriage lasts forever, that it endures beyond death, might be understood as an attempt to pass off shopworn goods. We know, of course, that marriage is in crisis—when not? It is not only high divorce rates and single-parent families that are tearing marriage apart. It is also the high rate of cohabitation that suggests that people can't be bothered and gives the impression that marriage is in its twilight. The fact that US marriage rates have diverged increasingly along class lines in the last decade, with higher income and more educated couples marrying more often, indicates that this is a luxury good that increasingly few need or want.[9] The economic necessity and tight interdependency that used to bind families together no longer serves that purpose, and the desire for marriage seems more clearly ideological, and halfheartedly so. Marriage seems to appeal to same-sex couples on similar grounds, amid a shower of custom cake-toppers, gay-friendly honeymoon destinations, and, indeed, lavish hers-hers showers. But if recent research suggests that married same-sex couples' incomes are in line with other couples (with male couples earning more and female couples earning less), there are other reasons for same-sex couples to marry. The list of rights that accrue to married couples are both novel and more pressing for couples still vulnerable to dismissal, derogation, and stigma. Where parental rights or medical decision making is still likely to be precarious, marriage can be a high-stakes affair. In addition, queers' long history of exclusion from marriage and family is like a fresh coat of paint on this weather-beaten institution, making it appear desirable once again. But although that longing is real, the content of the fantasy of everlasting marriage is derived as much from the history of idealized friendship as it is from paeans to companionate marriage.

The tradition of friendship now being retailed back to queers as a dream of inclusion is in fact deeply embedded in queer history, with its implication of secrecy and punishment. Critics Alan Bray, George Haggerty, and Eve Kosofsky Sedgwick have considered the charged and volatile boundary between idealized friendship and sodomitical relations ("the alternative licence of the Greeks").[10] In this tradition, what Sharon Marcus has called the "deviance paradigm of homosexuality," the language of longevity, stability, or calm, drops away.[11] Instead, through what we now know as queer history, there are images of abomination, crime, and sin, morphing in the twentieth century into a romantic discourse of tragic and impossible love. I have long been magnetized by this strain of representation and have felt that it offers an important counterweight to arguments about gay marriage as the end of history. Same-sex relations are certainly transformed by legal recognition, but not in ways that float free of the history of queer exclusion. For those who have always been denied access to it, marriage can look like the cure to inequality and existential loneliness too. But in this context, it is humane and necessary to point out the limitations of marriage. Such an impulse motivates the popular reframing of the right to marry as "the right to be miserable too." Putting the brakes on idealization can help to ease the pressure, already immense but particularly charged for queer couples, on the need to have a perfect marriage and family.[12]

Although I am committed to this strategy of deidealization and believe that it remains a crucial tool in the queer arsenal, such a persistent concern entails other forms of disavowal and repression. In particular, it is at odds with my own relatively long-standing tenure in a same-sex partnership (unmarried, with children). Over the past decade I have attempted to come to terms with the contradictions of contemporary queer theory and politics, attending in particular to the institutionalization of the field and its self-understanding as an activist and outsider field.[13] As awkward and difficult as it has been to reconcile my tenured status with the antinormative and subversive stance of queer scholarship, it is more difficult for me to avow the fact that, despite my attachments to queer heartbreak and impossibility, I have spent much of my life in relatively stable and enduring partnerships. The challenge is to offer a critical perspective on what I see as the lies and false promises of gay marriage discourse without lying myself. I have tried to address these tensions between my personal life and intellectual and political commitments recently in writing about Maggie Nelson's *The Argonauts* (2015).[14] Nelson attempts to reconcile a queer discourse of impossible love (via Roland Barthes's *A Lover's Discourse*) with a feminist commitment to domesticity and care, offering a richly detailed and ambivalent portrait of queer family life. I experienced Nelson's memoir as a spotlight on the contradictions of my own life; by writing about it, I have attempted to more fully avow otherwise backgrounded or simply disavowed attachments to the couple and the family form. But it was also a balm: avoiding the discourse of eternal love, Nelson describes the deep spell of intimacy, binding and nourishing but without guarantee.

It is clear that I prefer my accounts of married life seasoned with ambivalence. When it comes to friendship, however, I have fewer reservations and fewer defenses. Despite some attempts on my part to see friendship otherwise, it remains a highly idealized topic for me and a wellspring of my queer optimism.[15] Over the years this cleavage has developed as a division between writing and teaching. My writing has focused on the effects of homophobia and other forms of inequality and exclusion on gender and sexual outsiders: my persistent concerns have included failure, stigma, deviance, self-hatred, loneliness, and longing. Meanwhile, I have parked my queer idealism elsewhere. Since 2002, I have been regularly teaching a course called "Friendship," in which we read canonical texts on the nature of friendship and its relation to democracy, ethics, and intimate life, from Aristotle to Montaigne. But it is also a survey of the variation in the meaning and nature of same-sex attachments. Although this is not a course in queer studies, I frame the course by suggesting that friendship is where queer intimacies have historically flourished alongside or in place of romantic bonds. The course reliably appeals to students grappling with questions of identity, relational ethics, and with ordinary quandaries of social and romantic life. I take a lot of joy in observing the students in the midst of this practical-theoretical reflection and in the thought that the readings and discussions in the course may be of some direct use to them. But I also see the course as a chance to explore the paradoxes of queer life after *Obergefell*.

No single piece of writing is as important in this context as Michel Foucault's brief, electric late interview, "Friendship as a Way of Life." Foucault's interview dates from a moment (the early 1980s) before the emergence of *queer*, but it anticipates the curious mixture of same-sex relations with a universalizing and disruptive desire that the term designates. With its expansive definition of friendship and its suggestion that we should understand homosexuality as "something desirable" rather than "a form of desire," this piece disrupts student expectations and sets the stage for an experiment in queer pedagogy. In his final comment, Foucault calls for a renewal of social relations: "We must think that what exists is far from filling all possible spaces. To make a truly unavoidable challenge of the question: what can we make work, what new game can we invent?" The students are provoked by Foucault's suggestion that there are relational forms that are yet to be invented; we spend some class time speculating about those nascent forms and discussing the classroom as a common space of work and play. But the translation of Foucault's account of friendship into the terms of the class is not seamless. Foucault attends to the relations that can be elaborated among men, in sexual but not only sexual ways. "How is it possible for men to be together?" Foucault asks. "To live together, to share their time, their meals, their room, their leisure, their grief, their knowledge, their confidences? What is it to be 'naked' among men, outside of institutional relations, family, profession and obligatory camaraderie?"[16]

We are not among men (nor "naked") in the classroom, and the reason that we are together in the first place is institutional: "Friendship" is an upper-level undergraduate seminar, answerable to the requirements of the university curriculum. Nonetheless, despite the slight awkwardness of translation, "Friendship as a Way of Life" is a crucial text for this class, primarily because it offers an account of intimacy outside of family and outside of the couple. This is the minimal but expansive definition of friendship that we rely on in class. But Foucault offers an account of friendship that emphasizes intimacy and attachment minus the language, familiar from *Obergefell*, of romantic fusion ("two people become something greater than once they were") or eternity ("marriage embodies a love that may endure even past death"). Instead, the absence of institutional structures enables and may even be understood to require creativity. In this context, instability is not only a deficit: it also offers an opportunity for reinvention. Comparing age-discrepant relations between men and women to those between men, Foucault considers the absence of a form to legitimate and frame the latter: "But two men of noticeably different ages—what code would allow them to communicate? They face each other without terms or convenient words, with nothing to assure them about the meaning of the movement that carries them toward each other. They have to invent, from A to Z, a relationship that is still formless, which is friendship."[17] Foucault suggests that relations can flourish outside of institutional forms and that alongside stability and duration we might also value qualities such as singularity and invention in our relations.

One of the defining tensions in the history of friendship is that it can both refer to the most stable and lasting of relations (Montaigne's "holy bond of friendship") and to relations that are intense and significant but not necessarily lasting. There is perhaps no greater expression of this paradox than Nietzsche's aphorism "Star Friendship." Using the occasion of a friend breakup, the passage juxtaposes "the tremendous invisible curve and stellar orbit" of a "sublime" friendship with the occasional encounter on Earth, when, as Nietzsche writes, "we may cross and have a feast together, as we did."[18] One of the pedagogical aims of "Friendship," and indeed of all my teaching in queer studies, is to destigmatize and, moreover, to celebrate intimacies that are intense and significant but not necessarily lasting. Nietzsche suggests that even the most fleeting relations may have a basis in eternity. This is a suggestion that can be extended to cover many different instances of contingent, aleatory, and impersonal relations. Along the way, we consider Walt Whitman's "Among the Multitude," in which the speaker imagines a stranger in the crowd, "picking me out by secret and divine signs, / Acknowledging none else, not parent, wife, husband, brother, child, any nearer than I am"; the visiting culture of the spinsters and bachelors of Sarah Orne Jewett's *The Country of the Pointed Firs* (1896), who, despite long absences and deep social reserve, establish intimacy through ritual and a sense of place; Samuel Delany's argument, drawing on Jane Jacobs's writing about urban planning, about the value of public sexual cultures in sustaining democratic life; and the sexual encounter between Eric and Vivaldo at the center of James Baldwin's *Another Country* (1962), which, although it lasts just one night, is understood by both of them as a lifelong bond.[19]

These examples, as different as they are from one another historically, formally, and tonally, are marked by a similar willingness to interleave short-term and long-term forms of intimacy. They supply an occasion to propose the idea that value is not the same as duration. They allow us to frame friendship as a rich ecology made up of both long- and short-term commitments, of relations of greater and lesser intensity, of personal and impersonal forms of intimacy. The long history of queer attachment allows for such variability in a way that is at odds with the ascendance of same-sex marriage. One of the ironies of this moment is that while the gay couple has taken over the transcendent and eternal pole of the discourse of friendship, representations of impossible and fleeting connections have begun to appear in texts not otherwise marked as queer. This shift is registered subtly in the increasing number of representations of female friendship that I have been drawn to teach in this class. Certain texts remain canonical within representations of female friendship and highlight its vexed relation to same-sex eroticism— for instance, Henry James's *The Bostonians* (1886) and Toni Morrison's *Sula* (1973). But recently I have begun to teach more contemporary texts that are part of the publishing boom in narratives of female friendship, including Elena Ferrante's novels, Jacqueline Woodson's *Another Brooklyn* (2016), and Sheila Heti's *How Should a Person Be?* (2010).

The queerness of these texts, as I understand them, does not inhere in their invocation of same-sex relations but rather in their account of the remaking of social bonds outside of normative expectations for women's biography. Rachel Cusk's *Outline* (2014) is a key example. The novel is structured as a series of monologues by people the narrator encounters during a short stint teaching creative writing in Athens. Cusk has described the book as part of a turn away from narrative fiction that she links to her experience of divorce. In *Aftermath: On Marriage and Separation*, published in 2012, Cusk wrote in a more directly autobiographical vein. An example of the genre that Lauren Berlant has called "the female complaint," the book describes up close the dissolution of a marriage.[20] In *Outline* this knot of attachment and disappointment has morphed into a more distanced and alienated perspective. In an interview, Cusk ties the shift in genre to the experience of divorce as a kind of exile. Echoing Foucault in "Friendship as a Way of Life," she describes the experience of being cast out of familiar forms of relation:

> You are chucked out of the house, on the street, not defended any more, not a member of anything, you have no history, no network. What you have is people, strangers in the street, and the only way you can know them is by what they say. I became attuned to these encounters because I had no frame or context any more. I could hear a purity of narrative in the way people described their lives. The intense experience of hearing thus became the framework of the novel.[21]

Outline is narrated from a similarly "denuded" perspective. Named only once, minimally described, and involved in very little action, the narrator is a mere outline: "a shape . . . with all the detail filled in around it while the shape itself remained blank."[22] After her divorce, the narrator has "definitively left" (70) behind familiar social scripts and has devoted herself to "living a life as unmarked by self-will as possible" (170). She has moved from a condition of wanting and willing to a state of intensive watching and listening; the novel alternates between descriptions of an unfamiliar world and other people's stories as they relate them to the narrator. The conversations, a mix of personal narrative and philosophical reflection, involve a colleague, a few friends and acquaintances, and students. Beyond this circle, there is a humming background of strangers, whom Cusk invokes in an early account of her flight from London:

> The air hostess stood in the aisle and mimed with her props as the recording played. We were strapped into our seats, a field of strangers,

in a silence like the silence of a congregation while the liturgy is read. She showed us the life jacket with its little pipe, the emergency exits, the oxygen mask dangling from a length of clear tubing. She led us through the possibility of death and disaster, as the priest leads the congregation through the details of purgatory and hell; and no one jumped up to escape while there was still time. Instead we listened or half-listened, thinking about other things, as though some special hardness had been bestowed on us by this coupling of formality with doom. When the recorded voice came to the part about the oxygen masks, the hush remained unbroken: no one protested, or spoke up to disagree with this commandment that one should take care of others only after taking care of oneself. Yet I wasn't sure it was altogether true. (4–5)

Outline repeatedly couples "formality with doom": the measured description and the detached perspective emerge because of rather than in spite of the imagined proximity of death and destruction. If the other passengers are only half-listening, the narrator is giving the scene her full attention—not to escape disaster but because, in the face of disaster, attention has become a sacred practice: "What you have is people, strangers in the street, and the only way you can know them is by what they say."

What is at stake, in this scene and throughout the novel, is not just survival but what we owe to others. In relation to one's children, the claim might be absolute: at one point the narrator steps out of class to accept a call from her son, who is lost on his way to school. But in other cases the situation is ambiguous. The closed world of the plane creates new forms of intimacy and dependency, but it also creates new forms of impersonality, as people are turned into passengers: all alike, all anonymous. Out of this impersonal matrix, a more intimate connection emerges between the narrator and "her neighbor," an older Greek businessman who is never named in the book. The hint of a plot attaches to this figure; the narrator discusses marriage, divorce, and family with him on the plane, and he later takes her out on his boat, makes an awkward pass at her, and is rejected. Married and divorced three times, the neighbor exemplifies the mix of demand and self-delusion that drives romantic attachment.[23] The narrator accuses him of bad faith several times, noting at one point that his words about his children "reminded me of the oxygen masks" (31) in their elaborate but empty promise of care. But the problem with the neighbor is less his flawed character than the fact that he has landed in the wrong genre: this is not a love story. The book is composed of philosophical conversation between friends rather than passionate conversation among lovers. When the neighbor tries to make things more personal ("Has there really been no one?" he asks), the narrator returns to the terrain of ethics: "There had, I said, been someone. We were still very good friends. But I hadn't wanted to carry on with it. I was trying to find a different way of living in the world" (171). When physical contact occurs, it is not only awkward but, somehow, unlikely. Cusk's characters are not drawn that way. When the neighbor attempts an embrace, "Through the whole thing I stayed rigidly still, staring straight ahead of me at the steering wheel, until at last he withdrew, back into the shade" (177).

The narrator refuses to enter into the destructive cycle of the marriage plot, taking it instead as an object of thought. Foucault writes that "homosexuality is a historic occasion to re-open affective and relational virtualities, not so much through the intrinsic qualities of the homosexual, but due to the biases against the position he occupies; in a certain sense diagonal lines that he can trace in the social fabric permit him to make these virtualities visible."[24] In *Outline* it is not homosexuality but conversation that virtualizes intimate relations and opens diagonal lines in the social fabric.[25] By means of this virtualization, Cusk keeps open possibilities for connection "in a field of strangers." This insistent virtualization—along with many other features, including a shared setting—links *Outline* to Plato's *Symposium*. Both books feature conversations about love by people who are not lovers. In both cases the commitment to dialogue is challenged—by the neighbor's dry, fumbling embrace in *Outline*, and by Alcibiades's crashing, drunken entry at the end of the *Symposium*. Just after Socrates has related Diotima's speech, Alcibiades arrives and attempts to turn the discussion of the nature of love into a love story. Alcibiades flirts with Socrates, who engages him but resists his advances. Eventually, almost everyone at the party falls into a drunken sleep, and Socrates continues to discourse until dawn. In "Friendship" I teach *Outline* and the *Symposium* together—as books about friendship and about the social space of the classroom.[26] The symposium is a space where drinking can take place but you don't get drunk, where people may flirt but not have sex, and where speech rather than action is primary. *Outline* features two chapters set in a classroom, where the narrator meets the students—the "curious group—a mixed bag" (132)—who have signed up to take her writing class. The students respond to assignments—*describe something you saw on the way to class today; write a story involving an animal*—delivering their stories in the form of speeches. In addition to sharing these stories, the students also negotiate the boundaries of the classroom—should the windows be open and the doors closed, or vice versa?—and the rules of engagement.

In a replaying of the end of the *Symposium*, a student brings a pink box with almond cakes to the last day of class, which the narrator "shares out" with the students (226).

The social spaces represented in the *Symposium* and in *Outline* resemble what Ellen Rooney, in a passionate defense of the seminar, describes as a "semiprivate room." Rooney elaborates the concept of the "semiprivate" with reference to the relations between people sharing a hospital room. Brought together by means of "an indifferent public process," these "accidental room-mates do share an ontological condition: the semiprivate room shelters strangers who have in common the quite particular neediness that brings them there, in close proximity to each other and, crucially, available to a host of other people, most of them strangers as well." Rooney is interested in the vulnerability and exposure—what she calls the "impersonal intimacy"—that are engendered by this proximity but also in the exclusions that it depends on: "Not just anyone can walk into your classroom and take a seat." Through this elaboration of the "peculiar intimacy" of the classroom, Rooney intends a polemic against the notion of unfettered access and, in particular, early proposals for online education. Although it might seem paradoxical, it is only through restriction that the democratic space of dialogue can flourish. Rooney understands the semiprivate room not "as a set of protocols or rules, or as a content or datum, but as a form of rhetoric and a mode of address."[27] As the continuities between the *Symposium* and *Outline* would suggest, this is a remarkably durable structure, although it is one that, as Rooney proposes, is under threat. The efficiency imperative in higher education and hardening lines between public and private can make the seminar seem an impossible luxury: a threat to democracy rather than, as Rooney believes, its guarantee.

Similar charges of elitism might attach to the peculiar intimacies of queer friendship. For instance, W. H. Auden's poem "For Friends Only" announces the exclusive nature of its address in its title.[28] The poem opens by delineating a space—a semiprivate room—to which the "friends" of the title are invited:

> Ours yet not ours, being set apart
> As a shrine to friendship,
> Empty and silent most of the year,
> This room awaits from you
> What you alone, as visitor, can bring,
> A weekend of personal life. (532)

This invitation is only possible because the "we" of the poem—a couple, pre-sumably, and householders—have set aside the room, keeping it empty. But this ownership is provisional and impersonal: the room might be said to belong more properly to those who occupy it and make it, if temporarily, their own. But that possession is provisional too, for the "personal life" that visitors bring is thinned out, or virtualized, by the framework of friendship: "You are unlike to encounter / Dragons or romance: were drama a craving, / You would not have come."[29] In the era of gay marriage such spaces, consecrated to the serene (nonnarrative, discursive) pleasures of friendship, are increasingly rare. *Obergefell* enables the kind of stability that allows for the poem's "we" to issue this invitation. Still, it is the looseness of the ties that bind that allows them to assure their guest

> That whoever slept in this bed before
> Was also someone we like,
> That within the circle of our affection
> Also you have no double. (533)

This peculiar form of recognition, both intimate and impersonal, is characteristic of the classroom and of the tradition of friendship. If it can be spared, if it can be "set aside," it may prove a more durable container for queer intimacy than the love that endures beyond death. This is not because we are married to our students or because we have become one with our weekend guest. Each semester brings new students, and guests are occasional, not permanent. Recognizing the singularity and significance of these bonds requires a dedicated space and the possibility of renewal rather than a solemn vow.

NOTES

1 *Obergefell v. Hodges*, 576 U.S. 644 (2015), available at https://supreme.justia.com /cases/federal/us/576/14-556.

2 The "dawn of time" opening was included on *McSweeney's* facetious "Student Essay Checklist": "Since the dawn of time, man has. . . ." Shannon Reid, "Student Essay Checklist," *McSweeney's Internet Tendency*, November 1, 2017, www.mcsweeneys .net/articles/student-essay-checklist.

3 On the racial and gendered dimensions of marriage, see, for example, Jackson, *American Blood*, and Carter, *The Heart of Whiteness*.

4 It is worth noting how much Justice Roberts's dissenting opinion relies on the strategy of temporalizing same-sex relations in particular and homosexual life in general: "Indeed, however heartened the proponents of same-sex marriage might be on this day, it is worth acknowledging what they have lost, and lost forever: the opportunity to win the true acceptance that comes from persuading their fellow citizens of the justice of their cause. And they lose this just when the winds of change were freshening at their backs" (27).

5 In such arguments (in contrast to *Obergefell*), the benefit to same-sex couples
   is cast as fungible: legalizing gay marriage is a necessary step to promote family
   values and civic stability more broadly. See, for instance, an interview with Ted
   Olson, Bush II's solicitor general, who argued and won *Bush v. Gore*: "We're talking about an effect upon millions of people and the way they live their everyday
   life and the way they're treated in their neighborhood, in their schools, in their
   jobs. If you are a conservative, how could you be against a relationship in which
   people who love one another want to publicly state their vows . . . and engage
   in a household in which they are committed to one another and become part of
   the community and accepted like other people?" Cited in Nina Totenberg, "Ted
   Olson, Gay Marriage's Unlikely Legal Warrior," NPR, December 6, 2010, www.npr
   .org/2010/12/06/131792296/ted-olson-gay-marriage-s-unlikely-legal-warrior.

6 Cicero, *Letters of Marcus Tullius Cicero*, 15–16.

7 Montaigne, "On Affectionate Relationships," 205–19, 209–10.

8 Montaigne, "On Affectionate Relationships," 210.

9 In the words of sociologist and demographer Daniel Lichter, "The latest results
   seem to indicate that marriage, as a context for childbearing and childrearing . . .
   is increasingly reserved for America's middle- and upper-class populations."
   Quoted in Hope Yen, "More Couples Who Become Parents Are Living Together
   but Not Marrying, Data Show," *Washington Post*, January 7, 2014.

10 Bray, "Homosexuality and the Signs of Male Friendship in Elizabethan England";
   Haggerty, "Desire and Mourning"; Sedgwick, *Between Men*.

11 Marcus, *Between Women*, 31.

12 For a powerful argument on the broader utility of deidealization for queer studies, see Amin, *Disturbing Attachments*.

13 See, for instance, Love, "Doing Being Deviant."

14 Love, "Playing for Keeps."

15 My attempts to deidealize friendship in print include "The End of Friendship," a
   chapter in *Feeling Backward*, and "Truth and Consequences."

16 Foucault, "Friendship as a Way of Life," 308–12.

17 Foucault, "Friendship as a Way of Life," 309.

18 The full text reads: "We were friends and have become estranged. But that was
   right, and we do not want to hide and obscure it from ourselves as if we had to be
   ashamed of it. We are two ships, each of which has its own goal and course; we
   may cross and have a feast together, as we did—and then the good ships lay so
   quietly in one harbour and in one sun that it may have seemed as if they had already completed their course and had the same goal. But then the almighty force
   of our projects drove us apart once again, into different seas and sunny zones,
   and maybe we will never meet again—or maybe we will, but will not recognize
   each other: the different seas and suns have changed us! That we had to become
   estranged is the law above us; through it we should come to have more respect
   for each other—and the thought of our former friendship should become more
   sacred! There is probably a tremendous invisible curve and stellar orbit in which
   our different ways and goals may be included as small stretches—let us rise to
   this thought! But our life is too short and our vision too meagre for us to be more

than friends in the sense of that sublime possibility. Let us then believe in our star friendship even if we must be earth enemies." Nietzsche, *The Gay Science*, 159.

19 See, for example, Delany, *Times Square Red, Times Square Blue*.

20 Berlant, *The Female Complaint*.

21 Rachel Cusk, interviewed by Kate Kellaway: "*Aftermath* was creative death. I was heading into total silence," *Guardian*, August 24, 2014, www.theguardian.com /books/2014/aug/24/rachel-cusk-interview-aftermath-outline.

22 Cusk, *Outline*, 239–40. Further page references to this novel will be given parenthetically in the text.

23 The narrator responds at last: "I said I wondered how he could fail to see the relationship between disillusionment and knowledge in what he had told me. If he could only love what he did not know, and be loved in return on that same basis, then knowledge became an inexorable disenchantment, for which the only cure was to fall in love with someone new" (175).

24 Foucault, "Friendship as a Way of Life," 311.

25 See Bersani and Dutoit on the virtualization of intimacy from the sidestepping of the couple in *Contempt* (1963) to the scene of sociability in *All About My Mother* (1999) in *Forms of Being*.

26 The course is structured through a series of what I call "pedagogical experiments," in which two students take over the course and design how we interact. The experiments can include anything from traditional pedagogical exercises such as fishbowl, classroom debates, or round robin to more singular exercises, often based on relational forms represented in the texts we are reading. Over the years students have undertaken a number of experiments, including letter writing within romantic triangles (Henry James, *The Bostonians*); small-group discussions taking jazz improvisation as their model (James Baldwin, *Another Country*); speed dating (Sarah Orne Jewett, *The Country of the Pointed Firs*); and the increasing use of new technology (anonymous chat room).

27 Rooney, "A Semiprivate Room," 131, 135, 134, 130.

28 "For Friends Only" is the ninth of twelve poems that make up "Thanksgiving for a Habitat," the first part of Auden's 1965 collection *About the House*. Page references are to Auden's *Collected Poems*, edited by Mendelson.

29 The poem continues in this vein: "Should you have troubles (pets will die, / Lovers are always behaving badly) / And confession helps, we will hear it, / Examine and give our counsel: / If to mention them hurts too much, / We shall not be nosey" (532).

BIBLIOGRAPHY

Amin, Kadji. *Disturbing Attachments: Genet, Modern Pederasty, and Queer History*. Durham, NC: Duke University Press, 2017.

Auden, W. H. "For Friends Only." In *Collected Poems*, edited by Edward Mendelson, 532–33. New York: Random House, 1976.

Berlant, Lauren. *The Female Complaint: The Unfinished Business of Sentimentality in American Culture*. Durham, NC: Duke University Press, 2008.

Bersani, Leo, and Ulysse Dutoit. *Forms of Being: Cinema, Aesthetics, Subjectivity.* London: British Film Institute, 2004.

Bray, Alan. "Homosexuality and the Signs of Male Friendship in Elizabethan England." In *Queering the Renaissance*, edited by Jonathan Goldberg, 40–61. Durham, NC: Duke University Press, 1994.

Carter, Julian. *The Heart of Whiteness: Normal Sexuality and Race in America, 1880–1940.* Durham, NC: Duke University Press, 2007.

Cicero, Marcus Tullius. *Letters of Marcus Tullius Cicero, with his treatises on friendship and old age*, translated by E. S. Shuckburgh. And *Letters of Gaius Plinius Caecilius Secundus*, translated by William Melmoth. Edited by Charles W. Eliot. Harvard Classics, vol. 9. Originally published 1937 by P. F. Collier. Available online at https://openlibrary.org/books/OL24212386M/Letters_of_Marcus_Tullius_Cicero.

Cusk, Rachel. *Outline.* New York: Picador, 2014.

Delany, Samuel R. *Times Square Red, Times Square Blue.* New York: New York University Press, 1999.

Foucault, Michel. "Friendship as a Way of Life." In *Foucault Live (Interviews, 1961–1984)*, edited by Sylvère Lotringer. New York: Semiotext[e], 1989.

Haggerty, George. "Desire and Mourning: The Ideology of the Elegy." In *Ideology and Form in Eighteenth-Century Literature*, edited by David H. Richter, 184–206. Lubbock, TX: Texas Tech University Press, 1999.

Jackson, Holly. *American Blood: The Ends of the Family in American Literature, 1850–1900.* Oxford: Oxford University Press, 2013.

Love, Heather. "Doing Being Deviant: Deviance Studies, Description, and the Queer Ordinary." In "Queer Theory without Antinormativity," edited by Robyn Wiegman and Elizabeth Wilson, special issue, *differences* 26, no. 1 (2015): 74–95.

Love, Heather. *Feeling Backward: Loss and the Politics of Queer History.* Cambridge, MA: Harvard University Press, 2009.

Love, Heather. "Playing for Keeps." In "The Ontology of the Couple," edited by S. Pearl Brilmyer, Filippo Trentin, and Zairong Xiang, special issue, *GLQ* 25, no. 2 (2019): 257–72.

Love, Heather. "Truth and Consequences: On Paranoid Reading and Reparative Reading." *Criticism* 52, no. 2 (2010): 235–41.

Marcus, Sharon. *Between Women: Friendship, Desire, and Marriage in Victorian England.* Princeton, NJ: Princeton University Press, 2007.

Montaigne, Michel de. "On Affectionate Relationships." In *The Complete Essays*, translated and edited by M. A. Screech. London: Penguin, 1987.

Nietzsche, Friedrich. *The Gay Science.* Edited by Bernard Williams. Translated by Josefine Nauckhoff. Cambridge: Cambridge University Press, 2001.

Rooney, Ellen. "A Semiprivate Room." *differences* 13, no. 1 (2002): 128–56.

Sedgwick, Eve Kosofsky. *Between Men: English Literature and Male Homosexual Desire.* New York: Columbia University Press, 1985.

LISA ADKINS is professor of sociology and head of the School of Social and Political Sciences at the University of Sydney. Her contributions to the discipline of sociology lie in the areas of economic sociology, social theory, and feminist theory. Recent publications include *The Asset Economy* (with Melinda Cooper and Martijn Konings, 2020) and *The Time of Money* (2018). She is joint editor-in-chief of *Australian Feminist Studies*.

MARYANNE DEVER is professor and associate dean in the faculty of Arts and Social Sciences at the University of Technology Sydney. She researches in the area of critical archival studies. Her recent publications include *Paper, Materiality and the Archived Page* (2019) and the collection *Archives and New Modes of Feminist Research* (2018), which was awarded a Mander Jones Award from the Australian Society of Archivists. She is joint editor-in-chief of *Australian Feminist Studies*.

CARLA FRECCERO is Distinguished Professor of Literature and History of Consciousness at UC Santa Cruz, where she has taught since 1991. She is the author of *Father Figures* (1991); *Popular Culture* (1999); and *Queer/Early/Modern* (Duke University Press, 2006). She coedited *Premodern Sexualities*; a special issue of *American Quarterly* on "Species/Race/Sex"; and a special issue of *Yale French Studies* on "Animots." She has published essays on European early-modern culture, queer and feminist theories, and animal studies. She is currently working on a book about animals and figuration, *Animate Figures*.

ELIZABETH FREEMAN is professor of English at the University of California, Davis. She is the author of three books published by Duke University Press: *The Wedding Complex: Forms of Belonging in Modern American Culture* (2002); *Time Binds: Queer Temporalities, Queer Histories* (2010); and *Beside You in Time: Sense Methods and Queer Sociabilities in the American Nineteenth Century* (2019). She has also guest-edited "Queer Temporalities" (a special issue of GLQ, 2007) and, with Ellen Samuels, "Crip Temporalities" (a special issue of *South Atlantic Quarterly*, 2021). She is currently working on a monograph on caretaking, queer theory, and reading practices, as well as a coedited collection, "Queer Kinship: Erotic Affinities and the Politics of Belonging," with Tyler Bradway.

SCOTT HERRING is professor of American Studies and Women's, Gender, and Sexuality Studies at Yale University. He is the author of several books, including, most recently, *The Hoarders: Material Deviance in Modern American Culture* (2014).

ANNAMARIE JAGOSE is a scholar of feminist studies, lesbian/gay studies, and queer theory. She is the author of four monographs, most recently *Orgasmology* (Duke University Press, 2012), which takes orgasm as its scholarly object in order to think queerly about questions of politics and pleasure, practice and subjectivity, agency and ethics. She is also an award-winning novelist and short story writer.

AMY JAMGOCHIAN is the chief academic officer of Mount Tamalpais College (formerly known as the Prison University Project), an Associate of Arts degree program that runs inside San Quentin State Prison. Prior to this, she was a lecturer in the Rhetoric Department at the University of California, Berkeley, where she also earned her PhD.

E. PATRICK JOHNSON is Carlos Montezuma Professor of Performance Studies and African American Studies at Northwestern University. He is the author of *Appropriating Blackness: Performance and the Politics of Authenticity* (Duke University Press, 2003), *Sweet Tea: Black Gay Men of the South—An Oral History* (2008), *Black. Queer. Southern. Women: An Oral History* (2018), and *Honeypot: Black Southern Women Who Love Women* (Duke University Press, 2019), as well as a contributor to several edited and coedited volumes.

JAYA KEANEY's research explores the racialization of kinship in changing biotechnologies and reproductive forms. She currently holds a postdoctoral fellowship at the Alfred Deakin Institute for Citizenship and Globalization at Deakin University, where she is completing a project about queer families, race, and reproductive technologies.

HEATHER LOVE is professor in the Department of English at the University of Pennsylvania. Her research interests include gender and sexuality studies, twentieth-century literature and culture, affect studies, sociology and literature, and critical theory. She is the author of *Feeling Backward: Loss and the Politics of Queer History* (2009), the editor of a special issue of GLQ on Gayle Rubin ("Rethinking Sex"), and the coeditor of a special issue of *Representations* ("Description across Disciplines"). Her forthcoming book is *Underdogs: Social Deviance and Queer Theory* (2021).

SALLY R. MUNT is professor emeritus of cultural politics at the University of Sussex UK, taking early retirement following COVID-19 in 2020. She is the author of *Queer Attachments: The Cultural Politics of Shame* (2007) and remains chief editor of the journal *Feminist Encounters*. She is also a cognitive behavioral psychotherapist in private practice and founder and clinical director of a local charity: Brighton Exiled/Refugee Trauma Service.

KANE RACE is professor of gender and cultural studies at the University of Sydney. He has published widely on questions of HIV infection, sexuality, biomedicine, drug use, digital culture, risk, and care practices, motivated by the capacity of bodies and pleasures to intervene in the disciplinary production of knowledge, subjects, technologies, and life. He is the author of *Pleasure Consuming Medicine: The Queer Politics of Drugs* (Duke University Press, 2009), *Plastic Water: The Social and Material Life of Bottled Water* (coauthored with Gay Hawkins and Emily Potter, 2015), and *The Gay Science: Intimate Experiments with the Problem of HIV* (2017).

AMY VILLAREJO has been the Frederic J. Whiton Professor of Humanities at Cornell University, where she has taught in the Department of Performing and Media Arts and the Department of Comparative Literature. Her publications include *Lesbian Rule: Cultural Criticism and the Value of Desire* (Duke University Press, 2003) and *Ethereal Queer* (Duke University Press, 2014), along with a number of edited collections and teaching resources, the most recent of which is the *Oxford Handbook to Queer Cinema*, coedited with Ron Gregg. Her essays on cinema, media, queer theory, and critical theory have appeared in journals such as *Film Quarterly*, *Cinema Journal*, *New German Critique*, and *Social Text*. She joined the Department of Film, Television, and Digital Media in the School of Theater, Film, and Television at UCLA in the fall of 2020.

LEE WALLACE is associate professor of gender and cultural studies at the University of Sydney. She has published on Pacific sexual encounter, sexual historiography, and lesbian representation in post–Production Code film. Her most recent book is *Reattachment Theory: Queer Cinema of Remarriage* (Duke University Press, 2020).

Blondell, Joan, 227
Blue Velvet (film), 226
"Bodily" (DiFranco song), 126
body genre: rereading and, 33; sentimental literature and, 30
body language, prisoner-volunteer relationships and, 159–66
body phobia, illness and, 71–73
Bookanista, 145
Book of Martyrs (Foxe), 80
The Bostonians (James), 258
Boston marriages, 241
Bourdieu, Pierre, 78, 233–34
Bray, Alan, 127, 255
Breckon, Anna, 224–32
Brown, Rebecca, 124
Brown, Rita Mae, 147
Burns, Olivia, 118

California Department of Corrections and Rehabilitation (CDCR) Code of Regulations, 158–66
Calinescu, Matei, 33–34, 38
capital: illness and, 74–75; neoliberal financialization and, 206–8
Carel, Havi, 66, 82
caretaking: bibliography of fiction on, 44n28; gendered labor of, 74–75; queer theory, 25–42; Sontag's fiction and, 38–42
Carriageworks (Sydney, Australia), 226–32
Carter, Steven, 141
Cassavetes, John, 224, 227–28, 239
Castañeda, Claudia, 191
Cavell, Stanley, 9–11, 239–44
Centers for Disease Control and Prevention, 39–40
Centrelink (Australian welfare agency), 214–17
Chambers, Ross, 90
choice, alternative families discourse and, 180–81
chronic fatigue syndrome (CFS), 64–67
chronic thinking, 17
Cicero, 252
Cindy & Barb's Wedding, Boston, 1986 (Sohier), 12–13
citizenship discourse, queer reproduction and, 182–83, 188

Civil Marriage Collaborative, 178
class: homonormativity and, 202–5; illness and, 76–78; obesity crisis and, 74; prison volunteerism and, 167–72; queer reproduction and, 181–82; same-sex marriage and, 254–56
Clinton, Bill, 3
The Cloud of Unknowing, 81–82
Clowning in Rome (Nouwen), 81–82
club drugs, HIV/AIDS therapies and, 95–100
Cobb, Michael, 234–35
cognitive behavioral therapy(CBT), 66–67, 84n5, 86n27
Coldness and Cruelty (Deleuze), 169
college courses, prisoners' access to, 159–66
colonialism, animal-human interaction and, 117–20
combination antiviral therapy, HIV/AIDS and, 90–92
comedy, commitment and, 9–11
commitment: animal-human connections and, 120–27; aversion to, 7–8; body phobia and lack of, 72–73; definitions of, 6–7; framework for, 9; gay-parented families and racialization of, 176–95; prisoner-volunteer relationships and, 159–66; transferability of, 237–38. *See also* long-term commitment; serial commitment
commitment ceremony, definitions of, 7
commitment phobia, evolution of, 141–43
complaint: genealogies of, 79–81; illness as, 76–78
Confucius, 252
Contagious Divides (Shah), 139
Contesting Tears (Cavell), 9–10
Cooper, Melinda, 207
correctional philosophy and practice, prisoner-volunteer relationships and, 159–66
The Corrections (Franzen), 144
countercommitments, 8
The Country of the Pointed Firs (Jewett), 258
"Couples Are Couples" public information campaign (Australia), 214–17
Crimp, Douglas, 124
Critical Inquiry, 2–3, 9
Cruel Optimism (Berlant), 9, 139
Cruising Utopia (Muñoz), 176–77
crying, cultural and racial aspects of, 170–72

ceutical amnesia and, 100–104; silence of patients with, 105–8

Hocquenghem, Guy, 108–10

Hoffmann, Gaby, 53

homoinnocence, multiracial gay parenting and, 192–94

homonormativity: Australian same-sex entitlements and, 208–12; costs of inclusion and, 212–17; financial framework for, 205–8; long-term commitment as finance capital guarantee, 217–18; neoliberal sexual politics and, 201–5; political economy of long-term commitment and, 199–201; queer critique of, 2

homophobia, HIV/AIDS and, 108–10

Homosexual Desire (Hocquenghem), 108–10

homosexuality: animal-human interaction and, 127–32; deviance paradigm of, 255; Foucault on, 261–62; as pathology, 64–67

hospice care, animal-human interaction and, 118–27

household units, neoliberal financialization and, 206–8

Howard, John, 209, 212

How Should a Person Be? (Heti), 258

How to Survive a Plague (film), 55

human artifice, attachment and, 48–49

Human Fertilisation and Embryology Act 2008 (UK), 203–4

human interactions: disavowal in prison volunteerism and, 166–72; prisoner-volunteer relationships and, 159–66

Human Rights and Equal Opportunity Commission of Australia (HREOC), 209

Human Rights Campaign, 178

The Human Condition (Arendt), 60–61

hysteria, chronic fatigue syndrome and, 64–67

"I Believe I'll Run On" (gospel song), viii

identity, race as cosmetic and, 189–94, 196n36

"I Feel Love" (song), 243

illness: in animals, 117–27; awareness and spirituality and, 81–82; capital and, 74–75; complaints *vs.* disorders, 76–78; *Lebenswelt* (lifeworld) of, 68–71; medicalization of, 124–27; mind/body split and, 71–73, 79; mortality and, 82–84; queer feel-

ings and, 64–67; sick methodologies and, 75–76; subjectivity and, 78–79

Imitation of Life (film), 224

immigration policy, same-sex couples protections and, 204–5

incarceration: gay male sex and, 155–58; race and, 155–72; trauma of, 169–70. *See also* prisoner-volunteer relationships

Indian surrogacy industry, 175–76, 183–88

inheritance laws, same-sex couples and, 204–5

interest rates, neoliberal financialization and, 207–8

internet, drug procurement and, 101–4

interrelationality, quiet attachment and, 48–49

intestacy, same-sex couples and, 204–5

Intimacy (Berlant), 2–4

intimacy, racialization of, 183

In Translation (Jagose), 233

Jacobs, Jane, 258

Jagose, Annamarie, 223–54

James, Henry, 144, 258

Jamgochian, Amy, 155–72

Jean & Elaine, Santa Fe, 1988 (Sohier), 13

Jewett, Sarah Orne, 258

Johnson, E. Patrick, viii–ix, 18

Johnson, Marsha P., 55–56

Joseph, Ralina, 191

Jungermann, Ingrid, 53

K9Kidneys

Kaplan, Alice, 238

Keaney, Jaya, 175–95

Kennedy, Anthony (Justice), 134, 250–52

ketamine, 109–10

Keynesian economics, employment and social welfare under, 205–8

Kierkegaard, Søren, 240

kink.com protest, 169

kinship: queer reproductive technology and, 177–95; quiet attachment and, 48–49; same-sex family and inheritance laws and, 204–5; surrogacy economics and, 184–88

Lebenswelt (lifeworld), chronic illness and, 68–71

Lee, Ang, 232

Leibovitz, Annie, 234

domesticity of, 234–35; gay-parented families and, 176–95; homonormativity and, 201; legalization of, 250–54; minority populations and impact of, 203–5; performances of intimacy and, 232; psychological benefits of, 134–36; queer-of-color critiques of, 5–6

Same-Sex Relationships (Equal Treatment in Commonwealth Laws—General Law Reform) Bill 2008, 212, 214

Same-Sex Relationships (Equal Treatment in Commonwealth Laws—Superannuation) Bill 2008, 212

Same-Sex: Same Entitlements report (Australia), 209–17

San Quentin State Prison: ethnic breakdown of inmates at, 166–67; prisoner-volunteer relationships in, 158–66; University Prison Project in, 156–58

Sapphic Slashers (Duggan), 245n9

Saturday Night Fever (film), 243

Schechner, Richard, 223–24, 232

Schnall, Maxine, 141

The Second Woman (Breckon & Randall), 224–32, 238

Sedaris, Amy, 53

Sedgwick, Eve Kosofsky, 3, 9, 18, 81–82, 233, 236, 255

self-care: family support and, 107–8; illness and capital and, 74–75

sentimental literature, care work in, 26–32, 38–42

serial commitment: performance studies and, 223–32; repetition and, 232–39

Seuffert, Nan, 204–5

"Sex in Public" (Berlant & Warner), 3

Sexual Encounters: Pacific Texts, Modern Sexualities (Wallace), 233

sexuality scholarship, homonormativity and, 201–5

sexual relations, prisoner-volunteer relationships and risk of, 162–66, 171–72, 173n14

Shadow, San Francisco, 2002 (Sohier), 13–15

Shadow & Sky, San Francisco, 1987 (Sohier), 15

Shah, Nayan, 139, 146

Shakespeare, William, remarriage in plays of, 242

short-termism, 236–39

short-term relationships (STRs), 2, 236–39

Showalter, Elaine, 65

sickness. *See* illness

"The Sick Child" (Sigourney), 29–31

Sigourney, Linda, 29–31, 37

Sirk, Douglas, 224

The Slope (web series), 53

Slow Water (Jagose), 233

Smile or Die (Ehrenreich), 73

social security policies, Australian same-sex entitlements and, 214–17

social welfare: asset-based welfare policies and, 213–14; Australian same-sex entitlements and, 208–17; Australian same-sex policies and, 205–8

sociocultural conditions: HIV/AIDS therapy and, 97–100; long-term commitment and, 235–39; mental and physical health and, 73–74; prison volunteerism and, 167–72; queer reproductive technology and, 186–88; race as cosmetic and, 189–94

Sohier, Sage, 11–15

Sokol, Julia, 141

somatoform disorders, 67–68

somatophobia, 72

Sontag, Susan, 38–42, 44n30, 72–73, 233–34

Spacks, Patricia Meyer, 38

Spade, Dean, 202

Spahr, Juliana, 34

spatiotemporality: of attachments, 237–39; in caretaking, 28–32, 35–38; drug use and, 101–4; in performance studies, 223–32; recovery and, 54–55; rereading and, 32–34

Spillers, Hortense, 5

Spinoza, Baruch, 82

spirituality, illness and, 81–82

Stein, Gertrude, 34, 42, 237, 240–41, 245n40, 246n37

Stewart, Kathleen, 47

Stonewall Riots, 56

Stop AIDS Project, 93

Street Transvestite Action Revolutionaries (STAR), 56, 59

subjectivity, Foucault on, 78–79

Sula (Morrison), 258

Sullivan, Andrew, 3, 95–100, 102

Summer, Donna, 243